History of
Criminal Justice

THIRD EDITION

HERBERT A. JOHNSON

Distinguished Professor Emeritus of Law
University of South Carolina

NANCY TRAVIS WOLFE

Distinguished Professor Emerita of Criminal Justice
University of South Carolina

 anderson publishing co.
2035 Reading Road
Cincinnati, OH 45202
800-582-7295

History of Criminal Justice, Third Edition

Copyright © 1988, 1996, 2003
Anderson Publishing Co.
2035 Reading Rd.
Cincinnati, OH 45202

Phone   800.582.7295 or 513.421.4142
Web Site   www.andersonpublishing.com

Library of Congress Cataloging-in-Publication Data

Johnson, Herbert Alan.
    History of criminal justice / Herbert A. Johnson, Nancy Travis Wolfe.-- 3rd ed.
        p. cm.
    Includes bibliographical references and index.
    ISBN 1-58360-515-0 (pbk.)
     1. Criminal justice, Administration of--History. 2. Criminal justice, Administration of--
    United States--History. I. Wolfe, Nancy Travis. II. Title.

HV7419 .J64 2001
364.9--dc21

                                                    2001034110

Cover design by Tin Box Studio, Inc.   EDITOR Elisabeth Roszmann Ebben
COVER PHOTO CREDITS: CORBIS IMAGES   ACQUISITIONS EDITOR Michael C. Braswell

for Jane and Mary

Acknowledgments

Once again we take pleasure in thanking the students and faculty members who have helped us revise this book. We have tried to include answers to their critical questions and to incorporate their valued corrections. Without them the book would be less accurate and less "user friendly." Our colleagues across the United States who have adopted the book for class use have also provided helpful input by explaining their reasons for using this textbook. Those who did not have kindly made suggestions that in several cases permitted us to create a "better mousetrap" in this Third Edition. In making this acknowledgment we freely admit our need for further assistance and generosity on the part of our readers. This book has developed from its use in the classroom, and its improvement in future years depends upon all who have suggestions concerning the text and its presentation.

Work on this Third Edition has been greatly facilitated by Elisabeth Ebben, Legal Editor in the Criminal Justice Division of Anderson Publishing Company. She originated the idea of including the Time Capsules and Time Lines, not only to enhance the text, but also to provide needed assistance to students who lack familiarity with World History and American History. In addition, she has been diligent and creative in obtaining and incorporating new illustrative materials that enhance the visual attractiveness of the text and provide insight into historical events that can only be obtained through pictures. Finally, she has done painstaking work in overseeing the copyediting of the text and saving us from errors in grammar, style, and history.

H.A.J.
N.T.W.

Preface to the Third Edition

Almost eight eventful years have passed since the Second Edition of *History of Criminal Justice* was sent to the printer, and the field of criminal justice has burgeoned in its importance for university curriculum planning and in its bibliographic scope. Historians and political scientists have increasingly been drawn into the field, and their work has enriched the materials available for additional student reading. While this alone was sufficient reason for a new edition, recent events suggested that a major revision of the last chapter was very much needed. Like many historians, we tended to view our task as an effort to "look backward" and to explain the past's contribution to the present. However, the events of September 11, 2001, have forced us (along with millions of others) to take a new look at the world and its history.

This Third Edition is the beneficiary of Professor Wolfe's research and teaching in the field, both prior to and after her June 2000 retirement from the University of South Carolina's College of Criminal Justice. She has expanded and updated the bibliographical apparatus, and authored more than half of the Time Capsules that have been added for the first time to this text. Both students and faculty find their work enriched by access to a variety of communications media. This serves two functions: (1) it alerts us to more detailed coverage of topics discussed in the text, and (2) it provides graphic proof of the interconnectedness that exists among all fields of human knowledge.

Professor Johnson shared in the preparation of Time Capsules, prepared the Time Lines, and drafted an entirely new Chapter 14. The new chapter takes globalization as its theme, a topic that has become critical in the wake of the September 11 terrorist attacks. It also touches on new trends that are emerging rapidly—international trial of war criminals, multinational cooperation in drug traffic suppression, and the rise of personal criminal law in the case of Native Americans (American Indians) and American armed forces personnel. Chapter 14 also looks at growing concern for human rights in criminal justice practice throughout the world. The European Declaration of Human Rights, the United Nations' Declaration of Human Rights, and countless regional and national charters of rights and liberties, attest to this development. The humane quality of a nation's criminal justice system is no longer an issue isolated within national boundaries; it has become a significant matter in the conduct of diplomatic and commercial relations.

Like the Second Edition, this revision continues to provide 14 chapters of material to accommodate either a 14-week semester, or a seven-week quarter system. Shorter academic calendars require a more cursory glance at Chapter 1, and a reduction in time spent on Chapter 11, which deals with constitutional themes that may well duplicate topics covered in courses on constitutional law or American federalism.

The publisher has generously agreed to expand the scope of this Third Edition, permitting us to make it more useful to students. We hope that it will prove to be even more useful to the reader than the earlier editions have been, and as always, we welcome any and all suggestions for its improvement.

Nancy T. Wolfe
Wilmington, Delaware

Herbert A. Johnson
Franklin, North Carolina
October 7, 2001

A Note on Political Correctness and Historical Accuracy

In this edition the authors and editors have struggled with the standards of "political correctness" that have resulted in some changes that need explanation. The most obvious involves conversion to gender-neutral language, because "he" no longer can be acceptable as referring to all human beings. However, there are well-established distinctions between men and women, particularly when writing about the history of criminal justice. First and foremost, men and women differ in their historical patterns of criminal behavior, and there always have been far more male criminals than female criminals. Not only have punishments varied, but the expense of segregating prisoners by sex has frequently resulted in less-than-adequate women's prisons. Second, the legal (jural) status of women has historically been inferior to that of their male counterparts. At times this has resulted in the denial of all rights before the law when women committed offenses for which they were to be punished. The substantive law dealing with individual responsibility and the right to own or dispose of property has frequently imposed sweeping limitations on the legal capabilities of women. With adequate scholarly research it might be possible to deal with these factors and reflect when given rules of law, procedures, or punishments, were applicable to both sexes. Unfortunately, the place of women in the criminal justice system has not been the subject of extensive research. It would be wildly speculative to make general statements given the current state of knowledge.

Consequently, we have decided that when the evidence is not known, we should use the term "he." This reflects the predominance of males as those prosecuted, tried, and imprisoned for criminal activity. Our use of the terms "he or she," or a neutral plural such as "they," indicates that both males and females are included, or most likely are included, within the group to which we refer. We believe that this usage will most accurately reflect the conditions affecting both men and women, to the extent current scholarship permits us to make these determinations.

H.A.J.
N.T.W.

Table of Contents

Chapter 1

Introduction

Crime and its punishment are among the oldest problems faced by humankind; however, academic degree programs in criminal justice are relative newcomers to American colleges and universities. Most of these academic programs were launched in response to the federal government's initiative in passing the Law Enforcement Assistance Act (LEAA) of 1968. This law stressed federal assistance to state and local governments, as well as to academic institutions, in the hope that increased study of crime, law enforcement, and penology would result in a decrease in the crime rate.[1] Just as LEAA emphasis was on the solution of immediately pressing problems in the law enforcement field, so the new academic programs were primarily concerned with the professional subjects essential to graduates who would become law enforcement officers, forensic scientists, and corrections officials. The success of criminal justice programs and their general acceptance as part of the university curriculum have begun to modify this emphasis on current problems and practices. The full panoply of humanities and social science techniques are now applied to criminal justice problems. The student of today needs broad education in these fields, as well as in the forensic and legal sciences, if he or she is to function adequately and knowledgeably in the law enforcement profession.

Yet more than professional competence is involved in the liberal education of those who wish to enter the criminal justice field. Our nation and world desperately need informed law enforcement leadership that deals not only with the mechanical "how" criminal justice is operated, but also with the philosophical and moral "why" it should or should not continue to be conducted in a traditional manner. What is perhaps the major problem in human existence—criminal activity and its suppression—requires creative and innovative thought from those in professional leadership positions. Graduation from a criminal justice degree program cannot be the end of study for the professional; it can only be the beginning of a lifetime of hard study, applying good judgment, and the communicating ideas by articulate speech and writing.

Progress in any form of human endeavor comes only when men and women rise above the performance of routine day-to-day functions, only when they have dared to ask "why" and aspired toward constructive change.

1

While the human intellect and imagination have their limitations, these limitations have hardly been reached in the administration of criminal justice. We are right in striving to improve our system of law enforcement. We are wise to question the rationale and fundamental assumptions that support our penology. We do well to question what crime is and whether it can be prevented. That these are age-old questions does not make them less pressing in the twenty-first century; it proves that they are among the most complex problems facing humanity.

However, progress can be achieved only if an individual or a society has a firm understanding of where it has been and what has been achieved in the past. A knowledge of history provides a special sort of orientation for the leader of tomorrow.

First of all, history provides a sound perspective concerning the nature of human growth and development. Change takes place over time, and in most cases the elapsed time between the statement of a new idea or invention on one hand, and its full acceptance on the other, may well be more than one lifetime. Discontent with the slow tempo of change is more easily borne by one who recognizes this peculiarity of individual humans and their societies.

Second, historical knowledge brings with it some assurance against "reinventing the wheel." Modern society needs history much more than our ancestors did; the tragedy is that, in most cases, we do not realize it. Human beings badly need a sense of where they and their civilization have been before they can decide where they and their world should try to go. History is in many ways the "memory bank" of humankind. It does not repeat itself very frequently, if at all, but it gives to those who study it with care a very good idea of the mistakes past generations have made. It is only human to make mistakes; it is stupid to repeat them. Viewed in this way, the study of history is the accumulation of experience over time.

Third, history demands critical analysis and careful thought from its students. One of the worst charges that can be brought against the study of history is that it is the mere memorization of dates. The relationship of historical events, which is the study of cause and effect, is vastly more significant than dates. Historians must struggle with the weighty question of why individuals and societies acted as they did in the past. Why are some historical events so difficult to explain, and why do others seem to lend themselves to easy solutions? Spending time with human history makes the historian inquisitive about the nature and psychology of men and women throughout the ages. Has humankind really changed since the time of the Pharaohs? Historians seek to shape their findings into coherent patterns, and to draw generalizations from what people and societies have done at various times and in different places over the course of human existence. In this sense, history is always the application of a comparative method, for it is by comparisons, across time periods as well as across cultural and national experiences, that the general principles of human behavior can be most easily discerned.

This introductory survey of the history of criminal justice deals with the ways in which human beings and their societies have dealt with the serious issues of crime and its punishment. Throughout this text, an attempt has been made to engage the reader in his or her own analysis of historical events, and to raise issues from both a historical and a contemporary perspective. Focusing on the American experience, the book nevertheless devotes a substantial amount of space to the coverage of European and British developments, both as an antecedent to our national experience and as a parallel evolution of ideas and practices that have influenced American criminal justice. In addition, the treatment of ancient and medieval history has been included to illustrate not only the antiquity of the issue of crime and punishment, but also to provide the reader with an overview of the earliest developments. At the outset, it will be useful to direct some attention to the nature of crime itself, the general trends in law enforcement and the various approaches to punishment. These are themes that will recur throughout the chapters and are subjects that will become more clearly defined as the reader proceeds through the book.

Crime

One of the fastest ways to stop a glib speaker is to ask for a definition; that also works for college professors in the middle of a lecture. The definition of crime, supposedly a very simple concept, is actually very difficult. Webster's *New Universal Unabridged Dictionary* (New York, 1972) provides us with three useful definitions and one indirect definition:

1. An act committed in violation of a law prohibiting it, or omitted in violation of a law ordering it; crimes are variously punishable by death, imprisonment or the imposition of certain fines or restrictions.

2. An extreme violation of the law; wrongdoing of a criminal nature, as felony or treason, which affects the whole public and not just the rights of an individual; distinguishable from a misdemeanor.

3. An offense against morality; sin.

4. The acts of a criminal; habitual violation of the law.

If we exclude the fourth, which defines crime as what criminals do and thus defines criminals as those who commit crimes, we are left with two basic positions: (1) crime is defiance of a positive law and (2) crime is a breach of moral law. Henry Campbell Black, the compiler of the most widely used American law dictionary, defines crime as "a positive or negative act in violation of penal law; an offense against the State." He proceeds to discuss crimes that are *mala in se*, that is, evil in themselves or inherently evil, and those that are *mala prohibita*—not basically or morally wrong, but simply wrong because a statute or rule of common law makes them wrong. Placed side by side, it seems the two writers suggest that there is a positive definition that crime is the act or omission that the state condemns, and that there is also a moral or ethical dimension to the definition of crime. Indeed, their definitions and the historical experience of humankind suggest that, in the latter instance, crime may actually be identical with sin. When the ruler was considered the earthly manifestation of a god, such as in Pharaonic times, legal compulsion was indistinguishable from moral rules and sanctions.

Even this initial exploration into the accepted definition of crime does little to explain why a given act is a crime and another act, perhaps similar, is deemed acceptable and not punishable as a crime. It is best to approach the subject in terms of how societies in the course of history have decided what conduct should be prohibited. At the most basic level, societal prohibitions of conduct must focus on the relationships between individuals that most need protection. A person's life, the welfare of his or her family, the security of the individual against bodily harm, and the security of his or her possessions are among the basic needs of people in society. By far, the most significant collection of criminal law rules touches upon these basic human requirements. A second level of interest and concern is the need for a society to ensure order, stability, and productivity. Private wars, like family feuds in the American West, are not only costly in life and limb to the individuals directly involved, but they also pose a threat to innocent bystanders. As economic relationships become more complex, private battles and revenge may exact an unacceptable level of waste to the society and the state that depends upon prosperity for its well-being. At a still more abstract and third level of crime prohibition, there is the need for the state to ensure against being weakened by individual action. For example, the ruling monarch, president, or civil magistrate must be protected against violence; the public highways and places of legislative assembly must be given special attention and places of religious devotion must be made secure and kept inviolate. Individuals perform state-related functions, such as military duty, labor on highway maintenance, and undertaking public office; in appropriate cases, penalties may be prescribed for failure to keep oneself ready for such duties, as well as for failure to accept them gracefully and to perform them acceptably.

Crime as a concept does not emerge full-grown in any society. Quite to the contrary, it develops out of experience and is conditioned by social and cultural attitudes. For example, let us consider the act of killing another human being. In American society, unprovoked homicide committed knowingly and without justification has always been considered wrongful and punishable either as murder or manslaughter. However, in primitive societies, killing prevailed as a way of exacting private retribution, or revenge, upon one who killed a kin member. As we shall see, the killer's state of mind may also alter the criminal nature of the offense. If he or she lacked a certain level of mental capacity or was "insane" at the time the offense was committed, society may accept that as an adequate defense against prosecution. The state, by declaring war, may render legal, in both national and international law, a killing that otherwise could be prosecuted as murder or manslaughter. The further one attempts to define criminal homicide, the more apparent it will become that over the course of the history "crime" has changed, just as the reasoning that condemns it has changed.

In working through a definition of crime, we must take into account the variety of cultural perspectives that shape the concept. What might be considered murder in Western Europe is acceptable as a method of acquiring food in a cannibalistic tribe. For the most part, the criminal law in any state or territory is uniformly imposed upon all present within its boundaries. The law finds itself in difficulty when one of varied cultural background acts "criminally" according to territorial law but not in accordance with the law he or she knows. How does the cannibal in Washington, D.C., go about getting lunch without being prosecuted for murder or manslaughter? Indeed, could such an individual be effectively defended on the plea of cultural ignorance? Consider for a moment the bizarre and intriguing case of *The Queen v. Dudley and Stephens*, decided by the English Court of Queen's Bench in 1884. Three Englishmen and a young boy were cast adrift from a sinking ship without provisions in their lifeboat; after a time it became apparent that unless they could get food, they would all die. It was also obvious that the young boy would die much sooner, and two of the men took steps to hasten his death by cutting his throat with a knife. All three then ate his flesh and drank his blood. Picked up by a rescuing vessel a day after the young boy's body had been fully consumed, they were brought to trial in England, and the two who slit his throat were convicted of murder.

The *Dudley and Stephens* case raised some interesting questions in its own day, and it continues to fascinate law professors and students today. Among the strong arguments made on behalf of the cannibalistic men was the contention that the killing of the boy was essential for self-preservation and that no evil motive was involved, merely a decision to preserve life in the manner that seemed most appropriate under the dire circumstances of the case. Modern technology has, in fact, brought us back into the *Dudley and Stephens* situation because the current routine use of organ transplants involves the removal of vital organs from a body that is "brain dead" but may not be dead in terms of its circulatory system. In effect, the removal of the vital organs precipitates the process of dying, and while the circumstances and underlying societal attitudes differ widely from the 1884 English case, it is arguable that the necessity of preserving life (the organ recipient's) is the principal justification for the organ transplant donation. During the last century, we have seen medical developments that may require a closer look at the certainty of the English murder judgment in 1884.

Other evidence of the impact of culture upon the concept of crime is the degree to which a law generally applies only to the territory of the tribe or nation that promulgates the law. This assures that the cultural preferences of that particular region are implemented by the legal system. In the *Dudley and Stephens* case, English criminal law was held to apply because the men were shipwrecked from a British vessel; thus, English courts might try them under admiralty law for an offense committed on the high seas. However, had the two who killed the boy been under the same strictures of necessity in a territory ruled by a cannibal king, would they have been free to act as they did? Might it not be argued that even though they were by nationality English, they had the right to act as the law permitted in a land of cannibals: "When in Rome (in this case, in cannibal territory) do as the Romans (or cannibals) do."

When widely diverse cultures with differing views of law come into contact, legal and philosophical dilemmas are frequent. The concepts of private property ownership that European settlers carried with them to seventeenth-century America were not held by the eastern woodland Indians they met upon their arrival. The native Americans considered land to be without restriction except regarding hunting rights, and these rights were held not by individual tribesmen but, rather, by the tribe that occupied the land. Misunderstanding, litigation, and at times open violence resulted from the colonists' inability to deal with Indian attitudes toward property. Individual colonists raised in a legal system that provided harsh penalties for offenses such as larceny, robbery, and burglary found it difficult to adapt to Indian tendencies to appropriate unattended property for their own use. A few years prior to the English conquest of New Amsterdam in 1664, the Dutch authorities found themselves involved in suppressing an Indian uprising that originated from the fatal shooting of an Indian "stealing" peaches from a Dutch farmer's orchard.

Anthropologists tell us that culture is what shapes individuals into a civilization; it is the cement of tribes and nations. It is not surprising that law was once also a matter of belonging to a given clan, tribe, or nation, rather than being in a particular territory. Among nomadic tribes rules of law applied only within a tribe or cultural group; outside that group, one would be free to act as one pleased. Thus, the rules against killing another human were applied only within the tribe, and no formal action was necessary to permit a tribesman to kill a human being outside the tribal ranks. On the other hand, a tribe might specifically prohibit such homicides if they were found to bring warfare and hardship to the offender's people. Birth into a tribe or nation brought with it the right to appeal to tribal law for both privileges and protection. In the case of one of the graver offenses, an individual might lose this birthright and be "outlawed"; outside of the law's protection, he or she might be injured, robbed of possessions, or even killed without any punishment being imposed on other members of the tribe. Obviously, as interaction between different tribes and cultural groups became more frequent, the system of a tribal law that protected only individuals within the tribe became cumbersome and self-defeating. The need to trade with other tribes required a certain level of physical security to those who came to trade in tribal lands. This recognition of the need to expand beyond a tribal system of law worked two changes in customary law: (1) it broadened its applicability to include friendly strangers and (2) because it had to deal with strange new customary laws, it gradually was influenced by them and adapted its rules to those more generally accepted by adjacent tribes.

Across cultural boundaries and throughout historical time, there are a few constants that seem applicable to our definition of the term "crime." Despite variants, there is general agreement that taking another person's life is an evil act. Certain rules concerning family life (those prohibiting incestuous marriage, adultery, and other acts detrimental to the marital union) also tend to be common. There is also a general tendency to use penal sanctions to uphold the social structure; for example, harsher penalties may be applied to one who kills an overlord or chief than to one who kills an equal on the social ladder. Where societies have placed the father of an extended family in the role of judge and law enforcer within his household (as in republican Rome or in China), there are stronger penalties for patricide. Whenever the political powers are able, the tendency is to suppress blood feuds and revenge killings.

Crime and Sin

At the beginning of the previous section, we noted that the definition of *crime*, by common usage, also includes the idea of sin; lawyers tend to exclude this moral dimension in the discussion of crime and treat crime as something that is either prohibited or required by some rule of man-made law. At the outset of our study of criminal justice, it is important that the two concepts be discussed at some length, and that they be compared and contrasted in such a way that their distinctions and similarities are highlighted. However, at the same time it is important to realize that, historically, the concept of crime had the same roots as sin. Secular rulers, such as the Egyptian pharaoh, Chinese emperor, and even obscure tribal chieftains, were viewed as gods residing on earth, or as emissaries of gods who spoke authoritatively on behalf of the godhead. That being the case, the rules made by leaders had divine sanction as well, and offenses against those regulations might at the same time be considered both crimes and sins.

Of course, there is a moral dimension to the definition of crime. One of the most formative influences upon human culture is that of religious belief and practice. Theology, or the way in which men and women understand their relationship to their gods, determines the manner in which they will view society; it has been, and in many societies continues to be, the major source of ethical and behavioral rules. Not surprisingly, when legislators or judges participate in the lawmaking process, they are strongly influenced by their religious beliefs. Every rule of criminal law thus has a moral dimension derived in large measure from cultural views concerning theology.

On the other hand, even before the leaders of the American Revolution implemented the separation of church and state, it had been discovered that social diversity on matters of religion made it more difficult to agree upon one moral, or theological, basis for law. Just as ecclesiastical authority has, over time, become more and more separated from political sovereignty, so also has the attempt been made to secularize the concept of crime. From this has emerged the lawyer's simple definition that a crime is an offense against the laws of society, leaving sin to be dealt with as a matter of private religious belief. In asserting the state's authority to condemn behavior or demand actions by its subjects or citizens, society has caused a division between the concepts of crime and sin. The state may establish standards that govern human relationships and conduct, but it cannot and should not attempt to deal with the individual's relationship with his or her god. Indeed, transgressions of divine law (sins) are not, by modern standards, issues of state concern. This divergence of crime from sin is an important factor that has great significance in the study of criminal justice.

The early identification of crime with sin meant that offenses against human laws had the added dimension of being transgressions against divine commands. Those who committed crimes were offenders against the divinity, as well as against the state and other inhabitants; condemnation of such individuals who turned their backs upon both man and god was not a particularly complicated matter. The evil impulses of people and societies puzzle theologians and philosophers; essentially, the two major camps divide over whether there is one god who represents good or if there are two contending gods or forces that represent the struggle between good and evil. For the most part, the Judeo-Christian tradition has held the first position: that the evil in the world is due to human nature or to the temptations of the devil, who vainly opposes God and tries to draw men away from allegiance to God and into acts of evil. The society that equates crime with sin can easily judge the convicted felon to be either possessed by the devil or irredeemably evil. Ridding the earth of such a depraved creature makes the earth safer for others and also accords with what is perceived as God's purpose; it assists him in the heavenly struggle against the forces of evil. However, when society differentiates crime from sin, it refrains from such a moral judgment and is prepared to move in the direction of reforming, retraining, and rehabilitating the offender. Added to these considerations is the impact of Christian belief in the redemptive power of a loving God; even the most degenerate offender against the laws of society and God might be saved through repentance. As a consequence of these developments through recorded history, criminal law no longer considers the offender a person totally beyond the protections afforded to human beings. In this sense, an individual can never be completely outlawed in a society that believes that divine love and forgiveness is available to the most depraved of humankind. A secular version of this Christian view of humanity is contained in the Enlightenment philosophy of the seventeenth and eighteenth centuries.

Based upon a profound confidence in the perfectibility of humankind and the persuasiveness of reason, the Enlightenment had a profound influence over the development of law enforcement and penology.

The Human Sources of Crime

The Renaissance of the fifteenth century turned the focus of scholarly activity away from theology and toward the study of humanity. Thereafter, writers undertook the task of explaining why people acted as they did, and the modern social sciences began to take root as one of the primary tools used to understand human beings. As the National Rifle Association states, "Guns don't kill people, people do." That leads to the inevitable conclusion that human psychology is a vital key to the nature and source of crime. In times of despair over the venality of humankind, one is apt to conclude that Charles Darwin's theory of evolution—that human beings are evolved from anthropoid apes—is bound to be wrong. In fact, it is an outright insult to most monkeys, gorillas, and orangutans of our acquaintance. Yet some scientists assure us that humans are truly descended from a small, aggressive (and mean), meat-eating monkey. Even a brief survey of the cruelties of humankind, along with the extent and variety of criminal activities, leads one toward acceptance of such a verdict.

Whatever our ancestry may be, humans are extraordinarily attracted to crime. That tendency is part of the very characteristics that have permitted *homo sapiens* to populate even the most desolate areas of the earth's surface. Even under primitive conditions, people are adaptable to virtually any climate; they have survived natural disasters and harsh warfare. Diseases such as the Black Death of the 1340s left the race decimated, but it went on. Among mammals, humans have the highest reproduction rates due to the ability of the species to procreate at any time during the year rather than in isolated mating seasons. Aggressive, acquisitive, adaptable, and durable, the human race today is taller, better nourished, and more capable of self-destruction than any of its ancestors. This driving energy and force can, in the cases of many individuals, be turned to improper and even criminal purposes. Aggression and physical assertiveness may find outlets in assaults, batteries, murders, and rapes; acquisitiveness causes larcenies, burglaries, and robberies; accelerated to the level of entire societies, it can cause warfare between nations. Sexual urges can be adversely directed into a virtual encyclopedia of sex offenses, with attendant violence and homicide.

In earlier times, it was believed that people who had criminal inclinations might be identified by physical characteristics. Although no universally accepted anatomical mark of criminality was isolated, the studies (made in the nineteenth century) did much to advance the police science of identification through physical characteristics. Researchers paid careful attention to the shape of eyes, nose, and chin, and much was written on *phrenology* (the science of studying irregularities of the head, or cranium, which were said to disclose both good and evil characteristics in the personality). The question of whether women have historically been more or less prone to commit crimes than men is easily raised, but given the lack of documentation cannot be answered with certainty. Nor do historical records provide evidence about significant differences in the kinds of crime committed by women.

Behavioral aberrations in earlier centuries were not subjected to careful study but were attributed either to mental incapacity, physical illness, or the influence of the devil. As the humanism of the Renaissance was reinforced by the humanitarian impulses of eighteenth-century Europe, the subject of mental disease attracted students who laid the foundation for nineteenth-century research and progress in the field of human psychology. By the time Sigmund Freud began to publish his findings outlining the subconscious sources of human emotion and action, lawyers and judges were already dealing with the legal significance of mental illness as a defense against criminal prosecution. For the most part, they were concerned with the question of how essential it was for the perpetrator of an offense to have done so knowingly. Centuries ago, English common law contained a doctrine called *deodand*. This meant, for example, that a horse who bolted away from its master and dragged a cart over a bystander might be executed if the bystander died of the injuries. Eventually this foolish "punishment" of an animal, or even of an inanimate object (the cart might be burned if it rolled down a hill, killing a man), was deemed irrational. The nineteenth century dealt with the question of whether it was not just as unreasonable to "punish" a mentally ill person who was unable to form a criminal intent (*mens rea*) toward the activity for which he or she was condemned.

Substantial advances have been made in the study of human behavior, but it is still extraordinarily difficult to predict whether a given individual will become a criminal. The most that can be said is that certain personality traits may be keys to future inclination toward crime. Recently it has been suggested that criminal behavior may be hereditary. A group of physiologists identified particular chromosomes that occur most frequently in the cells of people who engage in criminal activity. Chromosomes carry an individual's DNA; they determine an individual's sex as well as physical characteristics, and it is possible that they also influence personality. If a particular genetic inclination to crime can be scientifically shown, then punishing a criminal's defiance of the law would be as irrational as punishing all members of society who are born with red hair or blue eyes. It could be argued that one who inherits a tendency toward crime is unable to stop him or herself from committing prohibited acts. Either on the ground of compulsion or on the basis of inevitability, he or she might be defended against prosecution.

TIME CAPSULE

What is a Crime? A Sign of Talented Individualism?

The French postmodernist historian Michel Foucault suggests a different definition of criminality than that set forth in this chapter. In *Discipline and Punish: The Birth of the Prison*, he advances the thought that the modern practice of imprisonment breeds delinquency, which he defines much as we would view the condition of habitual criminality. Following earlier scholars, he notes that recidivism—or repeated convictions of former prisoners—is very common. On the other hand, he posits the theory that the laboring poor form the majority of the delinquents because those individuals are the most creative and ambitious; were they members of the middle class, they would probably be highly successful businesspeople or political leaders. If that is the case, then the reformatory efforts of prisons are doomed to failure because crime is a product of class and personality, and prisons merely serve to perfect the skills of delinquents in perpetrating what law-abiding citizens call "criminal acts." At the very least Foucault's theories suggest that it may be time to reconsider the definition of crime and its possible origins within the social and economic classes.

Source: Michel Foucault, *Discipline and Punish: The Birth of the Prison*, trans. Alan Sheridan (New York: Pantheon Books, 1977), pp. 265-268, 286-291, 301.

Currently, the criminal justice system remains fairly rigid in its refusal to excuse crime except on the basis of proven insanity or mental illness. Excessive use of alcohol to the point of intoxication has regularly been rejected as a defense against prosecution, as has the use of habit-forming or hallucinatory drugs. The reason for this conservatism is that, in order to be effective, the criminal law must apply to all individuals within society. Permitting criminal behavior to be excused upon the receipt of evidence of "criminal heredity," intoxication or drug addiction leaves society unprotected against offenders who fit into these categories. On the other hand, the criminal intent (or *mens rea*) that is necessary to convict may be just as lacking in a habitual drunkard or drug user as it is in one suffering from mental illness.

Within the mysteries of human personality, there may well be the key to the eradication of crime from our society. Individuals, acting either singly or in groups, are the decisive elements in determining whether criminal activity will flourish or decline. Much of the study of criminal justice is involved with methods of influencing individuals to behave in a responsible and law-abiding fashion.

Our system of punishments is graduated to dissuade wrongdoers from committing more serious crimes after committing lesser offenses. The rationale for visible police patrolling is to make the presence of law enforcement personnel obvious and, thereby, to discourage those who would break the law. However, with all of these external incentives toward lawful behavior, it is also readily apparent that most citizens are inclined to obey the law even in the absence of harsh punishments or effective police action. The majority of the population accepts and abides by the provisions of the criminal law; it is only the minority, which already inclines toward crime, that might be deterred by the fear of punishment.

Social Factors and Crime

One reason for the citizen's ready acquiescence in traditional prohibitions against crime is the existence of a complex net of social relationships that inhibit criminal behavior. A number of historical examples illustrate the role of family and neighborhood relationships in law enforcement. In Anglo-Saxon England, it was the responsibility of local villages to police their members and accept punishment if wrongdoers were not apprehended and punished. As recently as seventeenth-century New England, we can find clear evidence of family ties working to inhibit criminal activity. This situation arose from the peculiar circumstances of New England colonization. Unlike the other English colonies, Massachusetts Bay and its sister colonies were settled by religious dissenters from the practices and beliefs of the established, or state-supported, Church of England. Entire congregations from small and closely knit English villages migrated to America together. Many families who were related by blood ties found themselves joining each other in establishing new and independent towns in sparsely settled New England. The extensive intermarriage that was common in England continued in America, as far as the traditional prohibitions against incest would permit. The crime rate was remarkably low due to these family ties between the inhabitants. Law enforcement was a private affair, where cousins kept a watchful eye on each others' backsliding, and elderly citizens, also related to the inhabitants, sat as town officials to administer justice. New Englanders also practiced "close watching," a duty imposed on all to keep a morally weak brother or sister from doing evil and, hence, offending against not only the criminal law but also against the moral commands of God. Perhaps at no other time in history was crime so closely identified with sin, and at few other times has the law been so well enforced by a population that strove mightily to be its "brother's keeper."

Seventeenth-century New England illustrates another social factor that had an impact on the historical crime rate: the stability in population that was characteristic of societies that were predominantly agricultural. That stability was characterized not only by the maintenance of a fairly uniform population but also by relatively little change in the identity of the inhabitants except by the natural processes of birth and death. Historically, the ability of a community to control criminal behavior has depended on the law-abiding citizen's ability to recognize any potential offender. The arrival of strangers in any town diminishes this capability and, therefore, increases the likelihood of crime. In the earliest years of New England colonization, the small rural towns were populated by families who knew each other, perhaps for many generations, and the most substantial migration into the communities came by way of marriage into an established family. Migration out of the town occurred only when the available land could no longer support those who reached adulthood, and they sought economic independence elsewhere. Those who decided to leave their native town or village found it necessary to ensure in advance their welcome in a new town. Poor laws required each town to support the needy residents within the town; as a result, only those economically able to support themselves were likely to find a welcome in a town with available land.

Such closely interrelated and stable town populations are actually the rule, rather than the exception, in world history. Only as commercial and industrial development has destroyed the agricultural basis of economic life have we seen the growth of a population that is not closely tied to the land, a society in which individuals most probably would spend their entire lives within a few miles of the place of their birth. Of course, those changes occurred centuries ago, and with them they brought the isolation of individuals from their society, the spiritual loneliness once typical only of the stranger, and a rising suspicion and fear concerning the motives and actions of others. Until about the fourteenth century, virtually all of the common people of Europe lived on manorial estates and earned their meager existence through farming. Bound by generations of intermarriage and close association, individuals knew each other and relied upon the good character of their neighbors. However, when disease and land redistribution destabilized European society, these conditions ceased to exist. Excess population drifted to the larger towns and cities, creating a faceless mass in desperate need of support and increasing the threat of criminal activity. It was amidst this turmoil that the discovery of the Americas opened the promise not only of riches but also of the chance to regain the comfort and stability lost with the passing of a traditional agricultural society.

The economic upheavals that shook early modern Europe had a profound impact upon the individuals of that time. For the first time in their lives, farm laborers were threatened with expulsion from the lands traditionally cultivated by their ancestors. The enclosure movements that turned substantial portions of English farmland into pasturage for sheep also turned dispossessed farmers into highly competitive materialists struggling to survive in a strange and terrifying new world. It alerted them to the need for self-help and turned them away from confidence in the benevolence of their social "superiors," the landowners. In the future, they would learn to prize certainty of property ownership and yearn for land that they held as freehold rather than by the copyhold rights (undocumented customary interests) that they had lost in their ancestral lands. Destruction of communal life in the manors released men and women into a new and highly competitive world; it was a time of change and excitement, even as it was a time of hardship and despair. Instability altered not only social patterns and individual attitudes toward life, but also turned many toward antisocial and criminal activity.

TIME CAPSULE

Government Interference with Individual Sovereignty

A perennial debate in the history of criminal justice concerns the degree to which government should be allowed to interfere with individual liberty in the effort to provide for the safety of the community. A classic statement of the libertarian view of government power was penned by John Stuart Mill in 1859:

The object of this essay is to assert one very simple principle, as entitled to govern absolutely the dealings of society with the individual in the way of compulsion and control, whether the means used be physical force in the form of legal penalties, or the moral coercion of public opinion. That principle is, that the sole end for which mankind are warranted, individually or collectively, in interfering with the liberty of action of any of their number, is self-protection. That the only purpose for which power can be rightfully exercised over any member of a civilised community, against his will, is to prevent harm to others. His own good, either physical or moral, is not a sufficient warrant. He cannot rightfully be compelled to do or forbear because it will be better for him to do so, because it will make him happier, because, in the opinions of others, to do so would be wise, or even right. These are good reasons for remonstrating with him, or reasoning with him, or persuading him, or entreating him, but not for compelling him, or visiting him with any evil in case he do otherwise. To justify that, the conduct from which it is desired to deter him must be calculated to produce evil to someone else.

Source: John Stuart Mill, On Liberty (New York: W. W. Norton & Company, 1975) pp. 10-11.

Question
Can you think of ways in which current law violates Mill's principle?

Sixteenth-century Europe witnessed the collapse of unified Christianity in the West as well as the rise of a number of denominations protesting against the doctrines and practices of the Roman Catholic Church. Protestantism provided still another factor moving people toward individualism and away from the community and stability of medieval society. With its emphasis upon the personal relationship between the individual and his or her God, this new form of Christianity was particularly attuned to the new economic conditions. Max Weber, an influential writer on history and philosophy, has suggested that Protestantism was an essential ingredient in the rise of capitalism. Growing acquisitiveness and the demand for security of property rights may well have preceded the Protestant Reformation, but it is apparent that individualism was further encouraged by the new religious beliefs. In terms of crime and violence, the Protestant Reformation can be seen to have had two effects. First, by weakening the unity of Christendom, it accelerated doubts concerning the traditional equation of crime with sin. The diversity of Christian denominations born of the Reformation resulted in secular states adopting criminal laws that would apply equally to all religious groups within their borders. The second impact of the Protestant Reformation was the beginning of a series of religious wars, which introduced even greater instability into society, increased the population's familiarity with violence, and heightened tensions between opposing religious groups.

Europe's turmoil during the religious wars was followed in the eighteenth century by the beginning of the industrial revolution, a widespread movement based on scientific discoveries that made it possible to use machines and large numbers of laborers to mass-produce consumer goods. Intensive use of labor required that workers be concentrated in urban centers, with an increase in the demand for food, shelter, and other necessities in those areas. The attraction of employment drew new migrants into the city and depressed wages in spite of the rising cost of living. Industrial capitalists grew wealthy while laborers starved. The widening gap between the rich and the poor, coupled with the intense overcrowding and competition of nineteenth-century urban life, caused great unrest in society. In Europe, Britain, and the United States, concerned statesmen addressed themselves to the problems of poor relief on the one hand and the need to combat the rising crime rate on the other hand. Harsh penalties for minor crimes failed to dissuade desperate men and women from stealing to sustain their lives and to protect their children. Scholars and reformers made careful studies of the existing modes of punishment and their effectiveness. Cities such as London and New York began to replace the ineffectual night watch with more formally organized police organizations. Under the prod of Enlightenment philosophers, the French system of criminal prosecution was reformed, and the prevailing sense of social responsibility and rationality caused the Italian philosopher Cesare de Beccaria to suggest that the law should carefully measure the severity of the punishment by the gravity of the crime.

The severe upheaval of the industrial revolution left such chaos in society that institutions had to be erected to prevent, detect, and punish criminal activity. As a consequence, the nineteenth and twentieth centuries witnessed the rise of police departments, specialized criminal courts, elaborate safeguards for accused persons, and the increase in the numbers of scholars and prison reformers attempting to find the most effective mode to punish criminals and discourage them from perpetuating their lives of crime. It can safely be said that before the industrial revolution, criminal behavior was considered rare enough that society could deal with the offender in a makeshift fashion. Untrained local officials handled much of the preliminary processing; appeals to higher courts were virtually unknown, and after a guilty verdict the execution of a sentence (usually death) came quickly. The great increase in crime after the industrial revolution made it necessary to institutionalize what earlier had been very informal.

Crime, Punishment, and Ideas

While all of the factos already discussed involved new ideas concerning individual psychology and social behavior, at various times ideas themselves have been adopted and applied by the state, producing striking changes in crime, punishment, and law enforcement. Thus, all aspects of criminal justice are influenced by the views societies take of people and their behavior. Christianity led to a new and optimistic view concerning human nature and the probability of redemption; applied to the behavioral sciences, the theological doctrine of redemption suggested that antisocial behavior might be altered by the proper incentives. The Renaissance and the thoughts of Enlightenment philosophers in the eighteenth century stressed the rational qualities of the human mind and relied heavily upon persuasion and training to alter criminal conduct. Beginning with the major work of Beccaria, a new school of thought evolved concerning the function that punishment should play in the criminal justice system. Enlightenment ideals also considered at length the relationship of people to the state; translated into American constitutional principles, these ideals became the foundation for the federal Bill of Rights and similar sections in state constitutions. Essentially, these procedural protections for persons accused of crime were designed to provide a fair trial—a proceeding that would most rationally decide the issues of guilt or innocence—and thus would be most acceptable to the society at large. Under these incentives, the French began to reform their modes of criminal procedure, eliminating some of its irrationality and duplicating to some degree the English practices that seemed more rational and more fair to accused persons.

The eighteenth-century political thinker saw the state as a fearful power capable of destroying human liberty and freedom if it were wrongfully used. This generated the great interest in constitutional limitations upon government, evidenced by the Constitution of the United States and by the English imposition of limits on their monarch in the Glorious Revolution 100 years previously. Political theorists were busy developing the delicate balance of powers that would so inhibit the actions of the state that citizens would be safe from oppression and able to pursue their personal happiness and well-being. Individualism in political matters echoed the free competition and classical liberalism that Adam Smith advocated in the area of economic activity. Of course, people of the eighteenth century, with the exception of the French Revolutionaries who brought it to a close, did not believe in equality for all people. Only individuals who had sufficient wealth and social standing were allowed to be part of the voting public, but others were free to work themselves into being a "stakeholder" in society. As we have suggested, the harsh realities of the industrial revolution raised questions about the fairness and rationality of such a system of free individualism, and the ideals of the eighteenth century were restated in the nineteenth.

Throughout the Western world, the nineteenth century was a time for increased concern for human affairs and conditions. Early in the century, the British Parliament began a series of commissioned studies on land distribution, public health and sanitation, housing for the needy, adequacy of food supplies, and similar topics that we would term "public welfare matters." These commissions ultimately published lengthy reports detailing their findings on the social and economic conditions of Victorian England, and those reports led to Parliamentary action aimed at altering the wretched conditions under which many of Britain's urban poor existed. Within the United States, the later occurrence of the industrial revolution and the division of authority between federal and state governments delayed such an outright inquiry into the state of society, but individual reform movements championed the rights of the imprisoned debtor, the condemned criminal, the oppressed woman, and most significantly, the black Americans held in slavery.

Humanitarianism was the focus of nineteenth-century social thought. Perhaps for the first time in the history of crime, reformers directed attention to the quality of life in prisons and penitentiaries and made efforts to influence convicts with religion, in the hope that some positive change might occur. Recognizing poverty as one motive for criminal activity, they also gave attention to the vocational training of prisoners held for short terms. They instituted elaborate systems of rewards for good behavior, including parole and early release. Toward the end of the century, they also made efforts to soften the punishment for young offenders and individuals likely to benefit from specialized treatment. As a consequence, even as criminal justice became more rigidly institutionalized, it also became more aware of the needs of suffering individuals and their society.

TIME CAPSULE

Why Do We Punish?

In examining the reasons given for punishing convicted persons, criminologists have identified five major categories of justification for punishment (each of which has subcategories). These five purposes are not mutually exclusive; nor are they specifically related to particular cultures or time periods. It is, however, often possible when reading contemporary accounts or judicial opinions to discern which reason was primary. As you read this text, ask yourself which purpose was predominant in the Anglo-Saxon period, in medieval England, in the American colonies, on the western frontier, and in the United States today.

1. Retribution

The principle of retaliation is that the person who has caused harm must suffer punishment, whether it be through physical pain, financial deprivation, loss of freedom, or other hardship. Often included in the concept of retribution is the principle of proportionality (*lex talionis*): the suffering inflicted on the convicted person should be equal to the harm he or she caused.

2. Deterrence

Under this principle, a sentence can be designed to deter the convicted person from committing further crimes (specific deterrence) by convincing him or her that the potential punishment for future violations would be too painful to risk. In an effort the impress this message on other members of the society as well (general deterrence), the sentence can be maximized and dramatized.

3. Incapacitation

The goal of incapacitation is to make it impossible for the convicted person to commit crimes. A death sentence is the ultimate example; other types of punishments severely limit the ability to violate criminal law, such as imprisonment, castration, or revocation of the license to practice medicine or law.

4. Rehabilitation

Based on the idea that the criminal violation resulted from inadequate socialization of the offender, rehabilitation represents an effort to provide counseling and practical training that can aid an offender and thereby weaken or remove the stimuli that led him or her to crime.

5. Divine Will

In societies that believed in an interactive god, divine will was the genesis of criminal law: When a person violated the law, he or she also offended god. The object of punishment was to bring the offender back to right relation to god and to avert the wrath of god against a community if it tolerated violation of divine will. Countries that have established the principle of separation of church and state do not, of course, overtly acknowledge a religious basis for punishment. However, it may continue to be significant in the attempt to rehabilitate offenders.

The thoughts of men and women are powerful forces in the history of humankind, and they form a significant part of any serious study of the way societies have approached the problems of crime and the administration of justice. Fortunately for the historian, ideas are communicated most effectively in the form of writings, and thus they tend to be preserved for historical study. In dealing with events, a student is frequently reduced to reconciling a variety of unrelated statements concerning the subject, bringing together all of the available statistical evidence, and then suggesting why people acted as they did. By way of contrast, the author who reduces his or her thoughts to written form wishes to influence others and is most likely to state with clarity the way in which he or she has arrived at given conclusions.

Summary

As with the studies of other areas of history, study of the antecedents of American criminal justice makes several demands on the student, because a number of factors must be kept in mind. Among the most important is the need to appreciate the complexities of the human being and the influences that motivate individual behavior; understanding human psychology is important not only for analyzing crime and those who commit criminal acts, but also to appreciate the reactions of law-abiding individuals and societies to crime and its punishment. Next, the student must look at the historical development of societies and economic systems (the changes and circumstances that may be far beyond an individual's control). Although people have, for the most part, succeeded in shaping the world to their own liking, individuals at times feel helpless against the forces of society as well as against the cruelties of nature. Part of appreciating humankind is identifying the relationship that people through the ages have attempted to define between themselves and their god. That identification defines not only the connection between crime and sin, but also shapes the individual's concept of good and evil. Cultural influences other than religion also have a great impact on a society's definition of crime and its decisions concerning punishment. It is in the variety of reactions, on the part of different societies and under vastly different conditions, that the serious student will find a basis for thought. Learning is a process of absorbing new material and gaining new insights into the world in which we live; it is also a process of reassessing past assumptions, rejecting false premises, and remaining open to new ideas. Studying criminal justice history may elevate one's spirit or depress the soul. It cannot leave one unaffected.

Discussion Questions

1. Is innate human nature unchanging throughout recorded history?

2. What factors limit the potential criminal´s choices?

3. Do you agree with the statement "Every rule of criminal law has a moral dimension that is largely based on cultural views on religion"?

4. Is it possible for a nation to eliminate all crime?

5. Are there occasions on which it would be moral to violate criminal law?

Notes

[1]   See Chapter 13.

References

For principles of culpability, see Hyman Gross, *A Theory of Criminal Justice* (New York: Oxford University Press, 1979). Theories of crime and punishment are examined in Philip Jenkins, *Crime and Justice: Issues and Ideas* (Monterey: Brooks/Cole Publishing Company, 1984); Robert C. Solomon and Mark C. Murphy, *What is Justice? Classic and Contemporary Readings* (New York: Oxford University Press, 1990); Lawrence M. Friedman, "Legal Rules and the Process of Social Change," *Stanford Law Review*, 19, no. 4 (April 1967), pp. 786-840; J.A. Inciardi, A.A. Block, and L.A. Hallowell *Historical Approaches to Crime: Research Strategies and Issues*. (Beverly Hills: Sage Publications, 1977), Chapter 1.

Although information concerning the role of women in criminal activity and in the criminal justice process is scarce, students will find useful references in general histories of sex: Gordon Rattray Taylor, *Sex in History* (New York: Vanguard Press, 1970); Reay Tannahill, *Sex in History* (Chelsea, MI: Scarborough House, 1992); Morton Hunt, *The Natural History of Love* (New York: Anchor Books, 1994).

Chapter 2

Criminal Justice in Ancient Times

The roots of Western civilization reach deep into antiquity, as do the problems of crime and punishment. In this chapter we shall be concerned with the experience of biblical Israel, classical Athens, and republican Rome; this is a period of nearly 1,200 years—longer by 200 years than from the time of William the Conqueror (1066 A.D.) to the present day. These cultures differed in their stages of economic development and in their fundamental attitudes toward human life, but each formed a vital part of Western civilization. The vast treasury of the Bible provides a rich heritage of history, theology, and philosophy that has had a persistent impact upon modern society. The Greek city-state of Athens provides the ideal of a culture governed by the active political participation of the people in the affairs of government, and the massive edifice of Roman legal and constitutional principles has shaped Western views of government through the ages.

Each of these civilizations made its imprint on recorded history at a crucial stage in its development. Biblical Israel moved from a nomadic existence, based upon herding sheep and goats, into an established farming society located in the promised land (c. 1200-650 B.C.). Athens in its classical period (594-404 B.C.) thrived upon Mediterranean commercial activity, its vast trade providing foodstuffs and other necessities of life imported from less advanced territories. With a long history of seeking freedom, Athenians placed a high premium on their city-state's ability to resist the rise of tyrants, although much of Athens' labor was performed by slaves acquired through conquest or purchased abroad. Republican Rome built upon the loyalty of the Roman citizen to erect a constitutional state, ruled by the interplay of aristocratic power in the Senate and plebeian strength manifested in the tribunate. At the time we study Rome (509-25 B.C.), it triumphed over most of the civilized world. It was heavily dependent upon trade for its necessities and employed a vast army of foreign slaves on its farms, manufactories, and households.

TIME LINE

Israel/Near East	Athens	Rome
1700 B.C. Code of Hammurabi		
c. 1280 B.C. Exodus from Egypt Ten Commandments Book of Covenant (?)		
c. 1000-961 B.C. Reign of David Cities of refuge established		
961-922 B.C. Reign of Solomon Two-witness rule established		
	753/752 B.C. Tenure of magistrates reduced to ten years	**713-673 B.C.** Compensation to be paid for accidental killing
	683 B.C. Tenure of magistrates reduced to one year	
	659-510 B.C. First Age of Tyrants	
640-609 B.C. Reign of Josiah **c. 625 B.C.** Deuteronomy text discovered Court of priests established	**621 B.C.** Draco's criminal law code	
	594 B.C. Solon becomes Chief magistrate	
	594/593 B.C. People gain right to appeal from magistrates	
		578-534 B.C. Law against patricide
		509 B.C. *Lex Valeria* limits magistrate's authority in regard to death sentences
	508/507 B.C. Cleisthenes expands Athenian citizenship	
	487-422 B.C. Cases tried by jury (*dicastery*)	
		451-450 B.C. The Twelve Tables, a penal code, promulgated
	410-404 B.C. Revision of laws by Nikomakhos	
		367 B.C. *Urban praetor* courts established

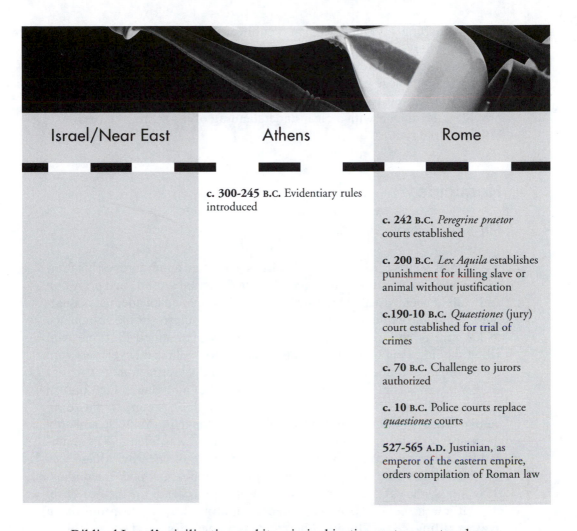

Israel/Near East	Athens	Rome
	c. 300-245 B.C. Evidentiary rules introduced	
		c. 242 B.C. *Peregrine praetor* courts established
		c. 200 B.C. *Lex Aquila* establishes punishment for killing slave or animal without justification
		c.190-10 B.C. *Quaestiones* (jury) court established for trial of crimes
		c. 70 B.C. Challenge to jurors authorized
		c. 10 B.C. Police courts replace *quaestiones* courts
		527-565 A.D. Justinian, as emperor of the eastern empire, orders compilation of Roman law

Biblical Israel's civilization and its criminal justice system centered upon the fact that the descendants of Abraham occupied the unique position of being the chosen people of the great god, Yahweh. Rules of behavior, as well as the structure of criminal law and punishments, reflected this profound religious influence. Wrongful conduct was offensive upon two grounds: (1) it destroyed the bonds of society, causing dissension among the people of Israel; and (2) the wrong of any member of God's chosen people could easily bring divine wrath down upon the entire nation. National rectitude was essential to the survival of a culture so closely tied to its jealous and all-knowing deity.

Athenians lived by a different code, although there is evidence that some of their criminal law, derived from an earlier historical period, also sought to prevent divine displeasure. Their experience with harsh rulers had convinced them that democracy, or the rule of the people, was essential to happiness. As their economic prosperity grew, so did their insistence upon governmental forms that would discourage any citizens from seizing power and establishing a tyranny. Roman republicans shared the Greek antipathy to kingly rulers, but their government was founded upon the concept of the citizen-soldier as the key to Roman dominance in the world. Conferring special status upon those privileged to be citizens of Rome, their system of criminal justice served to protect the citizen from unjust prosecution and to provide each citizen with a clear understanding of his rights and responsibilities to the state.

Homicide

Biblical Israel

Virtually all Near Eastern civilizations permitted a murderer or his family to pay compensation to the family of the deceased victim. In a primitive and violent society where labor was scarce, this seemed an adequate penalty for homicide while maintaining the labor of the culprit for the sustenance of his family and clan. However, Israelite law demanded that one who killed should be put to death, a relatively harsh principle that developed from the theological connection between the blood of the victim and the spirit of God. Yahweh was believed to possess the blood of a human, which in turn contained the spirit given to the individual by the Creator. In shedding human blood, a murderer took what rightfully belonged to Yahweh, and only the murderer's death and the shedding of his blood was adequate compensation. If a murdered person was found in a field, the nearby village was expected to sacrifice an animal if the culprit could not be found, and domestic animals who caused a person's death were put to death for their offense.

Although the Ten Commandments contain an absolute prohibition against killing, certain forms of homicide were permissible. The most obvious exceptions were killings required by warfare. Nonintentional killing was shielded by the existence of cities of refuge, to which a killer might flee to avoid conviction and the immediate imposition of the usual sentence: death by stoning. In a city of refuge, the killer awaited extradition from the place of the homicide, at which time the elders of the refuge city either turned the killer over to the prosecuting authorities or declared him guiltless and free to leave. Issues of criminal intent and proximate cause also played a role in Israelite homicide law, and these matters were so complex that they were removed to the Temple in Jerusalem, where the priests resolved these issues rather than the traditional court of town elders.

Athens

Because of its origins well before the classical period of Athenian history, the city-state's homicide law bore some similarity to that of ancient Israel. It was believed that a type of corruption, or miasma, attached to the person of a murderer. It also infected homicidal animals, or even a stone statue if it fell upon an Athenian citizen and killed him. Merely being accused of homicide made a person corrupt, and the accused person's movements were sharply circumscribed to keep him away from places of assembly and from sites of religious significance. The punishment for homicide, either intentional or unintentional, was expulsion from Athens and the surrounding countryside. Should the killer return from exile, he was tried at the Phreatto, a seaside location where a special court heard the evidence from a boat anchored offshore and then either reimposed exile or ordered death as a punishment. In the case of an unintentional homicide, the exiled culprit might secure a pardon from the victim's family and, thus, obtain permission to return to Athens.

In Athenian law, certain homicides were deemed justifiable. One could execute an exile who had returned without first obtaining a pardon. A citizen was justified in killing another who was attempting to set up a tyranny or to overthrow the democracy. A thief caught at night in the house of the intended victim might justifiably be killed by the householder. Deaths that occurred during brawls, in athletic contests, and in a passion over finding a wife or a concubine in the amorous embrace of another were also justifiable, and hence excused.

Rome

Roman law concerning homicide seems to have provided death as the penalty for intentional homicide and to have permitted the payment of blood money to the victim's family should the homicide be declared unintentional. From the meager evidence that survives, it appears that Roman views of homicide were more primitive than those prevalent at Athens, and we know that life was less valued in Roman society. In the early days of the republic, it was a common practice to expose deformed infants at birth, leaving them to die of exposure. Also, it was long the rule in Rome that a father might discipline his sons, even to the point of inflicting death, without running the risk of prosecution. It is not possible to say whether any special revulsion or religious taboo was involved in republican Rome's punishment of homicide.

Sex Offenses

Biblical Israel

Society and family life in biblical Israel was strongly patriarchal and heterosexual in its orientation. This preserved the genetic integrity of God's chosen people and also ensured rapid population increase to consolidate Israelite dominance of the Holy Land. Given this emphasis, it is not surprising that the major thrust of law was the punishment of adultery, defined as the sexual intercourse of one person with a married member of the opposite sex. With certain exceptions, both parties were put to death by stoning. Unlike other systems of Near Eastern law, Israelite criminal law did not permit the wronged husband to pardon his adulterous wife, because that would not make the criminal act clean. Should a free man engage in intercourse with a female slave betrothed to another, he was compelled to pay a fine, but no compensation was given to the betrothed husband of the adulterous slave. Fornication, or the unlawful sexual intercourse of two unmarried persons, was subject to mild sanctions. The father of a seduced virgin might demand the customary marriage present from the culprit, even if she did not marry him.

Athens

By way of comparison, Athenian punishment for sex offenses seems relatively mild. The rape of a free woman was punishable by a fine to be paid to her father or husband. Seduction was subject to harsher sanctions, presumably on the theory that her mind as well as her body had been corrupted. The seducer caught in the act might be killed outright by the woman's father or husband. If death was not inflicted, the seducer might be imprisoned and tormented. Two forms of torture were preferred: pulling out the culprit's pubic hair or forcing radishes up his anus.

The offenses of incest and fornication existed in Athenian law and usually were punished by compensation to the woman's husband or father, rather than by any physical sanctions. The presence of homosexuality in Athenian society required that the laws concerning rape and seduction be applied equally for the protection of men as well as women. Penalties against recruiting free persons into prostitution were also unisex in their application.

Rome

Early Roman legal texts do not deal with sex offenses, but the likelihood is that Greek rules may have provided a pattern for later Roman development. After 100 B.C., the offense of *inuria* (a malicious destruction of reputation) was developed by the Roman judges, and included within *inuria* was the right of a free woman whose chastity had been slandered to recover compensation from the wrongdoer.

Theft

Biblical Israel

The Ten Commandments prohibit theft in a statement that includes both property-taking and kidnapping. Originally, the sanction of death may have applied to both infractions, but by 620 B.C., only kidnapping was punished this severely. Property-taking was punished by fining the thief some multiple of the value of the animal or object stolen. That fine was increased if it appeared that the culprit exercised acts of dominion beyond mere possession; for example, if he either sold or destroyed the stolen animals or goods. This suggests that among a nomadic people whose wealth is in flocks of animals it was difficult to establish criminal intent by the mere fact of possession. However, either selling or killing another's animal involved the greater likelihood that the culprit knew that he was dealing with the property of another.

Property placed in the possession of a bailee (one who held goods for the owner) and subsequently stolen was subject to two rules of law. The taker was punished by multiple compensation if he was found. Otherwise, the bailee was put to proof and required to show that he did not take the goods himself. This rule, with increased compensation demanded because of sale or destruction of the stolen property, is an interesting demonstration of the way in which guilt was determined by weighing the probability of wrongful intent. A herdsman was expected to survey his flock regularly to prevent wrongful possession of another's animal. However, the inadequate performance of that duty was not as culpable as singling out an animal that belonged to another and selling it or killing it as if it belonged to the wrongdoer. Similarly, a bailee was responsible for returning the goods, and was subject to sanctions if the property was taken from his possession and he could not identify the thief; indeed, it was presumed that the bailee himself stole the goods unless he could prove the contrary. Violent seizure of another person's property, known as robbery in modern law, does not appear within the offenses enumerated by biblical law. Scholars have suggested that such an offense was outside the communal law of the people, something to be expected only of brigands and foreigners. Consequently, it was a matter to be dealt with by the military authorities and very likely punishable by death.

Athens

Athenian views of theft appear to be similar to the Israelite pattern of demanding multiple compensation to the owner. Harsher sanctions were provided for the thief caught in the act of a nocturnal burglary; if discovered by the owner, he could be killed by the owner. If his activities were later proven, the nocturnal thief would be executed. Stealing from Athens' sacred Temple or its precincts was punishable by death, as was theft from the public treasury or Temple property. Kidnapping a freeman was also a capital offense. Commercial aspects of life in Athens generated a new group of economic crimes that might be included within the general category of theft. Special courts imposed rules concerning fair prices and the forestalling (or monopolistic hoarding) of goods for profit. Counterfeiting coins and knowingly passing such coins were punishable by death.

Rome

Like biblical and Athenian law, Roman statutes imposed compensation as the penalty in situations of ordinary theft. If the thief was caught in the act, either at night or in possession of a weapon while stealing in the day, he could be killed by the victim and the homicide would be justified. However, such a killing during the day had to be preceded by the owner's shouting, presumably to draw the neighbors' attention to the owner's exercise of self-help. Unarmed thieves caught in the act during daylight hours were scourged and enslaved to the victim if the victim was a free person. Slaves caught in the act during the day, even if unarmed, were sentenced to be scourged and then executed by being thrown from the Tarpeian Rock.[1]

Selected for special punishment was the offense of cutting a neighbor's crops by night. The offender was sentenced to be "hung up" and then sacrificed (killed) to the goddess Ceres, presumably because the offender offended her as the patroness of the earth's fertility. The use of the term "hung up" in the provisions of Rome's Twelve Tables, a special legal code, suggests that crucifixion may have been used

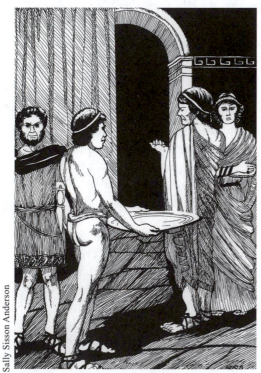

Sally Sisson Anderson

The "platter and loin cloth" search of fourth-century B.C. Athens and Rome was a strange rite employed to discover stolen goods.

as a way of enhancing punishment prior to actual execution. The punishment could be mitigated if the offender was under age, in which case he or she was usually scourged and enslaved to the victim.

Both Athenian and Roman law used a strange rite for the discovery of stolen goods. This was the platter and loin cloth search, which required the owner of the stolen goods to walk virtually naked through the premises of the suspect, holding a platter in both hands. Presumably this arrangement was to prevent him from touching any object and from carrying incriminating evidence into the house. The rationale was that if the lost object was present, it would reveal itself to its rightful owner. Clearly, this mode of search would have been most effective if the stolen property was a domestic animal that would recognize its master, even in his nakedness. How it would reveal inanimate objects is unclear.

Criminal Procedure and Sanctions

In all three systems of ancient law, the initiation of a criminal case depended upon the initiative of the person wronged or, if the person had been killed, by his family. Thus, criminal procedure perpetuated the primitive system of revenge, and the state acted not as a prosecutor, but as a weigher of evidence and as a sovereign power dispensing punishment. To a limited degree, the forgiveness of the prosecuting individual or family might serve to lessen the penalties imposed for an offense.

Biblical Israel

The ancient trial court of Israel, and the most common tribunal throughout its biblical history, was the "court at the gate." Originating in the authority of each clan's elders to determine controversies within the kin group, the court at the gate came into being with the establishment of towns and cities in the Holy Land. Usually convened in the morning hours, it met at the demand of litigants who waited at the gate of the town, demanding that the elders who passed through on their way to the fields should first stop to do justice. Both civil and criminal actions were tried at the gate, and, undoubtedly, the selection of this place for trial was made to allow the maximum number of people to witness the proceedings. In a criminal case, the accusing party stood to the right of the accused and, in the presence of the elders (who were seated), presented his or her complaint. Although this accusation was usually given orally, it might be written. The accused person might be assisted in his or her defense by a defender, who was in fact a witness for the defense. Each of the elders sitting as a judge acted as an arbitrator in the case and might himself give evidence pertinent to the matter being tried. The accusing witness bore special responsibility for prosecuting the case, and his role was emphasized by the rule that if the death penalty were imposed it was he who was responsible for throwing the first stone in execution of the judgment.

False witness was a serious matter in proceedings at the gate. Bearing false witness against a neighbor was prohibited by the Decalogue, suggesting that once a death penalty may have applied. When a person lied in a prosecution that could end in capital punishment, the rule was that the false witness should be punished as severely as the accused would have been if the false evidence had been accepted. The *lex talionis* (an eye for an eye and a tooth for a tooth) was strictly applied in cases of perjury. Aside from outright lies, witnesses might mislead a court by repeating evidence they received secondhand or by repeating unfounded conclusions they may have arrived at independently of their knowledge. Courts at the gate carefully instructed witnesses in capital cases (and most noncapital cases) that they were not to testify from supposition or to give secondhand or hearsay evidence.

Biblical courts required that at least two witnesses testify concerning the guilt of the accused. While this requirement may have originally been limited in application to cases of murder and idolatry, it became more general and applied to all criminal prosecutions by the time of King Solomon. There is reason to believe that if a thief was caught in the action of stealing (*in flagrante delicto*), only one witness was necessary to convict. In such a case, the surrounding circumstances might well justify abandonment of the two-witness rule; however, there was wisdom in always having corroboration of a witness's evidence. If the submitted evidence did not provide an adequate basis for a decision, the accused would be asked to take an exculpatory oath, denying his guilt. The accused would call upon God to curse him if the oath were false, and the case would be dismissed.

After the establishment of the Davidic monarchy, the religious activities of the nation shifted to the royal city of Jerusalem, where a Temple was raised to Yahweh. Difficult cases that could not be resolved at the gate were taken to the priests and judges at Jerusalem. Once there, additional exculpatory oaths might be used or the issue of guilt could be determined by oracular means. The breastplate of the high priest contained two objects for the purpose of determining guilt or innocence; a party wishing to prove his innocence was required to "draw lots," and the success of the accused's case would depend upon which of the two lots he or she drew from the breastplate.

Once the priests or judges ascertained guilt, sentencing and execution followed immediately. They usually inflicted death penalties by stoning, with the community casting stones at the convict until death occurred. Provisions of Israeli law that parallel those in the Code of Hammurabi stipulate that burning to death be the appropriate sanction against a priest's daughter convicted of prostitution, as well as against a man who committed incest by wedding both a mother and her daughter. Late in biblical history, perhaps as the consequence of Persian influence, flogging became a sanction for lesser offenses. We have already seen that theft was punishable by compelling the convicted thief to make multiple restitution.

Capital punishment might be rendered additionally harsh by providing that the convict's deceased body be exposed to the elements for a period of time on the day of his death. This could be done by hanging the body from a tree or impaling it in a public place. In both cases, the corpse was to be buried before nightfall. Although similar, the sanction of crucifixion was unknown to biblical law; while there is some evidence that it was used among the Persians and the Greeks, it became commonplace only among the Romans.

Athens

Athenian citizens prosecuting crime relied on self-help in arresting their adversaries, just as victims did in biblical Israel. However, they also had the option of asking a magistrate to accompany them to make the arrest; in a number of cases, the prosecution might begin with the simple filing of a complaint and service of a summons on the accused. When the parties were present, the magistrate held a preliminary hearing concerning the charge and then held the matter for the next session of the appropriate court.

Ancient Athenian procedure assigned the trial of homicide cases to a special tribunal composed of the serving magistrates, called *archons*, and all previously commissioned archons. Meeting in the agora (marketplace) or Areopagus (a hill in Athens where the tribunal met), this court tried all premeditated homicides and heard constitutional cases. Portions of the Areopagus tribunal, presided over by an archon, dealt with lesser homicide matters. These quasi-religious courts did not deal with other criminal offenses, which were left to the disposition of individual magistrates. Where the magistrates alone decided cases at the trial level, the matter might be appealed to the entire people of Athens for review. When this became cumbersome, Athenian procedure adopted a type of jury drawn from a broad cross section of the people, called a *dicastery*, to serve with the magistrate and render decisions in criminal cases. This could be as many as fifty citizens of Athens. As the practice matured, the panels from which jurors were drawn represented an ever-widening group of Athenian citizens. Each member cast a secret ballot to determine the guilt or innocence of the accused.

Before 404-403 B.C. there was no written text of Athenian law other than the inscriptions on stone (*stelae*) in the Areopagus or the *agora*. Consequently, the parties were required to submit to the court all laws relied upon in the prosecution and defense of the case. The *dicastery*, or the Areopagus court in homicide cases, was then responsible for deciding what law applied and how it should be construed. Lawmakers did not make a clear distinction between matters of law and issues of fact, resulting in a lack of precedent or even regularity in the application of law in Athens. Athenian jurors were impatient with excessive technicality in pleading and practice, viewing those sophistications as evasive attempts to avoid decisions on the merits. When paid orators assisted in either defense or prosecution, they took great pains to conceal their intelligence and learning, and in almost all cases they did not present the speeches orally but tried to conceal their identities. Athenian juries were also swayed by extraneous circumstances, it being said that many a jury acquitted an obviously guilty homicide defendant simply because his wife and children, present in court, were so loud in their wails of distress at his peril.

TIME CAPSULE

Attic Justice

Consistent with the Athenian principle of direct democratic rule, the trial of Socrates in 399 B.C. for impiety and corruption of youth was conducted by lay members of the community rather than by citizens with legal training. Whether the verdict was fair is a question that has occupied scholars ever since.

Despite the prominence of Socrates in philosophical discussion, he left no written record. The principal source for the events of his trial is Plato, who was present and wrote four dialogues concerning the trial and execution of Socrates (*Euthyphro, Apology, Crito,* and *Phaedo*). Two additional contemporary accounts by Xenophon and Aristophanes are supplemented by that of Aristotle, who wrote two generations later. On this slim documentary basis, a mountain of interpretation and controversy concerning the trial of Socrates has developed. For example, scholars disagree about the very purpose of Socrates' speech to the jury in his own defense. Did he deliberately attempt to antagonize the jurors to achieve an acceptable end to a life that had become disagreeable to him? Or was Socrates earnestly trying to convince the jury to acquit him as vindication of his moral principles?

Regardless of Socrates' intention, the trial offers the student of criminal justice history a dramatic example of Athenian prosecution, procedure, and adjudication in the fourth century B.C. Prosecution in Athenian procedure was initiated by citizens; it is known that three men (Anytus, Meletus, and Lycon) raised accusations against Socrates. By bringing the charges, the accusers put themselves at risk. Any citizen could bring an accusation, but as a safeguard against unwarranted or purely malicious attacks, accusers who failed to convince one-fifth of the jury were subject to paying a heavy fine.

The indictment, drawn up by Meletus, was put in writing and taken to the office of the King-Archon, who then forwarded the case to trial. No complete set of the charges leveled against Socrates in 399 B.C. has survived, but it is recorded that Meletus swore that Socrates was guilty of not recognizing the gods whom the state recognized, of introducing other new divinities, and of misleading the youth of Athens. The charges were vague and apparently did not cite specific violations of the criminal law.

Regardless of the questionable legality of the accusations, there is substantial documentation that Socrates had long antagonized political leaders in Athens. It was well known that Socrates was no admirer of democracy, preferring rule by those of knowledge and ability. Nor, with rare exceptions, did he take an active governmental role. Furthermore, Socrates had been friendly with men such as Critias and Alcibiades, who opposed the democratic rulers. Critias, a close associate of Socrates, was a member of the Council of Thirty, which exercised a short-lived reign of totalitarian rule before democracy was restored. Socrates' friendship with Alcibiades was suspected both of being a homosexual relationship and of being the cause of Alcibiades' treasonous behavior. Two of his other associates were involved in rebellion against the leaders. These alleged transgressions were compounded by Socrates' arrogant attitude.

The characteristics of the court that tried Socrates were quite different from today's criminal courts. Aside from a magistrate whose only duty was to keep order, there were no judges. Nor were there official prosecutors or defense counsel. The decision was to be rendered by jurors chosen from a pool of volunteers and randomly assigned to the court. The exact number of jurors in Socrates' trial is not known, but scholars estimate that there were probably 501. After swearing to judge according to the laws, the jurors heard from the prosecution and defense, each of which was allotted a limited amount of time so that the trial could be concluded before nightfall.

Following speeches by the accusers, Socrates spoke in his own defense. In essence, he argued that in seeking virtue and urging others to value wisdom above material wealth and reputation, he had both served the state well and followed the will of the gods. He saw himself as one who was "like a gadfly to a horse, which, though a large and noble beast, is sluggish on account of its size and needs to be aroused by stinging. I think the god has fastened me upon the State in some such capacity, and I go about rousing, urging, and reproaching each one of you, constantly alighting on you everywhere the whole day long."

As expected from the beginning, the jurors voted to convict Socrates, but by an unexpectedly narrow margin; a shift of 30 votes would have meant acquittal. Under Athenian procedural rules, there was no possibility of appeal from this verdict. The same jurors then heard arguments regarding sentence. Meletus proposed that Socrates be sentenced to death. It was then Socrates' turn to suggest an appropriate penalty. The jurors had to choose one or the other; no other sentence was possible. Some scholars believe that had Socrates proposed banishment, the jurors would have agreed. At first Socrates suggested that, because he had benefited the state, he should be allocated free meals for life, then backed off and offered to pay a token fine, and finally made the proposal that he pay a substantial fine.

With slightly more votes than for conviction, the jurors sentenced Socrates to death. Death sentences in Athens were carried out immediately. The condemned man was turned over to officials to be executed within 24 hours. At the time of Socrates' condemnation, however, the execution had to be delayed until a sacred boat that had been sent to the shrine of Apollo returned. It was delayed for nearly a month, and during this time Socrates' friends pleaded with him to flee. He chose instead to abide by the legal (if unjust) decision of the court. Once the boat reappeared, the execution ritual began. In the midst of his friends, Socrates drank the cup of hemlock handed to him and died quietly. Tradition has it that his last words concerned a request that his debt of a cock to Asclepius should be paid.

The trial and death of Socrates represents a paradox. The city of Athens, renowned for the principle of freedom of speech, had seen the prosecution, conviction, and execution of a man for words that alienated powerful members of the society.

Sources: Plato, *The Trial and Death of Socrates, Euthyphro, Apology, Crito, and Phaedo* (New York: Dutton, Everyman's Library, 1963); Irving F. Stone, *The Trial of Socrates* (New York: Doubleday, 1989).

Given the untrammeled discretion of the dicastery courts, it is apparent that rules of evidence, although present and applicable, were given interpretations that varied with circumstances. Hearsay evidence (a witness testifying about what someone else said) was prohibited unless the speaker was dead, and a litigant could not be a witness in his own cause. Adult male citizens could serve as witnesses, but women and slaves could not—unless their evidence was tendered against a homicide defendant. Slave testimony was considered unreliable unless it had been extracted under torture. Frequently, both sides would make slaves of the parties available for torture, in the hope that some advantage might be gained over the adversary. In classical Athens there were procedures for compelling a witness to appear and testify, and he could be penalized for failing to appear in court for this purpose. While evidence was originally delivered orally, by the fourth century B.C. it was presented in written form, with the witness swearing to it in open court. It was common for defendants at the conclusion of their trials to inform the jury that the evidence against

Jacques-Louis David's *The Death of Socrates*. Image credit: The Metropolitan Museum of Art, Catherine Lorillard Wolfe Collection, Wolfe Fund, 1931 (31.45). All rights reserved, The Metropolitan Museum of Art.

them was perjured and that they intended to bring an action against the witnesses at the end of the pending case.

Oaths played a significant role in Athenian criminal prosecution. The accuser and the defendant were both required to take an oath to the accuracy of their pleadings. At an earlier stage in history, an exculpatory oath procedure was available whereby defendants might invoke a curse upon themselves and their families in connection with their denial of guilt. If the "oath-helpers" that a defendant assembled outnumbered those who supported the accuser's oath, the case was dismissed. Later, during classical times, the oath procedures alone no longer disposed of criminal cases, but still gave weight to a party's evidence. The challenge oath was frequently used for the purposes of joining issues and bringing evidence before juries in a particularly dramatic way. It was customarily met with a cross-challenge, in which the respondent asserted that the challenger was a known atheist and perjurer whose oath was worthless. Decreased reliance upon oaths indicated not only a reduction in piety, but also marked an increased emphasis on the reliability and accuracy of evidence; these characteristics were enhanced, in at least some cases, by the solemnity of the oath.

After the submission of evidence and speeches by the parties in support of their cases, the jury gave its verdict. From this there was no appeal, but the losing party might ask for a new trial within two months of the judgment, or ask that the verdict be suspended or annulled for false testimony. The successful prosecutor of a public case was awarded a sum of money for his effort; if he failed to continue the case to conclusion, he was fined for his neglect. If the prosecutor lost a case, he usually escaped a fine unless he failed to obtain more than one-fifth of the jurymen's votes, in which case he would be fined 1,000 drachmas. This fine was instituted to discourage sycophants—individuals who made their living by threatening prominent citizens with prosecution for sham criminal offenses. By the end of the classical period, sycophancy was a public nuisance in Athens.

Athenian punishments took a variety of forms. Capital punishment in earliest times was accomplished by throwing the criminal into an open pit; in classical times, death by another means might be followed by an undignified burial in an open pit as an additional sanction. Stoning was the form of punishment most commonly applied in the time of Hesiod (c. 800 B.C.). In classical Athens, strangulation was a common punishment, and impalement on an upright board resulted in death through exposure. More common was death by drinking hemlock; this was the general mode for committing suicide and by far the most merciful form of execution. There is no record of Athenian executions by decapitation or hanging. In noncapital punishment, a variety of forms of *atimia*, or public degradation, were available, ranging from loss of the right to vote to various types of outlawry. Physical punishment by flogging was used for slaves but not for freemen; imprisonment was a rare punishment, the usual practice being to sell the convict into slavery.

Rome

Rome's republican constitution provided ingenious checks on the unbridled exercise of judicial power. Consuls, as the two principal magistrates, shared authority over the major affairs of state; in office for only one year, each consul was limited by the need to obtain the consent of his colleague. All magistrates, including the praetors and quaestors who were the major judicial officers, had the authority to veto a colleague's action, and this process (called *intercessio*) provided an effective check on arbitrary judicial power. Criminal judgments against Roman citizens were subject to an appeal. During the Republic, this appeal was to the body of the people, but after Caesar's establishment of the principate in 25 B.C., criminal appeals were heard by the emperor. Paul, the Christian apostle who was a Roman citizen, was permitted such an appeal from the adverse decision of Festus, governor of Judea. These appeals from a magistrate's judgments in serious criminal matters were called *provocatio*; they were available at all times except in situations of grave national emergency or civic disorder. A magistrate recognizing the likelihood of an appeal to the people could avoid such a review by bringing the matter before himself and his *consilium*, or council of advisors. Preliminary hearings were held in this forum, then the magistrate transferred the case to the popular assembly, which was responsible for judging the offense and to which the magistrate owed his selection.

Because magistrates were drawn from the senatorial class, the common people (*plebeians*) soon established their own claim to hold offices similar to those of the magistrates. These were the tribunes who, while not technically magistrates possessed of the *imperium*, were early declared sacred in their persons and granted broad governmental powers. The tribunes might present a criminal for trial before their own assembly, the *concilium plebis*, or to the assembly of the entire people, the *comitia centuriata*, which heard capital cases and other matters involving heavy penalties. During the closing days of the republic, prosecutions of unsuccessful generals and politicians before the *comitia centuriata* were commonplace.

Traditional procedures became too cumbersome and lengthy for the efficient administration of criminal justice. A solution was found in the establishment of special commissions, beginning in about 190 B.C., in which magistrates (usually *quaestors*) were authorized to assemble juries for the trial of a number of specified criminal offenses. The jurors were drawn from an equal number of patricians, knights and plebs. They decided issues concerning the guilt of the accused, and, upon their decision, the magistrate entered judgment; no appeal to the people was permitted in cases tried by this procedure. The *quaestiones* court system, utilizing one presiding officer and a jury ranging from 32 to 75 individuals, was based upon statutory authority. A law passed in 149 B.C. (the *Lex Calpurnia*) provided that this new method of trial be utilized in cases of extortion by provincial governors. In 81 B.C., the *Lex Corneliae*[2] imposed the new procedure in prosecuting those who carried weapons for criminal purposes, dealt in poisons, forged wills, and counterfeited coins, committed treason and sedition, committed election bribery, and embezzled public funds. Because the presiding officer was a *quaestor* or a lesser magistrate, these courts were not guided by men trained in the law; if any rules of law evolved, they escaped the attention of jurists and thus are unknown to us today.

What the new criminal procedures achieved in efficiency was accomplished at the cost of individual liberty. Loss of the right to appeal to the people was a serious restriction on Roman citizenship privileges; it involved the sacrifice of an opportunity to sway a large and presumably impartial assembly in favor of one's case. While the jurors used in the *quaestiones* proceedings were drawn from a broad cross section of the people, and due allowance was made for the representation of each order, the list of potential jurors ultimately became the prerogative of the emperor. Undoubtedly, public safety and the rising crime rate made necessary such an alteration in the ancient procedures, but taken together with the general decline of constitutional rights in the late Republic, these changes seem to mark the impending decline of Roman citizenship into the wretched condition that characterized it during the principate. Eventually, the jury courts were themselves superseded by police courts, which were established under the Caesars, staffed by imperial officials, and dedicated to the vigorous suppression of disorder and dissent.

Procedures before republican Roman criminal courts tended to provide a maximum flexibility in the submission of evidence. To the extent that the original procedures were tried before large assemblies, the oratorical ability of advocates played a significant role. Hearsay evidence was included and, frequently, testimony might be admitted in affidavit form even if the witness was readily available. Advocates were given license in their comments upon the evidence, in cross-examination, and in attacking the credibility of witnesses. In any criminal case, the reputation of the accused was a point in issue; therefore, the introduction of character evidence was not only permitted, but it was expected that the accused would take upon him or herself the burden of proving his good character.

Before the old courts, and in *quaestiones* jury courts, the mode of trial was adversarial: the prosecution and accused

Justinian I (483-565—Ruler of the Eastern Roman Empire 527-565. Collected all imperial statutes as codes *constitutionum* and preserved Roman Law for future generations.

were arraigned against each other, and issues were submitted to impartial triers of fact (the *iudex*, the magistrate's *consilium*, or the jurors assembled according to statute). As the emperors asserted their growing power, the locus of trial began to shift to police courts, which acted as investigatory agencies and based their decisions on information they had discovered. This inquisitorial method would become characteristic of criminal proceedings in the later years of the empire (called the *dominate*). These police court procedures continued in the courts of the eastern Roman empire and in the ecclesiastical tribunals of the Christian church.

TIME CAPSULE

The Emperor Justinian Proves that the Pen is Mightier than the Sword

In 527 A.D., Petrus Sabbatius Justinianus succeeded his uncle, Justin I, as Roman emperor in the East. The offspring of a Thracian peasant family, Justinian was earlier appointed co-emperor with his uncle, smoothing his ascent to the throne when Justin died. The reign of Justinian was marked by a disastrous attempt to reconquer the ancient Roman Empire and reunite it under his authority. After quick success in North Africa, Justinian's generals became bogged down in northern Italy, and misfortune followed in Palestine and Syria. The rise of Persian power threatened the eastern borders of Justinian's Empire, and his capital at Constantinople was wracked with plague. When Justinian died in 565 A.D., his limited military success augured badly for his place in history.

However, his contribution to legal science ensured his fame as one of the great lawgivers of the ancient world. Four months after his accession to the imperial throne, Justinian commissioned a group of distinguished jurists and learned officials to prepare

an edition of the codes issued by three previous emperors—Gregorius, Hermogenius, and Theodosias. Completed a year later, the new Code superceded the old codes, and the courts were directed to refer only to the text of the newly compiled edition as authoritative. In a subsequent edition, the commission added new constitutions (or statutes, as we would call them) and eliminated obsolete materials and contradictory matter.

In 529 A.D., Tribonian was appointed to chair a commission that undertook the collection and orderly arrangement of those portions of jurist's law that survived from the first through the fourth century of the Christian era. It required four years to review the 1,528 books of manuscript materials, and to place them in 50 books divided into 432 chapters. This was the famous Digest that, at the Emperor's command, superseded all old law within the Empire. Upon completion of this immense project, Tribonian and four other law specialists revisited Justinian's Code published in 527 A.D., including additional "new" statutes issued by Justinian since the code's publication.

The project was substantially completed by 540 A.D., and it was this body of law that Justinian hoped would restore the civil health of his empire. Historians suggest that this was a magnificent but impractical collection of law that probably received little attention outside of Justinian's capital, Constantinople. However, the rediscovery of the Digest in eleventh-century Italy resulted in the establishment of the University at Bologna in 1088, and renewed enthusiasm for the study of Roman law. As such, the work of Justinian's codifiers and digesters became the foundation upon which the *ius commune* of modern European law has developed. Thus the scholarly and legal efforts sponsored by Justinian earned him a prominent place in the history of western civilization, but his military efforts to reunite the old Roman Empire are largely forgotten.

The Code of Justinian, and some of the new materials added during his reign, suggest that the rules of law and approaches to crime, its prosecution, and its punishment were like many of today's legal rules.

Definitions of Crime

As many crimes are classed under the term "violence," and as force is often employed against those who resist, and blows are inflicted upon others who indignantly returned them, and murder not infrequently results, it has been decided that if any one, either on the side of the person in possession, or on that of him who rashly attempts to obtain it, should be killed, he must be punished who attempted to employ force, and was responsible for the injuries of either party, and he shall not be merely sentenced to relegation, or deportation to an island, but shall suffer death,

and the judgment pronounced against him shall not be suspended by appeal.
Emperor Constantine to Catulius, 317 A.D.

If anyone should hasten the end of either of his parents, his son, his daughter, or any of those relatives whose murder is designated by the term parricide, whether he committed the act secretly or openly, he shall suffer the penalty of parricide, and shall neither be put to death by the sword, or by fire, nor by any other ordinary method, but shall be sewed in a sack with a dog, a cock, a viper, and a monkey and, enclosed with these wild animals and associated with serpents, he shall be either thrown into the sea, or into a river, according to the nature of the locality; so that, while living, he may be deprived of all use of the elements, and during the remainder of his existence, he may be deprived of air, and at his death, of the earth.
Emperor Constantine to Varinus, 319 A.D.

When a woman is convicted of having secretly had sexual intercourse with her slave, she shall be sentenced to death, and the slave shall perish by fire. Every facility for the proof of this crime shall be afforded all persons, and any official can bring the charge, and even the slave himself shall be permitted to testify concerning it, and should it be established, he must be granted his freedom.
Emperor Constantine to the People, 326 A.D.

You will not permit persons guilty of crime to avail themselves of any privilege in order to avoid punishment; but you should only manifest indulgence toward those who are shown to be innocent of what they are accused. You must severely punish persons guilty of homicide, adultery, the rape of virgins, trespass with force and arms, and oppression; punishing culprits according to Our laws, in order that the penalties inflicted may enure to the safety of all persons.

17th Constitution, Emperor Justinian to Tribonian, c. 540 A.D.

Procedures and Judging
[P]roceedings in the case of crimes punishable by the laws . . . shall be instituted in the places where the offences were committed, or begun, or where the guilty parties may be found.

Emperor Constantine, 334 A.D.

We think that it should be perpetually established by this law that judges who are required to hear and determine cases should not arrive at sudden conclusions, but should render their decisions after careful consideration and reflection; and, after having revised them, and reduced them to writing with the greatest accuracy, they ought to deliver them in this form to the parties interested, and not afterwards be permitted to correct or change them . . .

Emperors Valens, Valentinian, and Gratian to Probus, 372 A.D.

[N]o one shall act as a judge in his own case or interpret the law for himself, as it would be very unjust to give anyone the right to render a decision in an affair which is his own.

Imperial decree of Emperor Valens, n.d. (372 A.D.)

Concerning *Res Judicata.* "If a case which has been decided could be revived under the pretext of a mistake in calculation, litigation would never end.

Emperor Antoninus to Stellator, n.d.

Questions

1. To what degree do the Roman definitions of crime seem similar to present-day American practice? How do they differ? Why?

2. How did a sense of fair play, or fair trial, affect the procedures in Roman criminal trials?

3. Are the Romans right that once a case is decided it should *never* be reopened? Not even if there was false testimony? Not even if proper procedures were ignored? Endless litigation is unfortunate, but should a person's life be lost because a judge made a mistake?

4. Why should a criminal trial be held in the vicinity where the crime was committed? Are there evidentiary reasons for this rule? Does such a trial provide an outlet for local vengeance upon the accused? Might a judge or quaestorial jury be influenced by popular animosity toward the accused?

Sources: George P. Baker, *Justinian* (New York: Dodd, Mead Company, 1931); James A.S. Evans, *The Age of Justinian: The Circumstances of Imperial Power* (London: Routledge, 1996); S.P. Scott, *The Civil Law, Including the Twelve Tables, the Institutes of Gaius, the Rules of Ulpian, the Opinions of Paulus, the Enactments of Justinian and the Constitutions of Leo,* 17 vols. (Cincinnati: The Central Trust Co., 1932; reprint edition, New York: AMS Press, 1973), vols. 12 to 16.

Sanctions in Roman criminal law varied according to the offense and the status of the accused. An intentional killer, one who gave false testimony, a citizen who incited a public enemy or betrayed a fellow citizen to the enemy, and an iudex who accepted a bribe were subjected to capital punishment, usually by beheading. However, the false witness was thrown from the Tarpeian Rock, and a defendant convicted of intentional arson was burned to death. The Twelve Tables, reflecting early superstitions, provided that a person convicted of singing incantations or casting spells and curses was to be clubbed to death. When a Roman citizen was sentenced to death, scourging, or a heavy fine, he was entitled to appeal the sentence to the people and remain at large until their decision was handed down. The result was that most Roman citizens convicted of serious crimes were never punished, but escaped into exile. Slaves, on the other hand, were imprisoned and dealt with harshly; they were perhaps simply thrown into prison and strangled shortly thereafter.

TIME CAPSULE

Islamic Criminal Justice

Students may be appalled, and perhaps intrigued, by references in the newspapers to the harsh corporal punishments of Islamic law (Shari'a) still in effect in countries such as Saudi Arabia, Pakistan and Sudan. In the centuries following Muhammad's death, four major schools of Islamic law have developed—Hanafi, Hanbali, Maliki, and Shafi'i—making it difficult to generalize about criminal law and procedure in the various countries that follow Shari'a. Nevertheless, it may be useful to include a brief explanation of the origin and principles of Shari'a and to indicate ways in which it differs from the civil law and common law.

The criminal law of Islamic countries derives from the revealed word of God; the basic principles of Islamic criminal law are found in the eternal and unchanging word of God expressed in the Qur'an. In addition, explications of these fundamental rules, found

in the recorded sayings of Muhammad (*hadith* or *Sunna*), consensus (*ijma'*), and analogical reasoning (*qiyas*), have offered further guidance and provided the flexibility to deal with contemporary legal problems.

The realm of acts considered criminal is far wider under Islamic law than in western systems. Because the eternal will of God governs all human acts and is to be obeyed at all times, any transgression is a crime, and in this sense there is no distinction between religious and secular offenses. Classification of crimes is determined by the punishment rather than by the harm caused by the offender, as would be the case in western law. Shari'a identifies three categories of crime: offenses against God (*hudud*) for which punishment is prescribed in the Qur'an and Sunna; crimes of physical assault and murder (*quesas*), which are punishable by retaliation and can be waived for compensation; and offenses (*ta'zir*) whose penalties are within the discretion of the judge. Included in this roster of offenses are acts such as blasphemy, which western countries do not punish.

The category of crime determines responsibility for initiating prosecution. Offenses against God (hudud) are to be prosecuted by the state. Crimes in the other two categories can be initiated by complaint of the victim or survivor and can be prosecuted by the state. As a protection against false accusation, the complainant can himself be punished if proof is not brought forth.

Penal law of Shari'a is indeed harsh by western standards, both in regard to the nature of the offense and the severity of punishment. For example, the crime of *apostasy* (voluntary renunciation of Islam) carries a death penalty. As is well known, a thief risks the loss of hand or foot, and adulterers can be stoned to death. The potential harshness of Islamic law is, however, modified by stringent evidentiary rules. The doctrines of presumption of innocence and a prohibition against ex post facto charges protect the defendant. In the absence of a confession the prosecutor must produce two witnesses (usually two male Muslims) with direct knowledge of the offense. The testimony of two women could be accepted in place of that of one man. The Qur'an requires that adultery be proved by eyewitness testimony of four male Muslims or by confession on four separate occasions by the defendant in open court; understandably, few charges result in conviction.

A criminal justice system based on divine law would, of course, contravene the hallowed principle of separation of church and state embodied in the United States Constitution in 1787, but as few as 150 years earlier, the colony of Massachusetts Bay had drawn up Bible Codes to restrict criminal activity (discussed in Chapter 6).

Question

Can you think of ways in which religion still plays a part in the criminal justice system of the United States?

Sources: J.N.D. Anderson, *Islamic Law in the Modern World* (Westport, CT: Greenwood Press, 1975); Sean McConville Lippman and Mordechai Yerushalmi, *Islamic Criminal Law and Procedure: An Introduction* (New York: Praeger, 1988); Malise Ruthven, *Islam* (New York: Oxford University Press, 1997).

Summary

Despite the cultural and chronological distinctions between the three cultures presented, certain common themes can be discerned. For example, all three placed the heaviest of sanctions on intentional killers and lighter penalties on kidnappers. Athenian and biblical theological positions appear to have added particular revulsion to intentional homicide, and in Roman law it resulted in death or exile, even for a Roman citizen. For the most part, sex offenses were dealt with less severely, but biblical Israel's emphasis on its status as Yahweh's chosen people altered the biblical law. In all three legal systems, theft was generally a matter of compensation; however, aggravating circumstances that made the property offense a possible occasion for physical violence, or that offended religious taboos, may have caused additional sanctions.

Turning to criminal procedure, there was a common pattern of self-help being required from the victims of criminal activities. Each system developed a number of rules of evidence, based upon logical analysis of the value of testimony. Probabilities of guilt or innocence entered into the assignment of burdens of proof. In the Roman and Athenian use of the platter and loincloth search and in biblical Israel's use of lots in the breast-plate of the high priest, we see a common thread of superstition and reliance upon the intervention of divine guidance into the evidentiary process.

Running through the organization of courts was a common thread of relying on group decision as being superior to the judgment of an individual. In the case of Athens and Rome, this was seen as a protection for the individual against the power of magistrates. Judgment at the gate in ancient Israel placed the accused before the elders of his or her town. There was an element of probability present also, for the populace represented by the dicastery, the quaestiones jury, and the council of town elders could not fail to be influenced by the reputation of the accused. Justice may not have been precise, but it tended to reflect public attitudes and judgments. As such, it maintained order, discouraged revenge, and advanced the interests of the community.

Endnotes

[1]   The Tarpeian Rock on Capitoline Hill was named for an early traitoress buried nearby.

[2]   Roman statutes were named after the first consul during the year of their enactment.

References

An excellent and readable introduction to Biblical law may be found in Roland de Vaux, *Ancient Israel*, Vol. I: Social Institutions (New York: McGraw-Hill, 1961). Another helpful survey is John M.P. Smith, *The Origin and History of Hebrew Law* (Chicago, IL: University of Chicago Press, 1931). Helpful for Jewish legal development in Biblical and post-Biblical times is Hyman E. Goldin, *Hebrew Criminal Law and Procedure*: *Mishnah, Sanhedrin, Makkot* (New York: Twayne Publishers, 1950). More detailed surveys may be found in A.C.J. Phillips, *Ancient Israel's Criminal Law: A New Approach to the Decalogue* (Oxford: Basil Blackwell, 1971); Ze'ev W. Falk, *Hebrew Law in Biblical Times* (Jerusalem: Wahrman Books, 1964); Brevard S. Childs, *The Book of Exodus: A Critical, Theological Commentary* (Philadelphia: Westminster Press, 1974). Among the best scholarship and the most exhaustive coverage of Biblical criminal law are Hans Jochen Boecker, *Law and the Administration of Justice in the Old Testament* and Ancient East, Jeremy Moiser, translator (Minneapolis: Augsburg Publishing House, 1980); David Daube, *Studies in Biblical Law* (Cambridge: Cambridge University Press, 1947); Martin Noth, *The Laws of the Pentateuch and Other Studies*, trans. D.R. Ap-Thomas (Edinburgh: Oliver & Boyd, 1966).

Greek studies are best approached through the survey by Antony Andrewes, *The Greeks* (London: Hutchinson & Co., Ltd., 1967); and an exhaustive fact book with an excellent discussion of Athenian constitutional and legal development is edited by Leonard Whibley, ed., *A Companion to Greek Studies*, 4th ed., revised (New York: Hafner Publishing Company, 1963). A well-written survey of Athenian law is Douglas M. MacDowell, *The Law in Classical Athens* (Ithaca: Cornell University Press, 1978); see also Douglas A. MacDowell, *Athenian Homicide Law in the Age of the Orators* (Manchester: Manchester University Press, 1963). Procedural matters are treated exhaustively in Alick R.W. Harrison, *The Law of Athens*, vol. 2: Procedure (Oxford: Clarendon Press, 1971). Although somewhat dated in interpretation, George M. Calhoun, *The Growth of Criminal Law in Ancient Greece* (Berkeley: University of California Press, 1927) is a very well-done and readable survey of criminal law and procedure. Specialized monographs for advanced study are Robert J. Bonner, *Evidence in Athenian Courts* (Chicago: University of Chicago Press, 1905); Robert J. Bonner and Gertrude Smith, *The Administration of Justice from Homer to Aristotle*, 2 vols. (Chicago: University of Chicago Press, 1930); Michael Gagarin, *Drakon and Early Athenian Homicide Law* (New Haven: Yale University Press, 1981); Joseph Plescia, *The Oath and Perjury in Ancient Greece* (Tallahassee: Florida State University Press, 1970); Thomas C. Brickhouse and Nicholas D. Smith, *Socrates on Trial* (Princeton: Princeton Press, 1989); Douglas M. MacDowell, *The Law in Classical Athens* (London: Thames and Hudson, 1978); Plato, *The Trial and Death of Socrates: Euthyphro, Apology, Crito, and Phaedo* (New York: Dutton, Everyman's Library, 1963); and I.F. Stone, *The Trial of Socrates* (New York: Doubleday, 1989).

Two thorough surveys of Roman criminal law may be found in Barry Nicholas, *An Introduction to Roman Law* (Oxford: Clarendon Press, 1962); and the somewhat more difficult text by Wolfgang Kunkel, *An Introduction to Roman Legal and Constitutional History*, 2d ed., trans. J.M. Kelly (Oxford: Clarendon Press, 1972). Also of value are the pertinent sections of H.F. Jolowicz and Barry Nicholas, *Historical Introduction to the Study of Roman Law*, 3d ed. (Cambridge: Cambridge University Press, 1972). An excellent guide to Roman criminal procedure is in Abel H.J. Greenidge, *The Legal Procedure of Cicero's Time* (Oxford: Clarendon Press, 1901).

For a fuller explanation of the three systems of law, see the following chapters in Israel Drapkin, *Crime and Punishment in the Ancient World* (Lexington: D.C. Heath, 1989): Chapter 1 regarding Greece and Rome, Chapter 4 regarding ancient Hebrew criminal law, and Chapter 9 regarding Roman criminal law. Examples of Greek trial procedure can be found in Kathleen Freeman, *The Murder of Herodes and Other Trials from the Athenian Law Courts* (New York: W.W. Norton & Company, 1963). A seminal work on early law is Sir Henry Sumner Maine, *Ancient Law: Its Connection with the Early History of Society and its Relation to Modern Ideas* (Boston: Beacon Press, 1963; first published in 1861). For a review of legal principles in various cultures, see Part I of Arthur Sigismund Diamond, *Primitive Law, Past and Present* (London: Methuen, 1971); J.N.D. Anderson, *Islamic Law in the Modern World* (Westport, CT: Greenwood Press, 1975); Sean McConville Lippman, and Mordechai Yerushalmi, *Islamic Criminal Law and Procedure: An Introduction* (New York: Praeger, 1988); and Malise Ruthven, *Islam* (New York: Oxford University Press, 1997).

Notes and Problems

1. One of the perennial debates in legal history is the degree to which economic development influences the laws that apply in any society. To what degree did pastoral, agricultural, and commercial influences change criminal law in biblical Israel, classical Athens, and republican Rome?

2. Appeals to the supernatural are recurring themes in the history of criminal law. Religion may be defined as the forms, rituals, and behavioral patterns by which an individual or group expresses worship for a superior supernatural being; magic may be defined as the use of supernatural forces to achieve earthly goals. To what extent did criminal law depend upon religion or magic in the ancient world?

3. There was a tradition in Rome that the Twelve Tables were drafted by a commission that had been sent to Athens to copy the laws of Solon and adapt them for Roman use. To what extent does the similarity of the two systems of criminal justice support this tradition?

4. What distinctions can be made between torts (injuries subject to private, civil court actions seeking damages for the victim) and crimes (wrongdoing of sufficient magnitude that it is subject to public prosecution and penalty) based upon the ancient world's experience?

5. A useful way to look at crime in the ancient world is to consider it to be conduct that society has previously considered subject to state prosecution and punishment. In other words, custom or usage results in societal agreement upon what is crime, and individuals who violate those usages are subject to prosecution. To what extent does this require that the individual wrongdoer be forewarned concerning new criminal law? How did ancient nations solve this problem of warning? How specific did notice of criminality have to be?

6. Describe the way in which membership in a given nation or society was of significance in the application of criminal law. How does the status of foreigners, slaves, women, and children vary, and how did it affect their responsibilities under the criminal law?

Chapter 3

Medieval Crime and Punishment Before the Lateran Council of 1215

The collapse of the Roman Empire was not a slow death, but rather a prolonged agony that created a sharp distinction in history between the peoples of the eastern Mediterranean and those of Britain and Western Europe. Rome itself went through a period of growing power for the emperor, and the empire was divided between an eastern emperor with his principal city at Constantinople (now Istanbul) and a western emperor in Rome. As the eastern empire moved toward increasing despotism, it also refined and reissued ancient Roman law texts in the Digest[1] authorized by Emperor Justinian. It was the eastern empire that survived until 1453 A.D., when the city of Constantinople fell to the Ottoman Turks and became the capital city of a vast Turkish territory that eventually stretched across North Africa to southern Spain in the west.

Our principal focus in this chapter is the history of portions of the western empire that, after the fall of Rome in 426 A.D., came under the control of a number of Germanic kings and ultimately emerged as the national states we know today. The process was complicated, taking the better part of six centuries; during that time, criminal justice changed markedly from the patterns of the ancient world. To begin with, the medieval world sank into a period of confusion and illiteracy called the Dark Ages. Christianity became one of the sole remaining unifying factors in Western civilization, and the Roman Catholic Church, with its pope resident in Rome, was one of the few remaining vestiges of Roman imperial authority. Yet the rapid disruption of ancient Roman systems of transportation (and thus communication) vastly increased the cultural distance between Rome and the rest of Europe. Increasingly, the church fell under the administrative control of powerful local bishops and archbishops, and, at the same time, the Greek social background of New Testament Christianity gave way to a special mix of Christian principles and local heathen customs and practices. For example, the midwinter date for Christmas drew upon a pagan festival held at the same time, and the so-called "Christmas tree" originated in the practices of Druids,

TIME LINE

Western Empire		Eastern Empire
	318-324 A.D.	Emperor Constantine recognizes Christianity as a religion within the Roman Empire, and declares himself a Christian
	325, 327 A.D.	At the call of Constantine, the Councils of Nicaea adopt a credal statement concerning the Trinity
	324-326 A.D.	Constantine unites the Western and Eastern Empires
Visigoths sack Rome	**410** A.D.	
Vandals conquer Carthage	**439** A.D.	
Pope Leo I asserts primacy of the bishop of Rome; his status affirmed by Emperor Valentinian III	**440-461** A.D.	
	451 A.D.	Ecumenical Council at Chalcedon clarifies church doctrine concerning the divinity and humanity of Jesus Christ
Odoacer deposes the last Roman Emperor in the West	**476** A.D.	
Clovis, King of the West Franks, becomes a Christian	**496** A.D.	
	527 A.D.	Justinian becomes sole Emperor of the East
	527-540 A.D.	Justinian's jurists compile the Corpus Juris Civilis
	535-553 A.D.	Justinian's general, Belisarius, conquers Carthage, evicts the Visigoths from Rome, and Justinian becomes Emperor of East and West
Pope Gregory the Great sends Augustine of Canterbury to Christianize England	**596** A.D.	
	633-732 A.D.	Islamic caliphs conquer Syria, Iraq, Palestine, Libya, Tripoli, Carthage, Spain, and Southern France. Their advance is halted at Tours by Franks
Charlemagne, King of the Franks, is crowned Holy Roman Emperor by the Pope	**800** A.D.	

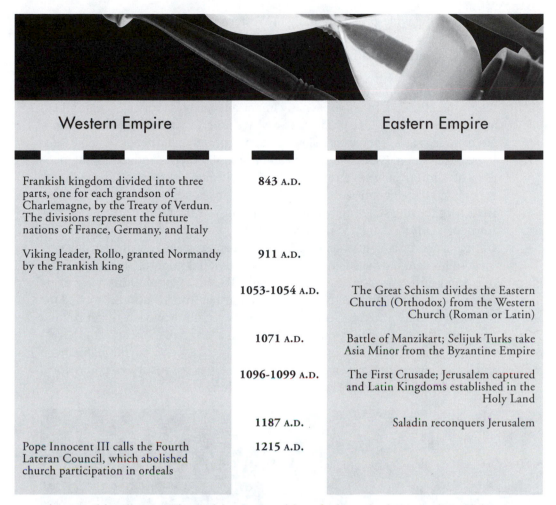

Western Empire		Eastern Empire
Frankish kingdom divided into three parts, one for each grandson of Charlemagne, by the Treaty of Verdun. The divisions represent the future nations of France, Germany, and Italy	843 A.D.	
Viking leader, Rollo, granted Normandy by the Frankish king	911 A.D.	
	1053-1054 A.D.	The Great Schism divides the Eastern Church (Orthodox) from the Western Church (Roman or Latin)
	1071 A.D.	Battle of Manzikart; Selijuk Turks take Asia Minor from the Byzantine Empire
	1096-1099 A.D.	The First Crusade; Jerusalem captured and Latin Kingdoms established in the Holy Land
	1187 A.D.	Saladin reconquers Jerusalem
Pope Innocent III calls the Fourth Lateran Council, which abolished church participation in ordeals	1215 A.D.	

who worshiped trees. The Celtic cross, with a circle at the intersection of the horizontal and vertical beams, incorporated the traditional symbol of Christianity with an older symbol used by those who recognized the sun as a god.

The declining power of Rome left in its wake a vacuum in political authority filled only in part by the rule of petty kings and would-be Holy Roman Emperors. Localities began to fall back on their own resources for instruments of government and crime control. Economically, it became important for poor farmers and merchants to associate themselves with a powerful lord, thereby securing protection in return for services or taxes paid to their overlord. Crime control became based upon kindred groupings; an individual's relatives became his supporters if he were injured by another, and they bailed him out of trouble by paying compensation if he maimed or killed a member of another kindred group. Expulsion from the kindred group deprived one of protection and permitted anyone to injure or kill the expelled person, or outlaw. At the same time, social rank depended upon the number and status of one's own kindred. Thus, recently-freed slaves with few free kin would be at the lower levels of society until their free children and numerous free descendants gave them a larger kindred grouping.

Given the widespread illiteracy in Western society during the Dark Ages, historians have limited sources of information upon which to draw, and many conclusions are speculative. However, there is little doubt that this period in history was very important to the development of Western government and society. In the millennium between the fall of Rome and the collapse of Constantinople and the eastern empire, vitally important changes took place in England and Western Europe. One product, as we have noted, was the beginning of modern national states. There was a slow buildup of power in the hands of noble families, based upon dynastic alliances and also upon their standing among peoples of similar language, culture, and traditions. As territorial magnates consolidated their control, their people found new cohesion in their differences from neighboring states and nations; the result was the rapid decline of a pan-European culture that had once been based upon Roman culture and upon the Christian church and its teachings. The other consequence was the rise of a new view of humankind based upon a person's individual importance as a member of a kindred group, a clan, and a society. To some degree, this was, at its inception, a perpetuation of Israelite, Athenian, and Roman attitudes toward the individuals who formed ancient societies. However, this new view of humankind was founded less upon religion or political philosophy and more upon the necessities of a more primitive and violent world. Chastened by the dangers of weak and uncertain government, Western societies reconstituted a new form of state through reciprocal rights and obligations.

TIME CAPSULE

Personal Law and Territorial Law in the Dark Ages

The New Testament narrative of the life of the apostle Paul introduces us to the impact of personal law. Accused by the Jewish authorities of blasphemy and defiling the Jerusalem Temple, Paul escaped a scourging by claiming his rights as a Roman citizen, a status he inherited from his father. At the time, Roman citizenship might be purchased, but under the Edict of Caracalla (213 A.D.) it was also awarded to all freeborn inhabitants of the empire. Unfortunately, Paul continued to claim Roman citizenship rights, which included the privilege of being tried in the courts of the emperor; the authorities who might have tried him in Jerusalem observed that, but for his claiming the right to a trial by the emperor, Paul would have been acquitted of the charges. In Paul's case, the decision to claim Roman citizenship rights may have been a mistake in the long run. However, the narrative suggests that trial by the emperor may have been the means he chose to spread the Christian faith to Rome.

Paul claimed a personal law that exempted him from a Judean territorial law. That tension between laws that governed all relationships within a geographical area, and laws that applied only to specific individuals qualified by birth or tribal associations, was typical of the collapse of the Roman Empire in the West after 476 A.D. As Germanic tribes moved into Italy and the other provinces formerly held by Rome, they brought customary law with them. In some cases, they eliminated Roman law and applied their own customary law throughout the conquered territory. In many other situations, they continued to allow the use of Roman law by the Romans living in their lands, but applied tribal customs to their own people. The Salic Franks were particularly generous in tolerating the continuance of tribal customs along with the rules of Roman law; as a consequence, France up to the time of Napoleon Bonaparte was governed by Roman law in the south and by a variety of customary laws in the north.

England, on the other hand, was not influenced by Roman law but derived its principles of law on a territorial basis, drawing heavily upon Anglo-Saxon and Norman customary law. The one exception to this rule was the exemption of clergy from the royal criminal law; as in continental Europe, English clergy were allowed the right of trial in church courts according to rules of canon law. As we shall see, these exemptions not only gave rise to the practice of "benefit of clergy," but they also encouraged lawlessness on the part of ordained clergy.

There are good and bad aspects of the resort to either territorial law or personal law. In territorial systems, all individuals located within the governed territory, whether they are natives or foreigners, are subject to the same rules. On the other hand, if they wish to break the territorial rules, they may do so with impunity by going to a territory where those rules do not apply. In personal law systems, the rules within a given land differ from each other, because each person may be entitled to a different set of customary laws. However, the person subject to customary law carries his law with him, and thus may be subject to punishment wherever he may be. He may also be punished by his homeland for offenses committed outside its territory. As Professor Simeon Guterman points out, the territorial system has been dominant since the 1648 Treaty of Westphalia. Will the preference for territorial law persist? Modern pressures toward establishing international rules of criminal law may begin to modify this tradition. American federal statutes concerning air piracy, for example, apply to persons subject to U.S. control, regardless of their citizenship or where the offense was committed. Another example may be the modern practice of punishment for war crimes that may not be offenses against the law of the territory in which they were committed, but that violate international law norms or treaty obligations.

Sources: Acts of the Apostles, 22:25-29; 25:6-12; 26:32; Simeon L. Guterman, *From Personal Law to Territorial Law: Aspects of the History and Structure of the Western Legal-Constitutional Tradition* (Metuchen: The Scarecrow Press, 1972), pp. 11-13, 17, 18, 22-23, 27, 29; Katherine Fisher Drew, *The Burgundian Code: Book of Constitutions or Law of Gundobad: Additional Enactments* (Philadelphia: University of Pennsylvania Press, 1949), p. 4.

Question

Do you think that criminal laws should be territorial in application, or is there room for some application of international laws as if they were personal laws binding all humanity? What difficulties arise when several systems of personal law coexist within one state or locality? How does one determine whether a crime has been committed if its definition depends upon the identity or ethnicity of criminal?

Even after the fall of Rome, Western societies and Germanic kings continued to recognize the personal nature of law; that is, individuals who had inherited Roman citizenship (and there were many in the Dark Ages) were entitled to the law of Rome, however imperfect the current understanding of what that law might have been. On the other hand, special tribal laws and customs applied to Germanic subjects of the same kings, resulting in complex rules concerning legal relationships between Romans and Germans. Over time, these differing laws produced a wide variety of local customs and usages. The English county of Kent and the borough of London each had inheritance laws that differed from other areas in England; the northeast of England, dominated for years by the Danelaw designed for the descendants of Viking conquerors, also had unique customs. It was the task of centralizing monarchs and their legal advisers to shape and impose a common law that would minimize both personalization of legal rules and the existence of distinctive territorial law.

One final point must be made concerning the rise of independent kingdoms and the growth of national cultures based upon shared languages and traditions. Shortly after the fall of Rome, western Europe and England enjoyed a common heritage of Roman law, the Latin language, and Christianity. By the year 1000 A.D., these remnants of Roman civilization had subsided into a literate subculture loosely clustered around the church. This subculture included newly founded universities and the bureaucratic staffs employed by chancellors and royal councilors. However, the language and customs of the common people and many of their landlords were either of Germanic origin or a barely recognizable version of the ancient Latin speech and culture. England early became subject to this sort of separation from its continental contemporaries. Conquered in 1066 by Norman French nobles, it was briefly drawn into the orbit of the Angevin empire, which included most of France. However, family dynastic ties could not restrain the pressures that drew England toward isolated nationhood. It is against this background that we must understand the similarities between English and continental criminal justice in the Dark Ages, and it is this factor that partially explains England's departure from continental Europe in its response to the mandates of the Fourth Lateran Council of 1215 A.D.

Vengeance, Wergild, and Dooms

Among Germanic peoples, kindred groups were formed by blood relationships. This meant that one's kindred were those who had a close biological relationship; it excluded, of course, one's spouse as well as the spouses of one's children. Closely connected to these considerations is the fact that in primitive societies there must have been considerable pressure to ignore the ecclesiastical rules concerning incest. A small population with a limited number of marriage partners might have applied incest rules more loosely, particularly in regard to the upper classes of society, where marriage would frequently be a means of amassing wealth. Nevertheless, canon law (church law) prohibited the marriage of first cousins, but great-grandchildren of the same couple (second cousins) could legally marry. It was acceptable that kindred ties might also be created by adoption or by the creation of blood ties through ceremonial means.

The basic relationship for purposes of vengeance was the blood relationship, but it was supplemented by other practices. For example, the widow of a murder victim might apply first to her husband's kinsmen (son, father, or brothers) to avenge his death, but if that request did not bring results, it was expected that she might appeal to her own kindred. She did this by a variety of methods, ranging from a simple demand for help to an elaborate ceremony of presenting the head or bloody garments of the deceased to her kinsmen. Women, small children, and elderly men were not expected to take part in the blood feud as actual avengers, but they played a vital role as aggrieved parties. A complex series of rules governed who among the deceased's male relatives were first entitled to seek vengeance, and the very complexity of the rules made it difficult for an accused slayer to pay *wergild* (compensation) to the proper representative of the family.

Despite its barbarity, vengeance progressed upon fixed rules that tended to limit its scope and ferocity. For example, indiscriminate killing was forbidden; a life could be avenged by the taking of a life from among the kindred of the slayer; exceeding the amount corresponding to the *lex talionis* in ancient law was illegal. Clans and kindred groups were careful to restrain the violence of their members because misbehavior that resulted in injury or death beyond the clan triggered revenge and brought disrepute upon the slayer's group. A rough sort of public opinion operated to discourage taking revenge when the victim's behavior might have justified the homicide. Revenge was dangerous and could erupt into countervengeance if viewed in an unfavorable light by the opposing kindred group.

Despite the complications inherent in a system of blood feud[2] and vengeance, it formed one of the most significant portions of the criminal law in Scandinavia, Germany, and Anglo-Saxon England, as evidenced by the Norse Sagas, the Niebelungen Ring legends, and the epic poem *Beowulf*. However, by the time Anglo-Saxon England emerged from the Dark Ages and laws began to appear on record, revenge and the blood feud had given way to a complex form of involuntary compensation for criminal acts, including the payment of money to a slain man's kindred.

The earliest recorded Anglo-Saxon laws were those issued by Aethelbert of Kent in 601-604. Called *dooms*, these proclamations treated theft as punishable by fines that ranged widely in magnitude. Stealing from the church or from persons in holy orders, was punishable by compensation ranging from three times the value of the property to the maximum of 12 times the value of the assets taken. Theft from the king was punishable by a fine of nine times the value of the goods, equivalent to the fine imposed when a priest's property was taken. These dooms evidence the beginning of the custom of the king's peace, a special protection that applied to those in the physical presence of the king, or to those located in a village or assembly area to which the king's protection had been extended. A similar form of peace, enforced by more modest fines, applied to the person and protected areas of an *eorl* (nobleman). The king's peace applied to all forms of wrongdoing, and it was imposed as an additional fine, supplementing the normal penalties and sanctions for the wrong itself. Aethelbert's dooms imposed a relatively heavy wergild of 100 shillings as the ordinary wergild; it was to be increased in proportion to the dignity of the victim. The dooms of Hlothaere and Eadric, issued in 685, perpetuated the wergild compensation imposed nearly a century before, but in the case of a servant who slayed a freeman, the dooms required that the servant be turned over to the victim's family in addition to the payment of the fine by his master.

The dooms issued by King Ine of the West Saxons (688-695) reflected a growing determination to control violent behavior. Fighting in the house of the king became an offense punishable by forfeiture of all property, and at the discretion of the monarch, the offender might be put to death. A detailed list of fines applied to fighting in the houses of nobles, churchmen, and common householders. Theft also became a problem, and these dooms imposed increased penalties if the taking of property was by a band of 7 to 35 individuals or an army of a greater number. One who plundered his fellows in the company of an army was required to pay his wergild to redeem himself. Wergilds were specially enacted to protect servants of the king as well as Welsh horsemen employed by him. During the reign of Ine, theft was also punished more harshly, and a thief caught in the act might be slain without incurring the payment of wergild.

Later, Anglo-Saxon dooms reflected the revival of commercial activity in England. By restricting trade to given ports or market towns and by requiring witnesses to sales transactions, the dooms were meant to deter disputes and criminal charges among merchants and the king's subjects. Increasingly after the ninth century, there was an emphasis on the need to bring criminal charges before the king's officials or courts before resorting to revenge. The dooms of Edgar (946-963) and Canute (1020-1034) established careful regulation for the creation and operations of local courts charged with law enforcement in the hundreds, shires, and boroughs.[3] While resort to private vengeance and reliance upon self-help remained a part of English law, by the eleventh century vengeance was clearly the last resort of a victim who had exhausted his or her opportunities for redress in the king's courts.

Oath and Ordeal

Once a system of trial was adopted as an alternative to blood feuds, it became necessary to develop means for determining the truth of testimony and other evidence presented to courts. Initially, this was done by means of a compurgatory oath, whereby an individual accused of crime or the wrongful withholding of property might take an oath that he or she was innocent of wrongdoing. If the accused gained the support of a sufficient number of his kindred, or "oathhelpers," he was acquitted. This procedure by oath has some similarities to early oath-taking modes of proof in Athenian procedure. Its reliability depended upon the widespread fear of divine retribution after perjury, and in the case of the medieval oath, the credibility of the party increased the likelihood that he would succeed in obtaining a sufficient number of helpers.

Should the exchange of oaths by the parties and the support of oath helpers not be sufficient to determine the issues of fact, medieval judges had the alternative of leaving the case undecided or proceeding to the ordeal, which would seek divine intervention to determine guilt or innocence. The ordeal took various forms, but only the most common need be considered to amply illustrate the procedure.

The ordeal of hot water required that the accused thrust a hand, or an arm up to the elbow, into a kettle of boiling water. When the hand was withdrawn, it was usually bound for three days and the divine verdict was determined by whether the individual emerged unscathed. An ordeal by cold water required that the accused be lowered into a body of water. If the accused floated on the surface, it was held that he or she was a sinner or wrongdoer, for it was believed that the spirit of Satan invaded the body of a perjurer, making its weight less than that of water. Careful calculations were, of course, necessary to preserve the life of an innocent party who sank to the bottom. Descriptions of the mode of placing accused persons in the water would indicate that a rope was attached to the body in such a way that only a short immersion would occur before the vindicated party was removed from the water. At times, divine intervention occurred in unusual ways; it was said that in some cases murderers and other felons were scalded by cold water, the unexplained change in water temperature indicating their guilt to the assembled multitude.

A variant of the hot water ordeal was the ordeal of the red-hot iron, which could be accomplished in one of two ways. The first method was to heat a bar of iron to red-hot heat and then require the accused to carry it a given distance before dropping it. The alternative was to heat a number of plowshares, ranging from 6 to 12 in number, and to require the ordeal subject to walk barefoot across the shares. The variations in the number of plowshares, and the weight of the bar of iron to be carried a given distance, depended upon the gravity of the crime. Ordeals by hot iron tended to be favored by the nobility while water ordeals were considered more appropriate for commoners. These two forms of ordeal were common throughout Europe, and were used extensively in Anglo-Saxon England and early Norman England. In English criminal procedure the ordeal by water or by iron was halted by the reforms of the Fourth Lateran Council of 1215, which prohibited the church from playing any role in the administration of ordeals. However, ordeals, particularly the ordeal of water, continued to be used in witchcraft cases into the nineteenth century.

The Ordeal of Queen Emma (c. 1043)

The queen was brought at the king's command from Whewell to Winchester and throughout all the night preceding her trial she kept her vigil at the shrine of St. Swithin. On the appointed day the clergy and the people came to the church and the king himself sat on the tribunal. The queen was brought before her son and questioned whether she was willing to go through with what she had undertaken. . . . Nine glowing ploughshares were placed on the carefully swept pavement of the church. After these had been consecrated by a short ceremony, the queen's shoes and stockings were taken off; then her robe was removed and her cloak thrown aside. Supported by two bishops, one on either side, she was led to the torture. The bishops who led her were weeping and those who were much more afraid than she were encouraging her not to fear. Uncontrollable weeping broke out all over the church and all voices were united in the cry "St. Swithin, O St. Swithin, help her!" If the thunder had pealed forth at this time, the people could not have heard it, with such strength, with such a concourse of voices did the shout go up to Heaven that St. Swithin should now or never hasten to her aid. God suffers violence and St. Swithin is dragged by force from Heaven. In a low voice the queen offered this prayer as she undertook the ordeal: "O God, who didst free Susanna from the wicked elders and the three youths from the fiery furnace, from the fire prepared for me deign to preserve me through the merits of St. Swithin."

Behold the miracle! With the bishops directing her feet, in nine steps she walked upon the nine ploughshares, pressing each one of them with the full weight of her whole body; and though she thus passed over them all, she neither saw the iron nor felt the heat. Therefore she said to the bishops: "Am I not to obtain that which I especially sought? Why do you lead me out of the church when I ought to be tried within it?" For she was going out and yet did not realize that she had gone through the ordeal. To which the bishops replied as well as they could through their sobs: "O lady, behold, you have already done it; the deed is now accomplished which you think must yet be done." She gazed and her eyes were opened; then for the first time she looked about and understood the miracle. "Lead me," she said, "to my son, that he may see my feet and know that I have suffered no ill."

Source: Henry C. Lea, *The Ordeal*, ed. Edward Peters (Philadelphia: University of Pennsylvania Press, 1973; first published in 1866 as Henry C. Lea, *Superstition and Force*).

This report of an ordeal by hot iron was prepared by Richard of Devizes, a late twelfth-century chronicler of Anglo-Saxon England. Historians note that Richard altered the legend of Queen Emma, the widow of King Aethelred the Unready who married the Danish conqueror of England, King Cnut (or Canute) in 1017, by adding details from the life of her daughter-in-law, Queen Edith, who was the wife of Emma's son, King Edward the Confessor. Thus the king mentioned in the narrative was actually the husband, and not the son, of the woman undergoing the ordeal. The charge of adultery apparently involved Queen Edith, who was suspected of extramarital relations with

Aelfwinet, Bishop of Winchester, and was accused by King Edward and Robert of Jumieges, the Archbishop of Canterbury.

Despite the confusion of persons in the rather complicated familial relationships of Emma, Edith, and Edward, the report illustrates the interrelationship between ecclesiastical ceremony and judicial trial of the facts. In recognition of their error, King Edward and the archbishop reportedly dedicated the revenue of nine manors to the honor of the local saint, Swithin. The Bishop of Winchester and Queen Edith were restored to their honors and released from confinement. For further details, see Pauline Stafford, *Queen Emma and Queen Edith: Queenship and Women's Power in Eleventh Century England* (Oxford: Blackwell Publishers, Inc., 1997), especially the prologue and Chapters 1-3.

The close connection between the ordeals and the church should be a matter of special note, because it demonstrates the degree to which a certain form of Christian belief could (and in some cases still does) influence modes of criminal procedure and the evidence produced before criminal courts. Because the ordeal anticipated divine intervention to determine guilt or innocence, it was not administered in a routine fashion. Quite to the contrary, the ordeal was preceded by an extensive religious ceremony that always included the celebration of the Eucharist (or Mass) and the exorcism of the water or iron to be used in administering the test. Finally, the celebrant delivered a lengthy prayer requesting God's assistance in conducting the ordeal and adjuring the accused that, if he had been guilty of perjury, he should recant and confess any guilt. An interesting variant might have been the requirement that the accused receive the consecrated bread during the course of the communion service, it being widely believed that if one guilty of crime or perjury took consecrated bread into his mouth he would choke or die. Before it was taken, a special prayer that emphasized the danger was recited.

Corbis Images

Tortures of the accused in medieval times included "the wheel."

Certain vestiges of the ordeals and their related superstitions persisted well after ordeals had been eliminated from criminal procedure. Bier-right was reportedly used before juries and as an investigative tool well into the seventeenth century. Bier-right was the belief that a corpse approached by its slayer would begin to bleed, regardless of how long ago the time of death might have been. Widely used in the Dark Ages to survey a number of suspected killers, bier-right may well have provided special encouragement for the confession of an accused person. There are reports of such unfortunate persons being immediately put to death upon the occurrence of bier-right and in the absence of any other evidence.

TIME CAPSULE

Adjudication by Battle

In the words of William Blackstone, writing in the eighteenth century, trial by battle was "another species of presumptuous appeals to Providence, under an expectation that Heaven would unquestionably give the victory to the innocent or injured party" (Blackstone IV, 346). Fortunately, Blackstone provided a detailed description of the ritualistic procedures of the duel. The duel in a felony matter was to be fought in a manner similar to that prescribed for civil trial by combat. A person appealed of a felony could plead not guilty, throw down his glove, and declare his willingness to defend it by his body. If the appellant took up the glove, they both swore an oath to the truth of their statements and a further oath against sorcery and enchantment:

Hear this, ye justices, that I have this day neither ate, drank, nor have upon me, neither bone, stone, nor grass: nor any enchantment, sorcery, or witchcraft, whereby the law of God may be abased, or the law of the devil exalted. So help me God and his saints.

A piece of ground is then in due time set out, of 60 feet square, enclosed with lists, and on one side a court erected for the judges of the court of common pleas, who attend there in their scarlet robes; and also a bar is prepared for the learned serjeants at law. When the court sits, which ought to be by sunrising, proclamation is made for the parties, and their champions; who are introduced by two knights, and are dressed in a coat of armour, with red sandals, bare-legged from the knee downwards, bareheaded, and with bare arms to the elbows.

The weapons allowed them are only batons, or staves of an ell [45 inches] long, and a four-cornered leather-target. . . . And if the appellee be so far vanquished that he cannot or will not fight any longer, he shall be adjudged to be hanged immediately; and then, as well as if he be killed in battle, providence is deemed to have determined in favour of the truth, and his blood shall be attainted. But if he kills the appellant, or can maintain the fight from sunrising till the stars appear in the evening, he shall be acquitted. So also if the appellant becomes recreant and pronounces the horrible word of *craven*, he shall lose his *liberum legem*, and become infamous; and the appellee shall recover his damages, and also be forever quit, not only of the appeal, but of all indictments likewise for the same offense (Blackstone III, 338-340; IV, 347-348).

Source: Sir William Blackstone, *Commentaries on the Laws of England*, 4 vols. (Chicago: Callaghan and Company, 1899), III, 338-340; IV, 346-348.

The compurgatory oath, ordeals, and bier-right were integral parts of the law in Anglo-Saxon England before the arrival of Duke William of Normandy. With him came a new form of ordeal: trial by battle. This involved the settlement of a legal issue by the combat of two champions (or substitute fighters) selected by the parties. It was used extensively in the trial of early claims to land, but it also was available when an individual was privately accused of a felony. The accusing party who brought the complaint (an appeal of felony) was responsible for dueling the accused or appointing a champion to do so. Theoretically, God would not permit the perjuring party to prevail, and thus the victor was held to win the case. This form of private prosecution died out as the state increasingly brought public actions for the punishment of crime, but trial by battle remained an option in English criminal law until 1819 when Parliament, reacting to a case in which a criminal escaped punishment by offering to do battle, abolished it by statute.

The Fourth Lateran Council (1215)

Active participation of clergy in preparations for, and in conduct of, ordeals long occupied the attention of the papacy. Over the course of time, an ambiguous attitude developed that sanctioned clerical participation in some cases and condemned it in others. The accession of Pope Innocent III did not indicate any substantial change, but the new pope had been educated at the University in Paris and determined to reform certain abuses that had developed within the church. Among those excesses was participation in ordeals, which brought revenues to local priests and bishops and violated a long-standing prohibition against clerical involvement in judicial proceedings that shed blood. Ultimately, Pope Innocent III's determination to exert spiritual supremacy over the western church resulted in critical attention being directed against ordeals and their supporting religious rituals. When Innocent III convened his bishops and theologians at the Fourth Lateran Council (1215), the stage was set for an abrupt curtailment of the ancient system of trial by ordeal.

The absence of records makes it impossible to determine why the ordeal procedure became a matter of pressing concern to Innocent III just one year before his death in 1216. His decision to submit the matter to the Fourth Lateran Council for its advice undoubtedly reflected his belief that a consensus among his cardinals and bishops would strengthen his action. There is historical conjecture that ordeals may have long concerned Pope Innocent III after his experience as a young theology student in Paris. During that time, Peter the Chanter was at the height of his influence as a theologian. Peter was in charge of church music at the cathedral of Notre Dame, but he also was one of the leading theological thinkers in Europe. His interest in the ordeal ceremony was heightened by the execution of one of his penitents. The man informed Peter that he was innocent of the criminal accusations against him but did not wish to undergo the ordeal. Peter advised him to refuse the ordeal; he did, and the civil authorities executed him. Had he lived, the ordeal might have continued, but his death triggered Peter the Chanter into action with his pen. A series of treatises emerged from his study, pointedly criticizing ordeals in both theological and legal terms. Perhaps his most effective publication was his extensive collection of ordeal cases that had wrongly resulted in the execution of accused persons; subsequent evidence proved that many of the condemned criminals could not have committed the offenses of which they were accused and cast serious doubt upon the infallibility of the ordeal. Peter took special aim at trial by battle, suggesting that if God really helped the champion of the innocent party, why should not one really obtain divine proof by selecting the most decrepit old man to be one's champion?

TIME CAPSULE

Pope Innocent III

At the end of his pontificate (1198-1216), Innocent III summoned the Fourth Lateran Council to meet with him in Rome to consider reforms in various church practices. Included within these was the requirement that all clergy abstain from participating in judicial ordeals. Closely related to this reform was Innocent's decision that relics of the saints should not be exposed for public veneration. Taken together, these two actions indicate that one of the Pope's major concerns was the degree to which religious practice was perverted by superstition and excessive involvement in the administration of justice outside of church courts.

However, the internal reforms by this council were even more far-reaching. It expounded the beginnings of a doctrine of transubstantiation, which would form the background for Roman Catholic-Protestant debate after the Reformation of the sixteenth century. The council instituted veneration of the consecrated Host (benediction), as well as private confession and the requirement that the laity receive at least one Holy Communion per year at Easter. Clerical discipline was strengthened by the adoption of a new code of canon law and by vesting disciplinary authority in diocesan bishops. Clerical responsibilities in the administration of pastoral care and preaching were re-emphasized, as were the obligations of bishops to visit their congregations on a regular basis.

Sources: Hans-Georg Beck, *From the High Middle Ages to the Eve of the Reformation*, Anselm Biggs, translator, Vol. 4; Hubert Jedin and John Dolan, eds., *Handbook of Church History,* (New York: Herder and Herder, 1970); L. Elliott Binns, *Innocent III* (London: Methuen & Co., 1931); Helene Tillman, *Pope Innocent III*, trans. Walter Sax (Amsterdam: North-Holland Publishing Co., 1970).

There is no direct connection known between Innocent III and Peter the Chanter, but the future pope studied with a student of Peter and may well have listened to Peter speak or read his treatises. If this was the case, it was perhaps one of the rare times when a teacher had a profound moral impact on the conscience of a student. In the case of Innocent III and the ordeal, it is clear that the decree of November 1215 at the Fourth Lateran Council, which prohibited clerical participation in preparations for ordeals, had immediate and significant impact throughout Western Europe. Within Normandy, England, and Denmark, ordeals stopped almost immediately; records as early as 1219 indicate that the practice no longer existed in England, but trial by battle still remained in a more secular garb.

Summary

The ending of church support for trial by ordeal created a void in all European legal systems, and new methods had to be found to determine issues of fact and the guilt or innocence of accused persons. Indeed, those new procedures were already in the process of development both on the European continent and in England. With the action of the Fourth Lateran Council, each separate kingdom was given the opportunity to institute its own substitute for the ordeal. In the vital area of criminal trials, there no longer existed a uniform transnational method approved by and supported by the western church. At this point in history, English and continental criminal procedure met a fork in the road and went their divergent ways.

Abolition of the ordeal may also be seen as a mark of increasing sophistication in judicial fact-finding and of decreased reliance upon divine intervention (or miracles) in the affairs of men. In biblical Israel, legal issues were tried by drawing lots from the high priest's breastplate; Athens and Rome used "platter and loincloth" searches. People were beginning to substitute reason and informed judgment for blind reliance upon these methods of superstition and chance. The Fourth Lateran Council's eighteenth canon on ordeals effectively ended a system of trial based upon superstition and magic. The change left a vacuum that would be filled in continental Europe by the rise of judicial inquisition (a form of investigation) and in England by the rise of the trial jury.

Endnotes

[1]   The Digest contained the laws of Rome as authorized by Emperor Justinian.

[2]   A blood feud developed when families or clans engaged in widespread vengeance over a series of generations, because efforts to resolve their differences had failed.

³ Saxon England was divided into hundreds composed of ten tithings, which in turn were made up of ten families. The shire, later called a county, was a larger division created by the grouping of hundreds. The borough was a walled town, usually incorporated or possessed of a royal charter of privileges.

References

Two old but still useful surveys are Sir Frederick Pollock and Frederic William Maitland, *The History of English Law before the Time of Edward I*, 2d ed., 2 vols. (Cambridge: Cambridge University Press, 1968); and the second volume of Sir William S. Holdsworth, *A History of English Law*, 4th ed. (London: Methuen & Co., 1936). On ordeals, see Henry Charles Lea, *The Ordeal*, ed. Edward Peters (Philadelphia: University of Pennsylvania Press, 1973); and James Bradley Thayer, *A Preliminary Treatise on Evidence at the Common Law* (Boston: Little, Brown and Company, 1898). On the blood feud and law of revenge, the reader might consult *Njal's Saga*, trans. Magnus Magnusson and Herman Palsson (Hammondsworth, England: Penguin Books, 1960); there is a useful collection of Anglo-Saxon dooms in Carl Stephenson and Frederick George Marcham, eds. and trans., *Sources of English Constitutional History*, 2d ed., vol. I (New York: Harper & Row, 1972).

See Chapter 3 on primitive Germanic criminal procedure in Adhemar Esmein, *History of Continental Criminal Procedure with Special Reference to France* (Boston: Little, Brown and Company, 1913); and Chapter 10 regarding government and law in Francis B. Gummere, *Germanic Origins: A Study in Primitive Culture* (New York: Charles Scribner, 1892). Two chapters (Chapter 2 on primitive Germanic criminal law and Chapter 4 on medieval Germanic law) provide more background on Germanic legal pinciples in Carl Ludwig von Bar, *A History of Continental Criminal Law* (Boston: Little Brown and Company, 1916). See also David A. Thomas, "Origins of the Common Law: Part II. Anglo-Saxon Antecedents of the Common Law," *Brigham Young University Law Review* (1985), pp. 453-503; Dorothy Whitelock, *The Beginnings of English Society* (Baltimore, MD: Penguin Books, 1956), Chapter 8; and William John Victor Windeyer, *Lectures on Legal History* (Sydney: Law Book Company of Australia, 1949).

For a brief history of canon law, see Chapter 2 in William John Victor Windeyer, *Lectures on Legal History* (Sydney: Law Book Company of Australia, 1949). Students interested in the Holy Inquisition can find useful information in Chapter 10 of George Ryley Scott, *The History of Torture Throughout the Ages* (London: Luxor Press, 1959). Regarding benefit of clergy, see Chapter 6 of Windeyer, *Lectures*; and Jeffrey K. Sawyer, "Benefit of Clergy in Maryland and Virginia," *American Journal of Legal History* 34 (1991), pp. 49-68. The right of sanctuary is discussed in George Ives, *A History of Penal Methods* (Montclair: Patterson Smith, 1970); and Andrew McCall, *The Medieval Underworld* (London: Hamish Hamilton, 1979).

Notes and Problems

1. This period in history provides great opportunity for the exercise of historical imagination. For example, what is the consequence of having a special law that applies to certain groups and not others living in the same geographical area? Why did Paul receive favored treatment by Roman governors (see the Acts of the Apostles) by virtue of his Roman citizenship? In a certain sense, the modern system of nation-states maintains a geographical or territorial system of law;

this raises special problems in federal states like the United States, where criminal law is usually state-determined. The law of the place where the crime is committed applies, but what law applies if the crime is a continuing one across state lines? And what happens if the crime occurs before and after crossing an international boundary?

2. Given the existence of one's personal "law" during this period in history, what did it mean to be placed outside that law, or to be outlawed? In addition to the life-threatening aspects of outlawry, what psychological impact might it have?

3. How well can a system of vengeance and blood feud discourage crime? To what degree does "might make right" in such a violent world? Icelandic practices sub-mitted many of these ongoing disputes to a gathering of family heads, called an Althing, either for regulation or for arbitration. Did the combined "force" of such an assembly help to impose limits on the spread of vengeance? Or did it simply involve clan leaders in the dispute and broaden the killing?

4. How much proof did the result of an ordeal provide? In what ways does it dif-fer from modern reliance upon lie detectors, blood, voice, and fingerprint analysis? Can it be distinguished from a jury verdict?

5. Can the ordeal be justified as a means for preventing revenge killing? It was the last resort, after a variety of oaths had been exchanged between the parties, and after their oath helpers had supported their veracity. When these proofs and the judge's knowledge of the facts were inconclusive, the ordeal was used. The judge could release the accused, but would that satisfy the kin group's demand for revenge? On the other hand, even one who prevailed in the course of an ordeal could be seen to suffer and, thus, the impulse toward revenge would be diminished.

6. Aside from the probative issues concerning the ordeal, what perversions of Chris-tian doctrine and sacraments were present in the ordeal ritual? Was the Eucharist designed as a test for criminal guilt? Is there sufficient evidence in either the Old Testament or the New Testament that God intervenes in human adminis-trations of criminal justice? Did church participation in the ordeal provide an aura of spirituality and legitimacy to a procedure based upon magic and super-stition?

Chapter 4

From the Lateran Councils to the Renaissance (c. 1150-1550)

While the abolition of trial by ordeal was the most notable development in thirteenth-century criminal justice, it was but one of many historical trends that caused the separation of English criminal procedure from that of continental Europe. The four centuries from 1150 to 1550 witnessed rapid and fundamental changes in all areas of economic and social life. Not surprisingly, the criminal justice system responded with new initiatives, striving to achieve efficiency in law enforcement and seeking to control mounting violence, spurred on by pressures of urbanization and the upheaval of economic growth and diversification.

Vast changes took place in daily life over the course of these 400 years. They were marked by the decline of feudalism, a political system founded upon relationships between lords and vassals in which the king was, in many cases, no more than the highest-ranking lord in a given territory. The feudal system of government provided a mode of land distribution; along with ownership of lands, feudal nobles were accorded certain judicial powers over their vassals and the farming classes laboring on their lands. When feudalism collapsed, down also went the local baronial courts, and the administration of justice fell once more into the hands of the kings. Royal power also grew by virtue of changed methods of conducting warfare, which destroyed the military value of feudalism. The entire complex system of feudal landholding and its supporting economic system of manorialism existed to field a combat army of mounted knights. By the middle of the fourteenth century, the evolution of the longbow and the subsequent invention of the more powerful crossbow made armored knights obsolete. Indeed, by that time, many of the armored knights were willing to pay the king enough cash to avoid the discomforts and danger of combat. In place of the feudal nobility arrayed in armor on the battlefield, kings now fielded armies paid by and loyal to the Crown.

TIME LINE

England		The European Continent
Rise of accusation by men of the country (grand jury)	**c. 1150**	
Assize of Clarendon	**1166**	
	1176-1226	Waldensee and Cathari heretics suppressed through use of inquisitorial procedures
Assize of Arms	**1181**	
	1215	Fourth Lateran Council prohibits clergy from participating in trials by ordeal
	1229	Church council at Toulouse authorizes Dominican clergy to launch the Holy Office (Inquisition) to stop the spread of heresies
Criminal trials by petit jury common throughout England	**1240**	
	1260-1295	The Venetians Marco, Nicolo, and Maffeo Polo travel to Bukhara and China to establish trading relationships
	c. 1290	First mention of gunpowder in European documents
	1300-	Use of extraordinary inquisitorial procedure (including torture) expanded in French civil courts
	1347-1377	Bubonic plague, or the Black Death, kills approximately 40 percent of Europe's population
Justice of the peace becomes a local judicial official	**1350**	
By statute, members of grand jury prohibited from serving on petit juries to try those they indicted	**1352**	
	1457	Johannes Gutenberg perfects the system for using movable type; his son-in-law prints an edition of the Book of Psalms
	1492	Christopher Columbus, sailing in the service of Spain, reaches islands off the coast of North America

England		The European Continent
	1494	Treaty of Tordesillas, later confirmed by a Papal Bull, divides the newly discovered world between Portugal and Spain
	1498	Vasco da Gama, sailing in the service of Portugal, reaches India
	1513	Nicòlo Machiavelli writes *The Prince*, a manual for statesmen that emphasizes *realpolitik*
	1517	Martin Luther posts his Ninety-Five Theses in Wittenberg, condemning the Church's sale of indulgences
Parliament declares Henry VIII to be Supreme Head of the Church in England	**1534**	
	1536	John Calvin's *Institutes of the Christian Religion* published in Basle, Switzerland
	1545-1563	Three sessions of the Council of Trent reassert the primacy of the Pope and restate Roman Catholic doctrine

Under feudalism, landholdings were established in self-sufficient economic entities called *manors*. These produced all of the food necessary to sustain the meager diets of Western Europeans and also provided the necessary craftsmen and manufacturing skills needed for the comfort of the manor lord and his retainers. Within the manor, the lord was virtually unlimited in his exercise of authority, both in civil disputes and in criminal justice. Unlike feudalism, manorialism persisted well into the seventeenth century, but its insularity and self-sufficiency were undermined as early as 1000 A.D., when a revival of trade caused a growing demand for new products. Small commercial villages and towns attracted excess labor from the manors, and enterprising men recognized that mercantile activity was the path to wealth.

Taken by themselves, these changes were of great magnitude, but they were also accompanied by a growing interest in learning and experimentation known as the Renaissance. Seeking to understand the world about them, and also to fathom the complexities of human nature and behavior,

Renaissance scholars reexamined the relationship of individuals to society. Ancient systems of science, based upon classical Greek authors, began to be challenged despite opposition by the Roman Catholic Church. Ultimately, the Church was unable to restrain this inquisitiveness, and the lines of debate shifted from matters of science and political theory to disputes over religion. From 1150 onward, the Papacy fought a continual battle against heresies by criminal prosecutions (the Holy Office, or Inquisition) as well as on the battlefield, and the judicial suppression of heresy provided a background against which a new system of criminal procedure would evolve. Ultimately, theological heresy did not shatter Christian unity in the West. Instead, growing pressure for clerical reform and demands for adjustment in church organization triggered the soul-shaking movement of the Protestant Reformation and the equally vigorous internal reform of the Roman Catholic Church in the sixteenth century.

TIME CAPSULE

Murder in the Cathedral

The dry distinction between ecclesiastical and rural jurisdiction is vividly evident in the struggle between King Henry II of England and Archbishop of Canterbury Thomas à Becket. Becket, student of canon law and Archdeacon of Canterbury, had been appointed Royal Chancellor by Henry II in 1154. In 1162 Becket was consecrated Archbishop of Canterbury. Perceiving a potential conflict of interest in holding both secular and ecclesiastical office, Becket resigned as chancellor. Once appointed archbishop, Becket's adherence to the principles of the Catholic Church strengthened and when King Henry required him to commit acts that violated church policy, Becket steadfastly refused, precipitating an open breach.

One of the major sources of conflict between Henry II and Becket was the question of judicial jurisdiction over members of the clergy who had committed crimes, the "criminous clerks." Henry, alarmed by increasing

clerical crime, decried the lenient punishments meted out in the ecclesiastical courts and insisted that clergy be tried in royal courts. In response to this demand, Becket cited the principle of clerical supremacy.

The conflict led to a direct confrontation during a conference in 1163. Calling on the principle of precedent, Henry stated in the Constitutions of Clarendon that he was claiming the judicial jurisdiction that had been customary at the time of his grandfather Henry I: a cleric who had been convicted in an ecclesiastical court and had been degraded (lost his clerical status) was to be turned over to the king's authorities for punishment.

Neither Becket nor the king would yield, and each had powerful tools to wield. Henry had the ability to deprive the Church of lands held under him and to withhold Church revenues. Becket could threaten to excommunicate the king, an act that would undermine his authority over his subjects. Although the symbiotic relationship between the royal power and the Church required both to temporize, the situation became so acrimonious in 1164 that Becket fled to France and remained there until he and Henry agreed that he could return to England in 1170. On his return, Becket again incensed Henry when he excommunicated three clergymen. In his rage, Henry is reputed to have said, "What miserable drones and traitors have I nourished and promoted in my household, who let their lord be treated with such shameful contempt by a low-born clerk!" (Barlow, 235). Four of Henry's knights took it upon themselves to arrest Becket. Finding the Archbishop in the cathedral, they attempted to take him into custody, but Becket, who had expressed his willingness to die for the Church, refused to leave. In a bloody struggle, the top of Becket's head was severed and his brain and blood stained the stones of the cathedral. There is no proof that the four knights had planned to take Becket's life. Neither is there documentation to support the claim that Henry deliberately sought the death of Becket. Inferences can be drawn, however, from the fact that the knights were never brought to trial for the murder, and they were later restored to the good graces of the king. Outrage at the murder and the violation of sanctuary brought public sympathy for Becket, and from the day of his death miracles were attributed to him He was canonized in 1173.

Who won? Becket had accepted death in order to uphold the rights of the Church and the ecclesiastical courts, and his martyrdom and canonization within three years could be viewed as a victory. Although the death did free King Henry from a serious rival for power, it was a mixed victory in that it also brought the wrath of the Church on his head. He faced excommunication and interdiction of his lands unless he could convince Pope Alexander III of his innocence or his true penitence. He eventually admitted being the unwitting cause of Becket's death and made substantial financial concessions to the Church. Perhaps of greater significance was the degradation of his being publicly scourged in Canterbury Cathedral by prelates and monks. The jurisdictional struggle between the royal courts and the ecclesiastical courts over "criminous clerks" remained rancorous until England abolished benefit of clergy in the early nineteenth century.

Note

The conflict between the Crown and Becket flared again in 1538, when Henry VIII revived the charge of treason against Becket, prompted perhaps by the lure of the fortune in gems and gold that had accumulated in Becket's shrine. It was said that Henry VIII had Becket's corpse disinterred, summoned him to trial, appointed a lawyer to defend him, saw him condemned, and had his body cremated. This tale, alluded to in a Bull of Pope Paul III, cannot be found in reliable historical records, but the fact that corpses of other long-dead traitors were brought to trial lends possible credence. For a dramatic presentation of the struggle between Henry II and Becket, see *Murder in the Cathedral* by T. S. Eliot.

Sources: Frank Barlow, *Thomas Becket* (Berkeley: University of Califormia Press, 1990); John Butler, *The Quest for Becket's Bones: The Mystery of the Relics of St. Thomas Becket of Canterbury* (New Haven: Yale University Press, 1995); Nesta Pain, *The King and Becket* (London: Eyre & Spottiswoode, 1964); Richard Winston, *Thomas Becket* (New York: Alfred A. Knopf, 1967).

Against this background of chaotic upheaval in the lives of people and nations, we must assess the way in which criminal justice changed, following the story of how English law took a separate path from that of the legal systems of continental Europe. Initially, we will trace the development of the French system of inquisitorial procedure, beginning in about 1150 and concluding with the enactment of the Ordinance of 1539. It will then be necessary to detail the evolution of the English system of jury trials, giving some attention to the ways in which both grand jury and petty (petit, or trial) juries shaped criminal law and procedure. Finally, we shall consider the impact of social and economic change on England and the continent, giving special attention to alterations in the criminal justice systems in rural England and rapidly urbanizing Italy.

The Rise of the French Inquisitorial System

The ancient and medieval criminal procedures already discussed were based upon two fundamental premises. First and foremost, the responsibility for accusing an individual of crime rested not upon the state or a public officer, but upon the person or group wronged by the accused's alleged criminal activity. In the event that no accuser came forward, prosecution was impossible. In such a situation, criminal cases and private actions to collect damages for wrongdoing tended to become indistinguishable. Protection from violence or property damage depended almost entirely upon the likelihood that the victim, or the victim's kindred on his or her behalf, would commence litigation.

In keeping with the first premise of private accusation, the second characteristic of early criminal procedure was its adversarial nature. In other words, the parties were arrayed against each other, charged with presenting evidence of crime on one side, and counteracting or disproving the evidence of criminality on the other side. Magistrates and triers of fact served as impartial referees of the contest, assuring that the parties followed certain rules in presenting their proofs and, ultimately, deciding between them. Only on rare occasions did a magistrate or fact-finding individual or jury independently develop evidence pertinent to the case. As we have seen in ancient Greek criminal procedure, the impact of public opinion might be very significant in the final outcome of a case.

Against this background, a new system of criminal procedure began to develop in the two centuries before 1215: the inquisitorial system. Essentially, its origins were in the efforts of church courts to discover and stamp out heresies. For example, southern France, beset by a corrupt clerical establishment and immoral behavior by churchmen, erupted into a series of heretical movements, including that of the Cathari (or Albigensees). The Cathari believed that there were not only forces of good (the spiritual side of man) and evil (his physical or material passions), but also that God had two sons, Christ (the good) and Satan (the evil son who rebelled against God).

They carried out these beliefs by remaining celibate and refraining from eating meat, milk, or eggs, all of which they considered to be material "fruits of reproduction." The rapid growth of the Cathari drew the attention of the Third Lateran Council, which authorized a two-year Albigensian Crusade (1179-1181); despite great bloodshed, the heresy continued to flourish until the arrival of Dominican friars. Authorized by the 1229 Council of Toulouse, the Dominicans began inquiries into the beliefs of accused persons and endeavored to eliminate heresy either by destroying the religious belief of the individual or, in the alternative, by keeping the suspect from spreading the heresy to others. These investigations were called *inquisitions*. In secular criminal procedure, which began to adopt the church's methods, they became the basis for modern continental criminal justice systems. Church courts ultimately applied the new inquisitional methods to combat the Protestant Reformation after 1517, and this led to the horrors of the Holy Inquisition.

There were sharp contrasts between the older adversarial system and the new methods of inquisition. Already noted in adversarial procedure was the role of the judge, who was to serve as an impartial referee between two contending parties. Adversarial systems were originally based on the private accuser, who was later replaced by the public prosecutor; consequently, the proof available for the judge's decision was essentially what the contending parties presented at their "battle," or trial. The judge in the inquisition received evidence discovered, not by a private accuser, but by an official investigator. If additional evidence was needed, the judge himself might conduct inquire further into the matter, including a secret hearing of witnesses at which the accused need not be present. In adversarial litigation, the judge played a passive role, but in the inquisitorial system he was an active participant in the trial process. The adversarial system utilized a trial by the accused's peers (or, earlier, a trial by ordeal), while the inquisitorial system afforded a modicum of protection to the accused by permitting him or her an appeal to a higher court or judge. Because the adversarial system presumed that the parties were contending with each other (if only in pleadings and words), it was basic to the case that the parties themselves should be present or the trial could not go forward. As we have noted, some significant phases of trial in the inquisitorial system might take place in the absence of the accused.

Both systems sought to determine the truth concerning the events in question, as well as to judge the criminal nature of the accused's behavior. Yet their concept of truth, as well as their mode of determining it, differed markedly. The adversarial system assumed that there were at least two sides to every controversy, and it permitted the parties to present their views for the judge and jury's consideration. Truth in the adversarial system was actually a determination of which opposed position was more likely to be correct. Truth was a matter of plausibility, of mature judgment, and of balancing two versions of a given event against each other. By contrast, the inquisitorial system demanded that one truth be ascertained by assembling all available evidence. Every effort of reason and all scientific knowledge had to be directed toward finding the truth. Only upon such overwhelming evidence, and not upon less proof or upon probabilities of guilt, could an accused be declared innocent or guilty.

This emphasis upon the conclusive nature of proof led to the stress upon confession in the inquisitorial system. This demonstrated to the world that the accused accepted the conclusiveness of the proofs against him or her. It exonerated judges and courts from the burden of deciding between conflicting bodies of evidence, and it reassured the public. As the inquisitorial system became more elaborate, it was standard practice to establish levels of proof adequate to convict for certain crimes. For the major crimes, it became almost impossible to obtain a conviction without having the confession of the accused person.

As confessions became a significant part of the state's case against those accused of crime, the methods used to obtain confessions were refined and perfected. Torture, limited by Roman procedure to extracting evidence from slaves, was expanded to all accused persons regardless of rank, and was also used to obtain evidence from witnesses or accomplices. There were few limits upon the form that tortures could take, but French law prohibited officials from causing the loss of life or limb through torture and also from using fire in its infliction. The most common method of torture was to stretch the accused naked on a wooden horse, throw water upon him, and then pour the water down his throat. After the cessation of this, or some other form of torture, the accused was permitted to regain his strength and then be reinterrogated. If the accused reaffirmed the confession, it was used as evidence, but if he did not ratify the confession previously given under torture, it was invalidated.

In the earliest stages of the French inquisitorial method, a system of ordinary trial was available. This provided an opportunity to hear the testimony of witnesses, to read depositions presented to the court, and to have a general knowledge of the case being presented by the state. Torture was not permitted in ordinary procedure, except in unusual cases. After 1300, more and more offenses came within the scope of extraordinary procedure, which did not give the accused any idea of the allegations against him and kept all testimony secret from him and the public. Interrogations and torture were performed in private, and the trial itself took place behind closed doors. By 1400, torture became a fundamental part of French criminal procedure.

By the mid-sixteenth century, the extraordinary method of criminal procedure was the rule in France. The Ordinance of 1539 provided for a two-stage process, consisting of examination before one judge, followed by formal trial before the entire bench of the court. The law abolished any right to be represented by counsel and prevented the accused from examining the accusation or depositions of witnesses; even the defendant could not argue in his own defense. Some defenses might be accepted: for example, one accused of homicide might obtain release by producing the victim alive. Self-defense and insanity were also available as defenses. All evidence by the accused was permitted only if the court granted the accused person's motion to prove these defenses by means of witnesses.

The English Jury System

Abolition of the judicial ordeal in England caused accelerated development of the English jury system, but not the introduction of a new method of criminal procedure. The origins of the grand jury (the body of local citizens who investigated and reported suspected crimes and serious wrongdoing to the royal justices) are unknown, but traces of the institution may be found in Germanic tribal law, in Anglo-Saxon dooms, and in the Norman Grand Inquest. On the other hand, the trial jury (or petty jury) seems to have evolved from some of the functions of the grand jury, a process that had begun before 1215 and that became a matter of urgency when the trial by ordeal was summarily removed from the law of western Christendom. To further complicate English criminal procedure, the practice of private accusation persisted in regard to felonies. These prosecutions began by an appeal of felony brought by an interested party, and the issue of guilt or innocence was decided by combat. Although the appeal of felony fell into disuse well before 1550, it was technically available as a mode of procedure up to 1819, when the British Parliament, embarrassed by its continued existence, abolished private accusations along with trial by battle.

The Assize of Clarendon[1] (1166) directed that 12 family heads of each hundred should be placed under oath and required to report to the King's justices all individuals accused or publicly known to be robbers, murderers, or thieves, or any persons known to have aided such wrongdoers. The accused were to be tried by the water ordeal, but, even if acquitted by that method, they might nevertheless be outlawed and exiled from the realm if they had poor reputations. Very clearly, the assize directed the use of a form of grand jury to bring criminal activity before the royal judges. Although ordeal was the mode of trial, the very fact that the grand jury had reported the suspect carried with it the inference of bad reputation. While supernatural ordeals might clear the accused of wrongdoing in the case at hand, his poor standing in the community could nevertheless serve as a basis for banishment. In this way, the character of the accused was as much an issue as it had been with the Greek dicastery or the Roman quaestiones jury.

It should be stressed that the use of a sworn body of local inhabitants characterized legal administration in early England. Henry II provided that certain questions concerning title to lands should be resolved by a body of 12 men drawn from the vicinity, and in the Assize of Arms (1181) he used a similar group to obtain detailed information concerning which of his subjects possessed weapons and in what quantity. Another use of a jury was in response to the complaint that an individual had been appealed of a felony[2] (and hence forced to submit to trial by battle) out of malice. A *writ de odio et atia* was available; under its terms, the person appealed was entitled to a jury decision on whether the appeal was improperly taken. This ensured that appeals of felony were reserved for the most serious crimes and that they were not used as instruments of oppression against the poor and weak, who were unable to hire champions or do battle themselves.

Matron's Juries

Until the twentieth century, jury service in England was restricted to males. There were, however, two exceptions to this rule. If a woman sentenced to death claimed to be pregnant, she could "plead the belly" and be granted a reprieve. The judge then would convene a special jury, composed of "twelve matrons or discreet women." The task of the matron's jury was to determine whether the woman was "quick with child"—that is, whether life in the fetus could be detected; merely being pregnant was not sufficient. Various tricks were utilized by condemned women, such as drinking to swell the belly or becoming pregnant during the pretrial period. A positive jury verdict meant that execution could be delayed until delivery or until it be shown that there was no child. A woman could call upon this form of mercy only once; if she became pregnant again, she could be executed before delivery. That pleading the belly could be a successful maneuver is attested to by the tale of *Moll Flanders* written by Daniel Defoe, a man personally acquainted with the jails and criminal justice procedures of England. The second use of a jury of women was to determine whether a woman accused in infanticide had recently given birth. The matron's jury was later replaced by medical examination.

Source: Sir William Blackstone, *Commentaries on the Laws of England, of Public Wrongs* (Boston: Beacon Press, 1962).

While the criminal procedure system for grand juries might seem to have provided ample basis upon which to construct a trial system for petty juries, it took several decades after 1215 to make the transition. At first, the royal judges were simply directed to order the banishment of criminals presented to them by grand juries. This was consistent with the past practice, in which the accused was acquitted by ordeal but was still of suspicious character. However, it did not provide the same verification of the grand jury's finding of probable guilt, and a rational alternative to the supernatural ordeal was needed. By 1240, the trial jury was in wide use; by 1275, it was rare that members of a grand jury would serve on the trial jury of an individual they had helped to present; and by 1352, such an overlapping of personnel was prohibited by statute.

Petty jury trials were sufficiently novel that it was felt that a person accused by the grand jury should be required to choose trial by this method. The alternative of banishment might be appealing because it did not carry with it the penalties of forfeiture of goods and lands attached to conviction before a trial jury. Because many defendants were inclined to take advantage of this loophole in criminal procedure, it was accepted practice to place them under torture to compel them to plead to the case and accept trial by jury. This torture, termed *peine forte et dure*, was also known as "pressing to death." The accused was placed in solitary confinement, starved, and then stripped naked. His body was then subjected to gradually increased weights of iron until he or she either pleaded to the indictment and accepted jury trial or died under the torture. Available until the nineteenth century under English law, pressing to death was ultimately replaced by the automatic entry of a "not guilty" plea on behalf of an accused person, with the resulting "acceptance" of jury trial.

The availability of *peine forte et dure* in English criminal procedure makes it clear that torture and barbarism were not unique to French and continental criminal justice. Reprehensible though both practices were, the English basis for pressing was to compel the accused to accept what the state had determined to be a rational form of trial. On the other hand, the continental reason for torture during inquisition was to make the accused person admit his or her guilt, thereby eliminating the need for additional proof of culpability. In England, torture could be a precondition of trial; in Europe, it was an integral part of the trial itself.

Almost from the beginning, grand and petty juries proved to be forces for the modification or nullification of law. Early thirteenth-century cases show patterns of petty jury convictions that suggest there was public dissatisfaction with the formal rules concerning murder and simple homicide. When a killing took place as a consequence of an ambush, or at night, or when the accused hid or buried the victim's corpse, conviction was highly probable. However, if the offense occurred in the course of a fight, or in circumstances that might today be considered worthy of a manslaughter conviction, the rates of conviction were extremely low. There is also some indication that early English juries manipulated the facts presented to them and reported to the courts a group of circumstances that justified pardoning the accused either on grounds of self-defense or justifiable homicide.

Modification of formal and unpopular rules of criminal law was not the sole function of trial juries. Their function as determiners of fact had, in many respects, the same finality that had hitherto attached to judgment by ordeal. Absent proof of bribery or intimidation, the jury's verdict could not be attacked nor could the jurymen be punished. Later generations of lawyers would say that there was no appeal from a jury verdict, but even at this early stage judges must have found it frustrating to deal with criminal prosecutions in which the good reputation or popularity of the accused prevented a guilty verdict. At a time when royal justice was becoming increasingly efficient and centralized, the trial jury ensured that the ultimate decisions in criminal prosecutions were still made in the light of local conditions and preferences.

It is remarkable that the English jury developed during an era of rapid centralization of English criminal justice. During the latter years of the twelfth century, itinerant royal judges heard cases in each county not more frequently than once every six years. By 1230, new systems of judicial appointment, based on commissions of gaol delivery[3] and commissions of oyer and ter-miner,[4] ensured semi-annual visitations and trials of presented individuals. Even this was not adequate to stem the growing tide of crime; by 1350, a system of royal justices of the peace had been established in each county, designed to try minor cases and to hold offenders accused of serious crimes for the arrival of the royal justices on circuit. The statutes of Parliament exhibited continuing concern for public safety and crime suppression, but, at the same time, no effort was made to modify or eliminate the institutions of grand and petty juries, both of which could be used to counteract the effectiveness of criminal prosecution. In a very real sense, the Crown and its judges were dependent upon the cooperation of each county's population for the suppression of local crime. Acceptance of that situation is apparent in the course that English criminal justice took in the years before 1550. Jury trial became the accepted rule, and public trials were insurance against investigative excess and judicial prejudice. Except for *peine fort et dure*, torture never became an integral part of English criminal procedure, and the presence of the accused in court at all times provided him with information and testimony useful in shaping his defense.

Society, Economics, and the Law

With the single possible exception of the industrial revolution (c. 1700-1850), no economic movement has had a greater impact upon Western civilization than the commercial revolution that began in about 1200 and continued into modern times. This was characterized by a gradual reestablishment of trade, not only within Europe and Britain, but also by sea routes in the Mediterranean, the Red Sea, and the Indian Ocean. Throughout this early period in history, transportation followed rivers and navigable waters rather than land routes, and for this reason, the Mediterranean areas of Europe were the first to experience commercial development. Their access by sea to the coasts of the Holy Land and the Near East (demonstrated by the ready transport of armies to fight the Crusades) ensured that the Italian city-states would become centers of wealth and commercial power, while northern Europe and Britain remained locked in an agrarian economic system, and thus had less wealth and prestige than their southern neighbors. Exploiting their advantages as trading centers, Venice, Milan, Florence, and Genoa established industrial activity early. This included specialized craft industries supervised by guild organizations; examples are the goldsmith and silver-smith guilds and the more mundane occupations of iron makers, carpenters, shipbuilders, and masons. Other industrial activity, for the most part also under guild control, included cloth-making, rope-making, tailoring, and leather work. These manufacturing processes added economic value to the raw materials that passed through the Italian cities and, as a consequence, added to the wealth of the craftsmen and guilds of those urban centers.

This sort of economic change and development was not limited to Italy, but the city-states on the Italian peninsula prospered earlier because of their geographical location. Throughout Europe and Britain there was related growth in the sense that commercial towns developed for the purpose of trading with Italian cities and for the sale of trade goods to smaller towns and villages in the rural areas of Europe. London served as such a commercial center in England, as did Paris in France. Over the course of the four centuries after 1150, these northern European trading centers became equal in wealth and prestige to their Italian counterparts. However, for purposes of historical study, it is important to remember that there was a considerable time lag between commercial development in Italy and the full impact of the commercial revolution in Britain and northern Europe. Commerce moved north slowly from the Mediterranean basin, awakening Europe to broader economic horizons and bringing with it the related problems of urbanization and social change.

Rising populations in cities caused an increase in theft and other property-related offenses. It is estimated that about 50 percent of the crimes prosecuted in early modern Europe were property crimes, while only 30 percent were violent crimes. Sources contemporary to the period, as well as historical research thereafter, suggest that the growing incidence of property crime is attributable to greater opportunity to participate in theft and other attacks on private property. Unlike modern cities, the trading settlements of the late Middle Ages and the Renaissance were not divided into sectors restricted to the wealthy and other areas designated as ghettos for the poor. The servants and retainers of wealthy nobles and merchants lived in the immediate vicinity of their master's residence, if not within the house enclosure itself. There was ample opportunity to observe the lifestyle and daily itinerary of the well-to-do victim in order to plan a burglary or theft with the advantage of good and reliable information. There was also strong incentive to engage in criminal activity. Economic prosperity resulted in a wide disparity between the standards of living of the rich and those of the urban poor. Economic necessity and class-related tensions helped to increase the likelihood of property-related crime. At the same time, cities provided an excellent facility for "fencing" stolen goods. Theft of valuable jewelry, other valuable personal adornments, and household items such as paintings and silverware, was encouraged by a ready market for stolen goods. To a lesser degree, this was also true of smaller towns near the cities, but thieves in rural areas were deprived of this urban-centered service. As a consequence, the rural thief concentrated on farm implements, draft animals, and food or clothing for him or his family.

Commercial growth depended upon the maintenance of peace, both with nations who were trading partners and within the city where trade was to be conducted. As a result, violence was discouraged, and the authorities did their best to ensure the safety of alien merchants and tradesmen. In Italy, they seem to have been less than successful, due in large part to the continuing taste of the nobility for blood vengeance and the degree to which the noble class did violence to individuals of lesser rank. Sex-related crimes are a good illustration of this tendency. In Venice, it was common for a nobleman to rape a woman of a lower class; for the most part, the penalties were so nominal that it was not worth the expense to bribe the judge or purchase the silence of the victim. On the other hand, no noblewoman over the course of nearly 200 years complained of being raped by anyone other than a member of her own class. To some degree, this may have been due to the common practice of secluding unmarried noblewomen, but it was also attributable to the harsh penalties provided for such an offense. Yet, even in an environment in which the machismo of noblemen was given relatively free rein, there were limits beyond which the rapist might not go. It was a taboo punishable by death to rape a girl under the age of puberty, and similar harsh punishment was available for those convicted of bestiality or homosexual activity.

The class of "important persons," ranking just below the urban nobility in status, was composed largely of merchants and owners of manufacturing establishments. This urban bourgeoisie was strongly devoted to the ideal of civic peace and tranquility. However, the virtual isolation of the nobility from the violence of the lower classes meant that laboring class resentment found its outlet against the "important persons." These "important persons" were the principal victims of property-related offenses and absorbed more than their share of the violent crimes. Nobles met with violence mainly as a consequence of their duties as leaders of police units charged with enforcing law and order.

Laboring and seafaring classes in Italian cities were the sources of most criminal activity. Most were unfamiliar with local customs and procedures because their population shifted frequently; all were kept at or below a subsistence standard of living. Easy access to the wealth of the upper class was a continuing temptation, as was the aggravating factor of the violence of nobles against the persons, wives, and property of the working man. In this shifting population, it was difficult to identify a person accused of crime, and the conditions of urban existence made crime an easy and relatively safe way of life. It was highly dangerous to move about the cities at night; the lack of any street lighting gave the advantage to criminals bent on robbery or murder. Special patrols were established to keep the streets clear, but they could not provide adequate protection in all areas at all times. In Venice, women carefully avoided certain ferries renowned for the number of assaults and rapes committed in the course of a trip across the Grand Canal.

Italian city officials reacted by establishing a police system based upon patrols commanded by noblemen. Heavy penalties were imposed for assaults on a member of the patrol, and attacking or killing a nobleman carried an extremely harsh punishment, rarely less than death. Magistrates had broad discretion in sentencing, and penalties ranged widely, depending on the social rank of the accused and the victim, the amount of property involved (if any), and the degree to which the crime disturbed public order. Capital punishment was designed to expiate community feelings of vengeance and to deter would-be criminals. The execution ritual required that the condemned man or woman be marched from prison to the place where the offense had taken place. There, he or she would be mutilated by the removal of the offending member (usually a hand in the case of theft or murder). Then the convict was marched back to the place of execution, to be hung if a male or burned alive if a female. In Florence, the crowds added to the ceremony by urging the official tormenters to keep torturing irons at high temperatures throughout these marches; executioners who failed to keep the convict howling by this method were occasionally killed on the spot by the mob.

England provides a striking contrast to Florence and Venice. No commercial centers were of great consequence beyond the city of London, and royal authority diminished as one moved away from the capital city. Local magnates in outlying areas exercised great influence on the deliberation of judges and local juries; they also maintained their own private armies for revenge and personal protection. In wooded and remote areas, bands of outlawed men preyed upon local residents and plundered merchants attempting to trade with provincial towns. There is reason to believe that the English nobility was less violent in criminal behavior than the Italian urban elite, and the statistics show a much lower rate of involvement in criminal activity. This is not to say that English nobles had lost their taste for mayhem. Quite the contrary, it had been directed into the form of the tournament or joust, in which many a noble contestant was either seriously wounded or killed under suspicious circumstances.

One striking thing about English criminality during this period was the intense involvement of clergy in a wide variety of offenses. Violence and theft by lower orders of clergy was common. Nuns

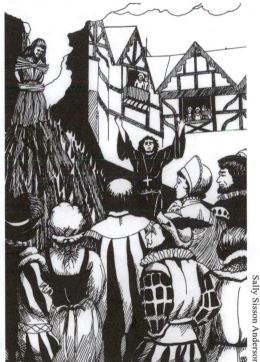

Sally Sisson Anderson

Public physical punishments during the Renaissance, in the forms of burnings at the stake, hangings, floggings and dismemberment, drew large crowds.

were recruited into schemes for prostitution; churches and priories served as places of refuge and refreshment for outlaw bands. Clerical literacy, and the access of clergy to the confidence of royal officials, made forgery of deeds and the counterfeiting of seals a clerical criminal specialty. Among the most enterprising of clerical criminals was Robert Colynson, a fifteenth-century priest who began his career as a confidence man by offering to represent fellow clerics before the Curia courts in Rome. He pocketed the fees they offered and never appeared to defend the cases. Discovered in this fraud, he moved on to obtain the savings of a wealthy widow through his assurances that her soul would never suffer pain while he prayed for her. Frequently visiting nunneries, he preached strong sermons urging the need for absolution and then collected a shilling from each nun to buy absolution in Rome. He retained the money and repeated the procedure several times before his reputation spread. Colynson lived openly with another man's wife, attempting at one point to kill the woman's husband. He also misbehaved with a young female parishioner and, on another occasion, romantically fondled a boy of 11. Despite all of these lapses, he avoided trial in a church court, was acquitted in royal courts on a charge of treason, and died in possession of the rectorship of Chelsfield in Kent and as the absentee bishop of Ross in Ireland.

Given the derelictions of English clergy in general, it should come as no surprise that the students and faculty at Oxford, who were all either ordained clergy or clerks in orders, were responsible for countless outbreaks of murder, theft, and mob violence. Because of their clerical status, all were entitled to the more lenient procedures of the church courts. As a consequence, the crime rate for Oxford was among the highest in England, and Cambridge was probably not far behind.

The crimes of outlaw bands and of bandits increased in number and magnitude in the instances in which English royal authority was weakest. These weak conditions might occur when the locale was far removed from London or when the king was absent from the country, indifferent to the administration of justice, or a minor under regency. All of these circumstances occurred in the years from 1150 to 1550. For example, the absence of Edward I, away at the Scottish wars, made possible one of the most celebrated crimes of English history. The wardrobe treasure was maintained in Westminster Abbey under close guard and careful control, but a merchant named Richard Pudlicott succeeded in removing £100,000 in gold and silver from the royal coffers with the assistance of a virtual army of monks and Crown officials who served as informers and staffed his burglary force. Professor John Bellamy has called this "one of the most enterprising of all medieval crimes."[5] It is remarkable in its illustration of how close criminal behavior might be to the very center of royal power, and how little distinction there was between criminal action and ordinary commercial activity. Pudlicott had long been a creditor of the king and may have viewed this as a mode of collecting what was due him. Certainly it ranks, along with Robert Colynson's confidence games, as one of the high points of inventive criminal behavior. Crime was becoming more sophisticated, and its perpetration required more planning and preparation than most commercial enterprises. In effect, professional criminals increasingly were being drawn from the ranks of learned men and women who used their skills for both legitimate and criminal purposes. A new age of criminal activity was dawning.

The late Middle Ages gave little thought to problems of penology. In a general sense, there was an effort to measure the severity of the punishment by the magnitude and circumstances of the crime, and there was clearly an element of public vengeance in many of the sanctions that were imposed. Perhaps the major change during the four centuries before 1550 was the movement toward imprisonment as a punishment. Hitherto, mutilation had been common, and this form of physical punishment had been followed by economic sanctions. However, fines quite frequently resulted in the offender serving time in prison as a debtor to the state when he or she could not pay the fine. Gradually it became the rule to impose a prison term in lieu of the fine, leading to the use of imprisonment itself as a form of punishment. Early prisons had served merely as places of detention for those awaiting trial, but now removal from society became an accepted form of sentence. By current standards, prison terms during these times may seem unduly short, but it should be remembered that the prison provided nothing but a place of confinement. Food, clothing, medical supplies, firewood, and all other necessities had to be supplied by friends or relatives or purchased from extortionate jailers. Privileges to leave a cell or to walk in the prison yard, for example, were also available at a price. For the wealthy, prison was an inconvenience; for the poor, it might easily lead to starvation, disease, and death.

The waning of the Middle Ages resulted in severe adjustments of the social and economic system, and it produced criminal behavior of greater magnitude and greater variety. A rapid increase of population, estimated at about 150 percent for the years from 1450 to 1599, put great urgency on the need to modernize the criminal justice system. Law enforcement procedures exacerbated the class divisions in society, and conflicting opinions of noblemen made constructive change difficult. For a time, at least, the crisis in criminal justice was subordinate to the turmoil of the Protestant Reformation and the religious wars, but it would also be accentuated by those troubled times and, in turn, be shaped by them.

Summary

The abolition of the ordeal launched European nations and England on two different courses in criminal procedure. Using methods devised by the church to combat heresy, continental nations such as France developed an inquisitorial system designed to provide an exhaustive investigation seeking the truth concerning an allegation of criminal activity. Gradually, the ordinary methods of inquisition gave way to extraordinary procedure, which stressed denial of information to the accused, isolation from counsel, and the use of coercion (including torture) to secure a confession. In contrast to the inquisitorial method, in which the judge was the principal investigator, the English system retained the adversarial nature of the older procedural system. Drawing upon pre-Lateran Council development of a type of grand jury, the English devised a system of trial through a petty jury that decided issues of fact. The parties themselves provided the evidence to be considered by the trial (petty) jury.

Revival of commerce in southern Europe set the stage for a shift of population to urban areas and an increase in the crime rate due to greater opportunity for property-related crime and increased probability of interpersonal violence. Increasingly, class structure played a role in the administration of criminal justice. The rise of certain privileged classes, such as the nobility in Italian city-states and the clergy in England, had a significant impact on the volume and nature of crime. At this time, there was a clear increase in crimes such as forgery, counterfeiting, and confidence games, all of which depended on the learning or social status of the perpetrator.

Endnotes

[1]   The term *assize* has had various meanings in English legal history. As used here, it refers to a pronouncement of law by the king, usually in consultation with his counsel, that had binding effect throughout the kingdom. Based upon such a law, new court procedures might have been introduced and also called assizes. During the reign of Henry II, the central courts began to travel on circuit, and sessions held away from Westminster, particularly those dealing with criminal matters, were also referred to as assizes.

[2]   As discussed above, the appeal of a felony was one of the remaining vestiges of self-help. Based upon the private complaint of a party claiming injury to oneself or one's family, it had become a mode of harassing those too poor to hire champions and too weak to participate in trial by battle. Long in disuse, the appeal of felony finally disappeared from English law in the nineteenth century. The use of the word *appeal* in this context differs from that in modern law, in which one "appeals" to a higher court from the adverse decision of a lower court. The appeal of felony, in contrast, was a proceeding at the trial court level.

[3]   Commissions of general gaol delivery authorized the royal justices to hear the cases of all individuals held in the jails of the counties of their circuit, whether or not charges had been filed against such individuals being held.

[4]   Oyer and terminer commissions empowered the justices to hear and determine all cases of treason, felony, and misdemeanor pending in the visited counties.

[5]   In John Bellamy, *Crime and Public Order in England in the Later Middle Ages* (London: Routledge & Kegan Paul, 1973).

References

On French developments, see Adhemar Esmein, *A History of Continental Criminal Procedure: with Special Reference to France*, trans. John Simpson (Boston: Little, Brown & Co., 1913); Carl Ludwig von Bar, *A History of Continental Criminal Law*, trans. Thomas S. Bell (Boston: Little, Brown & Co., 1916). A helpful comparative study of the continental and

Anglo-American systems, which contains historical material, is Gerhard O.W. Mueller and Fre Le Poole-Griffiths, *Comparative Criminal Procedure* (New York: New York University Press, 1969). The standard sources on English developments are Sir Frederick Pollock and Frederic William Maitland, *The History of English Law before the Time of Edward I*, Second ed., ed. S.F.C. Milsom, 2 vols. (Cambridge: Cambridge University Press, 1968); Theodore F.T. Plucknett, *A Concise History of the Common Law*, Fifth ed. (London: Butterworth & Co., 1956). For an interesting view of jury nullification of law, see Thomas A. Green, *Verdict According to Conscience: Perspectives on the English Criminal Trial Jury, 1200-1800* (Chicago: University of Chicago Press, 1984). For social and economic changes in criminal justice, a good general discussion may be found in Michael R. Weisser, *Crime and Punishment in Early Modern Europe* (Atlantic Highlands, NJ: Humanities Press, 1979). For detailed monographic studies, see John Bellamy, *Crime and Public Order in England in the Late Middle Ages* (London: Routledge & Kegan Paul, 1973); James B. Given, *Society and Homicide in Thirteenth Century England* (Stanford: Stanford University Press, 1977); John H. Langbein, "The Origins of Public Prosecution at Common Law," *American Journal of Legal History* 17, no. 4; James C. Oldham, "On Pleading the Belly: A History of the Jury of Matrons," *Criminal Justice History* 6 (1985); Keith Wrightson, "Two Concepts of Order: Justices, Constables and Jurymen in Seventeenth-Century England," in John Brewer and John Styles, *An Ungovernable People: The English and Their Law in the Seventeenth and Eighteenth Centuries* (London: Hutchinson, 1980); Malise Ruthven, *Torture: The Grand Conspiracy* (London: Weidenfeld and Nicolson, 1978); H.R.T. Summerson, "The Structure of Law Enforcement in Thirteenth Century England," *American Journal of Legal History* 23, no. 4 (1979); J.B. Post, "The Justice of Criminal Justice in Late-Fourteenth-Century England, *Criminal Justice History* 7 (1986); Davis Crook, "Triers and the Origin of the Grand Jury," *Journal of Legal History* 12, no. 2 (1991); J.S. Cockburn and Thomas A. Green, eds., *Twelve Good Men and True: The Criminal Trial Jury in England 1200-1800* (Princeton: Princeton University Press, 1988); Guido Ruggiero, *Violence in Early Renaissance Venice* (New Brunswick: Rutgers University Press, 1980); Marvin E. Wolfgang, "Socioeconomic Factors Related to Crime and Punishment in Renaissance Florence," *Journal of Criminal Law* 47 (1956). An interesting study showing the influence of vengeance, politics and class conflict is Sarah R. Blanshei, "Criminal Justice in Medieval Perugia and Bologna," *Law and History Review* 1 (1983).

Two books trace gender differential in penology: E.J. Burford and Sandra Shulman, *Of Bridles and Burnings: The Punishment of Women* (New York: St. Martin's Press, 1992); and Camille Naish, *Death Comes to the Maiden: Sex and Execution: 1431-1933* (New York: Routledge, 1991).

Historical views of the death penalty are discussed in Geoffrey Abbott, *Lords of the Scaffold: A History of the Executioner* (New York: St. Martin's Press, 1991).

For judicial process in Anglo-Saxon society and early English courts through the fifteenth century (including original documents), see Alan Harding, *Law Courts of Medieval England* (London: Allen & Unwin, 1973). For historical accounts of the development of the English jury, see Lloyd E. Moore, *The Jury: Tool of Kings, Palladium of Liberty* (Cincinnati: Anderson Publishing Co., 1973); John Dawson, *A History of Lay Judges* (Cambridge: Harvard University Press, 1960); Frank Barlow, *Thomas Becket* (Berkeley: University of California Press, 1990); John Butler, *The Quest for Becket's Bones: The Mystery of the Relics of St. Thomas Becket of Canterbury* (New Haven: Yale University Press, 1995); Nesta Pain, *The King and Becket* (London: Eyre & Spottiswoode, 1964); and Richard Winston, *Thomas Becket* (New York: Alfred A. Knopf, 1967).

Notes and Problems

1. Is there anything that can be deemed "the truth," or was Pontius Pilate's cynicism correct when he asked Jesus Christ, "What is truth?" (John 18:38). If you believe that there is an ascertainable truth, can you accept the adversarial method of trial? Does not the adversarial method incite at least one party to lie?

2. Is a confession obtained under torture more or less valid than one given voluntarily?

3. The English trial jury, along with the Greek dicastery and the Roman quaestiones jury, indicates a general preference for group decision over the judgment of a magistrate or judge. Do you agree with the basic premises upon which these various forms of jury trial depend? Why are juries drawn from the vicinity in which the crime was committed? Are they influenced by public opinion? Should they be?

4. If you were on the ruling council of an Italian city-state, how would you restructure the criminal justice system to combat the new crime wave? Should individuals (such as nobles in Italy and clerics in England) have immunity from prosecution?

5. Should criminal law be structured and administered so that it preserves class status and maintains stability in society? Was the "important person" in Renaissance Italy better protected from violence and more secure from public prosecution than the plebeian citizen of Rome in the late Republic?

Chapter 5

Criminal Justice and the English Constitution to 1689

The Protestant Reformation had an unlikely beginning in the austere cell of a German monk, Martin Luther, whose theological views were different enough from those of the Papacy that they eventually resulted in his excommunication as a heretic. Luther also objected to church practices of his day, most specifically the corruption of the clergy, the Papal authorization for selling indulgences, and the widespread practices of absentee bishops and parochial officers. When Luther nailed his Ninety-Five Theses to the church door in Wittenberg (1517), he launched both a theological and political revolution throughout Europe. Belatedly, the strokes of his hammer were to be felt even in the relatively isolated island kingdom of England.

Fifteenth-century Englishmen had suffered through a series of wars (called the Wars of the Roses) between the rival royal dynasties of York and Lancaster. Virtually all of the old feudal nobility had found themselves, at one time or another, on the side of a king defeated in battle. The result was that many were convicted of treason and lost their lives, but most others lost their wealth and power. Into this chaos came Henry VII, the methodical and strong-willed founder of the house of Tudor (a branch of the house of Lancaster). Under Henry VII's rule (1485-1509), England was stabilized; a new generation of nobles drawn from

Corbis Images

Martin Luther nailed his Ninety-Five Theses on the church door at Wittenberg, beginning the Lutheran protest that shattered the religious and social unity of Europe, leading to great changes in English constitutional government.

mercantile backgrounds gained power, and the nation began to take its place among the great nations of Europe. Given the tumultuous background of England in the fifteenth century, it is not surprising that his successor, Henry VIII, placed special emphasis on the tranquility of his realm. Among

TIME LINE

The English Constitution, 1215 to 1689

1215	An army raised by the barons defeats King John at Runnymede. During negotiations, the King grants Magna Carta, promising to respect the feudal privileges of the barons, to protect the borough towns and merchants, and to conduct criminal trials in accordance with the "law of the land." The "law of the land" provision is the forerunner of "due process of law" in modern judicial procedure.
	Thereafter, each English monarch at his or her coronation swore to uphold the principles of Magna Carta.
1327	Deposition of King Edward II for failure to uphold Magna Carta.
1485	Henry VII proclaimed King of England by Parliament after his victory at Bosworth Field; establishes the House of Tudor.
1529-36	Henry VIII obtains an annulment of his marriage to Catherine of Aragon, and Parliament separates the English Church from the authority of the Pope. A parliamentary statute declares Henry to be Supreme Head of the Church in England.
1603	James VI of Scotland succeeds Elizabeth I and establishes the House of Stuart as King James I of England.
1604	At a Hampton Court Conference, members of Parliament and James I disagree about the powers and privileges of the House of Commons.
1611	The "King James," or Authorized Version, of the Bible is published.
1616	James I dismisses Sir Edward Coke from his position as Chief Justice of the Court of King's Bench.
1628	Parliament addresses the Petition of Right to King Charles I, demanding that Parliament be consulted before new taxes are imposed, that similar approval be required before troops could be quartered in private dwellings, and that Parliamentary action be required before military law can apply to civilians.
1629-40	King Charles I begins a period of personal rule, omits calling Parliamentary elections.
1641	Long Parliament abolishes courts of High Commission and Star Chamber.
1642-46	English Civil War. The Royalist forces are defeated by the New Model Army under Oliver Cromwell.
1649	King Charles I executed after being adjudged a traitor.

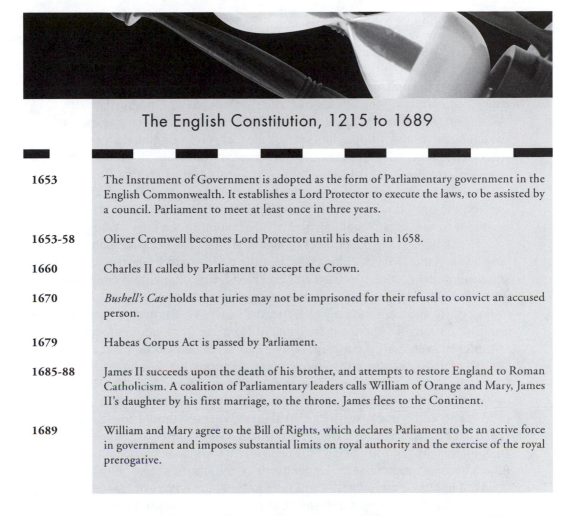

The English Constitution, 1215 to 1689

1653	The Instrument of Government is adopted as the form of Parliamentary government in the English Commonwealth. It establishes a Lord Protector to execute the laws, to be assisted by a council. Parliament to meet at least once in three years.
1653-58	Oliver Cromwell becomes Lord Protector until his death in 1658.
1660	Charles II called by Parliament to accept the Crown.
1670	*Bushell's Case* holds that juries may not be imprisoned for their refusal to convict an accused person.
1679	Habeas Corpus Act is passed by Parliament.
1685-88	James II succeeds upon the death of his brother, and attempts to restore England to Roman Catholicism. A coalition of Parliamentary leaders calls William of Orange and Mary, James II's daughter by his first marriage, to the throne. James flees to the Continent.
1689	William and Mary agree to the Bill of Rights, which declares Parliament to be an active force in government and imposes substantial limits on royal authority and the exercise of the royal prerogative.

other things, England's stability required maintaining close relations with the Roman Church and the vigorous suppression of any trace of Lutheranism. So successful was English policy in this regard that Pope Leo XI conferred upon the English King the title of "Defender of the Faith." The final project in Henry VIII's quest for this title was his authorship of a treatise against Lutheranism published with a large international circulation in 1521.

Ironically, this "Defender of the Faith" would, in less than two decades, lead his people out of allegiance to the Church of Rome and institute a modified form of the Protestant Reformation called the Church of England. A fascinating sequence of events led to this remarkable change in Henry's public policies and personal relationships. Perhaps the most significant factor was Henry's need for a male heir, dictated in part by the relatively recent date of Tudor accession to power. His marriage to Catherine of Aragon had produced only one surviving child, Mary. Dynastic consideration merged with the King's amorous interest in Anne Boleyn, a lady of the royal court who finally gave in to Henry's advances and became pregnant. The possibility that the baby might be a boy, coupled with Henry's ardent desire to marry Anne, drove him to seek a divorce or annulment from Catherine. It was his misfortune to be frustrated in this effort by events beyond his control. Pope Clement VII, who might otherwise have bowed to English diplomatic pressure, was at the time under virtual house arrest because Rome was under military occupation by the armies of Catherine's nephew, Emperor Charles V. With Anne's pregnancy advancing rapidly, Henry took the extreme measure of declaring himself Supreme Head of the Church in England, and, shortly thereafter, succeeded in obtaining the necessary marriage dissolution from a compliant English ecclesiastical court. Turning his attention to the new Church of England, Henry attempted to create a national church that preserved the orthodox Roman Catholic faith but at the same time was independent of the Papacy and politically subservient to the king of England.

Breaking the ties that bound England to Rome proved easier than fathering a son. Anne Boleyn's child was the future Elizabeth I. Shortly after this disappointment, Anne was tried and executed for treason, after which Henry successively sought other wives and managed to produce only one sickly son, who briefly succeeded Henry as Edward VI in 1547. Similarly, casting the English nation off from the main trunk of Roman Christendom proved to be simpler than shaping a coherent body of doctrine that would be acceptable to all subjects. Henry's insistence upon religious orthodoxy was undermined by Protestant-oriented counselors during the reign of Edward VI. Then, when the Catholic princess Mary succeeded her brother after his death in 1553, she and her consort (Phillip II of Spain) attempted to restore the Roman Church to England. Upon the death of Mary (known thereafter in English history as "Bloody Mary" for her violent purges of Protestants), Elizabeth became queen in 1559. Under her direction, the Church of England was revived to pursue a moderate Protestant path. The advisers of "Good Queen Bess" were quick to equate Roman Catholicism with treason to the Crown, and the long reign of Elizabeth I was marked by suppression of Catholics. At the same time, Elizabethan policy was hard-pressed to deal with growing Protestant elements within the English church that demanded that the national church be reformed and that its liturgy and theology be stripped of Roman practice and principles. Elizabeth wisely made concessions to these dissenting viewpoints, but undertook no harsh repressive measures. That course was left to her successor, James I. Fresh from struggles against Scottish Presbyterians, this first of the Stuart monarchs embarked on a policy of royal domination of the church and the political affairs of England. The result was a series of constitutional crises, a civil war, and the Glorious Revolution, which established Parliamentary supremacy in political matters and religious toleration as a state policy in ecclesiastical affairs.

Against this rich historical backdrop of Tudor dynastic intrigue and growing religious diversity, the seventeenth century emerged as the most important time in England history for the development of constitutional government. Ancient traditions, dating back to medieval times, were pitted against the Stuart dynasty's attraction for royal absolutism and the Roman Church. The struggle would be waged in Parliament, in the courts, and on the battlefield; from this struggle grew a form of constitutional government that shaped not only the future polity of England but also the thought and law of its colonies in North America. Much that is distinctive in the English and American systems of criminal law and procedure can be traced to this period in English history.

English Constitutionalism

England's dynastic and religious difficulties of the Tudor (1485-1603) and Stuart (1603-1689) periods prompted the transition of the nation into a modern state marked by strong central government and a special concern for the rights of the individual. These were times of immense change in both the criminal law and in the constitution of England. They were marked by religious persecution; numerous prosecutions for treason and countless lesser crimes; sharp shifts in political power between the Crown and Parliament; and a long, violent constitutional crisis and civil war stretching from 1629 to 1660. Only with the Glorious Revolution (1688-1689) were these matters resolved in a practical subordination of royal prerogative to the political supremacy of Parliament and in the strong affirmation of the traditional rights of Englishmen.

Those rights of Englishmen stretched into antiquity. Most ancient was the concept that a king was subject to law and required to respect the customs of his kingdom. This had served throughout early English history as the rationale for overthrowing one monarch and instituting another. Each king since 1215 swore to uphold the promises made in Magna Carta, and when Edward II was held to have violated this oath, he was forced to abdicate (1311-1327). In 1399, Parliament deposed Richard II, accusing him of criminal activities against the laws of England, and installed in his place Duke Henry of Lancaster, who succeeded to the throne as Henry IV. The Tudors had frequent recourse to Parliament to legitimize their rule. Henry VII procured an act of succession confirming his right to the Crown, previously seized by his victory on Bosworth Field (1485). When Henry VIII broke with the Church of Rome, he did so by a series of parliamentary statutes that abolished appeals to the papal court (1533), established the succession of his children to the throne (1534, 1536, and 1543), and secured royal control of the English church (1534).

Ancient tradition and recent practices of the Tudor monarchs confirmed the subordination of the kingship to law and custom. They also established the principle that matters of great state significance required parliamentary concurrence in royal actions. To deem this "government by consent of the governed" would state the matter too broadly, but it is clear that England in the sixteenth and seventeenth centuries was highly resistant to the novel and then-prevailing concept of the divine right of kings. This political theory, highly attractive to the Stuart kings of England and typified by Louis XIV of France (the "Sun King" who ruled from 1643 to 1715), traced royal power on earth to a direct grant of divine power from God. Anointed kings at their coronation, French monarchs saw themselves as possessing all political and moral authority. Unfortunately for the similar pretensions of the Stuart dynasty, English constitutionalism raised a formidable barrier to absolute monarchical rule.

Figure 5.1

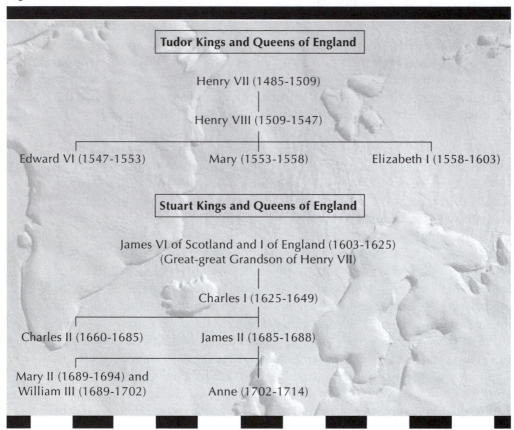

The bedrock of English constitutional government is the Magna Carta (1215), an old charter of privileges wrung from King John in 1215. Originally, it afforded John's rebellious barons relief from onerous and extraordinary taxation; it also made certain concessions to the church and provided protection for foreign merchants. Several specific guarantees (at the time closely limited to the protected classes) laid a foundation upon which subsequent rights of the people would be established. Most significant are the thirty-eighth, thirty-ninth, and fortieth articles, which read as follows:

> 38. No bailiff shall henceforth put any one to his law by merely bringing suit [against him] without trustworthy witnesses presented for this purpose.

39. No freeman shall be captured or imprisoned or disseised [dispossessed of property] or outlawed or exiled or in any way destroyed, nor will we go against him or send against him, except by the lawful judgment of his peers or by the law of the land.

40. To no one will we sell, to no one will we deny or delay right or justice.[1]

From these liberties in the Magna Carta, Englishmen in subsequent centuries gained the rights to trial by a jury of one's peers, to indictment only upon probable cause shown to a grand jury, and to a speedy and honest trial according to the law of the land. Even before the sixteenth century, Englishmen were protected against arbitrary prosecution by the state; individuals could be subjected to criminal prosecution and punishment only in accordance with accepted procedures.

As granted by John, the Magna Carta's sixty-first clause also provided for a committee of barons to police the king's compliance with its provisions. They were specifically authorized to raise a force to oppose him. In addition, the king directed that if he or anyone acting for him attempted to cancel any of the liberties, that attempted revocation would be null and void. Subsequent history demonstrates recurring royal attempts to nullify or circumvent the Magna Carta, just as the rise of a powerful representative legislature (Parliament) made reliance upon a baronial committee unnecessary. The sixty-first clause is illustrative, however, of the early emphasis upon countering power with equal force vested in other hands, something that later generations would call balancing (or separating) powers. It also shows

King John signed the Magna Carta in 1215, laying the foundation upon which subsequent rights of the people would be established.

Corbis Images

a primitive form of the constitutional principle that actions or laws that are beyond the traditional scope of governmental activity may be considered null and void, a concept that future generations would call judicial review or substantive due process.

Religion, Politics, and Criminal Justice

This ancient tradition of constitutionalism should not obscure the fact that social and political developments of the fifteenth century permitted the Tudor monarchs to make significant alterations in the criminal law and to provide more efficient methods than common law prosecution for its enforcement. For the most part, this was accomplished by expanding the judicial power of the Privy Council (exercised by the Court of Star Chamber), establishing a Court of High Commission to deal with high-level religious issues (1559), and giving additional authority and duties to the local justices of the peace. Although the consequence of each step was to enhance royal power, these new courts and officials did not supplant jurisdiction previously exercised by the common law courts. Historically, the English common law courts dealt with a very restricted number of felonies, and the modernization of English society and economic life created a number of other crimes not punishable at common law. English church courts had general jurisdiction in dealing with matters of heresy, blasphemy, illegal sexual activity, fraud, and perjury, but ecclesiastical sanctions were limited to fines, the imposition of public penance, and excommunication. This vacuum in criminal law enforcement permitted the Tudors to expand royal authority and to impose religious conformity throughout England.

From Henry VIII's break with the Roman Church until 1640, the Crown was actively involved in using the criminal law as a means of obtaining conformity with the theology and practices of the Church of England. In November 1538, John Lambert was tried for denying the doctrine of transubstantiation. This doctrine held, in accordance with the accepted belief of the Roman Church, that the physical elements of bread and wine actually became the body and blood of Jesus Christ during Holy Communion. Lambert was tried at Westminster Hall before the Privy Council, with the King himself presiding; upon his conviction of heresy, Lambert was burned at the stake. A year later, in 1539, Parliament passed the Act of Six Articles, which condemned as heretical the denial of the doctrine of transubstantiation. It also made heretical, and hence punishable by death, any speech or act that degraded the sacrament and any preaching that advocated altering the mode in which the Church of England administered communion to the people. As Sir James F. Stephens noted in his study of criminal law, writings or speech that earlier might be mildly punished as heretical now became matters of great political concern.[2] Personal religious belief that deviated from state policy was now punishable either as treason or as one of the many new types of felonies directed against irregular religious practice or belief. This intermixing of political loyalty with religious orthodoxy was characteristic of Tudor and Stuart England. Because of it, the Court of Star Chamber (charged with most criminal law enforcement) and the Court of High Commission (charged with the administration of ecclesiastical law and the punishment of heresy) had overlapping jurisdictions.

TIME CAPSULE

English Central Courts of the Seventeenth Century

All English royal courts evolved from the Curia Regis of the Norman kings, and began to be centralized in the twelfth and thirteenth centuries. The original and appellate jurisdiction of the House of Lords is also derived from this source, because Parliament at one time exercised some judicial authority and this has in modern times begun the work of the Law Lords. The Law Lords are composed of hereditary peers who have been trained as lawyers, or life peers appointed after distinguished careers as lawyers or judges.

With the rise of the overseas empire, the ancient Privy Council jurisdiction over the King's Channel Islands was expanded to include the American colonies and British India. Within Great Britain, the House of Lords exercised appellate jurisdiction over the Irish courts after 1719.

Admiralty jurisdiction was exercised by vice-admiralty courts in the colonies, subject to appeals either to the High Court of Admiralty in England or to the Privy Council.

Although the Reformation and the English statutes separated the Church of England from the authority of the Pope, the traditional courts of the Church remained in place. These included Archdeacon Courts, the Courts of the Ordinary (bishops), and the Prerogative Courts, which exercised the authority of the two archbishops. For the level of review previously exercised by the pope, the English Parliament substituted the High Court of Delegates and the Court of High Commission. The American colonies were considered part of the province of Canterbury until 1696, when they came under the ecclesiastical authority of the bishop of London.

The charts (Figures 5.1 and 5.2) that follow provide a graphic summary of the English court system as it existed in the seventeenth century. In 1873, the common law courts (King's Bench, Common Pleas, and Exchequer) were made separate divisions of the High Court of Justice. The Chancery court became a separate Chancery Division of the High Court of Justice, and the matrimonial and probate jurisdiction of the archbishops' Prerogative Courts were united with Admiralty, becoming the Probate, Divorce, and Admiralty Division; this last division is affectionately termed the court of "wives, widows, and wrecks." The appellate jurisdictions of King's Bench and Exchequer Chamber became the Court of Appeal. This Court of Appeal and the High Court of Justice together comprise the Supreme Court of Judicature.

Figure 5.2

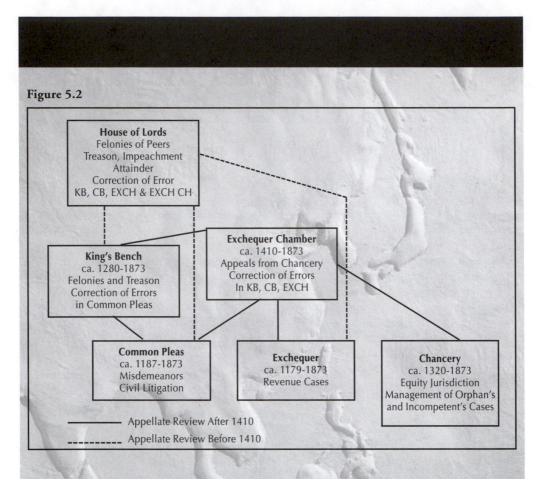

Figure 5.3

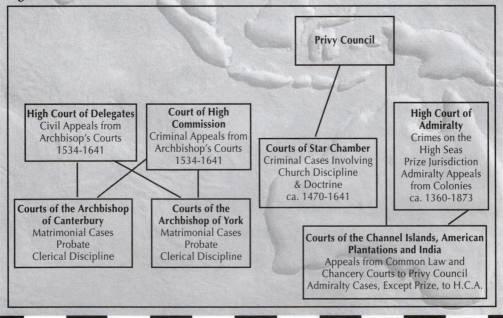

Prosecutions in the Court of Star Chamber and the Court of High Commission involved the examination of the accused by members of the court. Most frequently, this was done under oath and without the accused knowing the charges against him or her, the identity of prosecution witnesses, or the contents of their statements of evidence. The oath *ex officio* was used as a method to obtain statements from the accused that could subsequently be used to institute formal criminal proceedings against him. Both courts sat without juries and, as might be expected, very few defendants called before them secured an acquittal. Opponents charged these courts with following the harsh inquisitorial methods then in use on the continent. That they did so may be questionable, but it is clear that their existence challenged the constitutional traditions of England and, most specifically, weakened the protection of trial by jury.

Although the Tudor monarchs did not originate government by Privy Council or local administration through justices of the peace, they were responsible for refining these institutions into relatively efficient law enforcement systems. The justices of the peace, appointed for each county, were charged with maintaining law and order and adjudicating civil disputes. They also acquired minor criminal jurisdiction and eventually were responsible for preliminary hearings and commitments in felony cases to be tried before the Westminster courts or at the assize sessions of those courts. In this way, the justices of the peace, either individually or in a meeting of all justices, replaced the sheriffs as the principal judicial officers within the counties. Because they owed their positions to the Crown and not to local magnates, royal interests were better protected, and favoritism to local nobility was less likely to occur. New economic legislation was common in the years from 1485 through 1603, and the local justices of the peace were burdened with the administration of these new areas of law, frequently with penal sanctions. Sitting in general sessions and quarter sessions, the justices made certain that roads were maintained, bridges kept in repair, and vagrants supported by their towns of origin. This growing army of "J.P.s" was supervised by the Privy Council, which exercised virtually all of the executive powers vested in the Crown. The Council's ordinances and orders were as binding in law as statutes passed by Parliament, and it had the added authority derived from its close relationship with the king or queen. It was through the Privy Council that the Tudor monarchs influenced parliamentary action, calling upon selected members of the Council to stand for election and to articulate government programs in the House of Commons as well as in the House of Lords.

Dissent was dangerous in Tudor and Stuart England. Sir Thomas More, former Chancellor of England and former confidant of Henry VIII, was executed for questioning the validity of the Act of Supremacy (which established the king as head of the Church of England). A vast array of individuals not conforming to Henry's new church followed More to their deaths. However, it was not only major issues of religious or political dissent that drew official punishment. In 1612, a foreign trader was fined £2,000 for grumbling that in no other part of the world were merchants "so screwed and wrung upon as in England." This mild complaint against official corruption was punished by a six-year prison sentence when the accused refused to apologize to the officers in question. Three years later, two gentlemen were heavily fined and sentenced to a year in prison for expressing doubt concerning whether a convicted felon was actually guilty. These excesses, coupled with the religious and political partisanship of the Court of Star Chamber and the Court of High Commission, caused these two courts to be abolished in 1641 when the Parliamentary party, guided by nonconforming leaders, seized the power of government. As early as 1612, the common law courts began to assert traditional constitutional precedents in a struggle against the power of these two courts. Attempts were made to use writs of habeas corpus to free prisoners condemned to jail by one of the prerogative courts, and, at other times, writs of prohibition were issued to stop proceedings in the Court of Star Chamber or the Court of High Commission. Foremost in leading the common law's opposition to these executive courts was Sir Edward Coke, Chief Justice of the Court of King's Bench.

TIME CAPSULE

Treason

The offense of treason, the only act for which one can still be sentenced to death in England today, was clearly defined by Parliament in 1352. The statute passed during the reign of Edward III, although temporarily modified, has remained essentially the same.

Whereas divers opinions have been before this time in what case treason shall be said, and in what not; the King, at the request of the lords and of the commons, hath made a declaration in the manner as hereafter followeth; that is to say, When a man doth compass or imagine the death of our lord the King, or our Lady his Queen, or of their eldest son and heir; or if a man do violate the King's companion, or the King's eldest daughter unmarried, or the wife of the King's eldest son and heir; or if a man do levy war against our lord the King in his realm, or be adherent to the King's enemies in his realm, giving to them aid and comfort in the realm, or elsewhere, and thereof be provably attainted of open deed by the people of their condition. And if a man counterfeit the King's great or privy seal, or his money; and if a man bring false money into this realm, counterfeit to the money of England, as the money called Lushburgh, or other like to the said money of England, knowing the money to be false, to merchandise or make payment in deceit of our said lord the King and of his people; and if a man slay the chancellor, treasurer, or the King's justices of the one bench or the other, justices in eyre, or justices of assise, and all other justices assigned to hear and determine, being in their places, doing their offices.

Source: 25 Edw. III, c.2.

Sixteenth- and seventeenth-century England also was a battleground for free speech and freedom of the press, for the printing press made political and religious dissent a threat to bishop and king alike. Just as the invention of movable type and the printing press (1423-1450) aided in the spread of the Protestant Reformation, so did this new method of dispersing ideas play a vital role in English constitutional development and criminal law. Originally, the Privy Council assumed the authority to issue printers' licenses. As a consequence, whenever objectionable material appeared in print, the printer was arraigned before the Court of Star Chamber or the Court of High Commission. Should it develop that he had not obtained a license, he was prima facie guilty of seditious libel and subject to punishment. The Licensing Acts, which were reestablished in 1662 after royal government resumed, restricted printing in England to firms previously licensed, thus providing strong prior

Corbis Images

The invention of movable type and the printing press aided in dispensing ideas, playing a key part in English constitutional development and criminal law.

restraint over the publication of opposition opinions. When criticism appeared, it was harshly punished. William Prynne, convicted of seditious libel before the Court of Star Chamber in 1632, was disbarred from the practice of law, deprived of his university degrees, twice placed in the pillory, maimed by the loss of one ear, fined £5,000 and sentenced to "perpetual" imprisonment—the equivalent of a life sentence. Despite the sanctions available against seditious libel, opposition printers flourished, publishing a vast array of constitutional tracts attacking the excesses of royal government and stressing the constitutional value of trial by jury, the danger of examination by means of the oath *ex officio* and the theological ambiguities and objectionable liturgical practices of the established Church of England. Dissenters in seventeenth-century England were like the ancient Jews in Egyptian captivity: "the more they were oppressed, the more they multiplied."[3]

The Civil War and Law Reform (1640-1660)

Opposition to Charles I became so extreme by 1629 that he attempted the experiment of ruling England without calling Parliament into session. In normal times, refusing to ask Parliament for the right to tax would have made government difficult, but Charles was shortly faced with a rebellion in Scotland that placed heavy demands on the royal treasury. When Parliament was finally summoned in 1640, it proceeded to reassert its constitutional prerogatives and ultimately precipitated open warfare with the Royalists. Defeated on the field of battle, King Charles I was tried for treason and executed in Westminster Hall (1649). There followed a series of unsuccessful attempts to reconstitute government on a permanent basis, the last of which was the Protectorate (1653-1659),[4] established under the quasi-regal authority of Oliver Cromwell. In 1660, Parliament formally asked that Charles II resume the throne; the legislation and governmental forms of the Interregnum[5] were declared null and void and, with few alterations, royal government resumed on the same constitutional framework as existed in 1649.

For posterity, this period is of considerable legal and constitutional interest, for it contributed new ideas concerning criminal justice that deserve more than passing attention. In the course of the search for a permanent form of republican government, there emerged groups of political theorists known as Levellers and Fifth Monarchists. Believing that all law should be subject to rules of reason and conformable to Holy Scripture, they developed a law reform program designed to conform English law to biblical practices. An early product of this emphasis was a 1650 statute that made adultery and incest capital offenses. Subsequently, Leveller pamphleteers suggested that specific rights be guaranteed in criminal trials. These rights would include requirements that all charges be based upon the testimony of two or more witnesses, that the accused be permitted to confront his or her accusers, and that both parties be allowed to introduce evidence and examine their own witnesses. Those who brought false accusations were to receive the same penalty that would have been imposed if the defendant had been convicted wrongly. In the case of maiming or other physical injury, it was suggested that the biblical *lex talionis* ("eye for eye, tooth for tooth") would be an appropriate penalty. Considered by Parliament in 1653, these various proposals were referred to a committee for the regulation of the laws, which attempted to revise and codify all English law, shaping it in accordance with reason and the "law of God." However, divisions within the Leveller reform movements and partisan opposition in Parliament resulted in no such legislation being passed.

Contrary to earlier opponents of the royal prerogative, the Levellers took no solace in the protections of the common law. Many of them attacked the institution of jury trials, while others were harshly critical of the legal profession and judges, despite the fact that these groups were most effective in resisting Stuart absolutism. Constitutionally, the Levellers believed that all men should be treated equally before the law. As a consequence, they opposed special privileges such as benefit of clergy, which was available only to male defendants who could read. They also believed that the law should be based upon positive acts of Parliament, easily available to everyone and printed in English so that they could be understood. This emphasis on a statutory basis for criminal punishment would surface in American legal history, as would a number of the procedural guarantees advocated by the Levellers. The efforts of the 1653 law revision committee, destined to failure in England, were paralleled by similar work in the New England colonies. This produced the Bible Codes,[6] which had a significant impact on American criminal justice and constitutional development.

TIME CAPSULE

Sir Matthew Hale: He Perished Before He Published!

Lord Chief Justice Sir Matthew Hale (1609-1676) served as a justice in the Court of Common Pleas (1653-1658) during the Protectorate of Oliver Cromwell, following a brief time as a member of a law reform commission. He also was a member of the Committee on Trade, but retired from his judgeship rather than accept reappointment by Cromwell's son and successor, Richard Cromwell. As a member of the Parliament that called Charles II to the throne, Hale insisted that the offer should be made conditional upon the new king accepting certain limitations upon royal power. In this Hale failed to prevail, and the tender of the throne was made unconditionally. Despite Hale's Puritan leanings and his stand in the Restoration Parliament, Hale earned the support of the king, who appointed him Chief Baron of the Exchequer (1660) and subsequently elevated him to be Chief Justice of King's Bench (1671), where he served until shortly before his death in 1676. He also was the author of the parliamentary act providing governmental assistance to those made homeless by the London fire of 1666, and he subsequently served on the Court of Fire Judges that administered the relief provisions of the act.

Chief Justice Hale's remarkable record of public and judicial service was made possible by the approval accorded him by Parliamentarians and Royalists alike. His appointment by Oliver Cromwell was accepted only after the Lord Protector informed him that should he not accept, the "rule by red robes"—that is the use of judges to impose criminal law—would be replaced by the "rule by red coats"—or government by the Army. When Oliver Cromwell died in 1658, Hale refused to accept reappointment under the Protectorate, retiring to his home to write an essay criticizing the administration of the Poor Law. In this manuscript, he suggested that workhouses be established to serve the poor of several counties, and that the resulting establishments be places that would teach habits of labor and industry. This essay, published in 1684, was titled *A Discourse Touching Provisions for the Poor.*

Wisely, Hale declined to publish any of his writings during his lifetime. Many of them dealt with legal history, including the well-known *History of the Pleas of the Crown,* finally published in 1736 and his *History of the Common Law,* which was published in 1713. Hale's abilities as a barrister were of service to Royalists and Dissenters alike, and his concern for the poor and the tenants of London raised him in public esteem. Yet his writings on the law and legal history might well have placed him in jeopardy at a number of times during his long and illustrious career. For these reasons, he was determined not to publish his extensive writings on law, legal history, and even the social and natural sciences. Justice Edmund Heward writes of Hale:

> Matthew Hale was one of the outstanding judges of the seventeenth century. He was a lawyer of great learning and a fearless judge who resisted all pressures put upon him by Oliver Cromwell and Charles II and could not be solicited by bribes or other inducements.

Historian D.E.C. Yale agrees, pointing out that Hale was ahead of time in writing about the legal systems of the ancient and modern world in a comparative way. Professor Yale also points out that along with the antiquarian John Selden, Sir Matthew Hale developed a concept of legal history that stressed the continual growth and change of law and legal institutions, by alterations in society and by modifications dictated by an ever-refined wisdom concerning the role of law and its impact on the people.

It took fortitude, intelligence, and discretion to survive the transitions demanded by the political upheavals of the English Civil War, the ill-fated Cromwellian Protectorate, and the Restoration of the monarchy. One major factor in Hale's success was his willingness to forgo publication of his written work during his lifetime. Even today, much of his writing continues to exist only in manuscript form. However, the *History of the Common Law* and the *History of the Pleas of the Crown* now stand as fitting monuments to a judge who was also a profound and productive scholar.

Sources: Edmund Heward, *Matthew Hale* (London: Robert Hale, 1972); D.E.C. Yale, *Hale as a Legal Historian*, Selden Society Lecture, July 7, 1976 (London: Selden Society, 1976).

Levellers sought a higher, or fundamental, law that would limit the supremacy of Parliament and secure the people against excesses of tyrannical government. With the execution of Charles I, political authority shifted to Parliament, limited only by the actual power vested in the Army. To the Leveller, this was just as unsatisfactory as the exercise of monarchical power. Because men were equal before the law, there was no basis upon which any man or group of men should exert authority over another, particularly in regard to basic rights that they traced back to Anglo-Saxon times. Among the rights Englishmen held most dear was what we would today call freedom of conscience in matters of religion. Ultimately, these concepts would find their lasting impact not only in England but also in the newly established North American colonies.

Despite the limited impact of Leveller law reform, and despite the downfall of the Commonwealth in 1660, this troubled time of English history witnessed the permanent abolition of the Courts of High Commission and Star Chamber, with a resultant increase in the competence of the common law courts in criminal justice. The chaos of revolutionary society and government resulted in the expression of new and seemingly radical ideas that otherwise would have been suppressed. Although the locality of English law reform would shift to the colonial frontier, within the next three decades the constitution of English government at home would also be transformed.

Restoration and Glorious Revolution

The decline of Cromwell's Commonwealth meant the end to republican experimentation in government and law, but did not end English attachment to well-ordered parliamentary government or popular support for moderation and Protestantism in religion. It was the misfortune of the restored Stuart monarchs to be either unwilling or unable to adapt to these two political facts of life. When called upon to resume the throne, Charles II agreed with the Convention Parliament that statutes passed between 1640 and 1642 would remain part of English law, but that all other acts of the Interregnum period would be null and void. This meant that the new king agreed to the abolition of the Courts of Star Chamber and High Commission and thus heightened the constitutional position of the common law courts and their hallowed tradition of jury trial.

Two circumstances made it difficult for common law courts to protect constitutional rights or to provide due process to defendants in criminal cases. First, the judges continued to hold their offices at the pleasure of the Crown rather than on the basis of good behavior. Instead of a judge holding office until good cause could be shown for his dismissal, an office held at the king's pleasure was easily manipulated for political purposes. Second, ancient methods for judicial control of juries were revived and reinstituted. These methods included fining jurors who returned verdicts contrary to the wishes of the presiding judge and even imprisoning them on short rations until they altered their verdicts. Both of these situations made it possible for the Crown and its ministers to influence common law court decisions in vital cases. Many of the significant political trials of the day concerned seditious libel and unlicensed printing, with juries unwilling to return guilty verdicts. However, *Bushell's Case* (1670) involved the imprisonment of a jury that refused to convict William Penn (the Quaker and future founder of Pennsylvania) and others of riotous assembly. Edward Bushell, a member of the trial jury, along with colleagues, were thrown into prison for their resistance to the judge. The Court of King's Bench ordered the release of the imprisoned jury, reasoning that the jury's view of disputed facts did not contradict the manifest weight of the evidence. If it were the function of the judge to pass on the accuracy of the jury's verdict, he would in effect be judge of both the law and the facts of the case. Although this decision did much to affirm the independence of the common law jury, it did not stop Royalist efforts to obtain hanging juries or to coerce the decisions of jurors who resisted the authority of judges. Under Charles II and his Roman Catholic brother, James II, conformity to the Church of England was enforced by vigorous prosecutions of nonconforming Protestants. These prosecutions took place before common law judges subservient to the interests of the Crown; the most notorious of these was Sir George Jeffreys, Chief Justice of King's Bench, who held his "bloody assizes" throughout the realm. James II, during his short reign (1685-1688), took steps to enhance the ability of Roman Catholics to take public office in civilian government and in the military. These measures generated strong opposition among the English gentry and populace.

TIME CAPSULE

Juror Independence—Bushell's Case (1670)

The original record of the trial in the court of the Old Bailey of William Penn and William Mead for tumultuous assembly reveals the feisty insistence of Edward Bushell and his fellow jurors to fulfill their duty to try the case according to the evidence. Penn was accused, with the agreement of Mead, of preaching and speaking in Gracechurch Street, thereby causing a great concourse and tumult of people. The witnesses, for the Crown only, testified that they saw Penn speaking but could not hear what he said. The verdict of the jury was that Penn guilty of "speaking" in Gracechurch Street, a decision that was seen by the court as "nothing." Again the jurors were sent to deliberate and returned with a verdict that Penn was guilty of speaking or preaching to an assembly and that Mead was not guilty. The court then informed the jury that they would not be dismissed until they brought in an "accept-

able" verdict; that they were to be locked up without meat, drink, fire, or tobacco; the court would have a verdict or the jurors would, by the help of God, starve for it. Penn then addressed the jury:

The agreement of 12 men in a verdict is a verdict in law, and such a one being given by the jury, I require the clerk of the peace to record it, as he will answer it as his peril. And if the jury bring in another verdict contradictory to this, I affirm they are perjured men in law. . . . You are Englishmen, mind your privilege, give not away your right.

Again the jury was locked up without comforts, "not so much as a chamber pot, though desired." The verdict then was that

Penn was guilty of merely speaking in Gracechurch Street, a decision even less to the liking of the court and one for which the court held Bushell responsible. Penn then argued that, as they were indicted for a conspiracy and Mead was found not guilty, he could hardly be found guilty of conspiring with himself; that, he said, would make of the jury and Magna Charta but "a mere nose of wax."

Nevertheless, the jury was sent out and came back with the same verdict. In response to the ensuing diatribe by the court, Penn argued:

> Unhappy are those juries, who are threatened to be fined, and starved, and ruined, if they give not in verdicts contrary to their consciences.

The mayor, who presided over the court, called for Penn to be fettered and staked to the ground. The recorder (judge) said that he had never understood the policy and prudence of the Spanish inquisition but that it would never be well with us, till something like unto the Spanish inquisition be in England. When the jurors were directed to go

consider another verdict, they refused. The recorder then said that at the next session of Parliament that a law would be made that those that would not conform should not have the protection of the law. Under order of the sheriff, the jurors went to deliberate. The new verdict was that both Penn and Mead were not guilty. Finding that the jurors had followed their own judgments and opinions rather than the good and wholesome advice given to them, the recorder fined them 40 marks a man and ordered them imprisoned until it was paid.

As the text indicates, the jurors brought a petition for a writ of habeas corpus and the upper court confirmed the freedom of jurors to decide according to their convictions. To honor Thomas Vere, Edward Bushell, and the ten other jurors, a plaque was hung in the Old Bailey commemorating their courage and endurance.

Source: T.B. Howell, compiler, *A Complete Collection of State Trials and Proceedings for High Treason and Other Crimes and Misdemeanors from the Earliest Period to the Year 1783.* vol. 6 (London: T.C. Hansard, 1816).

The Crown's executive authority was, for the most part, left unaffected by the Restoration settlement; those powers included a sweeping power of arrest, restrained only by the common law writ of habeas corpus. This writ commanded jailors and others holding prisoners to deliver them before the issuing judge and to show some basis in law for the confinement. The Habeas Corpus Act of 1679 regularized these procedures and made them more effectual against the arbitrary use of royal authority. Multiple imprisonments on the same charges were declared illegal once the defendant had been released on habeas corpus. The 1679 act also required that individuals imprisoned for treason or felony (previously beyond the relief afforded by habeas corpus) would have to be indicted promptly, or habeas corpus would be available. Finally, the statute prohibited the transportation of persons outside of England to Scotland, Ireland or other dominions of the Crown, where the writ would not be available.

Sir James F. Stephen suggested that "the greater part of the injustice done in the reigns of Charles II and James II was effected by perjured witnesses, and by rigid enforcement of a system of preliminary procedure which made the detection and exposure of perjury so difficult as to be practically impossible."[7] One example of this injustice is the series of treason trials connected with the Popish Plot (1678-1680), a supposed attempt to overthrow Charles II and place James II on the throne. The defendants were held in close confinement; ignorant of the evidence against them, they were allowed neither counsel nor an opportunity to confront witnesses. Moreover, they were given no copy of the indictment nor information concerning the panel of jurors.

The political trials of the Restoration exhibited English criminal procedure very prominently. Countless men and women of modest income and obscure reputation may well have labored for centuries under the same restrictions in defending their lives and property. However, the highly publicized treason trials and the prosecutions for seditious libel and unlawful assembly focused public attention upon the need for law reform. That reform would come as a result of the peaceful overthrow of James II, known as the Glorious Revolution of 1688-1689.

Religious and dynastic considerations, rather than matters of constitutionalism or law, brought on the Glorious Revolution and the deposition of James II. The rule of Charles II had rested upon a coalition between the established Anglican church and a Parliament that represented a large Protestant majority. Charles II had followed a policy of de facto religious toleration, dispensing with the enforcement of many pro-Anglican statutes and ignoring others. At the same time, the Test Oaths (which excluded both Catholics and nonconformists from government) and the Corporation Act (which applied similar restrictions to holding city or borough offices) kept Anglicans in political power. What Charles II did not do, and what James II unwisely attempted to do, was disestablish the Anglican Church and to substitute Roman Catholicism as the state religion. When James' Roman Catholic wife gave birth to a son, thereby displacing the Protestant Princess Mary as heir to the throne, the stage was set for revolution. Mary and her husband, William of Orange, were called to accept the Crown by the Convention Parliament. Both had Stuart blood in their veins (William was a grandson of Charles I); however, their right to rule was founded not upon heredity, but rather upon the invitation of the people of England as expressed in Parliament.

Because that invitation to William and Mary was conditional, the Glorious Revolution was a significant constitutional event. First and foremost, it recognized the authority of Parliament, and, hence, was a further step in restricting government by royal prerogative. Second, it provided a bill of rights that restated some traditional rights of Englishmen and established new privileges and immunities for English subjects. Third, it established religious toleration for all Protestant denominations as the basis for future government policy and at the same time retained the principle that Roman Catholics were to be excluded from political life. The Anglican Church continued as the established (state-supported) church, but under William and Mary virtually all of the restrictions on freedom of conscience were removed for Protestant dissenters.

The impact of the English bill of rights upon constitutional and criminal law was of major importance. It provided that no standing army might be maintained in England without express consent of Parliament, thereby sharply limiting royal power over the military forces. In addition, the bill of rights guaranteed to Protestant subjects the right to bear arms for their own defense and exempted debates in Parliament from criminal prosecution. In criminal law and procedure, the bill made illegal the imposition of excessive fines or the demand for excessive bail. It sharply limited royal authority to give immunity from prosecution. Cruel punishments were prohibited, and the bill required that jurors be properly returned and empaneled. In treason cases, jurors were required to be qualified freeholders (that is, they had to own land of a set value). Supplementary legislation to the bill of rights provided that judges would hold office based on good behavior rather than at the pleasure of the Crown. A new statute made the offense of treason more specific and provided specific procedural protections, which included the right to receive a copy of the indictment and the right to assistance by assigned counsel. Conviction might be had only upon the testimony of two witnesses, but a confession obtained without violence and made in open court could be substituted for the evidence of witnesses.

Summary

The constitutional and religious conflicts of the sixteenth and seventeenth centuries resulted in sweeping changes in English law, giving increased protection against criminal prosecution and confirming the traditional reliance on the common law courts and trial by jury. At the same time, the unsettled environment of revolutionary times permitted men to consider revision of the criminal law. In the case of Interregnum theorists, that reevaluation included modification of secular law to conform to biblical guidelines. Although these substantial departures from common law rules were rejected, they left a legacy of enthusiasm for biblical precedent that would influence American legal development in the seventeenth and early eighteenth centuries. More permanent was the impact of the English constitutional struggle on the legal system of England. By virtue of the Glorious Revolution, Parliament emerged as the preeminent law-giving authority. Within the next century, the doctrine of parliamentary supremacy would flourish. The constitutional struggle also developed the common law courts as the primary force for upholding the constitutional rights of English citizens against royal power. Ultimately, English governmental practice would subordinate those courts to the supremacy of Parliament, but American constitutional practice would, through judicial review and written constitutions (themselves a legacy from the English Civil War period), subordinate legislative discretion to the moderating influence of constitutional litigation.

Alterations in governmental and institutional power should not obscure the advances made in criminal justice. The rights of accused persons were extended and enhanced by the bill of rights that emerged from the Glorious Revolution; the independence of judges was secured by the same document. Judicial decisions strengthened the ability of common law jurors to resist the punishments of corrupt judges. The privilege against self-incrimination arose from deep-seated resentment against the *ex officio* oath of the pre-rogative courts, and the inquisitorial system fell into extreme disfavor in English law. Finally, England learned the lesson that criminal prosecutions were ineffectual in enforcing religious conformity and that toleration was the only acceptable alternative if a tranquil society was to survive.

Endnotes

[1]   Carl Stephenson and Frederick George Marcham, *Sources of English Constitutional History*, 2nd Ed., vol. 1 (New York: Harper & Row, 1972), p. 121.

[2]   Sir James Fitzjames Stephen, *A History of the Criminal Law of England*, vol. 2 (London: MacMillan and Co., 1883), 302-303, 424.

[3]   Exodus 1:7.

[4]   The execution of Charles I left the way clear for the establishment of a republican form of government, and the various parties contended for popular sovereignty, elimination of the nobility, and a variety of other schemes. Ultimately, the army became the ultimate source of power, and England remained under virtual military rule until Oliver Cromwell established himself as Lord Protector in 1653. Thereafter, his government (called the Protectorate) closely followed the institutional forms of royal government. Cromwell's death in 1658, along with the inability of Richard Cromwell (Cromwell's son and successor) and a growing dissatisfaction with republican government, led to the restoration of the Stuart dynasty in 1660.

[5]   An interregnum is a time during which a throne is vacant between two successive reigns.

[6]   See Chapter 6.

[7]   Stephen, *History of Criminal Law*, vol. 1, pp. 369, 383.

References

Two surveys of this historical period are Maurice Ashley, *England in the Seventeenth Century* (Baltimore: Penguin Books, 1963); and S.T. Bindoff, *Tudor England* (Baltimore: Penguin Books, 1963); for constitutional developments, see Sir David Lindsay Keir, *The Constitutional History of Modern Britain Since 1485*, 9th ed. (New York: W. W. Norton & Co., 1966). A readable and enjoyable biography is Catherine Drinker Bowen, *The Lion and the Throne: the Life and Times of Sir Edward Coke (1552-1634)* (Boston: Little, Brown and Company, 1956).

Law reform in the Commonwealth period has attracted attention recently. Useful studies are Stuart E. Prall, *The Agitation for Law Reform during the Puritan Revolution, 1640-1660* (The Hague: Martinus Nijhoff, 1966); Barbara Shapiro, "Law Reform in Seventeenth Century England," *American Journal of Legal History* 19 (1975), 280-312; and G. B. Warden, "Law Reform in England and New England, 1620-1660," *William and Mary Quarterly 35* (3d Series) (1978), 668-690; Joanna Innes, "The King's Bench Prison in the Later Eighteenth Century: Law, Authority and Order in a London Debtor's Prison," in John Brewer and John Styles, *An Ungovernable People: The English and Their Law in the Seventeenth and Eighteenth Centuries* (London: Hutchinson, 1980), 250-298; Randall McGowan, "The Changing Face of God's Justice: The Debates over Divine and Human Punishment in Eighteenth-Century England," *Criminal Justice History* 9 (1988), 63-98; John Bellamy, *The Tudor Law of Treason; An Introduction* (London: Routledge & Kegan Paul, 1979); G.G.L. Du Cann, *Famous Treason Trials* (New York: Walker and Company, 1965).

Developments in criminal law and procedure may be traced in Sir James Fitzjames Stephen, *A History of the Criminal Law of England*, 3 vols. (London: Macmillan & Co., 1883); and volumes 4-6 of Sir William Holdsworth, *A History of English Law* (London: Methuen & Co., 1945 and 1937).

Useful background concerning social relations in England can be found in Douglas Hay, *Albion's Fatal Tree: Crime and Society in Eighteenth-Century England* (New York: Pantheon Books, 1975); and James Cockburn, ed., *Crime in England, 1550-1800* (Princeton: Princeton University Press, 1977).

The following three sources give a historical overview of English penology: George Ives, *A History of Penal Methods* (Montclair, NJ: Patterson Smith, 1970); Luke Owen Pike, *History of Crime in England*, 2 vols. (Montclair: Patterson Smith, 1968); and Leon Radzinowicz, *A History of the English Criminal Law and its Administration from 1750*, 3 vols. (New York: Macmillan, 1948-1957).

Notes and Problems

1. To what extent did the constitutional developments from 1485 to 1689 influence changes in criminal law and procedure?

2. Strengthening the jurisdiction and powers of local justices of the peace and placing them under Privy Council supervision was perhaps good policy early in the Tudor monarchy; did it continue to be an effective means of conducting business after the Court of Star Chamber supervision was abolished in 1641?

3. How did trial by jury change under the Tudor and Stuart monarchs? Was it an effective protection against executive tyranny? Did it help to combine jury trials with an independent judiciary that cannot be removed at the king's pleasure?

4. Was the Glorious Revolution a necessary consequence of the Interregnum? If Parliament already had extensive power, was it necessary to formalize the situation with a bill of rights?

5. To what degree did the events of the seventeenth century and the text of the English bill of rights serve as precedents for the American bill of rights?

Chapter 6

Criminal Justice on the North American Colonial Frontier (1607-1700)

Legal institutions do not readily adapt to changed economic and cultural conditions, and criminal law and penology also follow this rule. The establishment of English colonies in North America required that rules of criminal law, methods of enforcement, and modes of punishment be reconsidered and applied in an entirely new geographical, economic, and social situation. It is difficult for us to imagine the cultural shock and disorientation that must have confronted the earliest migrants to the North American colonies of England. It was not only a movement to a different part of the world; in many ways it was also a step back in history, back to a primeval forest, to the economic systems of pre-Bronze Age hunters and farmers, and into a total absence of external legal systems and authority. The highly sophisticated way of life and the system of criminal justice that had developed in western civilization over the course of 1,000 years suddenly became almost irrelevant in the face of primitive conditions in the colonies.

Survival dominated the first years of settlement, and the basic human requirements for food and shelter were paramount. In time, the colonists found it necessary to deal with the menace of Indian attacks. This made it prudent to restrict settlement to easily defended locations and to increase the number of men available for militia duty. A scarcity of labor discouraged capital punishment and lengthy terms of imprisonment. However, one benefit from the scarcity of population was the advantage it offered for law enforcement. Crimes that in the Old World depended upon anonymity for their success were impossible in the American wilderness. Everyone knew everyone else; in fact, most were related by blood or marriage. Identification of criminals (or strangers who were watched for illegal behavior) was a simple matter, and flight to avoid prosecution meant living a precarious existence among compassionate Indians or being tortured to a slow death by less friendly tribes. In the rough world of seventeenth-century America, every

TIME LINE

Criminal Justice in North America, 1607-1700

1607	First permanent English settlement at Jamestown, Virginia.
1611	*The Laws Divine, Morall and Martiall*, a military disciplinary code, established for the all-male settlement at Jamestown and surrounding areas.
1619	First meeting of the colonial assembly, called the House of Burgesses.
	The population changes from all white males. Young women are brought to the colony to marry the men and establish homes in the New World, and African laborers arrive and become indentured servants, leading to the establishment of slavery by 1660.
1620	English Separatists (Calvinists wishing to separate from the Church of England) arrive in Plymouth and adopt the Mayflower Compact as their form of political government.
1629-1640	Complete Puritan congregations—men, women, children, and pastors—arrive in Massachusetts Bay. This is the so-called Great Migration, caused by King Charles I's rule without Parliament and by the suppression of reform-minded clergy of the Church of England.
1634	English Roman Catholics establish a colony in Maryland.
1636-1648	To restrain the discretionary justice dispensed by Massachusetts magistrates, the legislature passed a series of "Bible Codes," which provided careful descriptions of what is a criminal defense and what the standard penalty would be if an accused person were convicted.
1636-1638	Anne Hutchinson, accused of teaching the predominance of personal revelation, tried for sedition and banished from Massachusetts Bay.
1652	As a fleet of Commonwealth warships lays at anchor in Chesapeake Bay, Virginia renounces its allegiance to Charles II and acknowledges the authority of Cromwell as Lord Protector.
1660	The Restoration Parliament enacts the Acts of Trade, limiting colonial trade to England and the colonies of England, and requiring trade with the Continent to pass through English ports.

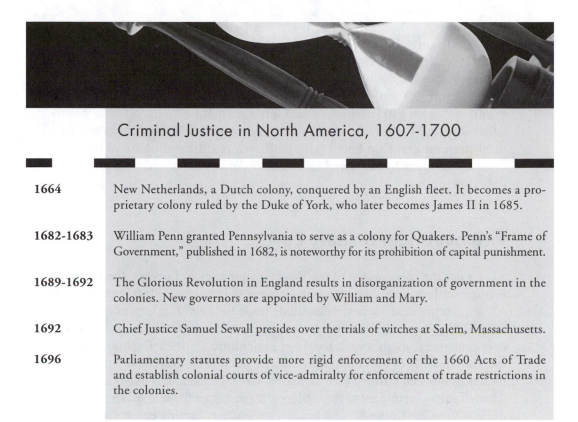

Criminal Justice in North America, 1607-1700

1664	New Netherlands, a Dutch colony, conquered by an English fleet. It becomes a proprietary colony ruled by the Duke of York, who later becomes James II in 1685.
1682-1683	William Penn granted Pennsylvania to serve as a colony for Quakers. Penn's "Frame of Government," published in 1682, is noteworthy for its prohibition of capital punishment.
1689-1692	The Glorious Revolution in England results in disorganization of government in the colonies. New governors are appointed by William and Mary.
1692	Chief Justice Samuel Sewall presides over the trials of witches at Salem, Massachusetts.
1696	Parliamentary statutes provide more rigid enforcement of the 1660 Acts of Trade and establish colonial courts of vice-admiralty for enforcement of trade restrictions in the colonies.

colonist was a police officer, and there was no extradition from the tender mercies or harsh cruelties of the neighboring Indian tribes. It made the would-be criminal think twice.

Much Old World criminal law was practically useless in North America. Many of the old laws were unacceptable to settlers who had fled from governmental imposition of harsh laws to limit religious belief. Both practical and cultural considerations entered into the growth of a new system of criminal law and punishment in seventeenth-century North America. Each colony functioned under unique conditions imposed by nature and by a variety of rules imposed either by the Crown, the corporate owners of the colony, or its feudal proprietor. Stretching along the vast expanse of the Atlantic Coast, the settlements exhibited great differences in climate, fertility of the soil, and accessibility to trade. Their people had abandoned the relative comfort and security of Old World homes, driven by adventure or necessity to seek a new life in the wilderness. Their reasons for migrating varied, from economic advantage to religious zeal, from the vibrant exuberance of a dreamer seeking personal and national glory to the grim choice of a condemned criminal offered the hard alternatives of transportation to the colonies (banishment) or death by hanging on Tyburn Hill.

Yet these colonists were still shaped by their experiences in the Old World. Although largely inapplicable to the situations in which they found themselves, their Old World experiences and culture were nevertheless a part of their outlook and thus shaped their opinions on law and order. Most of the politically influential settlers were of English or Scottish origin, and the events of recent English history had left a permanent mark on their political attitudes. Migrants from other nations brought differing views and cultural preferences. Combined with the harsh realities of colonial life, this diverse European heritage molded a unique American approach to crime and punishment.

Virginia Under Military Law

Under the sponsorship of the Virginia Company of London, the first permanent settlement in English North America at Jamestown (1607) was intended as a commercial outpost to facilitate trade between England and the Indians. Failing to find either gold or a quick passage to China or India, the colonists increasingly depended upon agriculture for their livelihood. Commercial viability of the colony was assured when John Rolfe learned the techniques of tobacco farming (1612), and by 1619 the Company extended a modicum of self-government to the settlers and permitted them to make purchases of land from the Company and begin independent farming enterprises.

Even before 1619, most of the significant adaptations to American conditions had been accomplished. Many of the first settlers were adventurers averse to manual agricultural labor in the sweltering fields of tidewater Virginia. Captain John Smith successfully bullied them into work, alternating threats of starvation with more terrifying sanctions of expulsion from the settlement into the hands of the Indians. To ensure order and to maintain centralized control, the Virginia Company permitted its resident governor to institute a system of military law. This gave maximum authority to the governor and his company-appointed council. It also provided harsh sanctions for those who deviated from the accepted norms of their society. *The Laws Divine, Morall and Martiall* of 1611 imposed harsh punishments for many offenses that might be considered "economic crimes." These punishments included a death penalty for mariners who came to Virginia and sold food and other necessities at prices above those fixed by the governor and council. Death was also prescribed for those inhabitants who attempted to leave without permission, and it also was the penalty for stealing crops from a garden one was employed to cultivate. The spiritual vigor of the inhabitants was reinforced by the penalties for failure to attend services or sermons. The first offense resulted in a loss of a week's rations, the second offense was punishable by loss of a week's rations coupled with a whipping, and the third was punishable by death. Sodomy, rape, sacrilege, trading with or attacking Indians, larceny, and murder were all punishable by death, as was desertion on the field of battle.

While the imposition of military law may seem an extreme measure, the vulnerability of Jamestown to attack either from Indians or from neighboring Spanish settlements in Florida made military discipline essential. There were few women or children in the colony, and in many ways the male-dominated settlement was more like an army camp than a civilian community. Imposition of a military code, based in part upon the martial rules of continental nations, was evidence of the lack of stability and internal self-discipline within the Virginia colony. The arrival of a substantial number of women in 1619 altered the social and cultural orientation of the Jamestown settlement. With the authority to participate in colonial government through a House of Burgesses, granted in the same year, Virginians ended martial rule and began the difficult task of adapting English laws to American conditions.[1]

The Old Dominion and English Law

Colonial statutes and court records indicate that Virginia's criminal law was taken almost in its entirety from English criminal law. Treason was punishable by death and forfeiture of property. In some cases, the punishment involved stretching the traitor on a wheel to break his back, disemboweling him while he was still living, hanging him until dead, then cutting off and exhibiting his head on a pole. The full sentence, derived from a statute of Henry VIII, was rarely used in America except when the convicted traitor was an Indian or a black slave. The offense of petit treason, or the murder of a master by his servant, was of special significance in Virginia because of the growing slave population. It served as the most frequent occasion for the application of the law of treason and the imposition of its heaviest sanctions.

Corbis Images

The ducking stool was a common punishment for women in colonial days.

Treason—along with murder, burglary, rape, robbery, and forgery—was punishable by death in Virginia as it was in England; none who committed such a crime received benefit of clergy.[2]

Virginia legislative action seems to have enforced what were termed *sumptuary laws* (regulations prohibiting excesses in dress or home furnishings) and prohibited free political speech through penalties for seditious libel. These libels were punished by fines, imprisonment, or public humiliation. Sitting with feet in the stocks (or standing with hands in the stocks) was a common penalty for such offenders. A peculiar form of humiliation was reserved for women who spoke irresponsibly of their neighbors. If the convicted woman's husband refused to pay the fine, she was subjected to "ducking." The process required that the accused woman be placed in a chair that was attached to the end of a long beam; then, while fully clothed, she was lowered into a pond or river in the presence of the community.

As in England, Virginia's early settlers had the morality of their behavior and the nature of their religious practices supervised very closely by civil authorities. Fines and imprisonment were used to discourage blasphemy, failure to attend church, and attacks upon ecclesiastical practices. In this regard it is helpful to note that Virginia remained loyal to the Stuart kings until a Cromwellian fleet in 1652 demanded its submission to the Commonwealth. Until that time it was treason in Virginia to claim allegiance to the Commonwealth or to any sovereign other than Charles II, who was then in exile. Church and state worked together in the colony, seeking to maintain the established Church of England. However, when, at the end of the seventeenth century, Commissary James Blair attempted to obtain trial of ecclesiastical matters in separate church courts, rather than in county courts, the Virginians successfully resisted this movement toward clerical meddling in judicial matters.

Throughout the seventeenth century, Virginia and its tidewater neighbor, Maryland, remained tied to English forms of justice and followed the procedures of the mother country. About three decades after the initial settlement at Jamestown, it became too cumbersome to continue all legal judicial activity at the provincial capital; separate county courts were set up to try virtually all civil cases and to sit as a magistrate's court in criminal matters. Thus, the county courts were responsible for deciding whether the accused person should be held in jail to await trial for a felony. Composed of the leading planters of the various counties, the county courts maintained law and order in their jurisdictions, aided by the sheriff and local constables. All criminal cases involving black slaves were tried before the county courts, as were minor cases involving free persons. Capital cases (which included virtually all felonies) were tried before the general court, which met at the Jamestown capital and was composed of the governor and members of his council.

Law enforcement does not seem to have raised a serious problem in early Virginia, but the presence of a growing number of slaves was cause for alarm. The individual master was responsible for the conduct of his slaves, and he was given a fairly free hand in their discipline. Although public opinion was harshly critical of masters who abused their slaves, very few cases, including those involving the deaths of healthy slaves who had been punished too severely, were prosecuted. On the other hand, the harsh penalties for petit treason discouraged slaves from violence against their masters.

Plymouth and a New Basis for Government

In sharp contrast to the settlement of Virginia, the second colony in English North America began with a new form of government by consent rather than with a system of military law. The separatist group that came ashore on Plymouth Rock in 1620 did not have a charter, but intended to settle on lands of the Virginia Company further south. What they did possess, however, was a strong Calvinist faith in the value of covenants. As a result, while they were still aboard ship, they had entered into a voluntary agreement stipulating that the group would make rules and regulations that would then become binding on all. This Mayflower Compact served as the charter for government until the Pilgrim colony was absorbed into Puritan Massachusetts Bay in 1662.

TIME CAPSULE

Compact Government

When the American colonists declared themselves independent of the English monarchy and turned instead to a contract form of government, they could draw on the experience of their forefathers as well as the theories of political scientists such as John Locke. Europeans who ventured to settle in the New World far from the seat of government, and who were concerned about the questionable efficacy of distant enforcement power, often voluntarily submitted themselves to a compact that determined the authority structure of a community. In addition to the Mayflower Compact, similar agreements originated in other colonies, pirate groups, settlements on the frontier, in the nineteenth century among members of caravans crossing the American "desert" and in the mining camps and vigilante organizations on the West Coast. Below is an example of prohibitions and obligations included in a pirate ship's articles:

1. Every man shall obey civil command; the captain shall have one full share and a half in all prizes; the master, carpenter, boatswain, and gunner [known as "artists"] shall have one share and a quarter.

2. If any man shall offer to run away or keep any secret from the company, he shall be marooned with one bottle of powder, one bottle of water, one small arm [weapon] and shot.

3.   If any man shall steal anything in the company, or game, to the value of a piece of eight, he shall be marroon'd or shot.

4.   If at any time we should meet another Marrooner [pirate shipt], that man that shall sign his articles without the consent of our company shall suffer such punishment as the captain and company shall think fit.

5.   That man that shall strike another whilst these articles are in force shall receive Moses' Law (that is 40 stripes lacking one) on the bare back.

6.   That man that shall snap his arms [weapons], or smoke tobacco in the hold without a cap to his pipe, or carry a candle lighted without a lanthorn, shall suffer the same punishment as in the former article.

7.   That man that shall not keep his arms clean, fit for an engagement, or neglect his business, shall be cut off from his share and suffer such other punishment as the captain and the company shall think fit.

8.   If any man shall lose a joint in time of an engagement he shall have 400 pieces of eight; if a limb 800.

9.   If at any time you meet with a prudent woman, that man that offers to meddle with her without her consent shall suffer present death.

Source: Davis Mitchell, *Pirates* (New York: Dial Press, 1976), p. 86.

While the Mayflower Compact was unique in asserting that governments might be instituted through the voluntary action of those to be governed, it followed earlier practices. It had been traditional for travelers aboard ships to enter into agreements for the regulation of their affairs in the course of a long voyage. English fishing fleets working the Grand Banks off Newfoundland during the sixteenth century usually submitted themselves to the governance of the captain of the vessel first to arrive, thereby establishing a method for administering both civil and criminal justice.

The government established on the basis of the Mayflower Compact had several advantages. First and foremost, the majority of individuals who landed at Plymouth were members of an English congregation at Scrooby. Harassed by church and royal officials because of their Calvinist criticism of the established Church of England, they fled to Holland and established themselves in Leyden. Dutch religious tolerance provided a safe haven until the group decided that they should settle in the New World, where their English manners and customs, as well as their religion, might survive and prosper. These shared experiences and common purposes contributed to the success of the Pilgrims and their Mayflower Compact. On the other hand, the original group of Plymouth settlers included individuals who were not members of the Old World congregation and thus were not subject to church discipline and sanctions. For those "nonbelievers," a secular and political form of government was required. The Mayflower Compact thus served two purposes: (1) it provided additional support for discipline within the church, and (2) it supplied a neutral political order to which both Pilgrim and non-believer would be required to adhere.

TIME CAPSULE

Compact Government II

Another example of the contract form of government is the Mayflower Compact:

In the Name of god, Amen. We, whose names are underwritten, the Loyal Subjects of our dread Sovereign Lord King James, by the Grace of God, of Great Britain, France, and Ireland, King, Defender of the Faith, etc. Having undertaken for the Glory of god, and Advancement of the Christian Faith, and the Honour of our King and Country, a Voyage to plant the first Colony in northern Parts of Virginia; Do by these Presents, solemnly and mutually, in the Presence of God and one another covenant and combine ourselves together into a civil Body Politick, for our better Ordering and Preservation, and Furtherance of the Ends of aforesaid: And by Virtue hereof do enact, constitute, and frame, such just and equal Laws, Ordinances, Acts, Constitutions, and Offices, from time to time, as shall be thought most meet and convenient for the general good of the Colony; unto which we promise all due Submission and Obedience.

Source: Kermit L. Hall, William M. Wiecek, and Paul Finkelman, *American Legal History: Cases and Materials* (New York: Oxford University Press, 1991), p. 11.

Although Plymouth colony did not survive as an independent settlement to the end of the seventeenth century, its laws and compact form of government had great impact upon American government and constitutional theory. Its larger, but more religiously orthodox, neighbor Massachusetts Bay was established by charter in 1629 and settled the following year. Like the Plymouth settlement, Massachusetts Bay enjoyed the advantage of being settled by groups of English dissenters who left the mother country not merely as family groups but also as entire congregations. The people of Massachusetts Bay, like those of Plymouth, shared common goals for their political and religious lives, and they also shared similar views concerning both the civil and the criminal law.

Plymouth colony's form of government by consent, or compact, was to serve as a model for many other English settlements. For example, the Fundamental Orders of Connecticut were drawn up by representatives of the settlers in the Connecticut River towns of Hartford, Wethersfield, and Windsor in January 1639. This agreement established a colony constitution that survived nearly 200 years as the basic governing document. Similarly long-lasting was the Plantation Agreement at Providence, which provided a government for the settlement on Narragansett Bay and which, after incorporation into the royal charter of 1662, would continue as the form of Rhode Island government until well after the American Revolution.

The Special Situation in New England

Homogeneity in population and belief were not the sole distinguishing characteristics of New England systems of law and government. Significantly, all of these colonies were established by groups that, at one time or another, were considered heretics, criminals, or traitors. The English establishment of the Anglican Church, and subsequent efforts by bishops and their ecclesiastical courts to stifle dissent, resulted in a broadly based migration to New England beginning in 1630 and continuing until the execution of Charles I in 1649. Throughout this period, Puritan pamphleteers (pamphlet writers), spurred on by the cruelties of the Stuart Court of High Commission and the inquisitions of the Court of Star Chamber, spelled out the constitutional right against self-incrimination. Marked as criminals and traitors solely because of their religious beliefs and practices, these pamphleteers became experts in asserting the ancient rights and privileges of Englishmen. A beleaguered people, they understood the helplessness of the individual citizen accused and prosecuted by powerful agencies of the state. This left those who ultimately migrated to New England with a profound attachment to trial by jury and to procedural rights against unreasonable searches and seizures, against compelled confessions, against the use of torture, and against the activities of all courts based upon the royal prerogative, including the courts of chancery (high courts of equity with common-law functions). They also felt strongly that laws should be drawn with sufficient certainty so that individuals would instantly know what was forbidden and what was permitted.

This demand for certainty in the criminal law moved New England officials in the direction of providing all law, both criminal and civil, to the public in a convenient and simple written form. During the earliest years of settlement, the administration of justice was in the hands of local magistrates appointed by the governor. Because the application of English criminal law was by no means required, the individual judge frequently was in the position of deciding what behavior was prohibited while, at the same time, concluding whether or not the defendant before him was guilty of the "offense." This discretion in magistrates and judges was inconsistent with the strict views of criminal law that had been developed by Calvinist dissenters in England. For this reason, the colonists began to voice objections and to demand that the criminal law be set forth in writing and that the full body of prohibited activities be stated with certainty.

TIME CAPSULE

Massachusetts Bible Codes

Discontent with English law in the seventeenth century led to initiatives for change—on both sides of the Atlantic. Given the religious fervor of the times, it is not unusual that the law contained in the Bible was suggested as an alternative to English criminal law. In England this was an integral part of the program of the Fifth Monarchy party, composed of radical dissenting groups who wished to change all of English law to conform to biblical standards. When Fifth Monarchy members gained a majority of seats in Oliver Cromwell's Barebones Parliament (elected by church congregations), the opportunity for such a reform existed, and a bill making adultery a capital offense was defeated by a narrow margin (1652). More sweeping amendments of the criminal law were proposed but also not enacted, and Cromwell shortly dissolved the Barebones Parliament after realizing that it was not only unrepresentative, but also likely to cause serious disruption in the orderly administration of government.

The same checks and balances on biblicism did not exist in New England during the middle of the seventeenth century. During the earliest period of settlement, Massachusetts towns were governed by magistrates exercising the authority of an English justice of the peace, but also applying law in a discretionary fashion. In response to this

autocratic rule, the settlers demanded that their laws be reduced to writing. The first product of this "codification" effort was *Moses His Judicialls*, printed in 1636 but never adopted as law by the legislature. Subsequent redrafting under the guidance of Nathanael Ward resulted in a *Body of Liberties* that was adopted by the legislature in 1641 and then reenacted in a slightly different form in 1648. Both of these compilations embodied elements of biblical law into the criminal law of the colony, but as we shall see from an examination of the 1641 *Body of Liberties*, there were significant differences between the criminal law provisions and the biblical originals.

Codification of the criminal law is important for American ideas of due process. It provides a convenient source of information concerning what is criminal activity, and it stipulates what punishment applies to any given offense. In this way it warns would-be offenders of the consequences of their acts, and serves as a deterrent. As later interpreted in our federal system of criminal justice, criminal prosecutions must be based upon a statute defining the offense before it was committed. In other words there is no federal common law of crimes in the United States. This represents one of the procedural protections that grew out of the early New England codification movement.

The following comparisons between Massachusetts's 1641 Bible Code and the Bible's text are examples of the variations between the two documents. They appear with more extended commentary in Edwin Powers, *Crime and Punishment in Early Massachusetts* (Boston: Beacon Press, 1966), 258, 259, 261, 263, 268-269.

Massachusetts Body of Liberties, 1641

Murder
If any person shall commit any wilfull MUR-THER upon premeditate malice, hatred or cruelty, not in a mans necessary and just defence, nor by meer casualty against his will, he shall be put to death, Exod. 21:12, 13; Numb. 35:31.

Manslaughter
If any person slayeth another suddenly, in his ANGER or CRUELTY of passion, he shall be put to death, Levit. 24:17; Numb. 35: 20,21.

Sodomy
If any Man LYETH with MANKINDE as he lyeth with a Woman, both of them have committed Abomination, they both shall surely be put to death, *unless the one party were forced, or be under fourteen years of age, in which case he shall be severely punished*, Levit. 20:13.

Adultery
If any Person COMMIT ADULTERY with a Married or Espoused Wife, the Adulterer and Adulteress shall surely be put to death, Levit. 20:19; 18:20; Deut. 22:23, 27.

The Bible

Murder
He that smiteth a man, so that he die, shall be surely put to death—Exod. 21:12. More-over ye shall take no satisfaction for the life of a murderer, which is guilty of death: but he shall be surely put to death—Numb. 35:31. Whoso sheddeth man's blood, by man shall his blood be shed: for in the image of God made he man—Gen. 9:16. Thou shalt not kill—Exod. 20:13.

Manslaughter
And he that killeth any man shall surely be put to death—Levit. 24:17. But if he thrust him of hatred, or hurl at him by laying of wait, that he die; Or in enmity smite him with his hand, that he die: he that smote him shall surely be put to death; for he is a murderer: the revenger of blood shall slay the murderer, when he meeteth him—Numb. 35:20,21. See also Numb. 35:22-25.

Sodomy
If a man also lie with mankind, as he lieth with a woman, both of them have committed an abomination: they shall surely be put to death; their blood shall be upon them—Levit. 20:13.

Adultery
And the man that committeth adultery with another man's wife, even he that commit-teth adultery with his neighbour's wife, the adulterer and the adulteress shall surely be put to death—Levit. 20:10. Moreover thou shalt not lie carnally with thy neighbour's wife, to defile thyself with her—Levit. 18:20. If a man be found lying with a woman married to an husband, then they shall both of them

Massachusetts Body of Liberties, 1641

The Bible

die; both the man that lay with the woman, and the woman: so shalt thou put away evil from Israel—Deut. 22:22. Thou shalt not commit adultery—Exod. 20:14. [See also Deut. 22:23-30.]

False Witness in Capital Cases
If any man rise up by FALSE-WITNESSE wittingly, and of purpose to take away a man's life, he shall be put to death—Deut. 19:16; 18:16.

False Witness in Capital Cases
If a false witness rise up against any man to testify against him that which is wrong; Then both men, between whom the controversy is, shall stand before the LORD, before the priests and the judges, which shall be in those days; And the judges shall make diligent inquisition: and, behold, if the witness be a false witness, and hath testified against his brother; Then shall ye do unto him, as he had thought to have done unto his brother—Deut. 19:16-19.

Cursing or Smiting Parents
If any Childe or Children above Sixteen years old, and of sufficient understanding, shall CURSE or SMITE their natural FATHER or MOTHER, he or they shall be put to death, unless it can be sufficiently testified, that the Parents have been very unchristianly negligent in the education of such Children, or so provoked them by extreme and cruel correction, that they have been forced thereunder to preserve themselves from Death or Maiming—Exod. 21:17; Levit. 20:9; Exod. 21:15 (1646).

Cursing or Smiting Parents
And he that curseth his father , or his mother, shall surely be put to death—Exod. 21:17. For every one that curseth his father or his mother shall be surely put to death: he hath cursed his father or his mother; his blood shall be upon him—Lev. 20:9. And he that smiteth his father, or his mother, shall be surely put to death—Exod. 21:15.

Stubborn or Rebellious Sons
If a man have a STUBBORN or REBELLIOUS SON, of sufficient years of understanding (viz.) sixteen years of age, which will not obey the voice of his father, or the voice of his mother, and that when they have chastened him, will not hearken unto them, then shall his Father and his Mother being his natural Parents lay hold on him, and bring him to the Magistrates assembled in court, and testifie unto them, that their Son is stubborn and rebellious, he will not obey their voice and chastisement, but lives in sundry and notorious Crimes: such a son shall be put to death—Deut. 22:20, 21.

Stubborn or Rebellious Sons
If a man have a stubborn and rebellious son, which will not obey the voice of his father, or the voice of his mother, and that, when they have chastened him, will not hearken unto them: Then shall his father and his mother lay hold on him, and bring him out unto the elders of his city, and unto the gate of his place; And they shall say unto the elders of his city, This our son is stubborn and rebellious, he will not obey our voice; he is a glutton, and a drunkard. And all the men of his city shall stone him with stones, that he shall die: so shalt thou put evil away from among you; and all Israel shall hear, and fear—Deut. 21:18-21. [This reference was probably the one intended.]

Discussion and Problems

The comparisons highlight the development of concepts of criminal intent (*mens rea*) premeditation, and conspiracy to commit crime. We also find a stress upon a minimum age, below which criminal sanctions either cannot be imposed or are of a less severe nature. Can you identify these cases?

Children who cursed or rebelled against parental authority did not fare well in either society, but notice that the Puritan code places an age limit on prosecution, and also provides that cruel treatment or unchristian neglect by the parents may be accepted as excuses for cursing or hitting a parent. Rebelliousness carries an age limitation, but the exceptions (which would seem equally applicable to the rebellion situation) do not apply. Gluttony and drunkenness are included in the Biblical offense of rebelliousness, but do not find their way into the *Body of Liberties*. Perhaps they are treated adequately elsewhere, but why were they deleted from the Bible Code of 1641? Is it possible that Ward, a Puritan clergyman, was a gourmet or a fancier of hard liquor?

Beginning in 1636, Massachusetts Bay approached this problem by drafting various "codes" of law that would establish norms for conduct not only in the criminal sphere but also in matters of civil law. The first of these codes, which were no more than a collection of statutes, was titled *Moses: His Judicials*. This particular code was not enacted into law, but its title suggests the strong influence of the Bible on the drafting of the New England Bible codes. Of all the Massachusetts codes, the most important for historical purposes was the *Body of Liberties* of 1648.

First enacted by the Massachusetts colonial legislature in 1641 and revised seven years later, the *Body of Liberties* provided capital punishment for a long list of felonies, including idolatry, blasphemy, witchcraft, murder, sodomy, adultery, kidnapping, bearing false witness, conspiracy, and insurrection. At the same time, it brought into American colonial law a number of provisions for the safety of persons accused of crimes. These provisions included a clause providing that both inhabitants and foreigners in Massachusetts Bay should receive the same justice and law throughout the jurisdiction, a rough parallel to the "privileges and immunities clause" of our federal Constitution today. Specific prohibitions were enacted against double jeopardy, cruel and unusual punishment, and certain forms of torture. Both the clear statement of criminal offenses and the enactment of procedural guarantees were seen as essential to the tranquility and stability of the state.

The Massachusetts *Body of Liberties* spurred the enactment of similar pieces of comprehensive legislation in many other North American colonies. While many varied in content and some departed from the Bible as a primary source of law, each incorporated the idea that criminal acts should be precisely defined and that persons accused of crime were entitled to particularly stated rights and privileges. After the English conquered the Dutch province of New Amsterdam and renamed it New York, they provided a New England-type code, the Duke's Laws of 1665, to govern the newly acquired territory.

Criminal law in Puritan New England moved even further from the English mode than the enactment of Bible codes would indicate. The secondary source of law was held to be not the common law of England, but rather the rules laid down in the Bible's first five books, called the Pentateuch. Secondary rules of law constitute the body of precedents and customs upon which a judge may draw in interpreting the positive commands of the written law. Instead of contemporary English common law, the Puritans substituted the more punitive laws of ancient Israel. This demonstrated their deep respect for the continuing value of the Old Testament and, at the same time, showed their profound distrust of the English law under which they had been persecuted. It was, of course, just a few years later when Levellers and members of the English committee on law reform would make their unsuccessful attempt to conform English criminal law to that of the Bible (1653).

When the *Body of Liberties* was first enacted, it drew criticism that it was not in accord with the laws of England. Dr. Robert Child and similarly minded inhabitants who were not Puritans in religion, attacked the colony's leadership for imposing laws that departed from the laws of England (1646). Because England was then moving toward civil war, this colonial dispute did not draw a negative response from the imperial authorities until after the 1660 restoration of royal government in England.

New England justice under the Bible codes appears more harsh than that applied to the same offenses in England, but the actual evidence of prosecutions under these codes indicates that maximum sentences rarely were imposed or carried out. Criminal procedure in New England seems to have been less arbitrary than that afforded in Virginia and other Southern colonies that were influenced by English precedents. This aspect of being less arbitrary was evidenced by the refusal on the part of the Puritan colonies to allow the practice of benefit of clergy. Another example of the egalitarianism of New England Puritan justice was its heavy reliance upon the independent judgments of trial juries. The trial jury long had been a strong check upon overzealous criminal prosecutions in England. The continuing vitality of the trial jury in North America is one of the strongest marks of colonial attitudes favoring the retention of certain English legal and constitutional forms.

Policing Seventeenth-Century America

Although formal police organizations did not exist in seventeenth-century America, there were at least two systems of law enforcement that operated in colonial society. The first was an informal system that had been effective from ancient times and that may still perform a useful role in modern society. This informal system involved the internal controls that exist in a small agricultural community, where virtually all of the inhabitants are related either by blood or marriage. Such a situation discouraged crime for many reasons. Disguise was impossible in a society where everyone was immediately recognized. Those who had criminal records were known and their modes of operation were easily identified. Also, punishment by public humiliation in front of relatives and long-term neighbors was a harsh sanction and a powerful deterrent. This system served the ancient world quite well until it became heavily populated and urbanized. It was revived in medieval Europe, which was intensely local in its politics and similarly provincial in the close economic and family relationships on each manor. From this background the ancient grand jury was drawn, a body of local inhabitants that reported on misdoings based on their own knowledge and their assessment of the probability that an accused person already well known to them might, in fact, be the guilty party. Historians of colonial America have found marked similarities between medieval manorial organization, the towns established in New England, and the plantations in the Southern colonies. Of course, the full-blown manorial and feudal system was not adaptable to American conditions, even though some efforts were made to implement it in New York, Maryland, and South Carolina.

The key to understanding the informal system of law enforcement in colonial America is demography. At the earliest stages of settlement, land was sparsely settled. In the case of New England towns, the original settlers were frequently members of the same English nonconformist congregation. Together they migrated to the New World, bringing with them church organizations and town governments based in part on their English practices and in part on their concept of the political covenant (that men could form governments by mutual consent, as in the Mayflower Compact). While similar religious ideas did not have such a decisive impact on the Mid-Atlantic and Southern colonies, those settlements also began with sparse populations and gradually evolved into established communities governed by a newly established elite. Apparently, social mobility was great at first, and a number of men brought to the New World as indentured servants[3] were able to amass considerable fortunes and achieve high political office. All colonies experienced rapid population growth, which presented difficulties in the distribution of land and dangers in public health, solved in part by the beginning of two centuries of westward migration. Within the settled communities, the crime rate rose rapidly in proportion to population growth.

Population was but one of many demographic factors that influenced crime rates and police systems. Another significant consideration was the rate of change in population, showing the numbers of individuals newly arrived in the community and the sizes of the groups emigrating to other settlements. This turnover in what was initially a static population decreased social control and created problems in identification. In its extreme form, the existence of transient populations caused growing seaport towns to resort to English law enforcement methods: constables, night watches, and special patrols. Even in the small agricultural towns and villages, the influx of new settlers was cause for great concern. Movement in seventeenth-century America was no simple matter. Just as Elizabethan Poor Laws required that each parish support its own poor, New England towns also took on this burden. Vagrants who could not assert a claim to the generosity of a specific town were usually driven out before they could establish residence and claim support. As a consequence, strangers were not only suspect in colonial America, but they were usually received with hostility.

The rule in the American colonies was that everyone was expected to work and everyone was expected to marry. A critical scarcity of labor required that all able-bodied males be profitably employed. The local courts administered terms of apprenticeship and assured that orphaned children received appropriate training in some needed skill or trade. As might be anticipated, judges were reluctant to imprison convicts but quick to assign sentences of hard labor or even to design penalties that would compensate a victim through the labor of the convicted criminal. In a similar vein, the family was viewed as a vital instrument of social control, and strong pressures moved both men and women in the direction of matrimony. Those who remained single were a source of concern to their neighbors, and court records abound of cases in which unmarried individuals of both sexes were involved in a wide variety of sexual offenses. Policing the activities of the unemployed and the unmarried was not difficult in small towns. It was accomplished by "close watching," a neighborly "sport" designed to identify suspicious activity that might be reported to the local court or grand jury. In New England this was particularly apparent in the large number of accusations for fornication, adultery, sodomy, and bestiality; the diligence of "close watchers" even resulted in some married couples being prosecuted for fornication after the early birth of their first child.

By the middle of the seventeenth century, a new demographic factor of major socioeconomic importance had appeared. Black servants, originally imported into Virginia in 1619, increased in numbers and declined in legal status until at some time after 1660 virtually every black held the status of a slave. As indentured servants, both blacks and whites had the obligation of laboring for a term of years either to repay the cost of their passage to North America or to satisfy their outstanding debts. The assignment of a term of service was made by the local courts if no precise time had been agreed upon beforehand. By mid-century it was generally accepted that Africans imported into the colonies were bound to servitude not only for their lifetimes but also for the lives of their descendants. Because of this historic development, control of a growing population of slaves became a special problem in all of the colonies. For the most part, this was accomplished by giving extensive disciplinary powers to the master and, at the same time, using the plantation and its staff of overseers as the enforcement authority. If a slave committed a felony, he or she was tried before the local town or county court.

Corbis Images

First imported into Virginia in 1619, black servants declined in legal status. Soon the slave population led to special problems that affected the formal system of law enforcement.

Some colonies established special courts charged with hearing criminal cases involving slaves. As a general rule, fewer procedural protections were given to slave defendants, and the sentences were always more harsh than those given to whites convicted of the same offenses. Throughout the colonial period, there were outbreaks of rebellion among the slaves. These were invariably put down with great cruelty, which demonstrated the underlying fears of the ruling and slaveholding classes. It is significant that most uprisings occurred not in the small rural communities dominated by plantation agriculture, but rather in the growing towns and seaport cities where itinerant slaves had the opportunity to mingle with free blacks and with slaves temporarily free of their masters' close control.

Supplementing this informal system of law enforcement was the traditional English structure of local courts and government. Enforcement of the criminal law was the duty of sheriffs and local constables, aided at their request by anyone within earshot of a call for assistance. All persons were obliged to assist the enforcement officer, but few were eager to risk injury or death in the discharge of the duty. The role of a sheriff or constable was not a happy one in colonial America, and the arrest of a suspect was frequently delayed or prevented by his or her resistance or by the occurrence of a riot. Riots and unlawful assemblies were subject to prohibition by a single justice of the peace; upon his reading of the Riot Act, a gathering became unlawful and was required to disperse. Harsh penalties, which might range as high as the sanctions for treason in opposing the forces of the sovereign applied.

Criminal cases were tried in the town or county courts if misdemeanors were involved. Those same courts heard arraignments of free inhabitants charged with felonies or treason and held the accused for the next meeting of the grand jury. It was customary for felony and treason cases to be tried either by the highest common law court of the colony or by a specially appointed court of oyer and terminer, composed of legally trained persons commissioned by the governor to hear and determine the guilt of the accused.

TIME CAPSULE

The Trials of Anne Hutchinson, 1637 and 1638

After the 1636 expulsion of Roger Williams from Massachusetts Bay, it was risky business to challenge the Puritan theocracy on theological grounds. The times were restless, with Indian wars threatening the western frontier, and threats in England asking the courts to revoke the Massachusetts charter. Yet Anne Hutchinson, a married woman who resided in Boston, proceeded in a seemingly harmless way. After attending the Sunday services in her congregation, she scheduled meetings in her own home, during which she critiqued the ministers' sermons. Although she was true to her Calvinist beliefs, she claimed the benefit of personal revelations from God. These experiences gave her the inner light to determine that the clergymen were undermining the Calvinist position that God predestined which man or woman would be saved, and that good works did not alter this divine judgment. Witty and personable, Anne gathered a large following among the community's women. She also found support from Sir Harry Vane, a refugee from the threat of church prosecution in England who for a while was the elected governor of Massachusetts Bay. By 1637, the orthodox leadership, clerical and lay (nonclerical), viewed Anne a serious threat to the Puritan elders and the leading pastors of the colony.

Anne Hutchinson's first trial—for sedition and contempt of the magistracy and clergy—took place in November 1637. The newly elected Governor John Winthrop presided at the trial assisted by members of the General Court, all of whom belonged to the anti-Hutchinson political faction. Governor Winthrop not only presided over the trial, but took an active role in prosecuting the defendant. A quick-witted woman, Hutchinson defended herself ably, contending that she acted within the law by teaching classes in her home, and denying that any men were present during those sessions. However, in the second day of the trial, she was goaded into the claim that God revealed to her that she was to prophesy against the Puritan clergy because they taught a covenant of works and not the covenant of grace. Her major supporter, the Reverend John Cotton, attempted to conform her teachings with orthodox Calvinist theology, but the court was not persuaded. Anne Hutchinson was convicted and sentenced to be exiled from Massachusetts Bay, and imprisoned until she might be able to leave.

In March 1638 Anne Hutchinson was brought to trial before an ecclesiastical court. While she at first renounced her unorthodox beliefs, she subsequently recanted the renunciation and was tried, convicted, and excommunicated from the church. She then was compelled to leave Massachusetts Bay, and traveled first to Rhode Island, then to Pelham Bay, New Netherlands, where she was killed by Indians in 1643.

At the time of Anne Hutchinson's trials, Puritans were being tried in England by King

Charles I's Court of High Commission. One of those prosecutions had earlier forced Anne's pastor, John Cotton, to flee to Massachusetts Bay, and she and her family followed him. It was the king's continuing efforts to force religious conformity within the Church of England that led to an unprecedented flight of English Puritans to the New England colonies; this was the Great Migration that historians consider the major cause for the rapid settlement and expansion of Massachusetts Bay. Ironically, once the Puritan dissenting groups arrived in the New World, they forgot about the religious toleration they sought within the Church of England. Anne Hutchinson and the Reverend Roger Williams were but the most prominent of many who were accused of sedition and heresy. Perhaps the most persistent persecutions in Massachusetts Bay were conducted against the Quakers; by the 1660s, many of these unfortunates were executed by burning at the stake.

Sources: Richard B. Morris, *Fair Trial: Fourteen Who Stood Accused from Anne Hutchinson to Alger Hiss,* revised edition (New York: Harper & Row, 1967), pp. 3-32.

Questions

1. Why would a religious group, itself the victim of persecution for sincerely held beliefs, become an enforcer of orthodoxy (strict religious rules) when it gained polit-ical power over a colony? Is it wise to have a government in which political and church authority are merged? That happened in England when Henry VIII became head of the Church of England, and heresy became a treasonable offense against the Crown. It happened in Massachusetts Bay until protections were afforded by the enactment of the 1641 and 1648 *Body of Liberties,* and subsequently by the 1685 revocation of the Massachusetts charter. Should the criminal law be enlisted as a means of ensuring orthodoxy of religious belief?

2. While we may well question some of the motives that moved the Massachusetts Bay authorities to bring Anne Hutchinson to trial, there is still the question of whether bringing the political leadership into contempt justifies the imposition of criminal sanctions. Clearly, Governor Winthrop and others felt that criticism of the colony's leaders, be they political dignitaries or Puritan pastors, represented a threat to the stability of society. How far can the state tolerate criticism before it imposes sanctions for undermining authority? Is there justification for suppressing speech, or the publication of dissenting opinions, when doing so would result in violence? To what degree is freedom of speech or religious belief necessary to sustain political freedom in twenty-first century America?

Judges of American colonial local courts were members of the leadership elite; they were determined to maintain law, order, and the dignity of their class. In theory, they were subject to the same supervision that the Privy Council exercised over their English counterparts. However, the governors of colonial America found that local justices of the peace and county courts were relatively isolated from centralized control. As a consequence, real political power became concentrated in the hands of local officials, and thus in the local gentry elected to represent the counties in the lower house of the colonial legislature. Throughout colonial America it was extremely uncomfortable to attract the disapproval of the local gentry. Many persons of blemished reputation were harassed by unwarranted threats of prosecution and decided to leave for other jurisdictions, notwithstanding the hostility of other townspeople to transients. Hence, a distrust of the gentry and the legal officers who upheld the status quo came to characterize the lower social classes, and resistance to the authority of constables and sheriffs was complemented by contemptuous speech directed toward the justices of the peace and magistrates. This formal system of law enforcement, despite its weaknesses and potential for abuse, persisted until the American Revolution.

Woodcut of a witch hanging in seventeenth-century England. Changes in society at the end of the seventeenth century helped contribute to a growing number of witchcraft cases, which strained the formal and informal law enforcement systems of that time.

Both the formal system of law enforcement and its unofficial "close watching" system were badly strained by the witchcraft agitations of the late seventeenth century. Beginning with prosecutions of old women in New England, the contagious fear of witches spread throughout the New World, just as it had infected the Old World in the sixteenth and seventeenth centuries. The famous Salem, Massachusetts, witchcraft trials before Judge Samuel Sewall resulted in the conviction and execution of a large number of women accused by hysterical children. Historians believe that witchcraft cases arose because of instability in society and shifts in political and moral power. At the end of the seventeenth century, the American colonies were experiencing a declining influence of the clergy, a rapidly growing and more diverse population, and an economy that was maturing into a mixture of commercial and agricultural activities. It was a time when the older, informal system of "close watching" no longer worked as a police system, and the formal structure of constables, sheriffs, and local courts was to experience difficulties in restraining crime and disorder.

Samuel Sewall

Alone among the persons involved in the prosecution of witches in Salem, Judge Samuel Sewall had the following statement read out in the South Meeting House in Boston in 1697 as he stood to acknowledge his penitence:

> Samuel Sewall, sensible of the reiterated strokes of God upon himself and family; and being sensible, that as to the Guilt contracted upon the opening of the late Commission [sic] of Oyer and Terminer at Salem (to which the order for this Day relates) he is, upon many accounts, more concerned than any that he knows of, Desires to take the Blame and shame of it, Asking pardon of men And especially desiring prayers that God, who has an Unlimited Authority, would pardon that sin and all other his sins; personal and relative: And according to his infinite Benignity, and Sovereignty, Not Visit the sin of him, or of any other, upon himself or any of his, nor upon the Land: but that He would powerfully defend him against all Temptations to Sin, for the future; and vouchsafe him the efficacious, saving Conduct of his Word and Spirit.

Source: Samuel Sewall's Diary (New York: Russell and Russell, 1963), pp. 139-140.

Summary

American colonial development in the seventeenth century was extraordinarily rapid, moving by 1700 from primitive settlement conditions to a complex society experiencing some of the ills of overpopulation and urbanization. For this reason, legal and social developments also occurred rapidly. Quite naturally, the settlers found much of value in their European and English traditions, and they reacted strongly to the persecution they had experienced in their home countries. The turmoil of the century and the frontier quality of colonial settlement provided opportunities for law reform that were stifled or short-lived in England, but flourished in the colonial wilderness. At the same time, political pressure from the royal authorities in London and the practical demands for effective police methods indicated that further changes would be required in the eighteenth century. American life drew closer to contemporary existence in England. Social mobility and access to cheap land decreased throughout the seventeenth century, and was to prove a serious problem in eighteenth-century America. An initial scarcity of labor softened harsh criminal sanctions in the early days of settlement, but a contrary trend was caused by unemployment and vagrancy in the cities and seaports. Law enforcement, like the law itself, became more formal and more in accord with English models. Experimentation of the early days gave way to the evolution of a mature legal system during the eighteenth century.

Endnotes

[1]   A later parallel to this Virginia movement from martial law to self-government occurred in New South Wales. Established as a penal colony in 1788, this Australian settlement by 1821 was well on its way to a representative form of colonial government.

[2]   Benefit of clergy was available to those who could demonstrate literacy, which by the seventeenth century gave rise to a presumption of clerical status. It was not available to women until 1692, and the course of English law in the seventeenth century was to exclude more offenses from the benevolent effect of this privilege.

[3]   Individuals were indentured so that they might work off a debt, which arose either from their passage being paid by their future master, or by judgment of an American court. Frequently young boys were indentured as apprentices to learn a trade or profession.

References

The best general survey of American legal history is Lawrence M. Friedman, *A History of American Law*, 2d ed. (New York: Simon & Schuster, 1985); the first part of the book, dealing with colonial law, has a good section on criminal law and law enforcement. Also useful is Kermit L. Hall, *The Magic Mirror: Law in American History* (New York: Oxford University Press, 1989). For more specific information, see Bradley Chapin, *Criminal Justice in Colonial America, 1606-1660* (Athens: University of Georgia Press, 1983); George L. Haskins, *Law and Authority in Early Massachusetts: A Study in Tradition and Design* (New York: Macmillan Co., 1960); Hugh F. Rankin, *Criminal Trial Proceedings in the General Court of Colonial Virginia* (Williamsburg, VA: Colonial Williamsburg, 1965); and Arthur P. Scott, *Criminal Law in Colonial Virginia* (Chicago: University of Chicago Press, 1930). Students particularly interested in the right against self-incrimination will profit from reading Leonard W. Levy, *Origins of the Fifth Amendment: The Right Against Self-Incrimination* (New York: Oxford University Press, 1968).

Colonial criminal policy is explored by Kai T. Erikson, *Wayward Puritans: A Study in the Sociology of Deviance* (New York: Wiley, 1966); Jeffrey K. Sawyer, "'Benefit of Clergy' in Maryland and Virginia," *American Journal of Legal History* 34, no. 1 (1990), p. 49-69.

For a more detailed history of witchcraft, see Wallace Notestein, *A History of Witchcraft in England from 1558 to 1718* (Washington: American Historical Association, 1911); Frances Hill, *A Delusion of Satan: The Full Story of the Salem Witch Trials* (New York: Doubleday, 1995); and Anne Llewellyn Barstow, *A New History of the European Witch Hunts* (San Francisco: Harper, 1994). Several sources provide perspectives on witchcraft in the American colonies: Edgar J. McManus, *Law and Liberty in Early New England: Criminal Justice and Due Process, 1620-1692* (Amherst: University of Massachusetts Press, 1993), 131-148; Gilbert Geis and Ivan Bunn, "And a Child Shall Mislead Them: Notes on Witchcraft and Child Abuse Accusations," in Robert J. Kelly and Donal E.J. MacNamara, *Perspectives on Deviance: Dominance, Degradation and Denigration* (Cincinnati: Anderson Publishing Co., 1991), pp.

31-45; James T. Richardson, *The Satanism Scare* (New York: A. de Gruyter, 1991); and Nanci Koser Wilson, "Taming Women and Nature: The Criminal Justice System and the Creation of a Crime in Salem Village," in Roslyn Muraskin and Ted Alleman (eds.), *It's a Crime: Women and Justice* (Englewood Cliffs, NJ: Prentice Hall, 1993), pp. 52-73.

Relatively little has been written about the criminal justice system in regard to American Indians, but the following publications are useful: John R. Wunder, *"Retained by the People": A History of American Indians and the Bill of Rights* (New York: Oxford University Press, 1994); Marjorie S. Zatz, Carol Chiago Lujan, and Zoann K. Snyder-Joy, "American Indians and Criminal Justice: Some Conceptual and Methodological Considerations," in Michael J. Lynch and E. Britt Patterson, eds., *Race and Criminal Justice* (Albany: Harrow & Heston, 1991), pp. 100-112; Marianne O. Nielsen, *Native Americans, Crime and Justice* (Boulder, CO: Westview Press, 1996); and Laurence French, *Indians and Criminal Justice* (Totowa, NJ: Allanheld, Osmun, 1982).

Criminal procedure in colonial and early United States history is examined in David J. Bodenhamer, *Fair Trial: Rights of the Accused in American History* (New York: Oxford University Press, 1992); and Douglas Greenburg, "Crime, Law Enforcement, and Social Control in Colonial America," *American Journal of Legal History* 16 (1982), pp. 293-325.

Notes and Problems

1. Because the first settlers in North America found such primitive conditions, was it wise for them to adopt biblical law as a convenient source of rules for a wilderness existence? Why did they select Jewish rather than Greek or Roman antecedents? What later caused them to abandon Bible Codes, but at the same time to continue their resistance to chancery courts, benefit of clergy, and the institution of church courts for minor moral offenses?

2. The experience of Pennsylvania provides an interesting counterpoint to those of the New England colonies and Virginia. Settled by Quakers, the Pennsylvania settlement experimented briefly with a code in which few offenses, other than treason, were subject to the death penalty; within the first decade, a series of law revisions restored the death penalty for most felonies that were so punished in the other English colonies. Does this prove anything? Were the Quakers wrong, or did they simply miscalculate the percentage of Quakers there would be in the population?

3. Bible Codes differ from English law in the sanctions available for the punishment of theft. As we have seen, the biblical method was to award compensation to the owner, usually in multiple amounts, for goods wrongfully taken. English law punished larceny in various ways, ranging from fines and imprisonment to death. Does this mean that the two systems of law had differing views concerning property rights, or that they placed different emphases upon the security of property? Did the rise of modern capitalism have anything to do with the harsher English laws?

4. It is interesting to speculate upon the interplay of Indian law with the colonial legal systems. In property law, we know that Indians did not recognize personal rights to land or possessions; as a consequence, they were frequently prosecuted for "stealing" goods of a European settler or for trespassing on "his" land. Which law should have governed, that of the Indians or that of the newly arrived colonists? The English position, taken by both the royal authorities and the colonial magistrates, was that English law (as modified by colonial laws and customs) was to prevail. Was that logical? Was it just?

Chapter 7

The Enlightenment and Criminal Justice

England's settlement of North America in the seventeenth and eighteenth centuries is eclipsed in significance by the upheavals caused by the Enlightenment. The Enlightenment was a philosophical movement that drew its initial driving force from the rise of scientific investigation in mechanical physics (marked by Isaac Newton's publication of *Principia* in 1687) and the application of reason, humanitarianism, and secularism to problems of philosophy and political theory, typified by the publication of John Locke's *Essay Concerning Human Understanding* and *Second Treatise on Government* (both published in 1690). Sparked by cynicism and satirical humor, the Enlightenment found ready acceptance in eighteenth-century France. Englishmen were, for the most part, preoccupied with the formidable task of reestablishing a stable and functional government after the upheavals of the seventeenth century. Yet, the Age of Reason would make its influence felt throughout the Western world. In the English colonies, it led to the American Revolution and the institution of republican government in a federal state marked by constitutionalism and limited political power. In France, it fueled seething discontent within the laboring and mercantile classes, generating a series of critical and satirical writings that survived both the censure of the authorities and the imprisonment of the authors. Ultimately, the Enlightenment was to be one of the leading causes of the French Revolution, which shook the old regime to its very foundations and caused a reconstitution of French society and political life. The impact in Britain was less dramatic, but within the first half of the nineteenth century the entire structure of English political power was radically altered by the gradual extension of the electoral franchise to virtually all classes.

Corbis Images

John Locke (1632-1704)—English philosopher.

TIME LINE

The Enlightenment in Europe and North America

1649	The parliamentary party, having defeated English King Charles I in battle, executes the king for treason and institutes a republican form of government.
1651	Thomas Hobbes publishes *The Leviathan*.
1653-1658	Oliver Cromwell serves as Lord Protector of the Commonwealth.
1660	Charles II, the son of the executed English monarch, is called to the throne by Parliament and reestablishes royal authority in England and Scotland.
1682	Augustin Nicholas, a French judge at Dijon, attacks the use of torture in French criminal procedure.
1689	English Bill of Rights is issued by King William III and Queen Mary II of England, newly called to the throne by Parliament to replace the deposed King James II.
1690	John Locke's *Second Treatise of Government* is published, arguing that political authority is derived from the consent of the governed.
1717	Voltaire is committed to prison in France and charged with writing a seditious poem.
1748	Montesquieu's *Spirit of Laws* is published, setting forth the concept that there should be a separation of powers in governments.
1766	Beccaria publishes *Essay on Crime and Punishment*, urging that punishments should be proportionate to the seriousness of the offense, and that certainty of punishment is more deterring than its severity.
1776-1783	The War for American Independence officially begins with a Declaration of Independence drafted by Thomas Jefferson; it ends with a peace treaty, by which Great Britain recognizes the independence of the former colonies.
1780	The French Estates-General abolishes torture in preliminary criminal procedure.
1787	The Philadelphia Convention drafts the federal Constitution, which is approved by the Confederation Congress and then sent to the states to be ratified by conventions elected by the people.

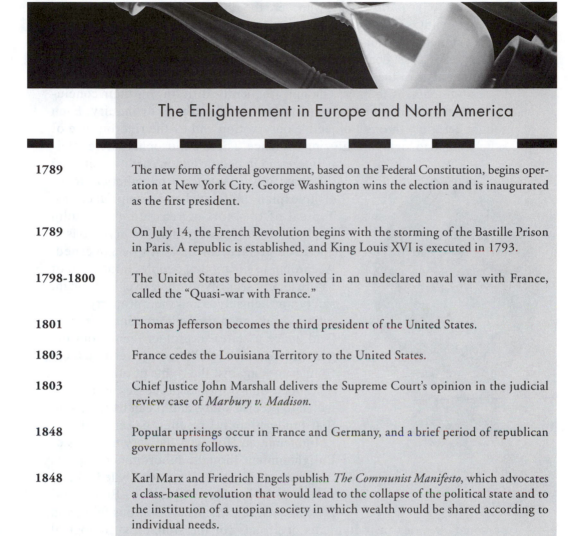

The Enlightenment in Europe and North America

1789	The new form of federal government, based on the Federal Constitution, begins operation at New York City. George Washington wins the election and is inaugurated as the first president.
1789	On July 14, the French Revolution begins with the storming of the Bastille Prison in Paris. A republic is established, and King Louis XVI is executed in 1793.
1798-1800	The United States becomes involved in an undeclared naval war with France, called the "Quasi-war with France."
1801	Thomas Jefferson becomes the third president of the United States.
1803	France cedes the Louisiana Territory to the United States.
1803	Chief Justice John Marshall delivers the Supreme Court's opinion in the judicial review case of *Marbury v. Madison*.
1848	Popular uprisings occur in France and Germany, and a brief period of republican governments follows.
1848	Karl Marx and Friedrich Engels publish *The Communist Manifesto*, which advocates a class-based revolution that would lead to the collapse of the political state and to the institution of a utopian society in which wealth would be shared according to individual needs.

The diversity of the Enlightenment makes it difficult to identify its main characteristics, but one of the primary aspects of the period was its emphasis on the role of reason in the enhancement of human understanding. Just as physical science used observation and measurement as the key to knowledge, so did the philosopher or political theorist study observable phenomena and then use logic to arrive at his or her conclusions. This required extensive research, not only of the variety of contemporary societies, but also of the historical evidence concerning long-dead civilizations. In the course of historical study, the Enlightenment philosophers discovered the ancient world and made it a model for their new view of life. However, they were careful to restrict their enthusiasm to the Athenian and Roman ancestors of western civilization, ignoring the Jewish experience so readily available in the Bible. To the *philosophes*, who were the Enlightenment philosophers of the eighteenth century, the Bible, along with other religious writings, was a product of superstition and ignorance. In this sense, the Enlightenment was a rejection of a past dominated by Christianity and a "rediscovery" of the secular humanism of the classical authors.

Enlightenment thinkers, though frequently differing in their conclusions, shared common modes of thought and methods of inquiry. Each sought certainty through objective observation and by the rigorous use of skepticism and logic in analyzing evidence. These philosophers were vitally interested in people and in earthly societies; they carefully constructed hypothetical models to explain individual and group functions. Typical of this sort of reasoning was John Locke's view of government as being based upon the consent of those to be governed. According to his model, people in the state of nature lacked security for their lives and sought safety for themselves and their property. They satisfied this need through erecting a society (and hence a state) to protect them from the greed of their fellows, but also to restrain them from crimes against the rights of others.

Corbis Images

Charles-Louis de Secondat, Baron de Montesquieu (1689-1755)—French political philosopher

Social and political processes were subjected to precise study, and it can truly be said that modern social science began with the Enlightenment. However, the very methods of Enlightenment thought subordinated aspects of human activity that do not readily lend themselves to objective evaluation. Emotional attachments, sentiments of religious faith, and personal loyalties to individuals or groups (or the simple psychological responses of hate and love) do not fit well into Reason's analytical scheme. As a consequence, most Enlightenment philosophers treated religion either with hostility or relegated it to a minor role in the affairs of mankind. Montesquieu in his *Spirit of Laws* (published in 1748) held two highly controversial views concerning religion. First, he indicated that no given religion was best for all societies and all situations; his detractors pointed out that this relativism undermined the very foundation of Christian missionary activity throughout the world. Second, he subjected religions to the test of utility; they were only as good as the benefit they conferred on the societies in which they existed. Because Christianity had long maintained its centrality as a source of public morality, and because political power had for centuries been enhanced by religious endorsement, it is not surprising that Montesquieu was attacked by the politically and ecclesiastically orthodox people of his day. For our purposes it is important to note his change of emphasis. Earthly institutions and societies were no longer to be judged by religious standards; rather, religion was to be measured by the new moral standard of utilitarianism: what good it did for humankind. While Montesquieu made this point respectfully and subtly, his contemporary Voltaire drove the matter home with satire and ridicule. Voltaire found himself frequently in prison or in exile for challenging the church, one of the fundamental institutions of European society. However, the greatest threat to theology and traditional religion was posed by men like Montesquieu, who chose not to attack Christianity but to ignore it.

The arrest of Voltaire and his niece by order of Frederick II. Undated illustration after a painting by Jules Giradet.

Minimizing or ignoring the role of religion in the lives of men resulted in an entirely new approach to crime and punishment. For the first time in the history of Western civilization, it was possible to think about crime as a secular phenomenon—something that had nothing to do with sin or moral standards based on theology. While biblical law represents the high point of religious influence upon criminal justice, the connection remained through the ages and was not really challenged until the Age of Reason. The Age of Reason originally stressed the importance of observing and measuring physical phenomena. It was expanded into the application of scientific methods and logic to the study of human beings and their society. Ultimately this latter phase of the Age of Reason became known as the Enlightenment. The *philosophes* viewed crime as an earthly phenomenon that had to be studied in a secular framework and explained in a logical way. Wrongful acts were evaluated in terms of their impact on the welfare of individuals and society. Entirely absent from the equation was a need to expiate the wrath of an angry god. Punishment served a utilitarian purpose—it was to discourage future criminal activity, both by the convicted person and by those who witnessed his or her chastisement. Social goals, rather than divine purposes, became the guiding light of Enlightenment penology.

When French proponents of Reason turned their attention to the criminal law of their day, they found a repressive system that had not only not changed in its particulars since 1539, but had become more arbitrary and class-oriented by the Ordinance of 1670. Still present was the secrecy of extraordinary procedure—the lack of a defendant's right to call or confront witnesses, the denial of defense counsel, and the use of torture to satisfy the need for a sufficient number of proofs of guilt. Practice had expanded the availability of royal pardons and remissions of penalty for those with sufficient influence or wealth to obtain them. On the other hand, the autocratic reign of the Sun King (Louis XIV) increased the use of the *lettre de cachet*, a royal warrant that might commit an innocent person to prison without trial or even an idea of the offense. Such a *lettre*, issued on the false suspicion that Voltaire was the author of a seditious poem, condemned him to prison as a young man (1717) and made him an inveterate critic of French criminal procedure. By way of contrast to arbitrary French law, the *philosophes* looked to England, recently restored to stability after its struggle with Stuart absolutism. They found much to praise in English institutions of criminal law and particularly prized the jury trial that formed such an important part of the liberty of English citizens.

Clarity in Law; Equality in Application

The *philosophes* considered the drafting of penal statutes to be one of the fundamental activities of the legislative power. They carefully distinguished between justice and law, viewing justice as a "higher law" that existed even before the establishment of political societies. In this sense, they rejected the political theories of Thomas Hobbes, a seventeenth-century English philosopher who reacted to the disorders of his day by advocating the preeminence of positive law, which held that what the sovereign power willed was both legal and just. Montesquieu, in his *Spirit of Laws*, made it quite plain that all laws should conform to natural law ideals. Furthermore, in shaping penal laws, the legislator should be certain to conform the letter of the law to the nature of the society in which it was to function. Laws should be adapted to the people for whom they were made and ensure both the health and stability of society.

Following the lead of Voltaire, Montesquieu also insisted that the criminal law should be clear and without subtlety. The person of common understanding should be able to comprehend each prohibition of the law and thus be dissuaded from violating any provision of the criminal code. In 1766, Cesare de Beccaria pointed out that when law is written in a clear manner and universally read and understood, the very fact of its existence will cause a decrease in crime. Clarity in regard to punishment was also desirable, for then the individual contemplating crime might accurately measure the inconvenience of conviction against the momentary pleasures of the crime. This preventative aspect of clear penal law was to be a powerful deterrent: "In moderate governments the love of one's country, shame and the fear of blame, are restraining motives, capable of preventing a great multitude of crimes."[1]

Another benefit of clear criminal statutes was the elimination of judicial discretion, which facilitated unequal application of the law. To the *philosophes*, the judge or magistrate should determine the facts of the crime and the identity of the accused. The definition of the crime, and the elements of proof necessary to convict, should be rigidly established by the written law. The principal function of the judge should be to apply the law to the facts, but at no time should he become involved in the interpretation of the law. Sharp limitations on judicial authority to interpret law were essential to the liberty of the citizen accused of crime and threatened with loss of property, liberty, or life. Discretion could result in unequal application of penal laws that might fluctuate according to the class or reputation of the defendant. In sentencing, the subjective decisions of judges were highly suspect, and Enlightenment commentators preferred precise legislative standards for punishment. As Beccaria phrased it,

> That a magistrate, the executor of the laws, should have a power to imprison a citizen, to deprive a man he hates of his liberty upon frivolous pretenses, and to leave his friend unpunished, notwithstanding the strongest proofs of his guilt, is an error as common as it is contrary to the bond of society, which is personal security.[2]

Judges had always had wide leeway in interpreting the law, and in many situations the punishments were finely tuned to the social or political status of the accused. However, the Age of Reason insisted upon the equality of individuals before the law. In France, and throughout most of Europe, this new attitude toward criminal law resulted in a precise codification of penal statutes and a sharp limitation upon any exercise of judicial interpretation. On the other hand, in Anglo-American law, this quest for certainty and equality has led to the general principle that criminal statutes should not be vague. The United States Constitution, written at the full flush of the Age of Reason, has been interpreted to read that vague penal laws are constitutionally void, that all federal crimes must be defined by statute, and that all accused persons must be afforded both due process and equal protection of the laws.

Procedural Guarantees

Enlightenment thought on criminal procedure sprang from a new view of the relationship of the individual to society; in the words of Montesquieu, "in moderate governments . . . the life of the meanest subject is deemed precious" and no one can be deprived of honor or property except after a long and careful inquiry during which he or she has been given every possible opportunity to make a defense.[3] This was supplemented by the principle that, in the eyes of the law, every person should be considered innocent until his or her crime had been proven beyond reasonable doubt. Departing from the viewpoint of earlier ages, the Age of Reason was more concerned with the moral injustice of a wrongful conviction than it was with the need for effective police and control of the masses. The main complaint of the philosophers during this age was against the European systems of inquisitory procedure. Although the excessive harshness of French criminal procedure was the background against which these philosophers wrote, the general principles of fair procedure and rights of the individual accused were also highly influential in Anglo-American legal development and constitutional thought.

Preliminary arrest was one of the widespread abuses of French criminal law, particularly during the reigns of Louis XV and Louis XVI. The infamous *lettre de cachet* could inflict imprisonment for an indefinite period, even without the accusation of a crime. The ordinary course of criminal prosecution utilized imprisonment before trial, leading Enlightenment writers to demand that a system of bail be instituted in noncapital cases. In addition, they suggested that individuals held under preliminary arrest should be separated from convicted felons, thereby softening the circumstances of imprisonment and mitigating its dangers.

Proposals for reforming the French system of trials included the demand that all criminal trials be held in public, that the accused be given an opportunity to confront the witnesses against him or her, and that no person be convicted in a capital case except on the testimony of two witnesses. It was stated that the accused should not be placed under oath and examined in such a way that he or she might accuse him or herself either by confusion or through compulsion. Following English practice, it was suggested that the most objective decision in criminal trials could be obtained only by the use of a jury with numerous members. This would provide additional security for the accused and also ensure impartiality in judgment. Where the accused was of a different social class than his or her victim, Beccaria suggested that one half of the jury should be drawn from the victim's peers and the other half from the peers of the accused.

Central to the *philosophes'* attack on criminal procedure was a logical and humanitarian critique of torture. By 1780 the vehemence of the effort convinced the French States-General to abolish the use of preliminary torture, a particularly objectionable method of obtaining incriminating evidence. In the seventeenth century, lawyers and judges had spoken out against the use of torture, claiming that it was an uncertain method of obtaining evidence and that more likely than not it would result in the conviction of innocent people. Augustin Nicolas, president of the parlemant of Dijon, penned a powerful attack against torture (1682) that criticized the execution of countless innocent people "upon confessions forcibly extorted by unbearable torments."[4] Nicolas questioned how a judge, faced with deciding the fate of an accused person, could possibly decide in favor of the death penalty without overwhelming evidence; indeed, torture resulted in confessions by the innocent as frequently as it resulted in admissions by the guilty. One of Nicolas' contemporaries, the Abbe Fleury, pointed out (1680) that torture was more of a trial of patience than of truth. However, these men were arguing for an idea whose time had not yet come. It was left to the Enlightenment philosophers, particularly Voltaire and Beccaria, to launch a full-scale attack upon the practice. By 1780 there was established an Academy of Chalons-sur-Marne dedicated to reform of the criminal law. Among the subjects for discussion and study was the abolition of torture.

TIME CAPSULE

The French Declaration of the Rights of Man and Citizen (1789)

The French Declaration (1789) preceded the Bill of Rights in the United States (1791) and exceeded the Bill of Rights in its presumptions regarding individual liberty. In addition to enunciating the principle that men are born and remain free in rights, the Declaration included in the designation of natural and inalienable rights not only the right to liberty and property, but also the rights to security and resistance to oppression.

The emphasis on inherent freedom is reflected in the Declaration's fifth and tenth articles, which limits governmental interference:

5. The law has the right to forbid only actions which are injurious to society. Whatever is not forbidden by law may not be prevented, and no one may be constrained to do what it does not prescribe.

10. No one is to be disquieted because of his opinions, even religious, provided their manifestation does not disturb the public order established by law.

The sixth article guarantees all citizens the right to concur in the formation of law, either personally or through their representatives—a principle at variance with common law. Several articles pertain specifically to criminal policy and procedure:

7. No man may be accused, arrested, or detained except in the cases determined by law, and according to the forms prescribed thereby. Whoever solicit, expedite, or execute arbitrary orders, or have them executed, must be punished; but every citizen summoned or apprehended in pursuance of the law must obey immediately: he renders himself culpable by resistance.

8. The law is to establish only penalties that are absolutely and obviously necessary: and no one may be punished except by virtue of a law established and promulgated prior to the offence and legally applied.

9. Since every man is presumed innocent until declared guilty, if arrest be deemed indispensable, all unnecessary severity for securing the person of the accused must be severely repressed by law.

Some of the clauses in the Declaration (a product of a liberal phase of the French Revolution) will seem familiar to Americans, since they are similar to ones in the Constitution of the United States. A comparison of the two documents, however, will indicate the wider scope of rights in the Declaration. For example, the Constitution, which was written during a conservative period, does not mention equality; the word "equal" first appears in the Fourteenth Amendment (1868); nor does the Constitution speak of presumption of innocence. Furthermore, the principle of positive law, which restricts designation of acts as criminal, is not inherent in the Constitution.

Note: A copy of the complete Declaration can be found in Walter Laqueur and Barry Rubin (eds.), *The Human Rights Reader* (Philadelphia: Temple University Press, 1979), pp. 118-120.

Corbis Images

Cesare de Beccaria (1738-1794)—Italian economist and jurist. The publication of his *Essay on Crimes and Punishments* in 1766 marked the beginning of the science of penology.

While Voltaire dealt with the subject of torture at various points in his correspondence and writings, it was left to Beccaria to mount a systematic campaign in his *Essay on Crimes and Punishments* (1766). It was widely accepted that Italian methods of torture had reached the ultimate in cruelty and barbarism. Hence, it is not surprising that Beccaria would be more effective in questioning its legitimacy. Referring to the use of torture in the course of the Holy Inquisition, Beccaria recalled the spectacle of "humanity groaning under implacable superstition . . . and the ministers of the Gospel of Christ, bathing their hands in blood in the name of the God of all mercy."[5] Torture had its origins in twelfth-century efforts to suppress heresy, and its survival in church courts ensured its incorporation into continental legal systems. As Beccaria

TIME CAPSULE

Bentham's Calculus of Pleasure and Pain

The term *utilitarianism* is often associated with Jeremy Benthan (1748-1832). He defined utility as the "principle which approves or disapproves of every action whatsoever, according to the tendency which it appears to have to augment or diminish the happiness of the party whose interest is in question; or, what is the same thing in other words, to promote or to oppose that happiness." Since a legislator strives for pleasure and avoidance of pain, Bentham argued, it benefited him to understand their nature. As a child of the Enlightenment, Bentham therefore analyzed the values inherent in pleasure and pain as a way of comprehending the hedonistic calculus a person might undertake when contemplating an action.

To a person considered *by him or herself,* the value of a pleasure or pain considered *by itself* will be greater or less, according to the four following circumstances:

1. Its *intensity*

2. Its *duration*

3. Its *certainty* or *uncertainty*

4. Its *nearness* or *remoteness*

These are the circumstances that are to be considered in estimating a pleasure or a pain. But when the value of any pleasure or pain is considered for the purpose of estimating the tendency of any *act* by which it is produced, there are two other circumstances to be taken into the account; these are

5. Its *fecundity*, or the chance it has of being followed by sensations of the *same* kind: that is, pleasures, if it be a pleasure: pains, if it be a pain.

6. Its *purity*, or the chance it has of *not* being followed by sensations of the *opposite* kind: that is, pains, if it be a pleasure: pleasures, if it be a pain.

And one other; to wit:

7. Its *extent*: that is, the number of persons to whom it *extends*: or (in other words) who are affected by it.

Source: Jeremy Bentham, *An Introduction to the Principles of Morals and Legislation* (New York: Hafner Publishing Co., 1948), pp. 2, 29-30.

pointed out, it shared the defects of the ancient trial by ordeal, long ago condemned by the church and society, for both procedures had no logical relationship to discovering truth. Could it be intelligently believed that truth depended upon the stamina of the prisoner; was it to be found in the muscles and fibres of the accused? People varied in their physical and emotional ability to withstand pain, but that had nothing to do with guilt or innocence. Indeed, the weaker persons who were innocent of crime were more likely to be condemned than the strong and robust individual who was guilty. Furthermore, it was contrary to logic to use torture to compel an accused person to become his own accuser. It was equally unreasonable to inflict the same pain upon an innocent person as upon one who was actually guilty. Because punishment was to serve as a deterrent to crime, the use of torture as a part of the criminal process made it clear that one would be tormented not for guilt but, rather, as a simple consequence of having been accused.

As the French Revolution approached, the attacks of the *philosophes* upon criminal procedures and the barbarities of torture began to have their impact. Shortly after the abolition of preliminary torture in 1780, there were a series of criminal prosecutions in which individuals were convicted and executed for crimes later shown to have been the deeds of others. However, prominent lawyers and judges continued to defend the system of criminal procedure, asserting that without torture it would be virtually impossible to convict persons accused of crime.

The Birth of Penology

The publication of Marquis de Beccaria's *Essay on Crimes and Punishments* (1766) represented the high tide of Enlightenment thought on criminal justice and was also the beginning of the modern science of penology. A true product of the Age of Reason, the *Essay* was influenced by theories of public utility and moderation in the exercise of political power. It demonstrated a deep compassion for those convicted of wrongdoing, but at the same time it attempted to provide a realistic appraisal of the nature of crime and to suggest methods for its control. Beccaria saw the increase of population, with the consequent clash of private interests, as the reason for the increase of crime. Certain steps might be taken to suppress criminal activity, such as the illumination of the streets at night and the establishment of security guards and street patrols, but the greatest deterrent to crime was the certainty of punishment and not its severity. Indeed, the harshness of penalties might cause the populace to become hardened to cruelty and render punishment less effective as a warning to future offenders.

Public utility was the central focus of Beccaria's system of punishment. He was deeply concerned that the bond of society be strengthened, not weakened, by the imposition of criminal sanctions. That bond he called justice, by which he meant the very minimum of behavior necessary to maintain tranquility in society and also the very minimum of punishment necessary to discourage misbehavior. Quoting Montesquieu, Beccaria asserted, "Every punishment, which does not arise from absolute necessity . . . is tyrannical."[6] Necessity was found in the need to suppress crime, to deter its future commission, and to protect society from criminal behavior. Sanctions that did not serve these purposes were both unjust and counterproductive. For example, Beccaria believed that capital punishment was unnecessarily harsh in the case of convicted murderers. The major concern was the protection of society against a future offense, which could be more humanely achieved through the banishment of the criminal. Because banishment traditionally had been associated with the forfeiture of property rights, Beccaria again applied utility as the measure. The banishment of the murderer, if it were a permanent break with society, might justify some seizure of property. However, forfeiture punished the innocent heirs of the convict, and should it impoverish them to the point of desperation, it might easily cause them to resort to crime out of necessity. Thus, Beccaria noted that the best interest of society would be served by banishment, coupled with very limited forfeitures of family property.

Deterrence was a major factor in Beccaria's penology. To serve as a good example, punishment should be both quick and certain. Penalties were to be fixed by law, not subject to the whim of the ruler, who might pardon the accused or remit the sentence. Clemency was to be found not in the heart of the ruler but, rather, in the precise provisions of the penal statutes. Prosecutions were to be prompt, thereby insuring that the public did not forget the nature of the crime before it viewed the extent of the punishment. Sanctions should be graduated to fit the severity of the crime. By this, Beccaria intended to insure that no would-be offender would be tempted to commit a more serious crime simply because it bore the same penalty as a lesser crime. One example of this is the variant treatment he accorded to what American law terms larceny (the nonviolent taking of property) and robbery (seizure of property coupled with violence or the threat of violence to the owner). Larceny was to be punished by pecuniary sanctions, either fines or multiple restitution, but robbery was to be subject to these penalties plus corporal punishment, the preferred method being public whipping.

Throughout his treatise, Beccaria emphasized the need for public punishment, even of minor crimes; he felt that it was the shame and ignominy of such sanctions that provided the strongest deterrent to future would-be offenders. In this, he followed Montesquieu's admonition, "Let us follow nature who has given shame to man for his scourge; and let the heaviest part of the punishment be the infamy attending it."[7] According to Beccaria, short prison terms for minor offenses lacked the value of deterrence, as did the practice of transporting minor offenders to penal colonies where their punishments might go unobserved.

The precise application of punishment was no simple matter. Each crime had to be studied and placed within the scale of severity. Severity in turn was a measure of the degree to which a given act undermined society or threatened the security of some individual or group. Matching punishment to crime required a consideration of the deterrent value of the sanction, as well as its effectiveness in protecting society. Finally, it was Beccaria's view that sanctions should be moderate, exceeding the anticipated gain from criminal activity only enough to discourage would-be offenders. Severity beyond that measurable limit was, in his opinion, superfluous and tyrannical.

Demography, Culture, and Crime

The essence of Enlightenment thought was the application of "Reason" to all areas of human knowledge. Given the right data, all human behaviors would also conform to some predictable pattern—or so the *philosophes* thought. Yet the problem of crime has proven to be much more difficult to resolve than Beccaria surmised. Indeed, the complex origins of crime may lie deep within segments of culture and personality that we have yet to explore. On the other hand, we have made a beginning. One interesting case study is that undertaken by Douglas Greenberg, which looks at colonial New York from 1691 to the American Revolution. Virtually alone among the North American colonial settlements, New York was characterized by a wide range of nationalities in its population. There were also a substantial number of slaves, and the colony experienced slave revolts in 1712 and 1741. For most of the seventeenth century, the descendants of the original Dutch settlers were treated with suspicion by the English residents. They, in turn, retained many of their original customs and Dutch was spoken well into the eighteenth century. New York also welcomed Protestants fleeing from religious persecution in Louis XIV's France, and Jews expelled from the Spanish empire also found refuge in the colony. With such a mix of racial, ethnic, and religious groups, New York was the preeminent "melting pot" of colonial North America—and therefore an excellent subject for Greenberg's study.

As we might expect, the largest number (90%) of defendants in New York's colonial courts were white English males. Only 10 percent were women, but a higher percentage (16.8%) of city-dwelling defendants were women; Greenberg surmises that this was probably due to New York City being a seaport, with a large collection of brothels. Slaves constituted between 11 and 15% of New York's population, but they were less than eight percent of those prosecuted for crime. Perhaps their oppressed condition left them fearful of the consequences of criminal behavior, and even more likely is the possibility that most slave crime involved theft from masters, who took punishment into their own hands.

Another interesting comparison is the type of criminal activity for which men and women were arrested. For men the major category (22.6%) was violent crimes against persons, followed by violations of public order (drunkenness, street fighting, etc.). For women, maintaining "disorderly houses" (brothels and bars) was the highest basis for prosecution (40.4%), followed by illegal relations with slaves (usually selling alcoholic beverages) (32.4%), and theft (26.1%).

Among those accused of crime and brought to trial (about 50% of all accused persons), the highest percentage of those convicted (68.6%) applied to slaves, and 51.6 percent of Indians were convicted. On the other hand, the conviction rates of men (48.1%) and women (46.5%) are remarkably similar.

Greenberg provides many thought-provoking speculations, based in part upon his evidence. For example, he notes that single women accounted for an inordinate number of prosecutions, and quite likely the same is true for single men. Is the marital status of a population a significant factor in causing criminal activity? Does it alter the nature of criminal activity? We might also wonder whether the eighteenth century patterns persist even today, or have women become more violent and men more property-oriented in their crime patterns?

Source: Douglas Greenberg, *Crime and Law Enforcement in the Colony of New York, 1691-1776* (Ithaca: Cornell University Press, 1974).

Question

In light of these statistics, what can you say about sources of crime in colonial New York? Do you believe that Beccaria's view of penology—that is, the way in which punishment will deter people from crime—would have worked in New York? What other factors would you have to consider?

By modern standards, Beccaria's *Essay* presented an overly optimistic view of the potential of penology. Throughout, there emerged a confident assertion that each individual crime can be eradicated from society simply by discovering the "right" penal medicine. Certainty of punishment is impossible without effective policing and accurate procedures of criminal investigation, both conspicuously absent in Beccaria's day. The *Essay* rested upon the basic premise that all criminals will react in similar ways to the same sanction and that criminal activity is itself a rational form of behavior subject to logical deterrence. In this sense, Beccaria overlooked psychological diversity between individuals and the infinitely varied motivations for criminal behavior.[8] However, despite these reservations about its major premises, one cannot deny that Beccaria's masterpiece was a milestone in the history of criminal justice. For the first time, penology was subjected to vigorous and systematic analysis. Crime and its punishment was studied in an entirely secular framework, using public utility as the guideline for judging both the morality and the practical value of sanctions. After publication of the *Essay*, sin was to play a minor role in western civilization's discussions of penology.

Socialist Criminology

Enlightenment philosophy bore unforeseen fruit in the nineteenth century in the form of socialist theory and practice. Karl Marx (1819-1883), preeminent among socialist thinkers, followed the *philosophes* in emphasizing the ability of man rationally to form societies based on equitable principles, but he derived a far different concept of criminology.

Analysis of earlier societies convinced Marx and Friedrich Engels (1820-1895) that the principal dynamic of societies was the mode of production. Starting from the premise that labor is the source of all wealth, Marxism found inherent conflicts of interest between the class of persons who controlled the means of production (capitalists) and the class of actual producers (proletariat) who sold their labor to the capitalists. Marx and Engels believed this conflict would generate a series of revolutions. In their *Communist Manifesto* (1848), they wrote that the history of all previous society was one of class struggle. They predicted that the proletariat, which far outnumbered the capitalists, would come to recognize their common cause and rise up to overthrow their oppressors. Out of this class struggle would emerge a communist society in which the means of production would be communally owned and all persons would be equal.

TIME CAPSULE

A Communist View of Crime

The following passage from *Theories of Surplus Value*, written by Karl Marx in the 1860s, is seen by some as a serious argument, by others as satire. What is your opinion?

A philosopher produces ideas, a poet poems, a clergyman sermons, a professor compendia and so on. A criminal produces crimes. If we look a little closer at the connection between this latter branch of production and society as a whole, we shall rid ourselves of many prejudices. The criminal produces not only crimes but also criminal law, and with this also the professor who gives lectures on criminal law and in addition to this the inevitable compendium in which this same professor throws his lectures onto the general market as "commodities." This brings with it augmentation of national wealth, quite apart from the personal enjoyment . . . the manuscript of the compendium brings to its originator himself.

The criminal moreover produces the whole of the police and of criminal justice, constables, judges, hangmen, juries, etc.; and all these different lines of business, which form equally many categories of the social division of labour, develop different capacities of the human spirit, create new needs and new ways of satisfying them. Torture alone has given rise to the most ingenious mechanical inventions, and employed many honourable craftsmen in the production of its instruments.

The criminal produces an impression, partly moral and partly tragic, as the case may be, and in this way renders a "service" by arousing the moral and aesthetic feelings of the public. He produces not only compendia on Criminal Law, not only penal codes and along with them legislators in this field, but also art, belles-lettres, novels, and even tragedies. . . . The criminal breaks the monotony and everyday security of bourgeois life. In this way he keeps it from stagnation, and gives rise to that uneasy tension and agility without which even the spur of competition would get blunted. Thus he gives a stimulus to the productive forces. While crime takes a part of the superfluous population off the labour market and thus reduces competition among the labourers—up to a certain point preventing wages from falling below the minimum—the struggle against crime absorbs another part of this population. Thus the criminal comes in as one of those natural "counterweights" which bring about a correct balance and open up a whole perspective of "useful" occupations.

Source: Karl Marx, *Theories of Surplus Value,* vol. 1 (London: Lawrence & Wishart, 1969-1972), pp. 387-388.

In the ultimate classless society, the innate goodness of humankind would prevail and individuals and groups would live harmoniously in a community in which the "free development of each is the condition for the free development of all" (*The Communist Manifesto*). The state, being no longer necessary, could then wither away. However, before reaching this final stage, a society would, as Vladimir Lenin argued, pass through a socialist phase led by a dictatorship by the proletariat, which could educate individuals for life in a communal society. It is this dictatorial phase of development that spawned totalitarian criminal justice systems in socialist countries. So far, no nation has claimed to have moved beyond the socialist transitory period into full communism.

Although Marx and his collaborator Friedrich Engels wrote little concerning crime, passages in works such as *A Contribution to the Critique of Political Economy* (1859), *The German Ideology* (1845-1846), and *The Condition of the Working Class in England in 1844* (1844), indicate their conclusions regarding the causes of criminal activity, its nature, and possible means of curtailing it. If, as they contended, those who command the means of production can shape other fundamental institutions of a society by controlling the legislature, administrative bureaucracies, police, judicial systems, and prisons, then it is the economic elite who determine the legal definition of crime, the means of enforcement of criminal law, and the nature of sanctions to be imposed. Law, in the eyes of a Marxist, is a means of exploitation of the true producers of a society, the proletariat, and therefore an instrument in the class struggle.

Capitalists, who dominated the legislature and judiciary, could shape substantive law. By selecting the types of behavior to define as criminal, the ruling class created prohibitions that enhanced its power while at the same time avoided criminalizing their own transgressions. Therefore, emphasis was placed on "street crime" and those property crimes that adversely affected the capitalists. In particular, deviant thought was criminalized, thus stripping political opponents of a claim to legitimacy. The genesis of crime, Marx and Engels argued, lay in the inequitable economic relations of members of society. The capitalist system not only increases the wealth of the owners of the means of production by exploiting laborers, but it also fosters a sense of alienation of the worker from the product of his labor by depriving him of a fair share of its market value. Furthermore, when capitalists seek to maximize profits through laborsaving devices, they create an army of unemployed. These processes cause increasing misery among the proletariat, including hunger and homelessness. Some members of the oppressed class resort to illegal means to satisfy their needs. In 1844 Engels wrote, "If the influences demoralizing the working man act more powerfully, more concentratedly than usual, he becomes an offender as certainly as water abandons the fluid for the vapourous state at [its boiling point]" (*The Condition of the Working Class in England in 1844*).[9] Only in a fully developed communist society could the major economic and social causes of crime be eliminated.

At the lowest level of society, Marx and Engels perceived a parasitic "dangerous class" (*Lumpenproletariat*) that produces nothing and survives by criminal activity such as theft, prostitution, extortion and beggary. This class of criminals was denigrated by Marx and Engels as the enemy of the working class, both because they lacked the capacity to aid in the movement toward socialism, and because many actively served the capitalist state as police informers.

Marxists were not alone in urging fundamental transformation of the economic relations of man. In part, they drew on the concepts of earlier socialists such as Robert Owen (1771-1858) of England, and Charles Fourier (1772-1837), Henri Count de Saint-Simon (1760-1825) and Louis Blanc (1811-1882) of France.

Thus, although Marx, Engels, and other socialists followed the Enlightenment method of analysis in utilizing reason to understand societal dynamics and in viewing crime as a secular phenomenon, the model they posited and the goals they sought represented a sharply divergent trend. For them the fundamental causes of crime lay not within the individual but within society. Because individual free will was significantly curtailed by economic forces, solutions to the crime problem involved a radical transformation of economic relationships rather than deterrence of criminal activity or rehabilitation of individual criminals. Nor would Marxists look to existing political systems to guarantee procedural protections for the accused. Where legislatures serve the exploiters, no reforms could be achieved. These concepts, which remained peripheral to the mainstream of Enlightenment thought during the nineteenth century, provided the foundation for repressive criminal justice systems in the former socialist governments of Eastern Europe and in the People's Republic of China.

Summary

The Enlightenment formed a critical point in the intellectual history of Western civilization, just as the national revolutions that followed in its wake transformed the nature of politics and society. As a branch of learning, the study of crime and its punishment was inevitably influenced by the writings of the *philosophes*, but it was even more profoundly changed by the new world view espoused by the Age of Reason. Stressing the importance of the individual's freedom of action, the new philosophy readily accepted reduced social control. Both the structure and the mechanics of government were seen as instruments for moving men and nations toward perfectibility; hence, the U.S. Constitution's redundant but characteristic declaration that it sought a "more perfect" union. Past societies in Western civilization had been communal in their orientation; they placed theology in the primary place of academic study. The Enlightenment, however, sought the growth of the individual, and philosophy replaced theology as the central focus of academic training. As the Enlightenment poet Alexander Pope would phrase it, "The greatest study of mankind is man."

In balancing the interests of the individual against those of the state, the *philosophes* emphasized a view of limited government that had worldwide impact. Questioning the legitimacy of absolute monarchies, they found virtue in political systems that gave the greatest protection to the life, liberty, and property of the citizen. Criminal procedure was viewed as a fundamental guarantor of the freedom of the individual; it was praiseworthy only when it protected the rights of the accused and secured no more than the bare minimum of security for the continuance of the state and civilized society. Basic to the philosophers' respect for every human being was their demand for equality in the application of all laws, not only the penal laws. This reflected their philosophical model of society, in which the consent of each individual was necessary to the legitimacy of the state.

Concern for the condition of human freedom also triggered thoughtful study of Western Europe's social and economic order. As industrialization widened the gap between wealthy capitalists and the laboring poor, socialist thinkers blamed crime upon repression of the working class. They viewed criminal law and enforcement as capitalism's instrument to sustain an unjust social order. Thus they sought revolutionary change within society, and they considered crime to be a byproduct of unjust and inhumane social forces. In this way Enlightenment rationalism generated two fundamentally opposed views of crime: (1) that it originated in human psychology and could be discouraged by reasonable punishment, and (2) that criminal behavior was caused by a repressive economic and social system. While Enlightenment thinkers stressed the autonomy of the individual, socialists analyzed the impact of economic forces upon classes within society.

During the period that Enlightenment thought ran its course, the American colonies of European nations began to assert their political independence. In North America the colonies of Great Britain rebelled in 1776 and built a new nation based to a large degree upon the principles of the Enlightenment. For them, the traditions of English constitutionalism, the rich background of European history, and the philosophy of the Age of Reason combined to provide a bountiful resource for the creation of a new government. The new group of independent states and the federal government were soon to provide the world with ample cause to admire American ingenuity and inventiveness in dealing with the age-old problems of criminal justice.

Endnotes

[1]   Charles Louis de Secondat, Baron de la Brede et de Montesquieu, *Spirit of Laws*, Thomas Nugent, trans. David W. Carrithers (ed.) (Berkeley: University of California Press, 1977), p. 158.

[2]   Cesare de Beccaria, *An Essay on Crimes and Punishment*, François A.M. de Voltaire, trans., 5th ed. revised and corrected (London: J. Bone, 1801), p. 112.

[3]   *Spirits of Laws*, p. 155.

[4]   Quoted in Adhemar Esmein, *A History of Continental Criminal Procedure* (Boston: Little, Brown & Co., 1913), p. 353.

[5]   *Essay on Crimes and Punishment*, p. 19.

[6]   *Essay on Crimes and Punishment*, p. 7.

[7]   *Spirit of Laws*, p. 159.

[8]   Many of these oversights in Beccaria's pioneering work were taken up by Jeremy Bentham, particularly in his *An Introduction to the Principles of Morals and Legislation* (1789) and in his later proposals for *Panopticon*, discussed in Chapter 9.

[9]   Karl Marx and Friedrich Engels, "The Condition of the Working Class in England in 1844," Florence K. Wischnewetsky, trans., in *Marx and Engels on Britain* (Moscow: Foreign Languages Publishing House, 1962), p. 163.

References

The most thorough treatment of the Enlightenment is Peter Gay, *The Enlightenment: An Interpretation*, 2 vols. (New York: Alfred A. Knopf, 1966). More entertaining, and a helpful introduction to the major figures of the period, is Harold Nicolson, *The Age of Reason: The Eighteenth Century* (New York: Doubleday & Co., 1961).

On French criminal procedure and its reform, see Adhemar Esmein, *A History of Continental Criminal Procedure* (Boston: Little, Brown and Co., 1913).

An excellent source of information concerning early theories of criminology is Piers Beirne, *Inventing Criminology: Essays on the Rise of "Homo Criminalis"* (Albany: State University of New York Press, 1993). See also Randy Martin, Robert J. Mutchnick, and W. Timothy Austin, *Criminological Thought: Pioneers Past and Present* (New York: Macmillan, 1990); Francis T. Cullen and Robert Agnew, *Criminological Theory: Past to Present; Essential Readings* (Los Angeles: Roxbury Publishing Company, 1999).

For examples of more recent criminological theories, see Joseph E. Jacoby, ed., *Classics of Criminology* (Prospect Heights, IL: Waveland Press, Inc, 1994). Contemporary views of the causes of crime are discussed by James Q. Wilson and Richard J. Herrnstein, *Crime and Human Nature* (New York: Simon and Schuster, 1985); a historical review of theories of penal confinement is provided in Part I of Norbert Finzsch and Robert Jütte, eds., *Institutions of Confinement: Hospitals, Asylums, and Prisons in Western Europe and North America 1500-1950* (Washington, DC: German Historical Institute, 1996).

For an extended analysis of Marxist thought, see Robert N. Carew Hunt, *The Theory and Practice of Communism* (Baltimore: Penguin Books, 1963). Marxist criminology is discussed in Ian Taylor, Paul Walton, and Jock Young, *The New Criminology: For a Social Theory of Deviance* (London: Routledge & Kegan Paul, 1973), Chapter 7; and Philip Jenkins, *Crime and Justice: Issues and Ideas* (Pacific Grove: Brooks/Cole, 1984), Chapter 5. Students may enjoy the introduction and accounts of individual criminals in Philip Rawlings, *Drunks, Whores, and Idle Apprentices: Criminal Biographies of the Eighteenth Century* (London: Routledge, 1992).

Notes and Problems

1. Do you agree with the Age of Reason's attitude toward penology, or do you believe that the rights of society deserve greater protection?

2. Can torture ever be justified as a mode of criminal investigation? Is current police interrogation procedure a successor to torture? Why or why not?

3. Montesquieu claimed that crimes against religion should be punished only by religious sanctions, that is, exclusion from the church or from its services and sacraments. If that makes sense, how does one handle offenses like blasphemy, sacrilege, and sexual immorality, if they cause public disturbances?

4. What attitude would the *philosophes* take toward what we today call "victimless crimes," such as adultery, fornication, seduction, and the distribution of pornography to adults? Does society have an interest that must be protected? How does one apportion punishment?

5. Some writers stressed the Athenian and Roman roots of Enlightenment thought; can you identify aspects of Athenian and Roman criminal law in their thought concerning criminal justice? Did this have an impact upon United States law?

6. How realistic, in your opinion, is the Marxist explanation of the causes of criminal behavior? Can you think of contemporary criminal cases in which the defendant has argued that he or she was a "victim" of social forces?

Chapter 8

The American Revolution and Criminal Justice

Colonial America's frontier experience combined with the momentous events of the English Civil War, the Enlightenment, and the Glorious Revolution to form a unique background for the growth of American nationalism. From 1763 through 1776, this resulted in increasing tension between Britain and its North American colonies; matters of constitutionalism, law enforcement, and political theory were vital concerns in the last decades of colonial rule. At the same time, the sense of being different from Britain moved eighteenth-century colonists in the direction of independence. That feeling was reinforced by the subordination of colonial economic interests to those of the London, Bristol, and Glasgow merchants who controlled Parliament and the Privy Council and, thus, America's prosperity. Constitutional debate also involved American subordination. The Crown and Privy Council insisted that the colonies were not to be governed by Parliament, but rather by the Privy Council. The colonists felt that Privy Council rule was suitable for "non-English" possessions of the Crown, but that they, as the descendants of Englishmen, were entitled to representative assemblies with full autonomy in the colonies. In addition, they sought review of judicial decisions not in the Privy Council but in the House of Lords.

Americans were quick to assert that they were entitled to all of the rights of English citizens, including those obtained by the Glorious Revolution. Indeed, they were willing to press constitutional debate even further, adopting into their rhetoric and thought many of the principles first raised by Leveller pamphleteers during the Civil War and Interregnum. In effect, Americans were contending for what would later (in 1867) become recognized as "dominion status" within the British Commonwealth of nations. Many colonists, particularly New England inheritors of Leveller ideas, wished to go further and establish republican forms of government that were virtually free of any British imperial control. The prized independence of New England town meetings led to a decentralization of political power within colonies, and innovations in civil and criminal procedure sharply limited the ability of provincial governments to deal with seditious writings or actions.

TIME LINE

The American Revolution and Criminal Justice

1696	The English Parliament enacts a stricter navigation law, designed to impose stronger controls on colonial trade and eliminate smuggling.
1732	The number of hatmakers in the colonies is sharply restricted by Parliament's enactment of the Hat Act.
1750	Pennsylvania's embryonic iron industry is prohibited by the British Parliament's enactment of the Iron Act.
1754-63	The French and Indian War, triggered by colonial incursions into wilderness territory claimed by the French, involves Britain in an expensive and worldwide war with the French. The 1763 peace treaty awards Canada and lands east of the Mississippi River to Britain.
1761	James Otis of Massachusetts argues that the British statute authorizing colonial courts to issue writs of assistance is unconstitutional. He cites as precedent the seventeenth-century English opinion in *Dr. Bonham's Case* (1610).
1763	A British royal proclamation prohibits American settlement west of the Appalachian Mountain chain.
1764-70	The Sugar Act begins a series of taxation measures passed by Parliament to help pay for governmental expenses and debts incurred during the war. In 1766, the colonies meet in a Stamp Act Congress to devise uniform action against another British tax imposed on newspapers, legal documents, pamphlets, and broadsides. The Stamp Act is repealed, but new customs duties are imposed in 1767 and 1770.
1772	The British customs schooner *The Gaspee* is attacked and set afire; despite an official Commission of Inquiry, the identity of the culprits is never determined.
1773-74	Tea ships in Boston harbor are attacked by Bostonians disguised as Mohawk Indians; all of the tea is dumped into Boston harbor. In retaliation, Parliament passes the Coercive Acts, which suspend civil government in Massachusetts Bay, close the port of Boston to all commerce, and authorize the governor to grant immunity to Crown officials prosecuted in Massachusetts courts.
1775-76	First and Second Continental Congresses attempt to reconcile the differences between the British administration and the colonies. They also coordinate relief measures to assist Boston and surrounding areas.
April 19, 1775	Battles are fought between British troops and Massachusetts militia units at Lexington and Concord; the British march back to Boston without colonial munitions and gunpowder they were sent to seize.

The American Revolution and Criminal Justice

June 17, 1776	The Battle of Bunker Hill won by the British against 1,600 American defenders. The attacking British force sustains more than 1,000 men killed.
October 17, 1777	British General John Burgoyne surrenders his remaining 5,700 troops at Saratoga, New York.
March 1, 1781	The Articles of Confederation, the first federal constitution, is ratified.
October 19, 1781	British General Lord Cornwallis, surrounded at Yorktown, surrenders his army of 8,000 troops.
November 30, 1782	The United States, France, and Britain sign the preliminary Peace Treaty at Paris.
1785-1796	Thomas Jefferson's revisions of Virginia criminal law result in lessening of harsh physical punishment for crime. Capital punishment remains for first degree murder and murder through poisoning.
1788	The new federal Constitution, drafted at Philadelphia in 1787, is ratified by the states. A series of individual rights and liberties is proposed by the ratifying conventions, and the first federal Congress sends 12 amendments to the state legislatures for consideration.
1791	Ten proposed amendments are ratified and form the current federal Bill of Rights. Limiting the power of the federal government, the Bill of Rights protects citizens against unlawful searches and seizures, self-incrimination, and violations of due process of law. It also guarantees freedom of speech, religion, and the press, and assures equal protection of the laws.

Divergence of the English North American colonies from their mother country was not a product of the eighteenth century. This divergence began almost with the first days of settlement and became obvious in the seventeenth century, even though Americans at that time remained dependent upon British economic support and military protection. In New England, Bible Codes were instituted, at times in defiance of English protests. Slavery developed in the colonial South as local customary law contrary to the common law of England. Throughout the colonies, Americans faced special problems involving the enforcement of laws across colonial boundaries.

What precipitated the American Revolution was the rapid growth of the colonies, causing them to rival the mother country in population and institutional maturity. When Pennsylvanians ventured into the iron industry,

British interests secured the passage of the Iron Act (1750) to eliminate competition with manufacturers in Birmingham, England. When hatmakers began to flourish in the colonies, Parliament restricted their numbers through passage of the Hat Act (1732). When colonial assemblies began to mature into legislative bodies demanding rights secured to the Parliament by the Glorious Revolution, British statesmen resorted to a series of legislative prorogation (adjournments) and eventually a suspension of legislative powers in the Massachusetts Government Act of 1774.

Growth in population and in economic activity brought about change in colonial criminal law. At first this caused a rapid acceptance of English precedents into colonial procedure and substantive law. During the early days of settlement, the lack of labor and opposition to capital punishment restricted the death penalty to the most serious crimes. By the eve of the American Revolution, death was a widespread sanction for almost all felonies in virtually every colony. Density of population in colonial cities, coupled with a shifting group of seamen and itinerant laborers, resulted in a growing urban crime rate that was aggravated by the rise of political dissent with accompanying riots and other disorders. Once, in the 1760s, New York City was rocked by a riot started by prostitutes who clashed with a group of seamen, which illustrated an economic grievance more than a political protest.

Faced with the explosive nature of colonial discontent, the royal governors took refuge in the law of treason, which was applicable to riots and uprisings that did not disperse at the order of a justice of the peace or a magistrate. One such insurrection took place in Dutchess County, New York, after the repeal of the Stamp Act. As a means of protesting the tax imposed by British authority, American lawyers refused to bring cases in colonial courts that required the use of tax stamps on filed papers. Many of those cases involved suits for the collection of rents due from Dutchess County farmers. In 1766, when the courts were reopened (and the stamps were no longer required), a flood of rent collection actions were filed in Dutchess County. Sheriffs and their deputies were beaten when they attempted to serve process, and the governor was forced to restore order by sending royal troops into the county. Suspected organizers of the riots were imprisoned and brought to trial for "constructive treason," meaning that, while actual identification of the individuals present was not possible, the imprisoned persons were constructively guilty because they either instigated the riot from afar or were very likely present when it took place. Despite strong arguments by defense attorneys, the suspects were convicted and condemned to a traitor's death of hanging, drawing, disemboweling, and dismemberment. Only a royal pardon prevented their deaths, although it is questionable if the ancient Tudor punishment would have actually been used in the process. This and other examples of the broad application of English treason statutes were destined to make a strong impression on leaders of the American Revolution who, by their opposition to the Crown, ran the risk of similar treason convictions.

TIME CAPSULE

The Trial of Aaron Burr

Few criminal trials in American history have attracted the public attention that followed the treason trial of former Vice President Aaron Burr. This sensational court proceeding was held at Richmond, Virginia, from August 3 to October 20, 1807.

Burr was charged with having planned a military expedition into the Louisiana Territory with the purpose of starting a rebellion against the authority of the United States. The charge was based upon evidence that he and several others planned the venture, and that an armed force for that purpose gathered at Blennerhassett's Island in the Ohio River, then embarked in boats bound for the western territories of the United States. However, the evidence indicated that Burr himself was not present on the island when the armed men gathered there, nor when they launched their boats for the trip down the Ohio. President Jefferson, warned of the pending enterprise by Brigadier General James Wilkinson, issued a proclamation condemning Burr's expedition as treasonable, and alerted the territorial authorities to arrest Burr and the men associated with him. Several individuals associated with the expedition's planning were arrested, and Burr himself was captured by a detachment of U.S. Army troops on February 19, 1807. On orders from President Jefferson, Burr was taken to Richmond to stand trial before the U.S. Circuit Court for Virginia. Blennerhassett's Island was located on the Virginia side of the Ohio River, in what is now the state of West Virginia. This meant that the Federal Circuit Court for Virginia was the appropriate trial court.

Under the Judiciary Act of 1789, the U.S. Circuit Courts consisted of one justice of the Supreme Court and the district judges of each circuit. Chief Justice John Marshall was thus the Supreme Court justice who would preside over Burr's trial.

Arriving at Richmond under arrest on March 27, Burr was charged with treason against the United States. A second charge claimed that Burr and his associates planned to invade the territory of Spain, located beyond the borders of the Louisiana Territory. In committing Burr, Marshall found probable cause to believe that the misdemeanor of waging war upon a friendly nation might have been committed, but he refused to commit Burr on the treason charge. Thereafter, on May 28, the Chief Justice refused to accept affidavits as evidence of facts pertaining to the case, and the court awaited the arrival of the witnesses. On June 13, in response to a motion on Burr's behalf, Marshall issued a *subpoena duces tecum*, ordering President Jefferson to supply the Court with documents in the White House pertaining to the case. In a lengthy opinion, he reasoned that a person accused of crime was entitled to access to all evidence pertaining to his case, and that even the president was not immune from judicial process. After a short delay, Jefferson ordered the documents to be made available to the Court.

On August 18, Chief Justice Marshall issued an opinion concerning the trial agenda. He insisted that evidence of an overt act be provided before the submission of any corroborating testimony or documentation was introduced. Following the testimony of the first group of witnesses, Burr's counsel moved to suppress further evidence, asserting that because Burr was not present at the time of the purported act, it was impossible to prove his participation. Marshall ruled that because Aaron Burr had not actually taken part in advancing armed conflict with the United States, he could not be guilty of treason as defined in the U.S. Constitution. Merely conspiring to oppose lawful authority, or planning to do so, was insufficient to sustain proof of treason. "Levying war," as required by the Constitution for proof of treason, required that the accused have been physically present at the acts that represented opposition to the lawful authority of the United States. Mentioning the Supreme Court's earlier opinion in *Ex parte Bollman and Ex parte Swartwout* (4 Cranch 75, 1807), Marshall rejected portions of that opinion that implied that one might be guilty of constructive treason if the individual participated in a conspiracy to commit treason but did not actually commit an overt act by levying war. Instead he stressed that to be guilty of treason, the accused person would have to take part in the overt act of treason alleged in the indictment. Following Marshall's opinion setting forth the law of treason, the jury, after a short deliberation, returned a not guilty verdict on September 1, 1807.

The Burr treason trial was followed by a brief jury trial of the misdemeanor charge—that Burr conspired to assemble a body of armed men to attack Spanish territory west of Louisiana. Begun on September 1, the trial ended on September 15 with a not guilty jury verdict. While the government retained the option of prosecuting Burr for events that allegedly occurred in Ohio, Thomas Jefferson and his advisors refrained from taking any further action against Burr. Hounded by creditors, Burr traveled to the northeast and then sailed to Europe, hoping to improve his financial affairs while living abroad.

Sources: Mary-Jo Kline and Joanne Wood Ryan, eds., *Political Correspondence and Public Papers of Aaron Burr*, 2 vols. (Princeton: Princeton University Press, 1983), vol. 2, pp. 1017-1046; Charles F. Hobson, ed., *The Papers of John Marshall* (Chapel Hill: University of North Carolina Press, 1993), vol. 7, pp. 1-142; Herbert A. Johnson, *The Chief Justiceship of John Marshall* (Columbia: University of South Carolina Press), pp. 124-131.

Questions

1. The Revolutionary War generation were well aware of the perils of constructive treason, an offense at English common law that considered all who had a part in opposing the government to be traitors. As a consequence, the U.S. Constitution specifically limited treason prosecutions to those cases in which the individual had actually "levied war" against the United States, and further stipulated that two witnesses attest to the treasonable conduct. Is it wise to limit the offense of treason in this way?

2. In demanding a specific order for the submission of evidence, Chief Justice Marshall shortened the trial of both cases. Should he have been more flexible and permitted the prosecution to present evidence according to its own preferences? To what degree should trials be efficient? Does a court violate due process when it allows the prosecution to determine the scheduling of testimony?

3. The Burr cases involved the request that President Jefferson provide documents that would be necessary for Burr's defense. This was the purpose of the *subpoena duces tecum*, which ordered that documents be produced and attested to by a person who has them in his or her possession. The president was not required to be available in person. However, in a later case, *Clinton v. Jones* (520 U.S. 681, 1997), the U.S. Supreme Court decided that a sitting president is not immune from civil process in regard to cases pending against him in federal courts. Do you believe that this is a wise decision? Would national security be compromised by requiring the president to sit through court proceedings? Should the rule be different for criminal cases?

Smuggling was a popular and profitable pastime of American business; a seventeenth-century royal governor once referred to piracy and illegal trade as the favorite twins of New York merchants. Among the more economically repressive British regulations were those designed to regulate colonial trade. Essentially, these regulations prohibited commerce with any of the non-English colonies in the New World and also made illegal any trade with Europe that did not first pass through a British port. The chronic lack of gold and silver in the North American colonies could be relieved only by trade with non-English colonies or non-English nations. In a real sense, illegal trade made it possible for Americans to continue in the British system of mercantilism because their most profitable trade was illegal. Britain's efforts to combat this activity consisted of extensive use of naval forces to stop suspected merchant vessels at sea, and searching on wharves and in warehouses for illegally imported goods. Searches and seizures became high on the list of abuses colonists attributed to the Crown, culminating in the famous Writs of Assistance Case (1761), when attorney James Otis eloquently defended the subject's right to privacy in his home. A Massachusetts Superior Court jury upheld the defense. Of this case, John Adams later said that, as he heard Otis speak, he could hear the beginning sounds of the American Revolution. Adams was quite right; from the American colonial experience came not only the motivation to revolt but also the legal and philosophical foundations upon which American law and criminal justice would be established.

Procedural Rights in Colonial America

The eighteenth century was a time for growing conformity between English and American criminal law and procedure. It was also a time for the development of procedural rights of accused persons. Building on the English Leveller tradition, American lawyers early established the right against self-incrimination. This right was utilized fairly extensively in the defense of patriot leaders during the opening years of the American Revolution and appears to have been generally available throughout the colonies as a defense against coerced confessions and oaths *ex officio*. Significantly, a compurgatory oath was used in certain cases of paramount social concern: in prosecutions for selling arms or liquor to the Indians, for entertaining or providing refuge for slaves without a master's consent, and for engaging in certain forms of illegal trade.

American colonial legislatures elaborated upon English experience and put their faith in common law juries as a method of safeguarding those falsely accused of crime. Typical of this concern was the 1731 Jury Act of South Carolina, which specified a complicated method for the random selection of jurors that was designed to eliminate the possibility of bias in selecting a grand or trial jury. The need for establishing jury trials became paramount in the face of two situations. Most commonly, it became an issue when an American was tried before a court of vice-admiralty for smuggling or other breaches of the Navigation Acts. Vice admiralty courts were established in each colony in about 1696; they sat without juries and increasingly were the tribunals preferred by royal officials prosecuting illegal trade matters. With the enactment of the Sugar Act (1764), a vice admiralty court was established at Halifax in Nova Scotia and given jurisdiction over all illegal trade cases that might arise in any of the North American colonies. Not only was jury trial avoided by such a measure, but American merchants were forced to defend themselves before a court located at a great distance from the scene of the alleged offense. Making provision for the travel of witnesses and the process of employing counsel was vastly complicated. In addition, the judge was unlikely to be influenced by the public uproar that frequently attended smuggling prosecutions in the defendant's home colony. These grievances formed a significant part of the Declaration of Independence's indictment of the administration of King George III: that he forced them to stand trial before courts functioning without juries, that were distant from their homes and from the scene of the alleged offenses.

The other occasion for assertion of the right to jury trial came in a civil case, but it was equally necessary in criminal procedure. *Forsey v. Cunningham* (1764) involved a claim for damages, resulting from an assault and battery, in which the jury had returned an exceptionally high verdict. Shocked by the amount of the jury award, the governor contended that the case should be subject to review (on both the law and the facts) by the appellate court of governor and council. Virtually the entire New York bench and bar opposed the governor in this matter, and when it was finally decided against him by the Privy Council, it was hailed as a victory for individual rights. What the case established was the finality of a jury verdict in civil cases, as well as the independence of a common law jury from subsequent reversal by a higher court. It is an important precedent because it demonstrates the uniformity of American public opinion concerning the need for an independent jury.

Closely connected to the finality of jury verdicts was American colonial insistence on an independent judiciary. With the Glorious Revolution, English judges were guaranteed continuance in office during good behavior. This had been the rule concerning colonial judges until the accession of George III in 1760. With the accession of a new monarch, English practice required the reissuance of all commissions in the name of the new sovereign. To the dismay of the colonial legal profession, the new commissions were issued "at the pleasure of the King" rather than during good behavior, thus making the judges more susceptible to gubernatorial and royal pressure. Many judges refused to accept these commissions, precipitating a crisis in colonial affairs. Although the Crown and its advisers did not retreat from their position on the tenure of colonial judges, Americans considered this assault on judicial independence to be subversive of their liberties as Englishmen. New laws and constitutions enacted in the post-Revolutionary years were to reflect their concern for a free and independent judiciary.

Another example of colonial concern for fairness in criminal procedure is to be found in an evolving right to counsel. South Carolina's Jury Act (1731) provided for the appointment of counsel in treason cases and for all persons accused of felonies where the punishment was death. While this extensive grant of right to counsel was unusual, even in colonial America, it did represent a significant liberalization of the English practice that denied assistance of counsel in all felony cases until the beginning of the nineteenth century.

Freedom of the Press

The 1735 trial of New York printer John Peter Zenger drew attention throughout the British empire and resulted in basic changes in the law of seditious libel. Over four decades later, the Revolutionary leader Gouverneur Morris was to term the case the "morningstar of that liberty which subsequently revolutionized America."[1] The Zenger trial established that truth might be pleaded as a defense to a charge of seditious libel, and it also demonstrated that common law juries could (in the appropriate situations) take to themselves the decision of points of law and issues of fact in these cases. After Zenger's acquittal, the colonial press began to flourish as a significant factor in provincial politics, and the censorship authority of royal governors was virtually eliminated.

Corbis Images

The Zenger trial established that truth might be pleaded as a defense to a charge of seditious libel, and it also demonstrated that common law juries could (in appropriate situations) take to themselves the decisions of points of law and issues of fact.

This *cause celebre* began with a dispute over the salaries and perquisites of the governor's office. After his appointment as governor of New York, William Cosby delayed his departure from England for an extended period of time, during which the president of the council, a native New Yorker named Rip Van Dam, assumed the powers of the governor and received the salary. When Cosby finally arrived in the colony, he demanded one-half of the salary from Van Dam, who denied that it was payable and also set forth a list of counterclaims against the governor. Political factions within the colony quickly regrouped in support of one or the other contestant. Governor Cosby decided to sue for his salary in the Supreme Court of Judicature, but Chief Justice Lewis Morris was a member of the rival faction. To protect his personal interests, the governor dismissed Morris and appointed James Delancey (leader of the governor's faction) in his place. The threat of removal convinced the other justices that cooperation with Cosby was the only way to insure continuity in office. They readily decided that they had jurisdiction of the case and, ultimately, awarded the half-salary to the governor.

In the course of these legal proceedings, the *New York Weekly Journal*, printed by John Peter Zenger but written and edited by James Alexander, provided a running critique of the litigation and the governor's machinations. The pro-governor newspaper, the *New York Gazette*, replied with biting satire, terming Cosby's opposition baboons, mastiffs, and assorted other insults. When the *New York Weekly Journal* replied in kind, the governor felt himself aggrieved and had Zenger imprisoned on charges of seditious libel. Only with difficulty did the administration obtain an indictment; two successive grand juries refused to return a bill against Zenger. As the trial began, public sympathy strongly favored the printer. His wife continued to operate the newspaper, receiving at the cell door Zenger's report of his treatment in prison. Zenger's lawyer (and former editor) James Alexander was early held in contempt of court and barred from the courtroom. Andrew Hamilton of Philadelphia carried the case to completion. Arguing that the jury had the right to decide the law of the case, and that truth was a defense to seditious libel, he drew the sharp rebuke of the court. Hamilton pointed out that a free press was the foundation of the liberties of a people, and he made pointed criticisms of the governor's arrogant disregard for the law of the province and the procedures of its courts. The jury found Zenger not guilty, and he was released from prison. Shortly thereafter, his press was kept busy printing the text of the trial proceedings, edited by James Alexander. A year after the trial, Governor Cosby died in office, still smarting under the humiliation of the jury's verdict.

The Zenger case demonstrated the vulnerability of criminal courts to gubernatorial influence and manipulation, but it also showed that when public opinion was arrayed against the administration it was impossible to secure a conviction for seditious libel. In effect, the New York jury had done what common law juries had done for centuries: it nullified the unpopular rule of law by refusing to apply it to the case at hand. The law of seditious libel would subsequently undergo a series of changes until, by 1843, both England and the United States adopted the essence of the Zenger decision. Thereafter, truth would be a defense to seditious libel and, in both countries, the jury was assigned the responsibility of judging issues of law as well as issues of fact.

While it went a long way toward securing freedom of the press, the Zenger case did not accomplish that result. As historian Leonard Levy has shown, the colonial legislatures were by far more effective in suppressing newspaper publication than the courts have ever been. By imprisoning editors and other opponents for contempt, the assemblies were most effective in stifling dissent. It was only as the United States entered the nineteenth century that press freedom was widespread and this necessary foundation for republican government was secure.

Fair Trial in Violent Times

Britain and its North American colonies were on a collision course after 1763. The end of the French and Indian War left the mother country with a large war debt, and the leaders in Parliament attempted to increase revenues by imposing new taxes on the American provinces. Colonial newspapers and pamphleteers raised verbal challenges to these constitutional innovations, but violence surfaced early as a symptom of opposition. Some of the rioting arose from genuine political causes. Trade embargoes against British goods were enforced by the threat of tarring and feathering pro-British consumers who ignored the prohibitions established by the Sons of Liberty. Boycotting British trade increased the number of unemployed seamen, longshoremen, and warehousemen. British troops garrisoned in colonial cities aggravated the unemployment problem by their moonlighting activities, which displaced native Americans from jobs.

As the Zenger case shows, it was not easy to secure a fair trial even in the best of times, and the approach of the American Revolution created a period of increasing uncertainty and apprehension. By 1774 most royal judges were sufficiently apprehensive of their safety that they did not ride circuit in the outlying counties of the provinces. When they did so, they spent a substantial portion of their time lecturing the courtroom crowd about their duty of loyalty to the Crown and the need to preserve law and order. Growing popular resentment against royal authority challenged the legitimacy of government and reinforced the growing crime rate. The transition of allegiance from royal to American state government was far from being either instantaneous or orderly. Yet, it was at this time of crisis that Massachusetts lawyers graphically demonstrated their loyalty to the principles of fair trial for all accused of crime.

The trial of the soldiers accused of the Boston Massacre grew out of a series of events on March 5, 1770. While the full details of the situation will probably never be known, it is undisputed that a single British sentry was stationed in front of the royal Custom House. A small crowd had gathered about him and he, fearing violence or an attempt to enter the building, called for assistance. Immediately, he was reinforced by a group of six soldiers, a corporal, and Captain Thomas Preston, who took command of the men involved. Shortly thereafter, the soliders fired shots; three persons were killed instantly, and two others were fatally wounded. Public uproar was such that the authorities feared the reaction of postponing trial, but at the same time, it was readily apparent that no impartial decision could be reached until tempers cooled. Captain Preston and the men were turned over to the civil authorities and held in the Boston jail. Although there were murmurs that lynching was an appropriate fate for the captain and his men, no effort was made to carry out this plan.

On March 6, 1770, the day after the Massacre, John Adams was approached on behalf of Captain Preston and the imprisoned soldiers. Would he agree to serve as defense counsel, along with Samuel Auchmuty and Josiah Quincy? Adams later recalled his prompt agreement to undertake the burdensome assignment that brought great risk to his personal safety and professional standing: "I had no hesitation in answering that Council ought to be the last thing that an accused Person should want in a free Country."[2] We can guess some of the sacrifices Adams made in handling Preston's defense. His co-counsel, Josiah Quincy, was required to defend his actions to his own father and to point out that no man should be assumed guilty until proven to be so.

Defense counsel were hampered by the circumstances surrounding the Massacre and their need to protect both Captain Preston and his men. When

Preston's case came to trial in October 1770, the defense counsel introduced evidence of self-defense that would justify the homicide and require a jury verdict of acquittal. They succeeded in casting doubt upon the accuracy of testimony introduced to show that Preston actually gave the order to fire into the crowd. After three hours of deliberation, the jury returned a not guilty verdict, and Preston was free to deal with the numerous civil actions for damages that had been lodged against him. Adams and his colleagues turned to the soldiers' case, which they had separated from the proceeding against Preston. Despite the separate trials of the two cases, defense counsel was presented with a difficult tactical decision. Because Preston had been acquitted, presumably because of doubts relating to the order to fire, would the soldiers be convincing before a jury if they advanced the defense that Preston had ordered them to fire? Preston's acquittal deprived the Boston mob of its demand for blood vengeance. At the same time, it increased public pressure for the conviction of the soldiers. Fortunately for the soldiers, not a single member of the trial jury was a resident of the city of Boston.

The defense of the soldiers depended upon moderation in introducing testimony on their behalf. While it was necessary to prove their fear of the mob, it was important that the sensibilities of the jury not be affronted by proof that attacked the peacefulness of the province or the conduct of its people. In part, Adams shifted the blame to nonresidents of Boston, suggesting that the crowd was largely composed of visitors from surrounding areas and perhaps even other provinces or nations. To all but two of the soldiers, the jury returned a verdict of acquittal; the two remaining were found guilty of manslaughter and, after pleading benefit of clergy, were branded in the thumb and released from jail.

The acquittal of Preston and his soldiers and the release of the two convicted men (upon their pleading benefit of clergy) caused considerable resentment in Boston, which, until the Revolution, held a memorial celebration of Massacre Day on March 5. Adams claimed that Preston left Boston almost immediately after the trial of the soldiers and never expressed any gratitude to his defense counsel. However, Adams never doubted that he had done the right thing in accepting a part in the defense.

Patriots, Loyalists, and Those "In Between"

If international war is hell, then civil war must be the ultimate in torment. The American Revolution was both civil war and a war for national independence. Within the colonies, it divided families against each other, and it gave rise to a number of marauding bands that operated in the wastelands between zones of British and American authority, preying upon the civilian populations of both areas. The Revolutionary War novels of William Gilmore Simms provide a realistic, although fictional, account of the inhumanity of these outlaw bands as they existed in Revolutionary South Carolina. All phases of life were in disorganization as a result of the war, and numerous opportunities existed for both violent and property-related crimes.

Well before the colonies declared their independence on July 4, 1776, the break with Britain had taken place. Military battles had been waged in Massachusetts, Virginia, and North Carolina, and provincial congresses in each of the colonies began the slow process of developing new forms of civil government. Of paramount concern was the establishment of militia detachments and naval units that would afford some degree of security against the substantial military might of the mother country. A lesser concern, but one of persisting difficulty, was the problem of identifying those supporting the patriot cause and expelling or imprisoning those who remained loyal to the Crown. This task was assigned to local committees on conspiracy, staffed by patriot leaders, which searched out and punished actions that undermined the authority of the new states. In the early days of the conflict, it was something of a legal puzzle to determine

Corbis Images

The colonies declared their independence in July 1776—officially declaring their break from Great Britain, although the process was already well under way.

who owed allegiance to the new states, but the immediate need of suppressing espionage and sabotage obscured the legal issues. Once the states had declared their independence, it was a simple matter to demand that those favoring the Crown must make the choice: either leave American territory, and thus reaffirm their allegiance to George III; or remain and run the risk of prosecution for treason, sedition, or espionage if their actions were contrary to the interests of the United States. Those who chose the first alternative frequently found themselves the victims of sequestration, a process that seized their real estate and personal possessions, then gave ownership to the American state where the assets were situated.

Not surprisingly, many inhabitants chose to maintain a strict neutrality, neither supporting the American defense efforts nor assisting the British forces. Some estimates place the number of "neutrals" as high as one-third of the total colonial population. Many within this category were peaceful observers of the suffering and cruelty that were the inevitable consequences of the long and tedious War for Independence, but others were ruthless opportunists who found the chaotic situation a perfect backdrop for all sorts of criminal activity. A vacuum of authority introduced a new crime wave that added to the hardships of the war itself; the war's impact was particularly severe in states like New York and South Carolina, where the British military controlled part of the territory while the remainder was occupied by American forces.

The historical period from 1760 to the end of the war in 1783 has been identified as a time when American culture became attuned to violent behavior. For many reasons this is an accurate assessment. Well before the outbreak of the war, colonists living in areas distant from the seaboard centers of authority found it necessary to take law enforcement into their own hands. Noteworthy in this connection were the South Carolina regulators, a group of law-abiding citizens who organized patrols and tried members of criminal bands and others deemed to have committed crimes. Vigilante activity became a necessity because the only available criminal courts in colonial South Carolina were at Charleston, over primitive roads and trails. Only after 1768 did upcountry South Carolina obtain its own circuit courts, and it was not until the end of the American Revolution that the courts and law enforcement were fully functional in the area.

Penology in Revolutionary America

Patriot leaders of the Revolution were hard pressed to maintain law and order in the newly independent states. Despite this, there was a growing sentiment for a change in punishments. In part, this was due to discontent with the continued use of British criminal law; in part, it was an interest in the new penology advocated by Beccaria and the French *philosophes*; but it was also a recognition that harsh penal laws do not, in themselves, discourage crime. In 1768, New York lawyer Robert R. Livingston Jr. (who would become chancellor of the newly independent state) wrote about a woman convicted of petty theft who was under sentence of death. Her execution was delayed because of her pregnancy, but would be carried out shortly after the child was born. Livingston stressed the harshness and inhumanity of a legal system that left the infant motherless. In the same year a fellow New York lawyer, Peter Van Schaack, contemplated the penal law of the colony and concluded with resignation that, "to preserve Society Individuals must bleed; to secure a reverence for the laws that connect that Society the Violators must suffer"[3] However, both of these young men must have suspected that excessive punishments did not deter crime. A 1767 notice in the *New York Mercury* described a hanging of pickpockets at the public execution ground, and went on to advise that as the hanging took place one man in the assembled crowd had his pocket picked.

Dissatisfaction with English penal laws existed throughout the American colonies and the newly independent states, giving rise to far-ranging reform efforts once the Revolutionary War was safely past. One such reform was Thomas Jefferson's early unsuccessful effort to alter Virginia's system of sanctions. Originally drafted in 1776, his reform proposal was subjected to extensive revision and finally introduced in the Virginia Assembly's session beginning in October 1785. Jefferson proposed to reduce the number of capital offenses to two (treason and murder) and provide terms of imprisonment for most of the other felonies. Specific deterrents were provided to discourage dueling, and many property offenses were punishable by a term in prison coupled with multiple restitution. To Jefferson's dismay, the revisers had inserted the *lex talionis* into the revised code, including castration for rape and bestiality, and maiming in retaliation for similar injuries inflicted upon the victim. In keeping with Beccaria's view that justice should be equally administered, the bill eliminated benefit of clergy. It also followed a principle of proportionality in the assignment of punishments. Commenting on the failure of the reform bill to pass the General Assembly's consideration in 1785, Jefferson believed that it was the reduction in capital punishment that brought about its rejection.

In Virginia, as in most of the other states, executive clemency and pardons were utilized to soften the impact of capital punishment, and gradually the legislative climate became more receptive to penal reform. In 1796 a bill following the general lines of the 1785 proposal was enacted into law. It limited the death penalty to murder in the first degree, which included premeditated killing and murder by poisoning. Other crimes by free persons were punishable by terms in prison. Property crimes were subject to both restitution requirements and prison sentences, proportional to the severity of the offense. Multiple restitution and the *lex talionis* in regard to maiming were absent from the 1796 law, as was the sanction of castration for rape and bestiality. Historian Kathryn Preyer's study of the fragmented criminal court records of post-Revolutionary Virginia suggests that the failure of the 1785 bill may have been due in part to the reluctance of the legislators to reduce punishments in a society that retained a high incidence of violence in its frontier areas. During the intervening decade, it became clear that the harsh sanctions provided by English law were not reducing the rate of crime and, hence, some experimentation with less severe penalties was justified. Another influence, not mentioned by Preyer, was the growing tendency in American jurisprudence to require, as a matter of due process, that the definition of crime and the provision of penalties should be a matter of statutory law. As a result, codification of Virginia's penal law was much more acceptable in 1796 than it was in 1785.

The New Constitutions and Criminal Justice

Independence removed the last vestiges of British control over American law. As a result, the several state provincial congresses set about the task of drawing up new forms of government. These governments were based upon written constitutions that carefully balanced the powers allocated to the three branches of government: the executive, the legislative, and the judicial branches. Suspicion of executive authority was the result of past struggles against colonial governors. Dependence upon colonial assemblies to protect the people against royal authority led the new states to stress the preeminence of legislative power, and recognition of the need for an independent judiciary insured an enhanced place for judges and lawyers in the new American republic. State autonomy, recently won in battle against the mother country, was jealously guarded, and efforts to establish an effective national government were unsuccessful until 1789.

Criminal law reform might have proceeded slowly, but there was an immediate need to protect the individual rights of the people against governmental oppression. The leaders of the American Revolution were heirs to the traditions of the English Civil Wars and the Glorious Revolution. They were students of the Enlightenment philosophers and knew about the barbarities of continental criminal procedure. They had experienced oppressive searches at the hands of the British customs officers; they valued the right to defense counsel in felony cases and the protections afforded by a common law jury. All of these factors caused these leaders to pay particular attention to criminal procedure and the rights of accused persons. In preparing the new state constitutions, they inserted special clauses extending the most necessary procedural protections, and limiting the power of governments over the lives of citizens. These clauses insured individual freedom and recognized the dignity of all citizens before the law.

It is significant that all of the states adopted written forms of government, laying the basis for constitutionalism that would emphasize clarity in the distribution of power. Constitutional debates over state constitutions, and over the Federal Constitution in 1787-88, were directed toward the way in which political leaders could be given effective power without allowing them to oppress the people through tyrannical use of the authority provided. The political thought of Montesquieu was particularly influential in balancing one grant of power with another, as well as separating the powers in such a way that one agency of government checked and neutralized the possible excesses of another. These new republican states rested, in fact as well as in the theory of John Locke, upon the consent and support of their people: consent given by their ratification of the constitutional documents, and support demonstrated by their sacrifices throughout the long Revolutionary War.

These proud and autonomous states were reluctantly drawn into a federal union by the realization that a loose confederation was inadequate to provide economic growth as well as sufficient diplomatic power. Ten years passed between the Declaration of Independence and the Mount Vernon gathering (1786) that started American statesmen toward framing a new central government. Fear of a new imperial authority resulted in the creation of a federal government possessed of limited and carefully enumerated powers.

Bill of Rights

During the convention that drafted a constitution for the United States in 1787, the need for a bill of rights was suggested by George Mason and Elbridge Gerry, but the idea was rejected. The absence of a bill of rights, however, became a focus of controversy between the Federalists and Antifederalists, and several states refused to ratify the new constitution until a pledge was made to adopt a bill of rights. In agreement with this promise, in 1791 approval was gained for ten amendments, referred to as the Bill of Rights. Included were four of particular importance in guaranteeing criminal procedure, which would protect the rights of defendants: the Fourth, Fifth, Sixth, and Eight Amendments. To insure that a specific statement of rights would not imply that it was complete, the Ninth Amendment was added. In the ensuing decades, crucial terms in the clauses have been expanded or restricted through interpretation in courts of appeal.

Amendment IV:
The right of the people to be secure in their persons, houses, papers, and effects, against unreasonable searches and seizures, shall not be violated, and no Warrants shall issue, but upon probable cause, supported by Oath or affirmation, and particularly describing the place to be searched, and the persons or things to be seized.

Amendment V:
No person shall be held to answer for a capital, or otherwise infamous crime, unless on a presentment or indictment of a Grand Jury, except in cases arising in the land or naval forces, or in the Militia, when in actual service in time of War or public danger; nor shall any person be subject for the same offence to be twice put in jeopardy of life or limb; nor shall be compelled in any criminal case to be a witness against himself, nor be deprived of life, liberty, or property, without due process of law; nor shall private property be taken for public use, without just compensation.

Amendment VI:
In all criminal prosecutions, the accused shall enjoy the right to a speedy and public trial, by an impartial jury of the State and discrict wherein the crime shall have been committed, which district shall have been previously ascertained by law, and to be informed of the nature and cause of the accusation; to be confronted with the witnesses against him: to have compulsory process for obtaining witnesses in his favor, and to have the Assistance of Counsel for his defence.

Amendment VIII:
Excessive bail shall not be required, nor excessive fines imposed, nor cruel and unusual punishments inflicted.

Amendment IX:
The enumeration in the Constitution, of certain rights, shall not be construed to deny or disparage others retained by the people.

The Federal Constitution (ratified in 1788) was sharply criticized because it lacked a bill of rights that would secure to defendants in federal courts the same sort of rights they were guaranteed by state constitutional provisions. In spite of Federalist party arguments that these protections were part of English and colonial common law, the Antifederalist opposition succeeded in ensuring that many states did not ratify until guaranteed the passage of a comprehensive federal bill of rights. One of the first matters of business before the Congress that assembled in 1789 was the preparation of a bill of rights to be submitted to the states for ratification. Added to the federal Constitution as its first ten amendments (1791), the federal Bill of Rights guarantees freedom of the press, of speech, and of religion; it prohibits cruel and unusual punishments and mandates the use of a grand jury and a petty jury in criminal cases. Unreasonable searches and seizures are prohibited, as are self-incrimination and demanding excessive bail. Echoing the Magna Carta, the federal Bill of Rights protects citizens against being "deprived of life, liberty, or property, without due process of law." Other procedural guarantees include the right to a speedy and public trial, the right to confront witnesses, and access to compulsory process (to compel the presence of defense witnesses). While these protections originally applied only in prosecutions brought under the authority of the federal government, they became the model for similar grants in later state constitutions. Since the ratification of the Fourteenth Amendment (in 1868), there has been a strong judicial tendency to apply many of the Bill of Rights provisions to all criminal proceedings, even those pending in state courts.

Summary

The era of the American Revolution witnessed the maturity of the colonial legal system and the rise of distinct American views concerning the nature of the imperial constitution. American nationalism and injustices within the British Empire brought on the break in American relations with the mother country, but the newly independent states retained the criminal law of England as well as English modes of criminal procedure. While there was a growing feeling that penalties for crime were too harsh, it was not until the last decades of the eighteenth century that American legislatures altered the English common law of crimes. Constitutionalism in the new states was based upon written forms of government, drafted with due regard to the balance and separation of powers. Virtually all state constitutions and the federal Constitution of 1788 contained bills of rights that set forth an extensive set of procedural guarantees in the conduct of criminal prosecutions.

Endnotes

[1]   Quoted in Vincent Buranelli, *The Trial of Peter Zenger* (Westport: Greenwood Press, 1975), p. 63.

[2]   L. Kinvin Wroth and Hiller B. Zobel, eds., *Legal Papers of John Adams, III* (Cambridge: Harvard University Press, 1965), p. 6.

[3]   Van Schaack Papers, Special Collections Library, Columbia University.

References

On the writs of assistance, see Maurice H. Smith, *The Writs of Assistance Case* (Berkeley: University of California Press, 1978). On juries, see Richard D. Younger, *The People's Panel: The Grand Jury in the United States, 1634-1941* (Providence: Brown University Press, 1963); Carl W. Ubbelohde, *The Vice Admiralty Courts and the American Revolution* (Chapel Hill: University of North Carolina Press, 1960). The role of the Admiralty Courts is examined by George F. Steckley, "Merchants and the Admiralty Court during the English Revolution," *American Journal of Legal History* 22 no. 2 (1978), pp. 137-175.

The latest survey on freedom of the press and seditious libel is Leonard W. Levy, *Emergence of a Free Press* (New York: Oxford University Press, 1985); still useful is Levy's earlier book, *Freedom of Speech and Press in Early American History: Legacy of Suppression* (New York: Harper & Row, 1963). There are two editions of the Zenger trial proceedings: Vincent Buranelli, editor, *The Trial of Peter Zenger* (Westport, CT: Greenwood Press, 1975); and Stanley N. Katz, ed., James Alexander, *A Brief Narrative of the Case and Trial of John Peter Zenger, Printer of the New York Weekly Journal* (Cambridge: Harvard University Press, 1963). The second version, although earlier in date, is superior in annotation.

For further information on the Boston Massacre trials, see Hiller B. Zobel, *The Boston Massacre* (Cambridge: Harvard University Press, 1970); the documents are printed in L. Kinvin Wroth and Hiller B. Zobel, *Legal Papers of John Adams, III* (Cambridge: Harvard University Press, 1965).

The standard work on the South Carolina regulators is Richard Maxwell Brown, *The South Carolina Regulators* (Cambridge: Harvard University Press, 1963). On Virginia's criminal law reforms, see Kathryn Preyer, "Crime, the Criminal Law and Reform in Post-Revolutionary Virginia," *Law and History Review* 1 (1983), pp. 53-85. On the Bill of Rights, see Irving Brant, *The Bill of Rights: Its Origin and Meaning* (Indianapolis: Bobbs-Merrill Company, 1965).

Scholarly work on pirates in American history is scarce, but the following three might be of interest: Robert C. Ritchie, *Captain Kidd and the War Against the Pirates* (Cambridge: Harvard University Press, 1986); Clinton V. Black, *Pirates of the West Indies* (Cambridge: Cambridge University Press, 1989); and Alexander Winston, *No Purchase, No Pay: Sir Henry Morgan, Captain William Kidd, Captain Woodes Rogers in the Great Age of Privateers and Pirates, 1665-1715* (London: Eyre & Spottiswoode, 1970).

Lawrence M. Friedman analyzes the post-Revolutionary period of American history in Chapter 3 of *Crime and Punishment in American History* (New York: Basic Books, 1993).

The perennial problem of defining and prosecuting treason is examined in Bradley Chapin, *The American Law of Treason: Revolutionary and Early National Origins* (Seattle: University of Washington Press, 1964).

Notes and Problems

1. What did American Revolutionary leaders retain from their English heritage? What did they reject, and why?

2. Trace the specific provisions in the federal Bill of Rights to their origins in the English Bill of Rights, colonial tradition, and lessons learned during the struggle with the English over American independence.

3. Why are free speech and freedom of the press important? Should they be limited in any way? Should government officials be protected by a law of seditious libel?

4. Why is a grand jury important? A petty jury? How do juries function in criminal cases? If you were John Adams in the Boston Massacre trials, how would you have dealt with jury concerns and emotions?

5. What influence did Beccaria have upon the American Revolutionary leaders?

6. Vigilantism is an interesting phenomenon just touched upon in this chapter. Is there legitimacy in citizens resorting to "self-help" when law enforcement is inadequate or nonexistent in a community? Who determines inadequacy? It appears to be the case that civilized society demands some set of laws or rules, and when the government fails to provide them, along with the means of enforcement, informal systems of law and police arise. This raises significant questions concerning the nature of law and the societal needs it must satisfy.

Chapter 9

Freedom and Prisons in the Land of the Free

American conditions before the Revolution sharply restricted the number of individuals serving prison terms. Most jails and prisons existed for the temporary holding of offenders, either in anticipation of trial or after sentencing and before imposition of capital punishment. Lesser crimes were punished by physical means, such as whipping, branding, and mutilation. It was not uncommon for the culprit to be sentenced to serve his victim, in labor, for a period of time proportional to the magnitude of the crime. In labor-scarce early America, imprisonment simply was not a wise use of human resources. Burgeoning enterprise eagerly absorbed lesser criminals into the workforce and at the same time managed to absorb the substantial number of English convicts who were exported to the colonies in lieu of capital punishment.

Lack of freedom was not a new situation in nineteenth-century America; the most obvious evidence of this was the existence of chattel slavery, that peculiar institution of American life that survived long after its abolition in the British Empire and Europe. The fact that slavery existed in a nation pledged in its birth to the equality of men generated harsh condemnation and launched a long and bitter antislavery campaign that ended only in the bloodbath of the American Civil War.

Another restraint on freedom existed in the practice of debt imprisonment. Those unable to pay their creditors in pre-Civil War America frequently found themselves thrown into jail until the obligation was satisfied. Once imprisoned, the unfortunate man was deprived of the opportunity to earn money for repayment. Survival depended upon the kindness and aid of others; the prisoner bore the responsibility of securing food, clothing, firewood, and other necessities. Jailers customarily demanded gratuities when these essential supplies were delivered to debtors in their charge. As a consequence, the longer a debtor remained in prison, the larger the debt became. In colonial America, imprisoned debtors were traditionally granted "jail liberty," which permitted them to seek work within the town limits. However, with the passage of time, this liberality disappeared, taking with it the last hope

Freedom and Prisons in the Land of the Free

1703	Hospice of St. Michael established at Rome as a reformatory for boys.
c. 1715-1774	English felons sentenced to capital punishment are given benefit of clergy or have their punishment remitted on condition that they be transported to the North American colonies. It is estimated that some 50,000 individuals were sent to America under these conditions.
1766	Beccaria publishes his study of penology, *Essay on Crime and Punishment.*
1773	John Howard becomes sheriff of Bedfordshire and becomes an advocate for an improved prison system. His study, *The State of the Prisons in England and Wales*, is published in 1777.
c. 1785	Pennsylvania adopts the solitary system of prison discipline.
1788	New South Wales, Australia, is established as a penal colony.
1791	Jeremy Bentham publishes *Panopticon.*
1813	Elizabeth Gurney Fry makes her first visit to Newgate Prison and begins a lifetime of relieving the distress of female prisoners and their children.
1816	New York's Auburn Prison is established and operates on a "silent" communal system, which encouraged limited conversation but group labor.
1821	Milbank Prison is erected in conformity with Bentham's architectural ideas.
1826	The New York House of Refuge is established for juvenile offenders.
1827	Elizabeth Fry publishes *Observations on the Visiting, Superintendence and Government of Female Prisoners.*
1833	Johann Hinrich Wichern establishes the Rauhes Haus for boys at Hamburg, Germany.
1843	A panel of common law judges provides the House of Lords with a report that establishes the M'Naghten Rules to determine insanity in accused criminals.
1840-1848	Royal Navy Captain Alexander Maconochie introduces collective responsibility and early release for prisoners on Norfolk Island off the Australian coast. He publishes *Secondary Punishment, the Mark System* in 1848.
1854-1862	Sir Walter Crofton, director of the Irish prison system, introduces the "progressive stage" system, based upon the discoveries of Maconochie.

of earning funds with which to repay the prisoner's obligation. Given the fever of financial speculation that gripped the young American nation, it was common to find prominent people imprisoned for debt. Robert Morris, the "Financier of the Revolution," overextended his trading operations and ended his life in debtor's prison. An associate justice of the U.S. Supreme Court, James Wilson, got into difficulty while speculating in western Pennsylvania land grants; his death while on circuit prevented an undignified debt imprisonment. In the first three decades of the nineteenth century, there was a campaign to abolish imprisonment for debt. By 1840, virtually every state in the Union had eliminated debtors' prisons.

Local jails were also the depository for the mentally ill, the aged, and vagrants. As the population grew and poverty increased, many people in various conditions huddled together in crowded, unhealthy, communal cells. Curious multitudes flocked to pay their penny admission, viewing the degradation of the inmates and the antics of the insane, satisfying their taste for the macabre and their need to feel superior. However, accessibility to the general public was to prove the salvation of these unfortunate inmates. Responsible care through workshops and apprenticeships was substituted for imprisoning vagrants. Dorothea Dix took up the cause of the insane, arguing for care and treatment rather than imprisonment and neglect. Private charities assumed the task of housing, clothing, and feeding the aged poor.

TIME CAPSULE

Criminalizing Idleness

Is it a crime to be idle? Is it a crime to be a vagrant? Long before the appearance of workhouses in England, there were attempts to criminalize these conditions. At least since the mid-fourteenth century, when the Black Death caused a scarcity of laborers, England had a policy of penalizing idlers and vagabonds. The Statute of Labourers punished not only the idle, but those who supported them:

That every man and woman of our realm of England, of what condition he be, free or bond, able in body, and within the age of threescore years, not living in merchandise, nor exercising any craft, nor having of his own whereof he may live, nor proper land, about whose tillage he may himself occupy, and not serving any other, if he in convenient service (his estate considered) be required to serve, he shall be bounden to serve him which so shall him require. . . . And if any such man or woman, being so required to serve, will not the same do, that proved by two true men before the sheriff or the bailiffs of our sovereign lord the King, or constables of the town where the same shall happen to be done, he shall anon be taken by them, or any of them, and

committed to the next gaol, there to remain under strait keeping, till he find sure-
ty to serve in the form aforesaid (23 Edw. III, c. 1, 1349).

If any reaper, mower, or other workman or servant, of what state or condition that
he be, retained in any man´s service, do depart from the said service, without reasonable cause or licence, before the term agreed, he shall have pain of imprisonment
(23 Edw. III, c. 2, 1349).

Harsher measures, including corporal punishment, were stipulated under Edward VI in
the Statute of Vagabonds:

If any person shall bring to two justices of peace, any runagate servant, or any other
which liveth idly and loiteringly, by the space of three days, the said justices shall cause
the said idle and loitering servant or vagabond to be marked with an hot iron on the
breast, with the mark of V and adjudge him to be slave to the same person that brought
or presented him, to have to him, his executors or assigns, for two years after, who
shall take the said slave, and give him bread, water or small drink, and refuse meat,
and cause him to work, by beating, chaining, or otherwise, in such work and labour
as he shall put him unto, be it never so vile: and if such slave absent himself from his
said master, within the said term of two years, by the space of fourteen days, then he
shall be adjudged by two justices of peace to be marked on the forehead, or the ball
of the cheek, with an hot iron, with the sign of an S, and further shall be adjudged
to be slave to his said master for ever (1 Edw. VI, c. 3, 1547).

Note: For further information on this topic, see C.J. Ribton-Turner, *A History of Vagrants and
Vagrancy and Beggars and Begging* (London: Chapman and Hall, 1887).

Each of these reform impulses combined humanitarianism with faith in
the perfectibility of man. Many of the leaders had strong religious convictions, and all were strongly committed to freedom as a necessary attribute
of being American. It was not surprising that reform of the prison system,
already under way in England and Europe, should catch the imagination and
engage the energies of American reformers. Within a generation, American
penal systems became a matter of interest to European penologists, and the
New World truly began to lead the Old World in regard to prison discipline
and architectural design.

Initial Steps in Prison Reform

Beccaria's *Essay on Crimes and Punishments* (1766) did much to provide a logical analysis of punishment in terms of its deterrent effect. His essay
did not address prison conditions; quite possibly, he had not inspected even

one prison or given thought to the impact of a term in a jail or prison. Had he done so, it would doubtless have occurred to him that prisons, far from being remedies against crime, were actually institutions that fostered and perpetuated criminal behavior. This situation was based upon the relatively late development of imprisonment as a sanction. Normally, detention in a jail or prison was a method for ensuring the accused person's presence at trial or to hold him or her until the time of punishment. Fines developed as alternatives to physical punishment, and many convicts preferred to pay a fine rather than face the pain and humiliation of physical punishment. Because poor convicts could not afford to pay fines, but were entitled to respite from harsh physical punishment, imprisonment developed as a reasonable alternative. Unfortunately, early governmental administration was not attuned to the prison system. All public servants (such as sheriffs, court clerks, and even judges) were supported by fees paid by litigants or petitioners, and prisons did not readily fit into such a format. Keepers of jails and prisons provided virtually no food or other necessities of life without payment; inmates and their families were constantly coerced for fees and bribes, despite the fact that many of the inmates were imprisoned for poverty in the first place.

Erected as humanitarian alternatives to physical punishment, prisons soon proved to be unsatisfactory. Inmates were kept in large communal quarters; men and women lived together in a state of depravity and degradation. Young offenders consorted with prison veterans, learning new tricks of the criminal trade to be applied when they were released. Overcrowding produced sickness and death. The most virulent disease was gaol fever, a form of typhus that decimated prison populations and, at times, threatened all involved in the criminal justice system. At the Black Assizes, held at Oxford in 1577, gaol fever claimed the lives of 500 people within a period of five weeks. Among the dead was the Lord Chief Baron of the Exchequer, as well as a substantial number of jurors and witnesses.

Rapidly rising crime rates in eighteenth-century England would have overwhelmed the existing facilities if it had not been for capital punishment and exile. Capital punishment became common for virtually all felonies, the harshness of the law being softened to a degree by the existence of benefit of clergy. Taking this benefit saved the lives of first-time offenders, but recidivists stood a good chance of doing their last dance upon the gallows of Tyburn Hill. In addition to the use of the death penalty, English judges usually gave the condemned criminal the opportunity to select as an alternative the option of being exiled to the colonies. Before 1774, a large number of convicts sentenced to death chose transportation to one of the North American colonies. After the American Revolution halted this involuntary emigration from England, the judges ordered exile to Australia, which remained a penal colony for the first four decades of its existence.

Despite extensive use of capital punishment and exile to the colonies, English prisons found it difficult to deal with the growing number of inmates. Hunger, nakedness, promiscuity, and violent assault and rape by fellow inmates contributed to a persistent despair and regression to barbarism. Until John Howard (1726-1790) was elected sheriff of Bedfordshire in 1773, it seemed that no one in authority was concerned with the inmates' plight. After his first view of the Bedfordshire prison, for which he as sheriff was responsible, Howard went to the local justices of the peace to request funds for the repair of the building and the relief of its inmates. The court demanded that he show that such expenditures from public funds had been made in the past. It was this question that started Howard on a lifetime of inspecting prisons in Britain and Europe. Publishing *The State of the Prisons in England and Wales* in 1777, Howard became the acknowledged expert on the evil conditions prevalent throughout all of Western Europe's penal institutions. Perhaps the most charitable thing that could be said about English prisons was that they did not contain an array of torture instruments as did the institutions in France and Italy.

Throughout his career, Howard was concerned with the design of prisons, with disciplinary procedures, and with meeting the physical needs of the inmates. Having been held as a prisoner of war by the French in 1756, he knew firsthand many of the difficulties of prison life, but it was only after his inspection of English and Welsh prisons that he reduced his recommendations to written form. He noted that men should be separated from women, preferably in different prisons, but certainly in different rooms. Howard noted that young first offenders should be separated in individual cells during evening hours to provide time for privacy and meditation, and that they should be put to work in communal workrooms during the day to earn their keep and to learn habits of industry. Sanitary conditions made a lasting impression upon Howard; he wrote that the reek of his clothing after a day in prison made it impossible for him to comfortably remain in an enclosed place. His notebooks and papers also smelled of the prison's air. To counter this, Howard recommended that cells be well ventilated, cleaned on a daily basis, and scoured with lime at least twice a year. Howard seems to have had little contact with individual prisoners, and his report is most valuable for the statistics and management recommendations it contains. Yet it is clear that he felt that prisons should not be the cause of unnecessary suffering to the inmates, and that some effort should be made to preserve their lives and to turn them into better citizens.

Expanding his investigations to Europe, Howard came upon workhouses established in the Low Countries (Belgium, the Netherlands, and Luxembourg) for the relief of the poor and the training of petty criminals in useful crafts. During his visit to the Hospice of St. Michael in Rome, he discovered an institution that used labor in silence as a means of ensuring both diligence at work and meditation about past offenses. The hospice was dedicated to the care of young boys convicted of minor offenses who would profit from the training. It was on the basis of his observations at St. Michael that Howard coined the term "penitentiary" to describe an institution that would serve not merely as a place of safekeeping, but also as a training ground in self-discipline and moral meditation.

Three years after Howard's prison report was published, Elizabeth Fry (1780-1845) was born into the wealthy Gurney family, which was prominent in English wool manufacturing and banking circles. Raised as a "gay Quaker" (a Quaker who adapted to worldly ways), Elizabeth Gurney married banker Joseph Fry in 1800. His stricter religious views, coupled with her contacts with Quaker preachers from America, converted her to the strict observance of the religious practices and behavioral codes of the Society of Friends (another name for the Quakers). In addition to household duties and caring for 12 children born between 1801 and 1822, she established a school for poor youngsters in her neighborhood and spent many hours instructing them in reading and other basic skills. By February 1811, Fry was recorded as a Quaker minister, giving her words special weight in the Friends meetings and authorizing her to visit other congregations and to preach to them. At the suggestion of Stephen Grellet, an American Quaker visitor, she first visited Newgate Prison in January 1813. In his travel diary Grellet recorded what he and Fry discovered:

> I found many very sick, lying on the bare floor or on old straw, having very scanty covering over them, though it was quite cold; and there were several children born in the prison among them, almost naked.[1]

These conditions were appalling even to male prisoners in a separate ward nearby. Fry's immediate reaction was to get flannel cloth, assemble Quaker women to prepare clothing, and deliver children's clothes to Newgate the next day. This initial contact was not to persist, and four years elapsed before Fry began her prison visits once more. Against the advice of the keepers, she gained entrance to the women's ward in January 1817 and began to speak to them about the possibility that she could educate the children. With their cooperation, she started a school in a portion of the women's ward, attended by the children of the inmates as well as by juvenile delinquents committed to Newgate. The school was an immediate success, and Elizabeth Fry's commitment to the women of Newgate was firmly established.

Unquestionably, it was the mother-child relationship that made it possible for Fry to so influence the female prisoners. The prisoners themselves were utterly

Sally Sisson Anderson

During the sixteenth century, prisons began being erected as humanitarian alternatives to physical punishments, but they soon proved unsatisfactory.

without hope. Maintained on short rations, subject to the ravages of gaol fever, and meagerly provided with clothing for protection against the harsh winters, they were also totally at the mercy of their male keepers and the male prisoners who contrived to enter the women's ward. Into this state of hopelessness Fry carried the message that their children need not suffer the same fate, but that through education their future might be made more promising. It was that hope for their children that turned the vicious and depraved female inmates of Newgate into a cohesive community working toward common goals. Their first step was to provide a schoolroom; this was simply one of the sleeping rooms, made available through voluntary acceptance of its occupants into the other rooms.

Passive cooperation escalated into active support when Fry discovered that the Newgate women were willing and anxious to sew clothing for themselves and the children. Organizing the Ladies Newgate Committee, she secured donations of cloth and began training the inmates in sewing. Eventually she decided that the women's products could be sold commercially, providing funds to buy food and other necessities for the women and their offspring. The prison laundry, used only occasionally during the winter months, was converted into a work room, and its products were sold in far away New South Wales (Australia) to prevent any competition with English manufacturers or laborers.

A year after her work began, Elizabeth Fry discovered that force and disorder characterized preparations to transport female prisoners to penal servitude in New South Wales. Placed in heavy chains, the transportees were drawn in open carts through the city of London and placed below decks in the waiting transport ships. The terror of being driven through the gawking and jeering London crowd, coupled with the pain of enduring heavy chains cutting into their ankles and wrists, made the occasion one of anguish and fierce resistance to the keepers. In 1818, Fry succeeded in altering the conditions, persuading the authorities to dispense with the chains and use closed wagons. On the day before the departure, a gathering was held in the women's ward, marked by prayers for a safe journey and an exchange of farewells. From that year onward, the transport of female felons to New South Wales was marked by dignity and restraint. From 1818 to 1843, Fry organized the loading of more than 12,000 women inmates onto 106 ships, and her presence and example caused the preparations to go forward without any violence or unnecessary suffering.

Unlike John Howard, Elizabeth Fry did not begin her work at Newgate with a view toward publishing a report. Rather, she strove to work at the level of individual need within the prisons. However, by 1827 her work was widely known and her advice was sought not only in Britain but throughout Europe. Only then did she record her experiences and recommendations, and her *Observations on the Visiting, Superintendence and Government of Female Prisoners* was published in that year. Her contributions and discoveries are noteworthy. Moving beyond Howard, she had found that hope for the future was a powerful tool in influencing the behavior of inmates. Dealing with women, she used the mother-child relationship as a means of securing cooperation and acceptance of prison discipline. Even in the case of organizing inmates for transportation, she secured cooperation through avoiding humiliation and unnecessary physical suffering. She ignored the pleas of jailers that the female inmates were degraded beyond the level of humanity and began the process of treating them as individuals who could be inspired by hope, for their children and perhaps even for themselves.

Prison architecture and penal discipline also drew the attention of Jeremy Bentham (1748-1832), who published his treatise, *Panopticon*, in 1791. The book's theme was that prison life should be characterized by continual observation of the inmates. To achieve this goal, cell blocks were to be constructed around a central guard tower from which the keepers could observe inmates at every minute of the day or night. Initially favoring solitary confinement, Bentham was moved by considerations of economy to support the grouping of a small number of inmates in cells, their assignment being guided by the probable influence they would have upon each other. Believing that work should be presented as a pleasurable experience, he opposed hard labor but encouraged the development of workshops in penitentiaries. A man ahead of his time, Bentham suggested that private contractors might be engaged to use convict labor, and that the prisoners be permitted to keep the profits from the enterprise.

Milbank Prison, erected in 1821, incorporated Bentham's architectural ideas. It did not follow his disciplinary system, because there still remained the option of transporting inmates to Australia or Norfolk Island, which lay off the Australian coast. Milbank served as a temporary confinement facility where newly arrived inmates were kept in solitary cells for the first few months of their stay and then gradually integrated into work in association with fellow prisoners. Bentham's proposals, along with the suggestions of Howard and Fry, were fated to have limited application in England because most convicts were either executed or transported to the penal colonies. However, the new principles they proposed were known and in many cases acted upon in the United States.

Pennsylvania versus Auburn

Established by Quakers in 1681, the colony of Pennsylvania reflected the Friends' strong opposition to capital punishment and harsh conditions of imprisonment. During the colonial period, productive labor was introduced in Pennsylvania jails, anticipating one of the prime components of future penitentiary systems. Shortly after the Revolutionary War, a new form of prison discipline, known as the solitary system, or Pennsylvania System, was developed. It relied on the total seclusion of one inmate from all others and only occasional silent contact between the prisoner and his or her keeper. The

Walnut Street Prison in Philadelphia was constructed to provide no visual and little oral communication between the cells. The only opening in cell walls was a small window, far above floor level, designed to let in air and a small amount of light. Prisoners were brought to the jail in silence; once they were processed, a hood was placed on their heads, and they were led blind-folded to the cell where they would spend their entire sentence. They were expected to work at crafts and produce furniture, textiles, clothing, and other products for sale, but all of this labor was performed in the individual's solitary cell.

Each cell was equipped with a Bible and a variety of religious tracts. These were designed to turn the prisoner's thoughts in the direction of reformation and spiritual development. In addition to the keepers, only chaplains were regularly admitted to the cells. The solitary nature of confinement was designed to serve as a punishment, but of equal importance was the emphasis on meditation and repentance. While silence perhaps did not seem harsh to Quakers who used it effectively in their worship services, it caused some frightening reactions in the felons imprisoned at Walnut Street Prison and at its successor institution at Cherry Hill. After extended periods of confinement, many prisoners began to decline in health and exist in a stupor; others became incurably insane. Despite these developments, advocates of the Pennsylvania System of prison discipline continued to favor it over other, more social forms of punishment.

Clearly, solitary confinement with reading of the Scriptures was preferable to indiscriminate imprisonment of men, women, and children in single wards. However, the effects on physical and mental disease indicated that some modification in the Philadelphia system might be advisable. This modified system was devised by Louis Dwight and the Boston Prison Discipline Society. After an initial trial at New York's Newgate Prison, an alternative to the solitary system was implemented in the newly erected New York State Prison at Auburn. This was the "silent" system, or Auburn system, as opposed to the solitary Pennsylvania regime. Under the silent Auburn system, the inmates were kept in separate cells at night and required to maintain silence. During the daylight hours, they worked in communal shops but maintained quiet because of a number of behavioral rules. Prisoners were not to communicate with each other except by permission of the keepers; their eyes were always cast down, and when the group moved from one place to another, they did so in lockstep, with the right hand on the shoulder of the man in front. Respectful behavior toward the keepers was emphasized. Breaches of these elaborate rules, which were designed to reduce communication to a minimum, were punished either by banishment to the "dark hole" (a wet, interior, unlighted cell) on a diet of bread and water or by whippings with the cat-o'-nine-tails (a vicious leather thong designed to tear the maximum amount of skin with each stroke).

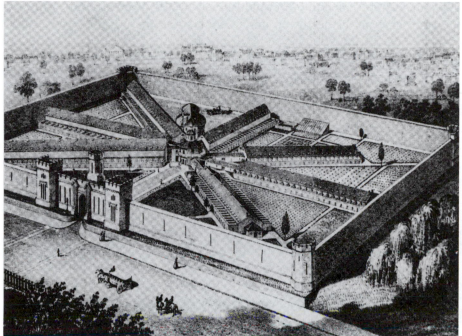

American Correctional Association

The Eastern State Penitentiary, designed by John Haviland and completed in 1829, became the model and primary exponent of the Pennsylvania "separate" system. The prison had seven original cell blocks radiating from the hub-like center, a rotunda with an observatory tower, and an alarm bell.

The Auburn system did not neglect opportunities for religious study and repentance. Chaplains made the rounds of the cell blocks regularly and, gradually, religious services were introduced along with Sunday schools and Bible study classes. As time went on, wardens learned that it was helpful to give prisoners times for relief from the strict discipline of prison life. On major national or religious holidays, a brief time might be allotted for conversation, carefully supervised by the keepers and warden.

European observers of the two American systems frequently confused the two, and even today's literature tends to blur the sharp distinction between silent and solitary imprisonment. "Silence" in the Auburn system was not complete silence, for ample opportunity was provided for essential communication. Solitary imprisonment in the Pennsylvania system meant virtually complete silence coupled with physical isolation from the world. Alexis de Tocqueville and Gustave de Beaumont of France, William Crawford of England, and Friedrich Demetz of Prussia made extensive studies of the two systems, and all preferred the Pennsylvania system because of its seeming lack of violence. Only Charles Dickens, the English novelist who visited the Pennsylvania institutions in 1842, disagreed. While he acknowledged the good intentions of the Quakers, he pointed out that incalculable damage was inflicted upon the inmates subjected to solitary discipline. Indeed, American penologists, except for a few fanatic defenders of the Pennsylvania system, came to prefer the Auburn system even after allowing for the excessive power bestowed upon keepers and the possibility of brutal enforcement of the silent system. There were also practical reasons for preferring the Auburn silent system. Penitentiaries stressing silent discipline were cheaper to construct than those with truly solitary cells, and the profits generated by Auburn shops helped to reduce the net cost of prison operations far more than the individualized craft activities of the Pennsylvania system.

In spite of the marked distinctions between the Pennsylvania and Auburn systems, it is abundantly clear that they both represented substantial improvements on the conditions described by John Howard in 1777 and those witnessed by Elizabeth Fry in 1817 when she began her work. Both American systems strove to obtain the inmate's repentance, both provided him or her with useful labor, both were concerned with physical health and well-being, and neither condoned wanton cruelty or neglect. What Elizabeth Fry succeeded in doing with the women in Newgate, American wardens were attempting on a larger scale with all of the prison populations committed to their care. Based on the pioneering work of Howard and Fry, American reformers and prison officials were taking the lead in finding new methods of prison discipline and administration. They were not alone, however; they formed but one part of a growing international movement to provide individualized treatment for prison inmates. They worked along with Sir Walter Crofton of Ireland and Captain Alexander Maconochie of Norfolk Island in developing new methods for influencing convict behavior.

Bringing Hope to the Prisons: Maconochie and Crofton

Captain Alexander Maconochie (1787-1860), a retired naval officer whose career had been cut short because of his departures from traditionally harsh naval discipline, relocated to Australia as a civil servant. He soon found himself in command of the penal colony on Norfolk Island. British felons were transported to Australia after 1788, but if they were convicted again, they were removed to remote Norfolk Island, where 1,400 of the very worst offenders lived in a state of siege, surrounded by approximately 150 Army troops and flogged at the slightest justification. Riots were frequent, and punishments tended to be brutal and brutalizing. Maconochie took charge of this settlement and instituted a mark system, by which each inmate collected credits for good behavior, exceptionally productive labor, or courageous deeds. Securing a certain number of marks obtained certain privileges, and, ultimately, a convict could reach the point that he had virtual freedom on the island and might qualify for conditional release to Australia. In addition, each prisoner was provided with a small garden plot, along with permission to sell his produce and use his profits to purchase whatever he wished.

This experiment in collective responsibility and early release was begun in 1840 and continued until Maconochie was recalled in 1844. By objective standards, it was highly successful. The convicts immediately set about earning marks and promptly began farming on their own accounts. The military troops maintained on Norfolk Island found little to do because disorder was rare and riots ceased. Among the convicts who left for Australia on conditional releases, very few returned to a life of crime. Most adapted easily to their new life of freedom.

Maconochie's experiment proved to be short-lived. His superiors disagreed with his liberating policies, feeling that prisons should exact punishment upon wrongdoers. Ordered back to Australia in 1844, Maconochie watched helplessly as his two successors applied draconian measures to maintain order. In 1846, a prisoner's revolt broke out and was suppressed with great difficulty. In 1848, Maconochie published his book, *Secondary Punishment, the Mark System*, setting forth his methods and their success with the convicts of Norfolk Island. While his experiment was both short-lived and probably limited in application to the conditions on Norfolk Island, it did demonstrate that convicted felons, and even multiple offenders, could be controlled and disciplined by a promised reward. Additional privileges or the possibility of a release before the end of a prison term were both powerful incentives toward cooperation and good behavior.

It remained to Sir Walter Crofton (1815-1897), as director of the Irish prison system, to build Maconochie's rough system of rewards into a comprehensive penal plan. Between 1854 and 1862, Crofton developed what became known as the "progressive stage" penal system. This plan involved an initial period of close, solitary confinement of up to nine months' duration, followed by a gradual lessening of restrictions and a moderate return to the society of fellow inmates. As imprisonment continued, the convict's tasks were increased in complexity, and privileges grew as the inmate progressed in behavior and skills. The key to the inmate's rehabilitation was the intermediate stage of imprisonment, where the tasks assigned were most closely related to gainful employment in society and the convicts worked without supervision. This intermediate stage permitted development of skills and habits of industry, and at the same time provided a test of the convict's self-discipline and ability to deal with freedom. Each prisoner released from the Dublin penitentiary had been carefully schooled by its teacher, James P. Organ, and, upon receiving conditional release (like parole), they were assigned to Organ's supervision. Organ not only kept track of the former prisoner's whereabouts and activities, but also was instrumental in finding each one of his charges some gainful employment and starting them back on their way to earning a place in society.

Crofton's system was a neat combination of all of the elements of penal discipline. At the initial stages, and with decreasing severity as the term of

imprisonment lengthened, it stressed punishment. For a considerable period of time, the convict was kept away from society, ensuring that the general public was protected from the criminal inclinations of the unreformed
inmate. Finally, recognizing that a time for return to freedom was somewhere
in the future, Crofton provided for schooling in useful trades and crafts and
a gradual social evolution from prison discipline to individual responsibility and independence. In this sense it was less lenient than the mark system
advocated by Maconochie, and it had the additional advantage of detailing
the steps by which convicts might safely be conditioned for release without
fear of recidivism (repeat offenses).

To a limited degree, American penology anticipated Crofton's methods,
even if American reformers did not articulate such a well-defined system.
Beginning in 1840, many states had enacted good-time laws, which permitted
release before the end of a prison sentence if the inmate had a record of good
behavior. In addition, Quaker concern for the reintroduction of former convicts into society had caused them to launch programs of aftercare for prisoners, a forerunner of today's aftercare system. Yet, even with these developments and a general knowledge of the work of Maconochie and Crofton,
the American states, by 1867, had not fully adopted the Irish progressive system of discipline, much to the regret of Enoch Wines and Theodore Dwight
in their *Report on the Prisons and Reformatories of the United States and
Canada*. Recognizing that prison overcrowding prevented application of the
individual attention required for Crofton's progressive system, they advocated construction of adult reformatories where the object is to teach and train
the prisoner in such a manner that, on his discharge, he may be able to resist
temptation and be inclined to lead an upright, worthy life.[2]

Their report heralded a new era in American penology, marked by the
heavy emphasis placed on reform of the inmate and his or her rehabilitative
education.

Houses of Correction and Juvenile Reformatories

The Wines and Dwight Report to the New York legislature has significance only because it linked rehabilitation to the situation of convicted
adult felons. It had long been the practice, in Europe and America, to use
retraining and socializing techniques with youthful offenders. Also, in an
effort to reduce vagabondage and unemployment, a number of nations had
used a form of vocational rehabilitation with their poor and idle classes. It
was the theory that if adequate training were provided, no individual need
be unemployed, and lack of an occupation was considered one of the primary
causes of criminal activity.

The first house of correction was established at Bridewell Palace in England in 1553. After listening to sermons by Thomas Lever and Bishop
Nicholas Ridley, the young King Edward VI decided to create an institution

to receive the vagabonds and those who were otherwise idle and destitute. Increasingly, the distinction was made between those who could not work to support themselves and those who, with proper training and the development of habits of industry, could earn a living. By 1576, the distinction was clearly made by parliamentary statute, and the helpless poor were put on the poor rolls of the counties and parishes; the able-bodied poor were assigned to houses of correction, or bridewells, for training. Early in their confinement, bridewell residents did the simplest and most menial of tasks, but as they showed promise, they were promoted to positions in which they learned skills marketable in the business and industrial community. Coercion was applied in securing the cooperation of inmates in the work of the bridewell, and the production was such that authorities felt that the bridewells were virtually self-supporting. Cloth-making, weaving, spinning, and ironmongering were among the crafts conducted within these institutions. Unfortunately, overcrowding and a decline in public and official interest had, by 1581, made the bridewells virtually indistinguishable from the prisons. Little actual production took place, and it was not uncommon for individuals who came to the notice of the local justices of the peace to find themselves in bridewells for punishment.

Established on the same basis as the bridewell, the Rasphuis and Spinhuis of Amsterdam (1596, 1596) were correctional institutions established for men and women, respectively. Designed to provide vocational training, along with punishment for idleness, both facilities began their inmates working on the simplest tasks and gradually increased their training as their skills became evident. The men's house drew its name from the rasping of wood to make dyes, while the women's was identified with the cloth production of its inmates. Both institutions were visited by European penal reformers, who brought the ideas home to their own countries and were responsible for establishing a number of houses of correction.

Closely linked to the rehabilitation of the poor and indigent classes was the question of juvenile offenders. Indeed, the initial impetus for the Amsterdam Rasphuis was the reluctance of the city fathers to commit a youthful offender to the city jail as a felon. European experiments with juvenile delinquents date back to the 1703 establishment of a correctional facility for boys at the Hospice of St. Michael of Rome. The inmates were isolated at night, but during the day they were kept busy in communal work marked by silence and frequent prayer. Punishment for infraction of the silence rules was whipping or solitary confinement. Gradually, the reformatory inclination of the hospice shifted to punishment, and the boys' house of correction was closed in 1827. John Howard, in the late eighteenth century, commented on the declining effectiveness of the bridewells in England and also upon the penal character of the St. Michael Hospice in Rome. It was left for a new century and a new generation of reformers to take up the task of reforming the treatment of juvenile offenders.

Swiss educators, following the lead of Henrich Pestalozzi (1746-1827), began to reestablish private institutions dedicated to the reform and training of wayward and destitute children. The first of these, Jakob Wehrli (? - 1855), brought the children into his own home, treated them as family, and taught them as much by example as by vocational training. The boys were involved in making decisions concerning the activities of the institution, and they took a part in administering discipline and in the financial management of "family" affairs. Wehrli's principles were applied on a larger scale by Johann Hinrich Wichern (1808-1881), who established the Rauhes Haus ("rough house") at Hamburg, Germany, in 1833. After his marriage in the same year, Wichern expanded his activities to include a girl's school in 1834, named the Mutter Haus ("mother house"). The children lived in cottages, a group of boys spending the entire day and night with a "brother" who was responsible for their work and discipline and who also served as a counselor and confidant. The routine was firmly established and included work interspersed with study and religious devotions. The institutions bore the mark of Pestalozzi's philosophy that love, decency, and happiness should be a natural, daily experience. These methods were so successful that they were instituted on a larger scale in Frederick A. Demetz' reformatory, Mettray, near Tours, France; and at Charles Lucas' agricultural colony at Val d'Yevre, near Bourges.

These European developments did not go unnoticed in the United States. In 1817, the New York legislature condemned the practice of confining youthful offenders in the common jails; by 1826, John Griscom was assigned the task of operating the New York House of Refuge for the reception of juvenile delinquents. The Boston House of Reformation was established in the following year and placed under the leadership of the Rev. E.W.P. Wells, and the Philadelphia House of Refuge was founded in 1828. By 1832, the Massachusetts institution was closed after charges that the discipline was too lax for a penal institution. It was not until 1856 that the Lancaster Reform School was established in Ohio, putting into practice the family methods of cottage living typical of the Swiss reformatories. However, the concept of correctional confinement, derived from European and English theories and practices, was beginning to have an impact upon American penology when Wines and Dwight prepared their 1867 Report.

Houses of correction for the idle and reformatories for juveniles were characterized by individualized attention. As Mary Carpenter, an English educator and juvenile rehabilitator, phrased it, "treatment should be according to the individual's need rather than being conditioned by the offense he or she committed." The stress was on the quality and adaptability of the offender. In a very real sense, this was preventive criminal justice, attempting to so condition behavior that future offenses were unlikely. It was in this light that the ad hoc contributions of Massachusetts Judge Peter Oxenbridge Thacher and John Augustus (1784-1859) deserve mention. Thacher hit upon the scheme of releasing young offenders on a recognizance; this was a legal procedure by which a judge could avoid placing a criminal or vagrant in jail pending trial. He stretched the rule somewhat in using the procedure to defer trial as long as the young delinquent behaved himself or herself. Similarly, John Augustus used bail as an instrument to keep drunkards, neglected children, and immigrants out of prisons and jails. Posting a bond for their return to court as needed, Augustus took control of his charges, found them jobs, and reformed their drinking habits and criminal tendencies. He made monthly reports on their progress to the judges in charge of their cases; when the work became too heavy for one man, the Boston Children's Aid Society, headed by prison chaplain Rufus R. Cook, took over Augustus' juvenile caseload. Judge Thacher's method would later be copied in modern methods for diverting first offenders from the full penalties of the criminal justice system. Augustus is known as the man responsible for establishing the system of parole and for serving as the first parole officer in the United States.

Insanity, Criminal Responsibility, and Penology

Closely related to the penal reform movements was the growing need to define the impact of insanity on criminal responsibility and the imposition of punishment. Before Dorothea Dix's successful campaign to remove emotionally disturbed inmates from American prisons, a rational approach to prison discipline would have been impossible. However, segregation of the insane from the convict did not remove the problem of insanity from the administration of criminal justice. The impact of mental disease had to be assessed to determine criminal responsibility, a key ingredient to prosecution for crime. An individual accused of a crime had to be adjudged sane at the time the offense was committed. Otherwise, it would be immoral to punish someone for something he or she did while deprived of his or her reason or free will. Likewise, it was unfair to prosecute someone who was not sane at the time of trial. This involved the due process consideration that a defendant with an unstable mental condition could not properly assist his or her attorney in preparation of a defense. Finally, a person convicted of a crime could not be imprisoned in accordance with the sentence until he or she regained sanity. Imprisoning a person who was incapable of understanding the conditions of imprisonment or the reason for the punishment was not only futile in a penological sense, but it was also immoral and inhumane.

Criminal law has always experienced difficulty in dealing with the concept of insanity. In 1843, a prisoner tried on a murder charge was released on a plea of insanity, and, in response to public outcry, the House of Lords solicited the opinion of 15 common law judges. Their report, setting forth the M'Naghten Rules, established the basis upon which future legal development occurred. The M'Naghten Rules provide:

1.   A man is presumed to be sane and presumed to have a suffi-
     cient degree of reason to be responsible for his crime. The
     defense of insanity must be clearly proved that at the time of
     committing the act he was laboring under such a defect of rea-
     son, or from a disease of the mind, as not to know the nature
     and quality of the act, or if he did know its nature and quali-
     ty, that he did not know that it was wrong.

2.   That if a man is laboring under a partial delusion, his act
     must be considered in the same circumstance, as far as respon-
     sibility is concerned, as if the facts with respect to the delu-
     sion were real.

The first rule set forth a standard based on the reasoning function, coupled with the ability of the accused to bring his or her moral judgment to bear
on the nature and consequences of the act. Significantly, it created a presumption of sanity and required that the defense undertake the burden of
proving such a defect of reason or moral judgment in order for the offense
to be excused.

The second M'Naghten Rule established a principle to govern the
actions of one who labored under a delusion, which is a belief (opposed to
fact) in which the person persisted even after having contrary proof. In
applying the M'Naghten Rules, the court and jury assumed that the delusion
was factually true and then judged the accused's acts accordingly. For example, if A believed that B intended to kill him, but B was innocent of any such
intent, A was not insane but had a partial delusion. Given these circumstances,
if B walked in the direction of A with a large hunting knife in his hand and
A shot and killed B with a shotgun, and if B were, in fact, planning to kill
A, A's firing the shotgun would have been justifiable as self-defense. Therefore, A's killing of B was excused, because he was laboring under a delusion.

Virtually all of the American states adopted the M'Naghten Rules in
deciding issues of insanity. However, as the nineteenth century gained new
insights into human psychology, the M'Naghten Rules were somewhat
modified. Specifically, the emphasis on the cognitive functions of the brain
began to be questioned as further study suggested that men and women are
not necessarily motivated by reasoned decisions. Was it not possible that,
although the accused knew what he or she was doing and knew that it was
wrong, the accused nevertheless was so overcome by other emotional factors that he or she could not prevent him or herself from so acting? This consideration led the Alabama Supreme Court in *Parsons v. State* (81 Ala.
577, decided in 1886) to set forth the *irresistible impulse* test. This added
freedom of will to the M'Naghten formula, requiring that, in order to be criminal, an act must be both knowing and voluntary. This division of the function of reason on one hand from control of behavior (volition) on the other
has fallen to the more recent psychological view that human personality is
integrated. Hence, it is unrealistic to separate mental processes into com-

ponent parts. Only about one dozen American jurisdictions now follow the irresistible impulse test in addition to the M'Naghten Rules.

The third test of insanity as an excuse for crime is the so-called *Durham* rule: that an accused is not criminally responsible if his or her unlawful act was the product of mental disease or mental defect (*Durham v. United States*, 214 F.2d 874, decided by the Court of Appeals for the District of Columbia, 1954). The *Durham* rule originated with the 1869 New Hampshire Supreme Court opinion in *State v. Pike* (49 N.H. 339). In *Pike*, the appellate court upheld a jury instruction that if the jury believed there was a mental disease (such as the one that the accused claimed to suffer), if the accused had that disease, and if the criminal act was a product of the disease, they might find him or her innocent by virtue of insanity. In effect, *Pike* treated mental disease as a force working upon the accused and depriving him or her of both reason and volition. However, its focus on whether the accused had a mental disease presented the difficulty of defining the mental disease and then measuring its causal relationship to the criminal act. These complications persuaded the District of Columbia court to abandon the *Durham* rule in 1972 (*United States v. Brawner*, 417 F.2d 969).

The weight of American law seems to incorporate the M'Naghten Rules as modified by the irresistible impulse doctrine of *Parsons*. In 1961, the American Law Institute adopted the following rule as section 4.01(1) of the Model Penal Code:

> An accused person is excused by reason of insanity if ". . . as a result of mental disease or defect he lacks substantial capacity either to appreciate the criminality of his act or to conform his conduct to the requirements of law."

Although mental disease is mentioned, there is no need to determine whether it produces the wrongful act. Rather, the understanding and volition of the accused are key issues, as is the criminality (right or wrong) of the act. The focus is on the mental capability and self-control of the accused, and not the probable manifestations of his or her psychological malady.

Conflicting views concerning what constitutes insanity are inevitable when the definition may relieve an accused person of criminal responsibility. Psychology does not recognize insanity as a medical condition, but it does classify a variety of mental aberrations that are adjudged abnormal. Some of these disrupt a person's reason and volition enough to appropriately be identified as conditions precluding the existence of criminal responsibility. On the other hand, crimes are behaviors that are so disruptive to society that sanctions are imposed to prevent their occurrence and to punish perpetrators of those acts. In a very real sense, all criminal behavior is aberrant, and thus might be viewed as insane. Understandably, the courts are hard-pressed to define insanity with enough precision that all crimes do not fall within its protection. Most men and women are criminally responsible for their actions; if they were not, civilized society would collapse. At the same time, there are a limited few whose mental disabilities make it impossible for them to have framed the criminal intent essential for guilt.

Summary

Reform of the penal system began with concern for the health and physical well-being of prisoners. As such, it was vitally concerned with prison architecture and the institution of a discipline that would maintain order but also ensure continued health and sanity. Slowly, prison industries began to develop, but before the American Civil War it was only in the area of juvenile reformation that work was seen as a method of rehabilitating inmates. Individual penologists experimented with individualized treatment of prisoners. Systems of early release, increased privileges, and gradual acclimatization to release into society were implemented. At a time when the science of psychology was in its infancy, substantial strides were made in positively influencing human behavior, and efforts were made to provide legal standards to determine criminal responsibility in light of current psychological knowledge. Yet for all their reformatory zeal, penologists already were struggling against rapidly growing prison populations and popular sentiment favoring retributive punishment. Reformers after the American Civil War campaigned through national and international prison reform societies, drawing on a growing body of scientific knowledge and statistics concerning criminal behavior and prison discipline.

Endnotes

[1]   Quoted in Janet Whitney, *Elizabeth Fry: Quaker Heroine* (Boston: Little, Brown & Co., 1937), p. 184.

[2]   Enoch C. Wines and Theodore W. Dwight, *Report on the Prisons and Reformatories of the United States and Canada, Made to the Legislature of New York* (Albany: Van Benthuysen & Sons, 1867; reprinted New York: A.M.S. Press, 1973), pp. 72-73.

References

The best comprehensive work on American nineteenth-century reform is still Alice Felt Tyler, *Freedom's Ferment: Phases of American Social History from the Colonial Period to the Outbreak of the Civil War* (Minneapolis: University of Minnesota Press, 1944; reprinted, New York: Harper & Row, 1963). A readable survey of penal reform is available in Torsten Erikksson, *The Reformers: An Historical Survey of Pioneer Experiments in the Treatment of Criminals*, trans. Catherine Djurklou (New York: Elsevier, 1976); or Bruce McKelvey, *American Prisons: A History of Good Intentions* (Montclair, NJ: Patterson Smith, 1977). An excellent scholarly treatment is Max Grunhut, *Penal Reform: A Comparative Study*

(Oxford: The Clarendon Press, 1948; reprint, Montclair, NJ: Patterson Smith, 1972). An old survey containing interesting materials from ancient times to the early twentieth century is in George Ives, *A History of Penal Methods* (London: Hutchinson Publishing Company, 1914; reprint, Montclair, NJ: Patterson Smith, 1970).

Among the multitude of specialized studies, the student will profit from consulting Harry E. Barnes, *The Evolution of Penology in Pennsylvania: A Study in American Social History* (Indianapolis: Bobbs-Merrill & Co., 1927; reprint, Montclair, NJ: Patterson Smith, 1968); Mary Carpenter, *Reformatory Prison Discipline as Developed by the Rt. Hon. Sir. Walter Crofton in the Irish Convict Prisons* (London: Longmans, Greeb, Reader & Dyer, 1872); Mary Carpenter, *Juvenile Delinquents: Their Condition and Treatment* (London: W. & F.G. Cash, 1853; reprint, Montclair, NJ: Patterson Smith, 1970); Derek L. Howard, *John Howard: Prison Reformer* (London: Christopher Johnson, 1958); John Howard, *The State of the Prisons in England and Wales* (Warrington: William Eyres, 1777; reprint, Abingdon, Oxfordshire: Professional Books, 1977); Norman Johnston, *The Human Cage: A Brief History of Prison Architecture* (New York: Walker, 1973); W. David Lewis, *From Newgate to Dannemora: The Rise of the Penitentiary in New York, 1796-1848* (Ithaca: Cornell University Press, 1965); Janet Whitney, *Elizabeth Fry: Quaker Heroine* (Boston: Little, Brown & Co., 1937); Enoch C. Wines and Theodore W. Dwight, *Report on the Prisons and Reformatories of the United States and Canada made to the Legislature of New York, January 1867* (Albany: Van Benthuysen & Sons, 1867; reprint, New York: AMS Press, Inc., 1973).

There is an abundance of material on the insanity defense. Students will find Donald H.J. Hermann, *The Insanity Defense: Philosophical, Historical and Legal Perspectives* (Springfield, IL: Charles C Thomas, 1983) a good introduction. Herbert Fingarette, *The Meaning of Criminal Insanity* (Berkeley: University of California Press, 1972) provides a detailed analysis and has an excellent bibliography; see also Herbert Fingarette and Ann Fingarette Hasse, *Mental Disabilities and Criminal Responsibility* (Berkeley: University of California Press, 1979). Helpful in regard to due process for the mentally disturbed defendant is Ronald Roesch and Stephen L. Golding, *Competency to Stand Trial* (Urbana: University of Illinois Press, 1980).

Two recent publications analyze English incarceration policy: Peter Linebaugh, *The London Hanged: Crime and Civil Society in the Eighteenth Century* (Cambridge: Cambridge University Press, 1992); and Lucia Zedner, *Women, Crime, and Custody in Victorian England* (Oxford: Oxford University Press, 1994); see also Philip Priestley, *Victorial Prison Lives: English Prison Biography: 1830-1914* (New York: Methuen & Co., 1985); Charles Campbell, *The Intolerable Hulks: British Shipboard Confinement, 1776-1857* (Bowie, MD: Heritage Books, 1994). The background of juvenile crime is traced in "Children and Their Offenses in History," in Arnold Binder, Gilbert Geis, and Dickson Bruce, *Juvenile Delinquency: Historical, Cultural, Legal Perspectives* (New York: Macmillan Publishing Company, 1988).

Changing penal policy in post-Revolutionary Massachusetts is explored in Linda Kealey, "Patterns of Punishment: Massachusetts in the Eighteenth Century," *American Journal of Legal History* 30 (1986), pp. 163-186; David J. Rothman, *The Discovery of the Asylum; Social Order and Disorder in the New Republic* (Boston: Little, Brown & Co., 1971); and Adam Jay Hirsch, *Prisons and Punishment in Early America* (New Haven: Yale University Press, 1992). An extensive, though somewhat dated, bibliography regarding American penology is that of Alexander W. Pisciotta, "Corrections, Society, and Social Control in America: A Metahistorical Review of the Literature," *Criminal Justice History*, 2 (1981), pp. 109-130.

Regarding juvenile detention in twentieth-century America, see Edmund F. McGarrell, *Juvenile Correctional Reform: Two Decades of Policy and Procedural Change* (Albany: State University of New York Press, 1988).

Notes and Problems

1. It is interesting to trace the role of religion and Enlightenment philosophy in nineteenth-century penal reform. Certainly scientific thought, such as it was, played a significant part in reform thinking, but religious zeal supplied the personnel and much of the motivation for prison improvement and new methods of dealing with juveniles and adult prisoners. If you had to decide which influence was paramount, which would you choose?

2. Can imprisonment be made rehabilitative and restorative without arousing public hostility on the basis that it is too lenient?

3. Is it possible to influence behavior once a convicted felon has served his or her time and been returned to society? Clearly it is possible through hope for early release, and through granting or withholding privileges, to greatly control conduct while in prison. But what will happen after release if there is no ongoing control in the terms of a conditional release or a parole system?

4. The nineteenth-century advocates of houses of correction, juvenile reformatories and penitentiaries argued that gaining skills would make convicts employable. Is that true, even in a high unemployment area of the country?

5. Compare and contrast the Pennsylvania and Auburn systems of prison discipline. Is solitude preferable to violence from fellow prisoners? Can either of these systems be considered rehabilitative?

Chapter 10

Early Nineteenth-Century Law Enforcement

Increased concern with law enforcement went hand-in-hand with prison reform in Western Europe and the new American republic. The emergence of national states centralized efforts for the prevention, detection, and prosecution of crime. At the same time, long-established cultural influences shaped the way in which police forces were established and how they functioned. In this chapter we will consider two European systems: those of France and England. Then we will focus upon the variety of American policing systems that functioned in various sections of the United States. Clearly, American practices modeled, but did not duplicate, those of England, and many characteristics of the French system were influential in the United States. Criminal law enforcement in the western democracies today still reflects the divergence of French and other European systems from those of Britain and the United States.

This variance between France and England began with the Norman Conquest. Although the French tendency toward a national policing system was within the Roman tradition, and thus preceded the conquest, William I and his successors elected to continue the Anglo-Saxon system of self-policing in their new island kingdom. Possibly it was felt that such an invasive, repressive, and expensive police policy was not necessary in a land less susceptible to chronic political instability.

For whatever reason, French law enforcement developments during the succeeding centuries caused little change in English methods of policing. In fact, only one major alteration had taken place in English police activities since the time of William the Conqueror, when local hundreds bore the full responsibility for policing their members. From about 1285 to the middle of the fourteenth century, a system of justices of the peace, supplemented by parish constables, was established under royal auspices. It was this system of justices of the peace (called magistrates in some American colonies and states) and constables that served both England and the United States before 1829.[1] While this system lacked efficiency and any significant amount of power, it did maintain some order in societies where ideals were shared and

TIME LINE

England	Europe	North America
	1066 Local hundreds (towns, villages) responsible for policing	
Justices of the peace and constables appointed for law enforcement duties	**1285** France continues Roman system	
Charles II restored to the English and Scottish thrones	**c. 1660** Centralized royal policing under Louis XIV	Justices of the peace (magistrates) police the colonies
	1699 Royal lieutenants-general of police established for French cities	
	c. 1700	Southern colonies establish slave patrols
Bow Street magistrate's post occupied by Sir Thomas DeVeil and Henry Fielding	**1730-1754**	
	1776	U.S. Declaration of Independence
Thames Police Act passed	**1800**	
	1808-1810 French Codes of Criminal Instruction and Penal Code adopted under Napoleon I	
	1815 Congress of Vienna formalizes the end of the Napoleonic Wars	
London Metropolitan Police ("bobbies") established	**1829**	

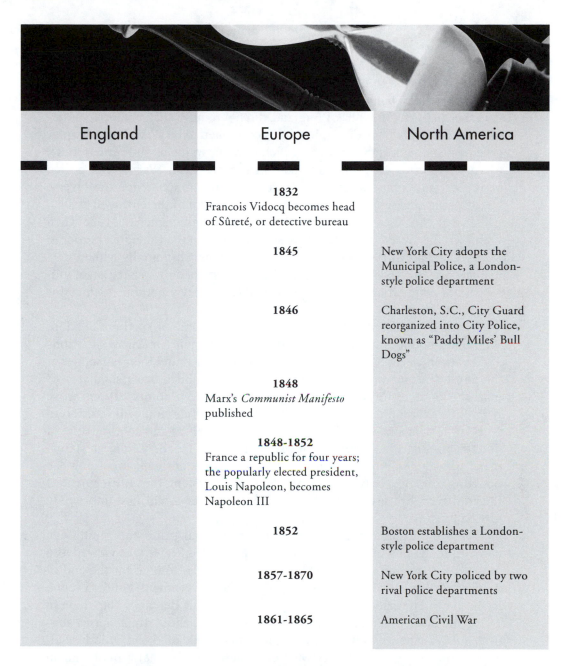

England	Europe	North America
	1832 Francois Vidocq becomes head of Sûreté, or detective bureau	
	1845	New York City adopts the Municipal Police, a London-style police department
	1846	Charleston, S.C., City Guard reorganized into City Police, known as "Paddy Miles' Bull Dogs"
	1848 Marx's *Communist Manifesto* published	
	1848-1852 France a republic for four years; the popularly elected president, Louis Napoleon, becomes Napoleon III	
	1852	Boston establishes a London-style police department
	1857-1870	New York City policed by two rival police departments
	1861-1865	American Civil War

class distinctions caused deferential obedience rather than conflict. A system perfectly attuned to the moderate law enforcement needs of an agrarian and manorial society, the justice/constable organization was more than adequate in early America.

After 1800, the United States was faced with law enforcement problems brought on by increased urbanization and industrial expansion. A growing tide of European immigration generated population pressure in the cities of the Northeast and Midwest; this immigration generated cultural and religious tensions between the new arrivals and native residents. American problems had earlier been faced in England, and in 1829 the London system of law enforcement was altered to establish a Metropolitan Police Department that served as a model for other British municipalities as well as for American cities. Of course, the rural areas of the northern United States, like the farm and grazing lands of England, did not require such elaborate policing arrangements. Those rural localities continued to be served by a simpler type of justice/constable system, which remains in place throughout much of rural America at the present day. In the pre-Civil War South, police activities and organization were influenced by the existence of slavery. Urban areas made careful provisions for the control of the enslaved blacks, while rural areas used slave patrols and local plantation-centered justice. Then there was the West—a vast territory stretching from the Canadian border to Mexico, and pressing onward to the Pacific. A land substantially without formal law, the frontier of the United States was seen not only as a region of violence and crime, but also as a place where society's natural instinct for justice, order, and humanity was triumphant.

While urban areas in the East and Midwest found it expedient to adopt the London police system, with modifications to suit American situations and tastes, men and women on the western frontier found their law either at the point of a gun or in the pragmatic need to establish basic standards of behavior in order for a settlement to survive. Further complications arose from the uncertainties concerning the nature and function of law enforcement in a democratic society. Some issues, such as the relationship of police activities to military dictatorship, had been faced by English statesmen. However, many problems were distinctly American, involving the operation of police activities within the federal system, the enforcement of the fugitive slave laws, and the introduction of criminal law into newly settled territories.

For Americans, these were matters of national pride and republican conviction. As one of the first republics, the United States was viewed as a model for the peoples of Europe and the world who longed for the end of monarchical rule and the institution of popular government. Yet the French Republic had reverted to a monarchy even before the defeat of Napoleon in 1815, and widespread disorder in the United States and Latin America suggested that anarchy was the only alternative to the rule of kings. Orderly societies and economic prosperity were convincing proofs that republicanism could survive as an effective and permanent system of government. The rapid growth of the United States, in terms of population, immigration, and economic development, made it increasingly more difficult to control the violence and criminality inherent in a changing and diversifying culture.

Examination of the policing system that had developed in England during the seventeenth and eighteenth centuries, and those of continental countries such as France, reveals fundamental differences. France, prior to the Norman Conquest, already manifested tendencies toward a national policing system in the Roman tradition, whereas England continued to rely on the principle of community self-policing that had prevailed in the Anglo-Saxon period. Although cause cannot always be distinguished from effect, it is likely that the chronic political instability in France was responsible for the invasive, even repressive, police policies characteristic of this period. Unlike English police, whose main duty was enforcement of criminal law, French police were also accorded a wide range of responsibilities that were assigned to the administrative realm in England. The divergence in policing systems was intensified during the political upheavals of the eighteenth and nineteenth centuries in France.

Nationalized Policing in France

The seeds of the centralized French police system were planted during the reign of Louis XIV (1643-1715). Capitalizing on the doctrine of the divine right of kings, he sought to overcome the patchwork of customary laws and lax police administration that had existed in France for centuries. Because of traditional aristocratic privileges and immunities, the first two estates (the clergy of the Catholic Church and the nobility) exercised considerable police power independently of the king and often to the disadvantage of the bourgeoisie, peasants, and urban workers. To subordinate the nobility and the Catholic Church, Louis XIV boldly modified their role in law enforcement. The traditional right of the nobility to enforce the law and to hold manorial court was undermined by a series of royal decrees during the 1660s. Additionally, Louis XIV separated the operations of high courts of France (the parlements) from those of the police, and appointed royal judges to serve in feudal courts.

Domestic tranquility was further enhanced by his bringing the military forces under royal control and by developing an organized system of police authorities. To subordinate the army to his will, Louis XIV transformed the old military system, which had relied on feudal levies and privately generated troops, into a modern army paid by the royal government and owing allegiance only to the king. One immediate civil benefit was the military police (provost corps), who were utilized to provide security along highways in rural areas of France. Although members of the army could not always be counted on to be loyal to the king, the army proved to be an effective instrument for civic order in times of domestic crisis, such as during the series of revolutions that shook France over the next century.

These reforms brought policing directly under royal authority and established a police system that was separate from the judiciary and independent from the control of other political leaders. The policing administration of Paris served as a model for other areas of the country. In the edict by which Louis XIV established the office of Lieutenant of Police for Paris, there is set forth the broad meaning of the term "police," which has continued to dis-

tinguish the French term from its narrower use in the context of English policing. Responsibilities of the lieutenant of police included, in addition to the
usual law enforcement roles, such diverse activities as supervising markets,
inspecting food and wine, press censorship, repairing municipal drainage,
constructing roads, establishing hospitals and schools for poor children, sur-
veilling foreigners, arresting blasphemers and sorcerers, directing fire-
fighting, coping with natural disasters such as floods, monitoring market-
places, and inspecting prisons. This comprehensive grant of police power
encompassed virtually all of the functions of modern local government in
the United States. However, in Louis XIV's France the power was not
shared, but entrusted to one man.

In addition to extensive duties regarding public welfare, the Lieutenant
of Police of Paris and certain police officials served as criminal judges in the
Châtelet, the center of royal police authority until the revolution. In the rest
of France, royal supervision was exercised by the Intendants who had been
established by Cardinal Richelieu in the reign of Louis XIV's predecessor.
In each of the 30 provinces of France, an Intendant of Justice, Police, and
Finance linked the crown and local government.

Jean-Baptiste Colbert (Minister of Finance under Louis XIV) nation-
alized the local police forces of France. Municipalities that had self-rule charters earlier had established police forces, but in 1699 the office of Lieutenant-
General of Police was instituted by royal decree for each of the major cities.
Because policies of the Lieutenant-General of Paris were binding on the
municipal lieutenants, there was thus some hierarchical structure to the
policing system. Later, Louis XIV established the position of Police Commissioner; appointees had limited judicial power and served under each of
the municipal Lieutenants-General.

As Lieutenant-General of Police, Marc-René Levoyer de Paulmy, Marquis d'Argenson, developed an effective espionage network in France and
in the French colonies. He and his successors supplied the king with daily
reports of information garnered by domestic and foreign spies. The extent
of domestic surveillance and the omnipresence of informers in France was
legendary. An often-quoted (but perhaps untrue) claim made to Louis XV
by Gabriel de Sartines (Lieutenant-General of Police from 1759-1774),
was that wherever three persons spoke to one another on the street, one of
them was sure to be his spy. Among his best informers were the prostitutes
of Paris and inmates of the jails. Another story, also of questionable validity, was told to demonstrate the efficacy of de Sartines' spy network. It was
said that de Sartines made a bet with a friend, a judge in Lyon, that it would
be impossible for him to come to Paris without the knowledge of de Sartines.
A few weeks later the judge slipped into Paris and took lodging in a remote
part of the city, only to receive within hours an invitation to dine with de
Sartines.

TIME CAPSULE

Foucault and Law Enforcement

Michel Foucault takes a dim view of French police methods, asserting that close observation began with the Panopticon prisons designs suggested by Jeremy Bentham. This plan permitted prison keepers to maintain a constant surveillance over all inmates in their cells. For Foucault this gradually became the standard of French police methods, for released prisoners became the accomplices of the police in maintaining surveillance over all citizens. With the establishment of the farm at Mettray, designed to "reform" youthful offenders, the keepers lived among the prisoners, creating a "network of permanent observation," and from these experiences there emerge a large number of individuals who are available to perform government surveillance of others. He notes that this was the same time that the science of psychology began to take shape.

Question

Did a nation like nineteenth-century France need to be concerned about the use of police methods to control freedom, to stifle dissent, and to maintain the status quo? Must freedom be sacrificed to ensure safety from crime?

Source: Michael Foucault, *Discipline and Punish*, pp. 268, 269, 295.

Not only did de Sartines seek control by promoting the belief that his police were everywhere and could learn everything, he also made progress toward specialization in police work. De Sartines was noted for his swift and severe reaction to violation of public order. He is reputed to have ordered his officers to say, when faced with rioters, that they had orders to fire only on rabble and to beg all honest men to return to their homes. According to the accounts, no one remained in the street.

With the accession of Napoleon Bonaparte as First Consul in 1799, the trend toward centralization of police was reinvigorated. In retrospect, it can be seen that one of the most significant acts of Napoleon I was his reform of French law. When he came to power, there were literally hundreds of legal systems (including Roman and Frankish elements) operating in the country, and statutory law consisted of accumulated legislation, ordinances, and edicts from previous regimes. Voltaire is reputed to have quipped that a person travelling in France had to change laws about as often as he changed horses. The Napoleonic Codes, which represented the first successful compilation of French law arranged in logical order, were drafted by a commission appointed by Napoleon in 1800. The codification provided a uniform, organized body of law applicable to all French citizens. A tripartite civil code appeared in 1804, a code of criminal instruction in 1808, and a penal code in 1810. Some of the libertarian principles of the French Revolution were incorporated, but the criminal codes also retained some of the harsh penalties of the revolutionary period.

For police control of rural areas, Napoleon augmented the Gendarmerie, a quasi-military force that was utilized by the Bourbons and accountable to the Ministry of Defense. Under the first Inspector-General, Adrien de Moncey, the Gendarmerie were used as both combat troops and as military police domestically. Napoleon had great respect for the ability of the Gendarmerie to keep order and valued their precise reporting. A significant part of their mission was to protect the regime from subversion. In this activity they sometimes resorted to disguises, but this was resented by the French, and after the collapse of the First Empire, the Gendarmerie were ordered to carry out their tasks in military uniform. This military aspect of policing is one of the principal characteristics that distinguishes the French system from the English system.

Historians concur in designating Napoleon's Minister of General Police, Joseph Fouché, the architect of France's modern national police system. By decree, the Prefect of Police for Paris was made subordinate to Fouché, and in each of the 12 districts of Paris police commissioners reported to the Prefect. Napoleon refused, however, to follow Fouché's suggestions that would have placed the Paris police commissioners and those of all the administrative departments of France directly under Fouché's authority. Instead, the local commissioners were placed under the supervision of the prefects of the 98 departments of France. The principal responsibility of the departmental prefects, who were nominated by Napoleon, was maintenance of law and order, and they were required to make regular reports to the Minister of Interior. Local policing, therefore, was under the authority of the Ministry of Interior rather than the Minister of Police.

It was during the period of Napoleon that one of the most dramatic figures in police history came to the fore: François Eugéne Vidocq. Vidocq, the friend of eminent novelists like Honoré de Balzac, Alexandre Dumas, and Victor Hugo, was known to embellish his tales, and historians have difficulty separating fact from fiction in his accounts. It is, however, agreed that he initiated a detective unit in Paris that came to be called the Brigade de Sûreté. A key to Vidocq's success was his extraordinary ability to observe and remember detail, a talent that enabled him to disguise himself effectively. He was also a pioneer in detection techniques. Not only did he utilize handwriting, paper, and ink analyses to solve cases, he also foresaw the day when fingerprints would be used to identify suspects.

The basic structure of the national police system instituted by Napoleon I, despite some modification during the administration of the Bourbon Restoration, survived the ensuing political disruptions of the July Revolution in 1830, which replaced King Charles X with King Louis-Philippe, and the revolutions that ushered in the Second Republic in 1848. The degree of centralization in the police system varied with the political shifts. During periods when liberals held power, an element of democracy in the form of election of lower police officials prevailed, only to yield to the practice of nomination and appointment when conservatives regained control. In 1851, the elected president of the Second Republic, Louis Napoleon Bonaparte, succeeded in making himself Emperor as Napoleon III. In implementing a centralized administration, he could call upon the French constitution of 1852 as a basis for executive power. Also, Napoleon III utilized principles of centralization that had been established by Napoleon I, and he claimed that his selection by the populace constituted a mandate to exercise general police powers in the name of general security. Authority over police was located in the Ministry of Interior, where it has remained despite a brief revival of the office of Minister of General Police (1852-1853).

The development of the police system of France did not proceed in a steady fashion. The bureaucratic structures initiated by the Bourbons, Napoleon I, and Napoleon III were not uniform in all urban or rural parts of France; nor was centralized authority over policing as effective in practice as it might appear on paper. Furthermore, the personal characteristics of those who ruled the nation and those who served in high police office determined in part how far along the libertarian-totalitarian scale the policing system would move one way or the other.

By the end of the nineteenth century, however, it was evident that the nature of policing in France differed greatly from that in England. First, political security and public order were accorded greater value than the rights of individuals against invasive police action. In France throughout the period being examined, rulers used police to suppress opposition, and there was an extensive system of surveillance of individuals. Second, there was a clear hierarchy of authority within the police bureaucracy from the minister in Paris down to the smallest commune. Third, the duties and responsibilities of police included social services and enforcement of regulations, which fell within the realm of administration in England. Fourth, France developed a bipartite structure of policing in which military units (Gendarmerie) policed rural areas and small towns under the authority of the Ministry of Defense and civilian units (National Police) policed municipalities under the authority of the Ministry of Interior.

The period saw the development of highly professional detective police forces (Brigade de Sûreté) that had been initiated by Vidocq. The Sûreté was institutionalized as a separate agency and achieved international renown. Its careful gathering of information and penetrating analysis were seen as a model for major investigation units of today, such as Interpol (International Criminal Police Organization). The effectiveness of the French detectives caught the attention of an English barrister, Howard Vincent, in the late nineteenth century. He went to France to examine the system and provided a report to authorities who were investigating corruption in Scotland Yard. As a result, he became head of the new Criminal Investigation Department in 1878, a unit that reflected the organization and operations of the Sûreté.

Respect for French methods and the attempt to emulate some of them did not, however, encourage the English to incorporate French administrative principles. Despite the claim of the French that a citizen in Paris was far safer than a citizen in London, concern about potential abuse of police power ensured the continuance in England of a decentralized, nonmilitary, and largely nonprofessional police force.

From Charlie to Bobby: The London Story

By the eighteenth century, the traditional justice/constable system was hopelessly inadequate to deal with the law enforcement requirements of the London Metropolitan area. The justice/constable system was organized around a group of constables appointed by the local justices, who patrolled the streets of their respective parishes by day. Limited in power, these constables were also delinquent in the exercise of their duties; this was understandable considering that, when they raised the traditional hue and cry against a fleeing criminal, bystanders were more likely to ridicule the constable than come to his assistance in making an arrest. Parish boundaries were also matters of great consequence; pursuit beyond the parish area was rare, and constables from adjourning jurisdictions neither helped each other nor exchanged information.

At night, not only did the occasions for criminal activity multiply, but the night watchmen were even less vigorous than their daytime counterparts. Charged with the duty of patrolling the deserted streets and maintaining street lamps in good order, these night watchmen were more likely to be found in a local pub or eating place. A critic of the times described a night watchman as a "person hired by the parish to sleep in the open air."[2] The butt of popular and theatrical jokes well before Shakespeare's time, the London constables after the reign of Charles II were known as "Charlies" because they were reorganized and reinforced by a statute passed during the Restoration period.

With rare exceptions, thieves and other criminals moved about the streets of London with impunity, the constables and watch providing only momentary sport to a truly dedicated felon. Merchants and other residents of London were left to their own resources to protect themselves from robbery, theft, assault, battery, and even murder. The well-to-do, of course, had servants and retainers to shield them from the so-called criminal classes, but no such private protection was available to poorer citizens. In the event of a theft, it was customary to hire a thief-catcher, usually a veteran constable well acquainted with the underworld and able to secure the return of the stolen goods. In this case, free enterprise proved to be a mixed blessing. While it inevitably resulted in the return of all or a portion of the booty, it did so at a considerable price to the owner. Not infrequently the thief-catcher with-held some of the property as an unauthorized supplement to his fee. The most notorious thief-catcher of all, Jonathan Wild, operated his profitable busi-ness for seven years before his racket was discovered. Not content with track-ing down goods that had been stolen, Wild found it worthwhile to employ a veritable army of thieves who stole on demand. Wild was then paid a com-mission to "find" the thief for the owner, and duly returned the property. Highly successful in this activity, Wild advertised himself as "Thief-taker General" of London and lived in luxury from his commissions until he was executed.

TIME CAPSULE

Peel's Principles

A major step toward professionalization of police was taken when Sir Robert Peel, Member of Parliament and Home Secretary, achieved passage of the Metropolitan Police Act of 1829. Peel's 12 principles of reform in the nineteenth century are still pertinent in the twenty-first century.

1. The police must be stable, efficient, and organized along military lines.

2. The police must be under government control.

3. The absence of crime will best prove the efficiency of police.

4. The distribution of crime news is essen-tial.

5. The deployment of police strength both by time and area is essential.

6. No quality is more indispensable to a policeman than a perfect command of temper; a quiet, determined manner has more effect than violent action.

7. Good appearance commands respect.

8. The securing and training of proper per-sons is at the root of efficiency.

9. Public security demands that every police officer be given a number.

10. Police headquarters should be centrally located and easily accessible to the people.

11. Policemen should be hired on a proba-tionary basis.

12. Police records are necessary to the correct distribution of police strength.

Source: William H. Hewitt, *British Police Administration* (Springfield, IL: Charles C Thomas, 1965).

Henry Fielding (1707-1754)—British novelist who became Bow Street magistrate in 1748, and whose efforts to improve the police brought about the Bow Street Runners, who specialized in thief-catching.

Thus, thief-taking undermined the criminal justice system in two ways. It always provided anonymity for the criminal, who was required only to return the stolen goods without penalty. Crime always paid under these circumstances, and prosecution simply provided a sanction that forced the felon to disgorge a portion of the profit he would have made if he went undetected. Second, it developed a group of thief-takers who operated on the very edge of the law, at times holding back some of the ransomed property for their own profit, or who, like Wild, actually encouraged thieves for the purpose of increasing their own business. It wasn't a good system, but it was the best that eighteenth-century England had to offer.

Even within this flawed system of indolent constables, sleepy watchmen, and venal thief-catchers, there was a glimmer of hope for a more efficient system of law enforcement. Sir Thomas DeVeil was appointed magistrate for the Bow Street district in 1730, and in the ensuing 17 years he established his police office as one of the most effective within the metropolitan London area. In 1748, DeVeil was succeeded as Bow Street magistrate by the novelist Henry Fielding who, somewhat to the surprise of his associates, took a serious interest in improving the function of his police office. These changes included the establishment of the Bow Street Runners, a group of highly skilled thief-catchers who received modest salaries for their work. Fielding also turned his literary talents to good purpose. Beginning with *An Enquiry into the Cause of the Late Increase of Robbers* (1748), he published five pamphlets on crime and its prevention before his death in 1754. Working on the assumption that the collection of good intelligence was essential to the detection of crime, Fielding also established the *Covent Garden Gazette*, which specialized in publicizing descriptions of criminals and their modes of operation. Advertisements inserted in the regular dailies asked citizens to report the descriptions and activities of suspected criminals to the Chief Magistrate of Bow Street, as Fielding described himself. Premature death did not halt Fielding's work in law enforcement; The chief magistracy of Bow Street and the campaign for an effective police was carried on by his half-brother and successor, Sir John Fielding. Sir John remained Chief Magistrate until 1779, and during his tenure the famous Bow Street Horse Patrol was established to maintain order on the highways leading into the metropolis.

By 1800, the Bow Street Police Office was recognized as the leading law enforcement agency in London. A historian of English criminal law, Sir Leon Radzinowicz, described it as:

the headquarters of a closely knit caste of speculators in the detection of crime, self-seeking and unscrupulous, but also daring and efficient when daring and efficiency coincided with their private interest.[3]

Within the framework of the old justice/constable system, the Bow Street Police Office represented the most that could be realized, and its runners were simultaneously "the most perfect creation and ultimately the most complete travesty of the system of incentives."[4]

Even if the evils of the justice/constable system had been eliminated from Bow Street Police Office operations, no local jurisdiction could combat the rising crime wave throughout London. Efficient patrol and thief-catching in one parish simply caused the felons to remove their activities to adjacent areas that might be totally devoid of any law enforcement. A patchwork system of law enforcement left entire segments of London's population to their own devices. Realizing the need for a universal control of law enforcement throughout the metropolitan area, Prime Minister William Pitt the Younger introduced a bill for a police force to be established throughout the city (1785). Defeated because of widespread fear that such a constabulary would undermine the liberties of Englishmen and lead to militarism, the bill was to serve as a prototype for the legislation that established the Metropolitan Police in 1829. While fear of police state suppression of liberties doomed Pitt's bill to failure, English statesmen recognized the need for a new police organization. In 1786, the Irish Parliament authorized the Royal Irish Constabulary, which followed the general outline of Pitt's bill. Significantly, Sir Robert Peel, later the founder of the London Metropolitan Police, was Chief Secretary for Ireland from 1812 to 1818.

Patrick Colquhoun (1745-1820), a Scottish-born merchant who spent some early years in Virginia, succeeded to leadership of the police reform efforts in 1790. Appointed a magistrate shortly after his removal to London, he began a painstaking study of law enforcement. His book, *A Treatise on the Police of the Metropolis*, was published anonymously in 1795 and went through numerous editions and reprintings before 1800. Estimating the indigent classes of Britain at more than 1,500,000 individuals, he claimed that more than 50,000 inhabitants of London composed a class of habitual criminals whose lives were spent in crime or in prison. Colquhoun estimated that approximately £12,000,000 per year was lost as a result of their activities. A combined effort to deal with the problem of indigence and to discourage crime by effective police activity was essential. He went so far as to suggest that the French police, widely viewed in England as subversive of French liberties, were a model for Britain to follow; to Colquhoun, effective police were perhaps even more important than the British constitution itself.

In a certain sense, Colquhoun was correct. England, and London in particular, was on the brink of criminal anarchy as it entered the nineteenth century. It was this widespread disregard for property rights and human life that rendered the constitution highly vulnerable. A highly complex and interdependent city that relies upon trade and commerce for its livelihood cannot tolerate extensive criminal activity. That fact was shown by the passage of the Thames Police Act (1800), which established a plenary police jurisdiction to cover the river itself and the adjacent land areas. Crossing numerous parish boundaries, the Thames Police Office soon proved an effective institution against the violence and property-related offenses of the waterfront. Most thieves in this area had developed highly sophisticated methods of operation. For example, as a method of removing whiskey and other liquids from wooden casks, a thief would move a barrel hoop from its location on the cask, drill a hole on one side to remove the contents and a hole on the other side to equalize the air pressure. When an adequate amount had been withdrawn, the barrel was plugged on one side and filled with water. The remaining hole was replugged, the hoop replaced, and the barrel sent on to its unsuspecting purchaser.

Patrick Colquhoun's 1800 treatise on the need for a marine police jurisdiction for the Thames was at least partially responsible for the establishment of this new and more effective police office. Yet despite its author's reputation, it was no more successful than his earlier works in stimulating an overhaul of the entire law enforcement system in London. That would have to wait for the outbreak of a new wave of crime in the 1820s and the decision by Sir Robert Peel to seek a Parliamentary reform of the London police system in 1829.

The necessities of the time, emphasized by the crime wave and frequent riots, created the stage for London police reform; however, little could have been accomplished without the political skills of Sir Robert Peel. It was the identification of the Metropolitan Police with Sir Robert that resulted in the police officers being called bobbies. (an earlier popular designation, "Peelers," has mercifully been dropped from the vocabulary). The jurist Sir William Blackstone (supplemented by the influential writer on moral philosophy, William Paley) saw a police force as detrimental to constitutional liberty. Following this viewpoint, most Englishmen opposed the adoption of more efficient systems of law enforcement. It was the utilitarians, led by Jeremy Bentham and supported by Patrick Colquhoun and Edward Chadwick, who were willing to view police activities in the context of efficiency rather than political theory. Coloring the entire discussion was the example of an efficient and repressive system of police in France, where extensive intelligence networks caught ordinary criminals as well as those who spoke

Corbis Images

Sir Robert Peel (1788-1850)—English statesman and reformer, whose connection with the Metropolitan Police led to the officers being called "bobbies."

and acted in ways that undermined the stability of the regime holding political power. Such a use of police to buttress unpopular government was contrary to England's concept of free and constitutional politics. Peel's approach to this conflict was to advocate a moderate approach to police activity. He stressed preventative measures, such as the establishment of regular patrols by uniformed police, the collection of intelligence concerning criminal activity only, and the centralization of all law enforcement activities within the London Metropolitan area. Mindful of the strong opposition, which the financial district of London had mounted to the 1785 reform effort, Peel was careful to remove the ancient City of London from the provisions of his proposal. As passed by Parliament, the bill retained this exception, but the separate City of London force very quickly copied the Metropolitan Police, making the exception a mere matter of political expediency that did not hamper the centralization.

Given the precarious political compromise that resulted in the passage of the Peel Act, it was clear that the image of the Metropolitan Police was a critical factor in whether the new force would survive. The two men chosen as justices, later named commissioners, were ideal leaders in the attempt to institute an efficient police system that would be free of the taint of repressive political behavior, but at the same time be an effective force to prevent and prosecute crime. Charles Rowan was a retired military officer with experience as a magistrate in Ireland, the home of the Royal Irish Constabulary; barrister Richard Mayne contributed both legal skills and political dexterity. Together they developed a uniform that made their growing force of patrolmen visible, but at the same time they avoided any color or decoration that suggested military dress. The hats of the patrolmen were flat top hats, designed with steel reinforcements that permitted the officer to stand on the headgear and peer over high walls and fences.

Preventative policing meant knowing what was going on throughout the London metropolitan area. On his beat, the bobby was expected to become familiar with the populace, to extend help as needed, and to remain alert at all times to indications that crimes were about to be committed. At the same time, it was felt that an officer should not be overly familiar with the residents of his beat. This was achieved by appointing officers drawn from other cities and from rural areas surrounding London; the few bobbies who were native to the city were assigned patrol duties well away from their home neighborhoods. As a result, the bobby was known in the area he patrolled primarily as a representative of the state and of the police commissioners. Officers were carefully trained in respectful behavior toward all classes and groups. Violent police behavior was discouraged in both training and in a policy that allowed officers to carry only truncheons (clubs made of birch wood), but no edged weapons or firearms.

Wilbur Miller, noting the tense political situation at the time the Metropolitan Police force was established, found little resentment toward the officers on the part of the laboring classes.[5] There were some complaints that

Metropolitan Police were more vigorous in administering law against working-class offenders than against members of the governing class. Marxist newspaper editors after 1850 were sharp in their condemnation of the officers as mere instruments for the oppression of the masses. However, as Miller explains, the police commissioners were generally successful in maintaining a reputation for restraint at a time when the English nation was sharply divided along class lines over the issue of extending the right to vote. Bobbies were forbidden participation in political activities, and, in later years, when the right to vote was broadened, they were still denied the right to vote.

The Metropolitan Police did not formally establish a detective office until 1842, at which time carefully selected patrol officers were assigned to this work. The close connection to the patrol force meant that detectives were assured the cooperation of their uniformed colleagues; it also provided an incentive for the bobby on the beat to perfect his skills of observation and crime detection. The new detective office also benefited from the reputation of the uniformed force for courteous and restrained behavior.[6]

Corbis Images

A turn-of-the-century London Bobby.

Restraint in routine law enforcement and in political involvement did not spare the Metropolitan Police the severe test of riot control in the years from 1830 to 1850. It was discovered that while police officers were helpful in the initial stages of disorder, they were unable to stop the activities of a large and determined mob. For that purpose, the Home Secretary (under whom the Metropolitan Police were organized) found that it was necessary to call out regular Army troops. On the other hand, the use of the armed troops usually escalated the casualty rate in any riot situation, and it was understood that bobbies were the preferred option in the case of minor disorders. Closeness to the inhabitants of the community, coupled with respect and confidence, made the Metropolitan Police the first line of defense.

Once established, the London Metropolitan Police created a law enforcement standard that would be widely emulated. Within England, bobbies were frequently sent on temporary duty to other cities and counties to help in establishing a "new style" police force. Their effectiveness in small-crowd control made them the obvious choice to assist in law enforcement activities outside the boundaries of London, and they were frequently assigned to these tasks. American police reformers, witnessing the transformation of law enforcement in England, sought to import the new system into American urban police organizations.

From Bobby to Copper in New York City

In 1845, New York City abandoned its earlier system of constables and watchmen and instituted the first London-style police department outside the British empire, but even by outward appearances, there was a sharp distinction between the two forces. Initially the New York City policemen did not wear uniforms, because of a combination of both official indifference and the individual officer's opposition to appearing in what he termed "subservient livery." Only after pressure from above, coupled with the commissioners and commanding officers wearing the uniform to social events, did the policemen accept the uniform, and even then it was customary to wear the heavy woolen coat only in inclement weather. For their mark of authority, the New York policemen relied upon a simple copper badge mounted on a leather circle; from this they gained the popular name of copper, later shortened to "cop." Originally, the new police force, called the Municipal Police, carried only a truncheon, but by 1850 the policy against firearms was weakened by the number of officers killed or seriously injured by armed criminals.

The London emphasis on careful patrol, familiarity with the community on the patrolmen's beats, careful supervision, and provision for adequate salaries were evident in New York's Municipal Police. However, the differing political and social situation in America produced a remarkable variation from the London Metropolitan Police format. Politically, the New York policeman was vulnerable to the "spoils system" that prevailed during and after the presidency of Andrew Jackson (1829-1837). This emphasized a democratic demand that public offices, both elective and appointive, should be accessible to all citizens. Indeed, the most significant factor in police appointments was loyalty to the party that was victorious in the most recent election. As a consequence, New York police officers were subject to immediate removal upon the failure of their party to win reelection. By contrast, the London bobby was insulated from changes in political office, not only because of his political neutrality but also because he reported directly to the central government and what would ultimately become the Home Office. Appointed by the elected alderman who represented a particular ward, the New York patrolman usually found himself working in the neighborhood in which he was raised or where he had lived for many years. Closeness in community relations was assured, but the image of the policeman was less that of an objective official and more that of an old friend. Because the officer's job depended on the success of his political party, he was strongly tempted to ensure the continuity of political power.

New York City politics were not divided along class lines, but rather in terms of native versus immigrant elements and, to some degree, ethnic lines. The selection of policemen by wards meant, to a considerable degree, that they represented the majority of the people within their wards. Thus, Irish policemen patrolled Irish wards; Germans dealt with German ward police problems, and Anglo-American officers predominated in the established middle- and upper-class neighborhoods. Political domination of police appointments eliminated the possibility of neutrality in the Municipal Police, but it did ensure acceptance of the individual officer within his native ward. Organization by wards meant that decentralization was the mark of the Municipal Police, and uniformity in deciding which crime should be prosecuted was vested not in the police, but rather in politically elected district attorneys.

One matter that New York City residents agreed on was the prohibition of alcoholic beverages. A majority of residents openly flouted the prohibition law of New York State, and their violation of the state "dry law" was widely ignored by the Municipal Police. This defiance, encouraged by the Democratic leadership of the city, caused the Republican and prohibitionist governor to secure passage of a state statute. This law abolished the Municipal Police and substituted a Metropolitan Police Force to be commanded by state-appointed commissioners (1857). Initially, the two police forces worked side-by-side, despite their conflicting sources of authority and attitudes toward prohibition. Ultimately, growing disorder brought the situation to a crisis, and an open battle broke out between rival police agencies. The Seventh Regiment of the New York National Guard (a militia under state control) established order at the point of the bayonet. Subsequently, the Municipal Police Force was disbanded, and the Metropolitan Police Force exercised police jurisdiction in the city until 1870, when home rule was reinstituted and a new municipal Police Force was established.

The exercise of police power in New York City was substantially different from what had occurred in London. London Commissioners Rowan and Mayne carefully created the image of a politically neutral and institutionally controlled policeman, familiar with the activities of his community while at the same time detached from them. A series of regulations defined the activities and limited discretion of the individual patrolman. By contrast, the New York City Municipal Police (and the Metropolitan Police from 1857-1870) depended on the prestige of the individual officer. Conferring a great deal of discretion on him, American practice limited the policeman's authority at the ballot box, where he and his superiors were either indirectly or directly answerable. The New York City policeman's standard of behavior was essentially to react as one of his fellow citizens would to the same situation.

While some police efficiency was gained when the Municipal Police was established in 1845, the political manipulation of the force was such that it verified the fears that earlier had impeded the reform of English police institutions. After 1848, American law enforcement became increasingly involved in the application of the controversial and inflammatory fugitive slave laws. Public sentiment grew against the increased political power and economic impact of immigrant laborers. Religious animosity between immigrant Roman Catholics and native Protestant groups caused conflict and violence. New York City police officers were not insulated from such disorder, but their political identification with their fellow citizens made it unlikely that resentment would be turned against them. Just as their prototypes in London could not effectively control riots, the New York City Police were ineffective in restoring order during the New York City draft riots of 1863.

Adapting the English Metropolitan Police model to American realities meant discarding virtually all of the institutional restraints that were so typical of the London police. Instead, the New York City police were marked by individual discretion and amenability to political influence. It was as if an excessively democratic spirit had sapped the Metropolitan Police model of all of its virtues, leaving only the simple outline of operations. This outline included improved methods of patrol and intelligence, and to that extent New York City was better served than it had been during the colonial past. However, in the future, citizens would at times wonder whether the operation of the city's police was as much a source of crime as a means for its prevention.

The city of Boston, after rejecting a proposal to follow the London police model in 1837, made extensive changes in its police organization in 1852. These changes included uniting the constables and the nightwatch into a single law enforcement body. Patrols were established, and this activity was monitored by superior officers. In 1855 the newly constructed station houses were connected by telegraph lines, facilitating the rapid transmission of information and the quick assembly of police forces where they were most needed. Between 1855 and 1857 the force was placed in uniform, causing more jeers from the general public than genuine opposition from the men themselves. Boston's ideal for police was simply stated: "The police, while it should be argus-eyed, seeing all things, should be itself unseen and unheard." In this sense, it closely paralleled the London Metropolitan Police and also represented the London ideal of detachment. Few, if any, Boston policemen were drawn from the city; most were from rural New England.

Southern Police Methods

By way of contrast to London and northern American cities, the South found little incentive to change its traditional police systems until the very eve of the Civil War. In his comparative study of criminal justice in Massachusetts and South Carolina, historian Michael Hindus shows how such contrast between North and South came about. Already at the vanguard of American industrialization, Massachusetts resorted to increased state regulation in all areas of economic and social activity, while South Carolina retained a traditional laissez-faire (hands-off) approach toward governmental power and economic regulation. Massachusetts strengthened law enforcement as a method of securing property rights and encouraging commercial activity; South Carolina was concerned with preventing violence in a slave-holding society dominated by racial fear and tension.[7] These general terms of distinction may suffer from some oversimplification, but they accurately portray the wide divergence between the urban North and the agrarian South.

Southern states relied upon slave patrols as a method of preventing slave insurrection and combating crime. All able-bodied white men aged 18 to 50 were subject to duty on the patrol, and female heads of household were also subject to call, even though they were expected to hire a substitute to perform the duty for them. Once every two weeks the patrol inspected roadways and inns, checking for passes that authorized blacks to be away from their master's plantation after the curfew hour. Those found abroad without such a document, and others found acting suspiciously or boisterously, were taken into custody and held for the court of magistrates and freeholders. This was a special court composed of one local justice of the peace and two to five landholders. This court had complete jurisdiction in all criminal matters concerning slaves and might impose capital punishment in appropriate cases. The usual penalty for being abroad without a pass was that the slave would be flogged and then given a passport for his unhindered return to his master's plantation.

While on the plantation, slaves were subject to the discipline of the master or his overseer, and punishments were inflicted for a wide spectrum of offenses ranging from assault, battery, and theft, to breaches of etiquette and surly mannerisms. This punishment usually involved legally controlled flogging, but occasionally punishments were carried to excess and slaves died under the lash. In other instances, planters starved their slaves, but in most cases the master's investment compelled him to deal with them in a more humane fashion. Excessive punishments that violated the mores of white society might cause the local justices of the peace to intervene, and there are instances of slaveowners being executed for the willful murder of their slaves. Yet white society for the most part was willing to let planters manage and discipline slaves as they saw fit.

If a South Carolina slave committed a felony, the case had to be brought before the magistrate and freeholder's court. The defendant was expected to be in court and could present witnesses on his or her behalf. Frequently, counsel was provided; however, conviction rates in the magistrate and freeholder's courts were much higher than those in the higher courts charged with trying white defendants. South Carolina's penal laws made most felonies punishable by death, and other offenses that would be considered minor if committed by a white man were capital offenses for blacks and slaves. Lesser penalties, such as flogging, sale outside the state (and hence separation from family and relatives), or walking the treadmill at the Charleston workhouse, were also imposed. When it was necessary to execute a slave as punishment for a crime, his or her master received either all or part of the fair market value of the slave, established on the basis of a jury verdict.

A mutual fear dominated racial relations in the South. For blacks, even those freed from slavery, there was the constant fear of white violence.

Blacks were expected to behave in a deferential fashion; city ordinances in Charleston required them to walk in the gutters and salute every white person they passed. It was a felony to strike a white person, even in self-defense or after extreme provocation. Even if a master was being attacked by another white, a slave could not act except at his master's order. Slaves had no standing before the law and could not bring a lawsuit. Neither they nor free blacks could testify in court against a white person. Slaves were subjected to a rigid curfew law, restricted to social gatherings that did not exceed a certain number, and were always kept under the surveillance of the white community. Whites had a different type of fear, but it was fear nevertheless. In 1830, the city of Charleston had a population of 30,289, of which 17,461 were blacks. Along with all other southern urban areas, it was a city under siege. Fear of slave uprisings governed the conduct of business, the architecture of houses, and the administration of the criminal laws. Curfews kept blacks off the streets in the night hours, and severe penalties were imposed for selling intoxicating liquor to blacks. Houses in the white community were strongly secured against entry after dark; few, if any, permitted easy access from the slave quarters that were situated in the yards of the mansions. In administering the criminal law, it was the custom that no white man could be flogged. Such a demeaning punishment toward a member of the white race was felt to be an incitement to slave rebellion.

Fear of slave rebellion was not a figment of a white man's imagination. In the 1790s, the black population of Haiti rose up and massacred virtually the entire white population of the island; those who survived fled to the American South, there to tell their experiences to slaveowners all too ready to apply the lesson to themselves. When in 1822 a freedman named Denmark Vesey was caught in the process of organizing a widespread uprising in the city of Charleston, the need for greater control became apparent. One initial step was an abortive attempt to prevent any black seamen from coming ashore at Charleston. This effort brought the city fathers into conflict with the federal government, and while they succeeded in restricting the freedom of seamen, they did not eliminate them from the transient population. More effective steps were taken to restrict the movements and activities of the free black residents of Charleston and the rest of South Carolina. They were required to obtain the protection of a white "guardian" who would vouch for their good behavior; failing that, free blacks were required to emigrate from the state.

A Charleston City Guard had been established in 1806. Operating on military lines of organization, the city guard was charged with patrolling the city after dark. Privates in the guard were equipped with a musket, bayonet, and cartouche (gun cartridge) box; sergeants, lieutenants, and captains wore swords; and the entire force was arrayed in blue uniforms. Guardsmen on patrol carried rattles, used to call for help and notify their officers of their location; five men and a sergeant patrolled each of the city districts. Given the dangerous state of the streets and alleys late at night, and the desperate nature of the criminals they apprehended, an individual rarely got separated from the main body of the patrol. In 1846 the city guard changed its named to Charleston City Police, and patrolling officers were charged with the identification of newcomers on their beats and the observation of suspicious circumstances that might give rise to crime. By 1856 the city police were in need of reorganization and expansion, and the task was undertaken by Mayor William Porcher Miles. Thereafter, the police consisted of one chief, two captains, six lieutenants, four ordinary sergeants, four patrol sergeants, and 150 privates. Taking to the streets in June 1856, the new force was known as Paddy Miles' Bull Dogs. Derision from the white residents was matched by fear from the blacks, particularly freedmen, who in 1857 were further restricted by a city ordinance requiring them to wear a numbered badge for purposes of quick identification. An English visitor to Charleston in 1857 remarked that the city looked like an army camp. The city police patrolled both night and day, displaying their uniforms and weapons. Some Charlestonians explained their presence as being the consequence of an unruly group of seamen; one of the more forthright and candid privates of the guard told a foreign visitor that the guard was for "keeping down the niggers."

From the little that is known about the Charleston City Police, it seems apparent that, while there may have been some effort to follow the London form of organization, the requirements for policing the "Holy City" were quite unique. Control of blacks, both slaves and freedmen, was of paramount importance. Trading with blacks, particularly selling alcoholic beverages, was strictly forbidden by ordinance, but blatantly practiced. Blacks were essential to city life: they were craftsmen, household servants, longshoremen, and seamen. The presence of a large percentage of free blacks, viewed as focal points of insurrections, was troublesome to the inhabitants, but the skills of the blacks were in demand. For the blacks, this contact with the white community provided a degree of protection against police harassment. Social control was the primary function of police in Charleston and the surrounding countryside. While there might be crime in the white community, it was of little concern to authorities concerned with suppressing black crime and assuring black subservience.

Urban Charleston, with its large black population and a growing number of itinerant black seamen from other American and Caribbean ports, cannot be considered typical of the rural areas of the South, which relied upon plantation discipline to control both the slave and free black populations. For the most part, the traditional system of passes and frequent slave patrols kept blacks from planning criminal activities and escapes from servitude. Urbanization and commercial growth rendered these informal methods of law enforcement inadequate, and popular sentiment supported the creation of an efficient military organization to control the black population. Public safety superseded any fear that southern leaders might have had of a military coup. This provides an interesting contrast to the situation in London and New York at that time, where the establishment of a new style of police force was seen as a threat to individual freedom and a step in the direction of a military dictatorship. The establishment of the city guard also removed slave discipline from the master, substituting an impersonal and public system of law enforcement that grew in repressiveness as northern abolitionists attacked the institution of slavery and the growing black population of Charleston increased the fear of insurrection.

Law and Violence on the American Frontier

Americans have long been fascinated with the westerly movement of the frontier, that "cutting edge" of western civilization where a thin line of settlers stood between the fierce Indian and the ravages of nature on one side, and the rapidly changing culture of the United States and Western Europe on the other. It was on the frontier, some historians believed, that the true character of America evolved. That character included rugged individualism, staunch independence in political and economic affairs, incorruptibility at the ballot box, and a simplicity of manners and behavior that lent republican dignity to American life. Others saw the frontier as a time and place where the deeply embedded culture of Western civilization was forced into adaptations to primitive conditions. Recently, a debate has evolved over frontier responsibility for the violent tendencies in American history. It is this last aspect of frontier historiography that holds the most interest for the student of criminal justice.

Crossing the great expanse of the North American continent is quite an experience, even with today's conveniences. It was a monumental endeavor for those who attempted it in the nineteenth century. For a brief period, Indian hostility took its toll in lives, but ultimately it was the geography of the continent that was the most formidable obstacle. From the banks of the Mississippi and Missouri Rivers, the land sloped upward, and with each foot of altitude it became more arid. Many perished of thirst or hunger on the Great Plains even before coming within sight of the next hurdle, the Rocky Mountains, where high passes tested the stamina of man and beast and fierce storms decimated wagon trains that risked the climb in late autumn or winter. Beyond the Rocky Mountains was a vast dry desert bordered on the west by the Sierra Nevada and Cascade mountain ranges. It was in the Sierras that an unlucky party found itself marooned in the Donner Pass and resorted to cannibalism before the ordeal was over. Arrival in Oregon or California provided a more hospitable climate, but did not give peace, for the institutions of government were only recently established and law enforcement was thinly spread. At times, only a handful of federal marshals policed an entire territory that today might include several of the western states.

Lack of effective law enforcement was not the only factor that produced crime on the frontier. Numerous studies have shown that the American West was the place of refuge for those reluctant to remain within settled eastern communities. Certainly many migrants sought adventure or wealth, but others found it expedient to "move on" from the East before they were arrested for unpaid debts, to avoid supporting families, or to escape criminal prosecution. There was a certain anonymity in westward migration; systems of communication were slow and unreliable, and it was not difficult to alter one's identity and begin a new life. In the colonial period, Americans complained about the English practice of transporting convicts to the colonies. Undoubtedly, many upright settlers in the West saw the same exportation of undesirables occurring in the nineteenth century; however, where the colonists at least knew something of the convicts' backgrounds, the honest westerners were left to learn by experience.

John Reid spent several years studying the experience on the westward overland trail in his "Elephant" articles.[8] Pioneers on the trail referred to the continent as the "Elephant," and they risked their fortunes and lives in an effort to see or conquer the Elephant. Almost none of these pioneers were lawyers, but they did not lack for law. Elaborate agreements governed the management of wagon trains and "messes" of individuals who joined together for the overland trip. Roughly approximating joint ventures (a simple form of business organization), these agreements provided for common ownership of equipment. They constituted a sort of insurance that the group would remain together until the end of the journey. These agreements also represented a pooling of the capital and resources of the individual pioneers and their families. Medical doctors frequently entered into contracts to provide care to the group, in return for food and protection during the journey.

Crossing the continent exposed the pioneers to conditions far more life-threatening than they had ever encountered before. Prices of goods rose as the number of wayside vendors decreased, and starving men at times arrived at a solitary trading post without sufficient funds to purchase food. However, even in such distress, it was uncommon for theft or robbery to occur. From their backgrounds the pioneers brought a thoroughly instilled respect for the right of private property. Beyond the restraints of traditional law, far removed from policy or law enforcement agencies and thousands of miles from the nearest courts, they conducted themselves in an orderly and law-abiding fashion. Reid's findings say much about the manner in which human behavior is controlled by early conditioning and self-discipline.

Selecting companions for the overland journey was a matter of great importance. It was also the key to good order on the trail. When the settlers reached their journey's end (such as the gold fields of California or the rich farmlands of Oregon), such selectivity was no longer possible. Competition for land or mining claims was intense, supplies were expensive, and neighbors were usually strangers. California experienced a rapid expansion of its population as gold speculators poured into the Bay Area, and its admission as a state in 1850 did little to alleviate the growing pains. Disorder and crime began to threaten stability and property rights, and in 1856 law-abiding citizens launched a vigilante movement. Vigilantism is an organized movement that seeks to impose law and order, independent of the existing legal authorities; at times it fills a vacuum in legal authority (such as the 1767 Regulator movement in western South Carolina, where there were no courts), and at times it operates simultaneously with legal institutions for law enforcement. The San Francisco Association, like many before and after it, insisted on holding "trials" of the accused persons and, thus, approximated formal court procedures. However, the defendants were always convicted and inevitably sentenced to death, with execution immediately following the trial. Richard Maxwell Brown, who has studied this and other vigilante movements, attributes much of American violent behavior to the vigilante tradition.[9] He finds that Americans are a people inclined to resort to violence, even when legal procedures are available; violence has thus achieved a neutral quality, with a perception that there is "good" violence (vigilantism) and "bad" violence (crime and banditry). Brown shows that there is a degree of admiration for the violent outlaw, enshrined in legends about a wide assortment of gunslingers, train robbers, and other felons. Indeed, the American fascination with leading criminals has resulted in Al Capone and Billy the Kid sharing the national pantheon with George Washington, Abraham Lincoln, and Robert E. Lee.

Reid and Brown illustrate two contradictory aspects of law enforcement on the frontier. On the overland trail and when social cohesion was vital, pioneers relied heavily on their concepts of legality. Without lawyers or judges, they made their arrangements for the mutual good of all, and for the most part they abided by their agreements, living up to the pledge of their honor that they would do so. It was in the more permanent, but less demanding, circumstances of frontier settlement that disorder developed. The lack of law enforcement created a severe vacuum that was filled by the private organization of vigilante groups. In a very real sense, both initiatives can be seen as similar in motivation and in execution. There was an abstract ideal of how societies should function and how individuals should behave toward each other. In the small, self-selecting group setting out on the overland trail, consent by all established a little government with common views and a shared trust in the integrity of each other. In the large, diverse, and fluid society of frontier cities, farms, ranches, and mining areas, such a consensus was impossible to achieve. Those in the community who owned property and sought a stable life free of violence joined together to provide a mechanism to restrain violence and protect property rights and life itself. Expulsion from a wagon train for noncompliance with the rules laid down by the company was a harsh sanction, as was summary justice at the hands of a vigilante committee.

The American frontier experience suggests that there cannot be a vacuum in law enforcement, nor can there be a situation in which there is no applicable law. Group consensus or community pressure establishes standards of conduct and methods for their enforcement. Vigilantism and other similar forms of self-help law enforcement arise because criminal activity cannot be allowed to threaten the existence of any society. The methods chosen for such informal police activities may be excessively violent and completely arbitrary by any legal standard, but their principal recommendation is that they work. By way of a corollary, police institutions must always be adequate to protect society. Failure in this vital task will cause the development of parallel extralegal organizations created to supplement, or even to replace, regular police activity.

While many historians identify the frontier as the source of American democratic virtues and self-reliance, others trace violence and disorder in national life to the frontier experience. Resorting to self-help law enforcement encourages violence and the likelihood of revenge killings. Widespread access to and use of firearms in the nineteenth century may well reflect how frontier attitudes penetrated the settled areas of the East. There is evidence that American individualism surfaced frequently in physical attacks that ended in mayhem or death.

Summary

Examination of the policing systems that developed in France and England during the seventeenth, eighteenth, and nineteenth centuries reveals fundamental differences. France, prior to the Norman Conquest, already manifested tendencies toward a national policing system in the Roman tradition, whereas England continued to rely on the principle of community self-policing that had prevailed in the Anglo-Saxon period. Although cause cannot always be distinguished from effect, it is likely that the chronic political instability in France was responsible for the invasive, even repressive, police characteristics of this period. Unlike English police, whose main duty was enforcement of criminal law, French police were also accorded a wide range of responsibilities that included matters left to the administrative realm in England. In the geographic area that became the United States, predominance of English institutions meant that the narrower definition of police power became the principle followed in American policing.

While a wide variety of circumstances were responsible for the institution of organized police departments in London, New York, Boston, and Charleston, it is clear that each of these institutions reflects the society that gave it birth. Each is a product of the historical forces at play when it was organized; and each reflects public attitudes toward crime, the liberties of citizens, the maintenance of order, and the necessary conditions for the stability of urban life. Because the cities were in the forefront of economic and social change, they were first to alter the old justice/constable system of law enforcement. Only after the middle of the nineteenth century did provincial towns and rural areas begin to follow the lead set by urban areas, but those law enforcement agencies faced different challenges and responded to crime in very different ways.

American diversity in law enforcement between the North, South, and West reflected the regionalism that would tear the nation apart in the four decades after 1860, first with the North-South conflict in the American Civil War, followed by the bitter Reconstruction period and, subsequently, by a farmers' movement that pitted the West against the financial East. Prison reform was a northern problem; slave discipline preoccupied the South; and the establishment of normal governmental and policing institutions was a continuing concern in the West.

Early nineteenth-century experience with police organization indicates that traditional forms of law enforcement change only when there is a pressing need for reform. Crime waves, new challenges to social stability, changing attitudes toward violence, and new emphasis on the security of property all play important roles in law enforcement reform. Different cultures place varying importance on police protection, but none is willing to do without a system of law enforcement. Where public police organizations are absent or inadequate, private initiative will supply either a consensual basis for orderly government or a forceful vigilante movement to enforce popularly accepted standards of behavior. A creation of the people, the police also depend heavily on the people. Each successful police reform dealt with public opinion. Each measured its actions by the popular acceptance of its programs, and each recognized that, while a people may give police organizations power to enforce the law, the gift is given grudgingly and with suspicion.

Endnotes

[1]   The justice of the peace and constable system is discussed in Chapters 5 and 6.

[2]   Quoted in W.L. Melville Lee, *A History of Police in England* (London: Methuen, 1901; reprint, Montclair, NJ: Patterson Smith, 1971), p. 184.

[3]   Sir Leon Radzinowicz, *A History of English Criminal Law and its Administration from 1750*, 5 vols. (London: Stephens, 1948-1986), vol. 2, p. 263.

[4]   Radzinowicz, *A History*, 263.

[5]   Wilbur R. Miller, *Cops and Bobbies: Police Authority in New York and London, 1830-1870* (Chicago: University of Chicago Press, 1977).

[6]   Detectives worked from the main office of the Metropolitan Police in Old Scotland Street; this gave rise to the investigative section being identified as Scotland Yard.

[7]   Michael S. Hindus, *Prison and Plantation: Crime, Justice and Authority in Massachusetts and South Carolina, 1767-1878* (Chapel Hill: University of North Carolina Press, 1980).

[8]   John P. Reid, "Dividing the Elephant: the Separation of Mess and Joint Stock Property on the Overland Trail," *Hastings Law Journal* 28 (1976): 73; "Sharing the Elephant: Partnership and Concurrent Property on the Overland Trail," *University of Missouri, Kansas*

City, Law Review 45 (1977): 207; "Tied to the Elephant: Organization and Obligation on the Overland Trail," *University of Puget Sound Law Review* 1 (1977): 139; and "Paying for the Elephant: Property Rights and Civil Order on the Overland Trail," *Huntington Library Quarterly*, 41 (1977): 39-64.

9   Richard Maxwell Brown, *Strain of Violence: Historical Studies of American Violence and Vigilantism* (New York: Oxford University Press, 1975).

References

There is vast literature on current police practice and organization; recent historical writing has begun to enhance our understanding of the origins of modern police institutions.

On the English experience, with emphasis upon the London metropolitan area, see David Ascoli, *The Queen's Peace: The Origins and Development of the Metropolitan Police, 1829-1979* (London: Hamish Hamilton, 1979); Thomas A. Critchley, *A History of Police in England and Wales*, 2nd ed. (London: Constable & Co., 1978); W.L. Melville Lee, *A History of Police in England* (London: Methuen, 1901; reprint ed., Montclair, NJ: Patterson Smith, 1971); Sir Leon Radzinowicz, *A History of English Criminal Law and its Administration from 1750*, 5 vols. (London: Stephens, 1948-1986); Phillip T. Smith, *Policing Victorian London: Political Policing, Public Order and the London Metropolitan Police* (Westport, CT: Greenwood Press, 1985); John J. Tobias, *Crime and Police in England, 1700-1900* (New York: St. Martin's Press, 1979); and good materials comparing London and New York police forces are found in Wilbur R. Miller, *Cops and Bobbies: Police Authority in New York and London, 1830-1870* (Chicago: University of Chicago Press, 1977).

On American police organization, the best general source is James F. Richardson, *Urban Police in the United States* (Port Washington, NY: Kennikat Press, 1974). For an overview of policing in the nineteenth and early twentieth centuries, see Clive Emsley and Barbara Weinberger, *Policing West Europe: Politics, Professionalism, and Public Order, 1850-1940* (New York: Greenwood Press, 1991). Students will profit from the historical articles published in Jerome H. Skolnick and Thomas C. Gray, *Police in America* (Boston: Education Associates, 1975). The New York City police are discussed in Gerald Astor, *The New York Cops: An Informal History* (New York: Charles Scribner's Sons, 1971); and in the more scholarly James F. Richardson, *The New York Police: Colonial Times to 1901* (New York: Oxford University Press, 1970). On Boston see Roger Lane, *Policing the City: Boston, 1822-1885* (Cambridge: Harvard University Press, 1967); students are cautioned that Lane has adopted the broad eighteenth-century definition of police, which holds that policing involves all activity, including fire protection, public health regulation, water supply, and governance, as well as what is today known as "police"—law enforcement. On South Carolina and particularly Charleston, there is no monograph dealing entirely with police organization and the lack of records makes it unlikely that one will appear in the future. The following materials will be of interest: Edward P. Cantwell, "A History of the Charleston Police Force," *Yearbook, 1908, City of Charleston* (Charleston: Daggett Printing Co., 1909); Howell M. Henry, *The Police Control of the Slave in South Carolina,* reprint ed. (New York: Negro Universities Press, 1968); Michael S. Hindus, *Prison and Plantation: Crime, Justice and Authority in Massachusetts and South Carolina, 1767-1878* (Chapel Hill: University of North Carolina Press, 1980); and John B. O'Neall, *The Negro Law of South Carolina* (Columbia: John G. Bowman, 1848). On police and race relations generally, see Robert F. Wintersmith, *Police and the Black Community* (Lexington: Lexington Books, 1974).

For materials on the West, students will want to read Richard M. Brown, *Strain of Violence: Historical Studies of American Violence and Vigilantism* (New York: Oxford University Press, 1975); and John P. Reid's articles, cited above in note 8. See also Roger D.

McGrath, *Gunfighters, Highwaymen, and Vigilantes: Violence on the Frontier* (Berkeley: University of California Press, 1984). For an historical and contemporary discussion of native American principles of criminal justice, see Marianne O. Nielsen, ed., *Native Americans, Crime, and Justice* (Boulder, CO: Westview Press, 1996).

Legal aspects of slavery are reviewed in Donald G. Nieman, *Promises to Keep: African-Americans and the Constitutional Order, 1776 to the Present* (New York: Oxford University Press, 1991).

For a general review of the development of crime control methods west of the Mississippi River, see Wayne Gard, *Frontier Justice* (Norman: University of Oklahoma Press, 1949). Details regarding private law enforcement are provided by Patrick B. Nolan, *Vigilantes on the Middle Border: A Study of Self-Appointed Law Enforcement in the States of the Upper Mississippi from 1840 to 1880* (New York: Garland, 1987); and William C. Culberson, *Vigilantism: Political History of Private Power in America* (New York: Greenwood Press, 1990). Stephen Cresswell views crime control from the governmental perspective in *Mormons, Cowboys, Moonshiners, and Klansmen: Federal Law Enforcement in the South and West, 1870-1893* (Tuscaloosa: University of Alabama Press, 1991).

For further information concerning the development of policing in France, see Barry M. Shapiro, *Revolutionary Justice in Paris, 1789-1790* (Cambridge: Cambridge University Press, 1993); Eric A. Arnold, *Fouché, Napoleon, and the General Police* (Washington: University Press of American, 1979); Thomas R. Forstenzer, *French Provincial Police and the Fall of the Second Republic: Social Fear and Counterrevolution* (Princeton: Princeton University Press, 1981); Richard C. Cobb, *The Police and the People: French Popular Protest, 1789-1820* (Oxford: Clarendon Press, 1970); Jean Galtier-Boissiére, *Mysteries of the French Secret Police* (London: Stanley Paul & Company, 1938); Louis Canler, *Autobiography of a French Detective from 1818 to 1858* (New York: Arno Press, 1976); and Philip John Stead, *The Police of France* (London: Collier Macmillan Publishers, 1983).

A swashbuckling, but not necessarily accurate, account of the life of Vidocq is to be found in Eugene François Vidocq, *Memoirs of Vidocq, The Principal Agent of the French Police* (Philadelphia: T.B. Peterson, 1859). A more reliable source concerning Vidocq is Samuel Edwards, *The Vidocq Dossier: The Story of the World's First Detective* (Boston: Houghton Mifflin Company, 1977).

Notes and Problems

1. A recurring theme throughout this chapter is the need to balance efficiency in law enforcement against the danger that police will destroy the liberties of a free people. When comparing patterns of policing in France and England, consider whether there is a causal link between political instability and repressive police policies. Is that fear realistic? How did nineteenth-century reformers attempt to deal with public fears? To what degree does each police department owe its existence to the need for control of an "out group" in society, such as political opponents, immigrants, slaves, or disenfranchised English workingmen?

2. Public acceptance and cooperation are essential to police work. What means were taken by the French police authorities of the nineteenth century to assure these prerequisites? What means were taken by the English and American police authorities? Does psychological distance between a patrol officer and civilians on his or her beat work better than close familiarity? In this regard, compare the London and New York police departments.

3. What functions do uniforms play in police operations and administration? Why did the London police wait until 1842 to place their detectives in plain clothes? And why did New York policemen resist wearing uniforms, while Charleston police seem to have glorified in their uniforms and weaponry?

4. Much ado was made in the nineteenth century about the need for a "preventive" police function, where the visibility of the police force made crime less likely because it put fear in the hearts of would-be criminals. This, of course, was the beginning of an emphasis on patrol; but the night watchmen and constables also patrolled. Is it just that there were more law enforcement officials on the beat, or was there a qualitative change in the way in which the individual patrolmen acted as a first line of defense against criminal activity?

5. To what extent was preventive patrolling a product of the idea that identifiable "lower classes" or "criminal classes" were responsible for crime? This can be seen in London police practice, which placed a larger number of policemen in the areas where middle-class homes bordered on working-class districts. Of course, that did not restrict crime in working-class areas, which tended to have fewer police if they were isolated from "respectable" parts of town. On the other hand, "respectable" areas out of the reach of the "criminal class" were not heavily patrolled. The question arises "What happened when public transportation made all parts of a city accessible to the 'criminal classes'?" Did all this contribute to the rise of the suburbs?

Chapter 11

Turning Points in Constitutionalism and Criminal Justice (1787-1910)

Two mountain ranges, the Appalachians and the Rockies, divide the land surface of North America, but there is only one dividing point in national history: the American Civil War. This monumental struggle—between the industrial and immigrant North on one side, and the agrarian, nativist, and almost feudal South on the other—permanently altered United States history. No student of criminal justice can afford to ignore the Civil War, because it changed the way the nation was governed, and it profoundly altered the way men and women looked on law and social issues. For nearly 90 years Americans had thought of themselves as citizens of a given state or geographical region; that provincialism carried with it a preference for long-established ways of life and an isolation from new ideas and political concepts. Police systems in the three major regions differed markedly and, to a degree, reflected local development and cultural preferences.

Prewar America was modeled on the preferences of the men who drafted the federal Constitution in 1787. Strongly influenced by the Enlightenment and resistance to British imperial policy, American Revolutionary leaders sought to restrict political power and thus ensure individual freedom and liberty. One essential principle was the vesting of most coercive power in the states and restriction of the authority of the federal government. That was particularly so in the case of criminal law and its enforcement. It was felt that the exercise of criminal justice was best retained by the states. There its abuse could best be controlled by the people, who, through close surveillance of an officeholder and control of the ballot box, would protect individuals against the abuse of law enforcement authority. Early in the history of the republic, the United States Supreme Court held that there could be no common law crime against the United States. All federal crimes had to

TIME LINE

Turning Points in Constitutionalism and Criminal Justice (1787-1910)

1787-1789	A convention of delegates from each of the states meets in Philadelphia to prepare a Constitution of the United States. The Constitution is ratified by state ratifying conventions held in 1787 through 1789.
1812, 1816	The United States Supreme Court declares that there are no federal common law crimes; all federal crimes must be established by the enactment of a congressional statute.
1819, 1824	Opinions of the U.S. Supreme Court declare the supremacy of the federal government in matters committed to it by the Constitution.
1820	The Missouri Compromise, adopted as a federal statute, divides the Louisiana Territory into "slave" and "free" sections. It was declared unconstitutional in 1857 by the *Dred Scott* case.
1833	South Carolina "nullifies" the 1828 federal tariff; President Andrew Jackson threatens to use federal troops to enforce the law, if necessary. The state finally agrees to compromise tariff measure, but passes an act "nullifying" the president's authorization to use the army to enforce the 1828 tariff.
1850	The Compromise of 1850 establishes popular sovereignty in the territory ceded to the U.S. by Mexico in 1848. It also abolishes the slave trade in the District of Columbia, and strengthens the administration of the fugitive slave laws.
1856	Civil war breaks out in the Kansas Territory, fueled by disagreements between slave-owning settlers and "free soil" proponents.
1857	The U.S. Supreme Court announces its decision in *Dred Scott v. Sandford*, declaring that the Missouri Compromise was unconstitutional because it deprived Southern slave owners of their property without due process of law. The case also defined state citizenship as primary and a prerequisite for U.S. citizenship. For this reason blacks could not become citizens of the United States unless the state in which they resided recognized them as citizens.
1859	John Brown, having murdered five proslavery settlers in Kansas in 1856, staged an attack on Harper's Ferry, Virginia, intending to start a slave insurrection. He failed in gaining support, and his small band of abolitionists was defeated and captured by federal troops. Brown was convicted of treason and hanged in October 1859.
1860	In the 1860 presidential campaign, Abraham Lincoln defeats Stephen F. Douglas, and southern political leaders begin to speak out for secession.

Turning Points in Constitutionalism and Criminal Justice (1787-1910)

1860-1861	South Carolina's legislature passes an ordinance declaring the state's secession from the Union.
1861	Southern state delegates adopt a provisional constitution for the Confederate States of America; U.S. military installations and post offices seized, and Jefferson Davis was elected President of the Confederacy.
1861-1865	The Civil War was fought, primarily in the south, with Confederate military incursions repulsed at Antietam, Maryland, and Gettysburg, Pennsylvania. General Robert E. Lee surrendered at Appomattox Courthouse in April 1865, but some scattered Confederate military units continued to fight in Texas until August 1865.
1863	President Lincoln signs the Emancipation Proclamation, declaring that Blacks held in slavery in territory occupied by the Confederacy were freed.
1865	The Thirteenth Amendment, abolishing slavery throughout the United States, was ratified on December 18, 1865.
1866-1871	"Boss" Tweed gained political control of New York City, and through manipulation of city contracts, became wealthy and controlled access to public office. Convicted in 1871, he served four years in prison before his death.
1867	The U.S. Secret Service, an agency within the Treasury Department, was authorized to investigate fraud against the U.S. government. It subsequently was assigned duties for the protection of the President, and to investigate the activities of the Ku Klux Klan.
1868	President Andrew Johnson was impeached by the House of Representatives for violation of the Tenure of Office Act of 1867. He was acquitted by the Senate on May 16, 1868.
1868	The Fourteenth Amendment was ratified on July 28, 1868. It granted U.S. citizenship to all persons born or naturalized within the U.S., and also required that these citizens be recognized as citizens by the states in which they resided. It also prohibited states from denying due process or equal protection of the law to U.S. citizens.
1887-1918	The federal government implemented a stronger enforcement of its power to regulate, and in some instances, prohibit, the flow of interstate commerce.
1907	The Bureau of Investigation of the Department of Justice was established. In 1924 it became the Federal Bureau of Investigation.

be clearly set forth in a congressional statute, giving warning to all would-be offenders. In addition, there was a belief that all federal law enforcement had to be tied to one or more of the express legislative powers delegated to Congress by the Constitution. Thus, penalties might be established for counterfeiting coins of the federal government, for bribing customs officials, or for violating trade restrictions in oceanic commerce, but the federal government could not prosecute an individual for murder or theft because no express congressional power related to those offenses.

If the states appeared to be the dynamic and active agencies of American government, that was exactly what the Founding Fathers intended and what their descendants preferred. However, such a compartmentalization of law into state jurisdictions did not entirely serve the broad purpose of the federal Constitution. The initial impulse toward drafting the Constitution came from the need to increase trade between the various states, thereby rendering them less dependent on European nations and creating an economic common market. These relationships between the states required some modification of state powers. This was particularly the case in regard to fugitive slaves, runaway indentured servants, and criminals who fled from one state to another to avoid either arrest or imprisonment. Trade requires the easy transportation of goods between one place and another, and this frequently necessitated crossing state boundary lines. The collection of debts in other states, the preparation of contracts between merchants of different states, and the recognition of the statutory law and the court judgments of sister states all formed a part of the legal apparatus upon which American economic prosperity depended.

The 1787 Constitution also erected a government that, while federal in its domestic politics, was a single nation in its conduct of foreign relations. The President and Congress (more specifically, the Senate) dealt with diplomatic affairs, a power denied to the various states. The supremacy clause of the Constitution provided that treaties entered into by the United States were to be the supreme law of the land. It also provided that congressional statutes passed in accordance with the powers granted by the Constitution would be superior to state laws and that state laws in conflict with federal statutes would be of no effect.

This balance between state and federal power existed tenuously, if at all, in the years from 1789 to 1833. At the latter date, a strong nullification movement on the part of South Carolina threatened to wreck the Union on the rocks of state sovereignty. The argument involved the economic impact of federal tariffs that protected northern industrial enterprise even as they subjected southern agricultural products to the full risk of worldwide free trade. South Carolina called upon its concept of state power to reject, or nullify, the federal law. If President Andrew Jackson persisted in enforcing the tariff, the state threatened to use force to prevent him. Thus was born the principle of state interposition, that a state government might shield its people from the force of a federal statute. The 1833 Nullification Controversy ended in a standoff between the president and the state authorities; Jackson threatened to use force to compel the state to obey, but, at the same time, secured a repeal of the tariff in question. The state did not oppose the new tariff, but, as a defiant gesture, nullified the congressional act that empowered the president to use military force against South Carolina.

The United States government and South Carolina might engage in political and constitutional debates over tariff legislation, but the real issue was one of state sovereignty against national power in dealing with slavery. This also had been touched upon in the federal Constitution, but by way of silence. Despite the vast hordes of blacks held in slavery, no provision in the Constitution contained the word "slave." Certain "persons" were to be enumerated for electoral purposes as being three-fifths of a person, and individuals who fled their states to avoid "servitude" were subject to extradition. Either unable or unwilling to deal with the issue of slavery, the Founding Fathers had retained the status quo, and the law of slavery remained the law of the several states in which the institution survived. The expediency of this solution is apparent in the fact that before 1848 slavery was, for all intents and purposes, a matter of state law. Well entrenched in the South and insulated from federal intrusion, the "peculiar institution" flourished in the balmy climate of state sovereignty. Success in the Mexican War (1846-1848) brought new territories into the federal Union and revived the issue of slavery in America's new western territories. Southern planters awoke to the need to expand westward into more fertile lands, taking their slaves with them; at the same time, the activities of abolitionists and the success of the underground railroad (a series of shelters to aid slaves fleeing north to freedom) triggered interest in a strengthening of the federal fugitive slave laws. In many respects, it was not slavery that brought on the Civil War but the southern demand for expansion of slavery into the territories and an equally strong southern insistence that blacks fleeing slavery should be subject to arrest and extradition from northern free states.

This summary of the constitutional situation before the Civil War provides nothing more than an inkling of the complexity of the constitutional and legal issues that preceded the conflict. It does suggest that neither North nor South was particularly consistent in its support of states' rights or national power. Each was willing to use constitutional theory for its own economic and political purposes; thus, each contributed to new modes of legal thought and constitutional principles.

That the Civil War occurred is of primary importance; that it happened when it did is also of historical relevance. Urbanization and industrialization began to alter the North and require the institution of formal police organizations modeled on that of London.[1] Economic growth and diversification was moving the United States toward a position in world power that could not be evaded even by traditional American methods of cultural isolation. The United States experienced a burgeoning enthusiasm and national pride in the mid-nineteenth century that, although deflected somewhat by the painful war years, pressed on to explore the great riches of the North American continent and to build the United States into one of the great nations of the world. Elimination of the institution of slavery from southern life meant a major restructuring of that regional society and its economic system, but it also meant that southern entrepreneurs shared in the values of their northern industrial counterparts. Relieved by the Confederacy's surrender of the need to debate slavery in the territories, southerner and northerner alike got on with the serious business of making money in the mines, farms, and grazing lands of the West.

To say that the United States was not a nation in 1789 is incorrect, for there were high points of national power even in the orientation toward states' rights. However, it is accurate to view the nation as one that was governed primarily by state agencies and institutions. The Civil War, both in its inception and in its conduct, challenged the primacy of the states and confirmed the growing power of the federal government. Yet the inexorable growth of the American economy and the transcontinental expanse of the national territory created new demands for federal authority that might well have surfaced independently of the Civil War.

Constitutional Issues and Criminal Law

One of the dominant characteristics of criminal law is that it works as a form of coercion upon individuals, requiring their behavior to conform to minimal standards established by their society. Penal laws operate on individuals, and historically the person subjected to sanctions has been one who is part of the state imposing the sanctions; he or she is, in modern terminology, a citizen of the state and, thus subject to its criminal law. That identity of citizen and state works well in the context of a centralized political unit, but is beset with difficulties when forced to operate in a federated government where sovereignty is divided between constituent states and a central government. The problem was most starkly presented in the *Dred Scott* case (19 Howard 393), decided by the United States Supreme Court in 1857. Scott, a slave belonging to an Army officer, traveled with his master to the free states of Wisconsin and Illinois. Scott claimed that, because the law of those jurisdictions did not recognize slavery, he was, in fact, a free man even after the two of them returned to Missouri, a slave state. The *Dred Scott* case clearly presented a question of status; Scott could not sue in the federal courts unless he was a citizen, and his citizenship had to be based upon his residence in a free state. Led by Chief Justice Roger B. Taney, the Court held that citizenship was a matter of state law and that each state had the right to determine who was entitled to citizenship. In other words, when Dred Scott moved from Wisconsin to Missouri, he could not take his citizenship with him. There was no national citizenship in prewar America, only state citizenship, which carried with it (almost as an afterthought) federal citizenship.

Because of the pro-state orientation of the *Dred Scott* case, antislavery activists directed their attention to the legal concept of citizenship. In the years immediately following the Civil War, it was deemed necessary to protect free blacks against actions by state governments that would deprive them of their civil rights, and the Fourteenth Amendment was ratified as the instrument to ensure the citizenship of free blacks wherever they might choose to reside:

> All persons born or naturalized in the United States, and subject to the jurisdiction thereof, are citizens of the United States and of the State wherein they reside. No State shall make or enforce any law which shall abridge the privileges or immunities of citizens of the United States; nor shall any State deprive any person of life, liberty or property, without due process of law; nor deny to any person within its jurisdiction the equal protection of the laws.[2]

Simply stated, the Fourteenth Amendment reversed the priorities of the *Dred Scott* case. In *Dred Scott*, state citizenship was the foundation on which federal citizenship depended. After July 28, 1868, federal citizenship was primary, and state citizenship resulted whenever a federal citizen chose to reside in any given state. Furthermore, the amendment recognized privileges and immunities of citizens of the United States, wherever they might reside, and protected them against state action. Also forbidden were state deprivations of life, liberty, or property, except through the use of due process of law. Finally, persons were guaranteed equal protection of the laws and states were forbidden to deny equality in the application of their laws. These are sweeping guarantees for the security of the individual against state action. Originally, the U.S. Supreme Court seemed inclined to limit their application to the specific situation of freed blacks, but ultimately the Fourteenth Amendment has become the focal point for the exercise of federal control over state criminal procedure. It applies to all citizens, male or female, and of all racial backgrounds; in certain cases, it has also been held to apply to resident aliens, minor children, and individuals who are mentally disturbed, retarded, or unable to act for themselves.

Corbis Images

Dred Scott (1795-1858)—American. The *Dred Scott* case in 1857 established a pro-state orientation that was later reversed by the Fourteenth Amendment.

The due process of law provision earlier appeared in the Fifth Amendment to the federal Constitution, adopted in 1791. It had been held to restrict federal action that took a citizen's life, liberty, or property, but not to inhibit the states in their criminal procedures or property seizures. Ironically, it was the Fifth Amendment's due process clause that Chief Justice Taney invoked to reason that, to the extent that the Missouri Compromise (which divided the Louisiana Territory into free and slave sections, making Wisconsin a free state) freed Scott from slavery, it took his master's property without due process of law.[3] As such, it was unconstitutional, null and void. The same phrase was inserted in the Fourteenth Amendment to protect individuals against harsh or irregular procedures on the part of state authorities. Subsequent legal development would expand the due process clause into two significant protections for individuals: Procedural due process requires that state (and federal) governments follow pre-established and fair procedures in taking criminal or civil action against a person. Substantive due process goes even further. It asserts that even if all the proper procedures are followed, there are limits beyond which a government may not go without unconstitutionally violating the rights of its citizens. Substantive due process restricts legislative, executive, and judicial aspects of political action, and both procedural and substantive due process have played a vital role in the federal Supreme Court's establishment of standards for state criminal procedure in the twentieth century.

Government at Flood Tide

The Civil War itself added a new dimension to governmental power. With few exceptions, the administration of federal power was nearly invisible in prewar American life, and when it emerged, resistance by the states or among the people tended to blunt federal initiatives. One assertion of federal power occurred in Jefferson's futile attempt to impede foreign trade through the Embargo Act of 1807. Totally dependent on state officials to enforce the federal statute, the president soon found that widespread opposition and evasion were undermining his objectives. Another example was the enactment of the Fugitive Slave Act provisions of the Compromise of 1850, which were designed to use federal officials and special procedures to secure the extradition of slaves from free states. Mob violence and state obstruction severely hampered the implementation of this law, exhibiting the dearth of coercive power in the central government and serving only to heighten northern antipathy to the growing pro-southern policy of the presidents and Congress. For the most part, Americans were lightly governed. They liked it that way and reacted strongly when federal officials attempted to introduce unpopular practices into the various states.

The first cannonball that Confederate General Beauregard sent into Fort Sumter, South Carolina, magically altered that simple world of the early republic and ushered in a period of vastly expanded federal presence in the daily life of all Americans. Initially, this stronger federal presence was the product of the war itself, because the need for economic mobilization demanded that each contestant wring the greatest possible support from all natural and human resources. In

Bombardment of Fort Sumter, Charleston Harbor, April 12 and 13, 1861, which initiated the Civil War, leading to an expanded federal presence in the lives of Americans.

addition, there was, in both the North and South, a substantial number of dissenting citizens who protested, by word and deed, the government's course of action. The control of internal disaffection, with the related task of combating espionage and sabotage, was a primary concern of Lincoln's administration. The task was complicated by the fact that disloyal activities were not prohibited by any federal statute. The sanctions for treason applied to the northern supporters of the Confederacy, and the constitutionally-defined offense of treason was one that had been narrowly construed and subject to stringent standards of proof. Lincoln and his advisers resorted to suspension of the writ of habeas corpus (thereby permitting military retention of civilian offenders without the privilege of recourse to civilian courts) and a series of emergency actions designed to maintain order, even as the Union army took form for the long struggle that awaited it. Ultimately, a series of federal statutes made provision for the prosecution of disloyalty in the form of espionage, sabotage, and resistance to the government.

TIME CAPSULE

Prosecution of Henry Wirz

At the end of the war between the states, in a precedent-setting case, Captain Henry Wirz was tried and executed for war crimes. In March 1864, Captain Wirz of the Confederate Army had been assigned the post of keeper of the inner prison at Andersonville, Georgia, and remained until the prison closed in April 1865. Soon afterward, Wirz was arrested and arraigned on charges of war crimes and murder. Wirz was accused of combining, confederating, and conspiring together with John H. Winder, Richard B. Winder,

Isaiah H. White, W.S. Winder, R.R. Stevenson, and others unknown, to injure the health and destroy the lives of federal soldiers held as prisoners of war. He was also charged with 13 specific murders "in violation of the laws and customs of war."

There was no dispute regarding the egregious condition of federal prisoners in the Confederate prisoner of war camp known as Andersonville; they suffered, and many died, from malnutrition, dysentery, and other diseases and from inadequate shelter and sanitation. The press fanned hatred of Wirz with labels such as fiend, savage, barbarian, and bloodthirsty monster. In his defense, Wirz claimed that he had struggled to provide humane conditions for the federal prisoners but was unable to do so. He cited the lack of supplies in a government that faced critical shortages of food, medicine, and housing for its own military and civilian personnel, and he also pointed to a lack of cooperation by government officials. The plight of the prisoners was exacerbated by the refusal of the federal govenment to exchange prisoners and by the policy of listing medicine as contraband.

On August 23, 1865, Wirz was brought to trial before a military tribunal. In the words of one historian, "Wirz was a dead man from the start" (Marvel, 1994: 243). Serious questions were raised then and later concerning the degree to which Wirz had a fair trial. At the time, critics protested trial by court-martial rather than civilian court. The testimony of government witnesses was in part internally contradictory and in part did not conform to known facts; furthermore, some key witnesses had received rewards from the government. Persons who wanted to testify in Wirz's defense claimed they were unable to do so. Whether Wirz deliberately and maliciously mistreated prisoners remains in dispute.

Wirz's superior officer at Andersonville, General John H. Winder, had died prior to the trial and none of the named conspirators was tried. Nevertheless, Wirz was found guilty of conspiracy. He was also found guilty of 11 of the specified murders, even though he was on sick leave at the time four of them occurred. An appeal for clemency was denied and he was executed in November 1865.

Bitter controversy surrounded the trial and it has continued to prompt analysis. Contemporaries and historians have questioned whether the demonization of Wirz and his execution were designed to serve the political purpose of forcing Confederates to face their responsibility for having caused the misery of war. Jefferson Davis rose to the defense of Wirz as a martyr to a cause through adherence to the truth, and the United Daughters of the Confederacy managed to have a monument erected in Wirz's memory.

Source: William Marvel, *Andersonville: The Last Depot* (Chapel Hill: University of North Carolina Press, 1994).

Given the threat to Lincoln's government, it is remarkable that harsher methods were not employed, but necessity drove Congress into wartime measures that were unheard of prior to the bombardment of Fort Sumter. One example was the enactment of a law permitting *conscription* (a draft—the forerunner of the modern Selective Service System). When it became impossible to obtain enough voluntary enlistments to fill the ranks of the Union army, the "draft bill" provided for the induction of all men capable of bearing arms. Among its provisions was a clause that permitted wealthy draftees to pay someone else to take their place in the ranks. It was the coercive aspects of the conscription law that triggered draft riots in New York City and other metropolitan areas. Protection of railroad and telegraph lines into the city of Washington was another vital concern that led to the use of federal troops and military trials to prevent disruption of communications with the capital city. The Civil War caused the enactment of the first federal income tax law; it established procedures for military contracting that persist to the present day; and it started the federal government on its long and controversial career as a printer of paper money, called "greenbacks," in the inflationary years ahead.

TIME CAPSULE

The Impeachment and Acquittal of President Andrew Johnson

The process of impeachment is established by the Constitution of the United States, and in the case of a number of senior federal officers, it is the only method to remove them from office. Frequently removal from office is a precondition for subsequent prosecution for criminal acts committed while in office. The Constitution provides that the U.S. House of Representatives must make charges against the federal officer, and this presentation of charges is called an impeachment. Once charges are presented to the Senate, the Senate proceeds to try the case and either acquits or convicts the individual of the impeachment charges. When the president of the United States is tried, the Constitution provides that the Chief Justice of the U.S. Supreme Court will preside at the trial. Only two presidents have been impeached by the House and tried by the Senate—Andrew Johnson in 1868 and Bill Clinton in 1998. Both cases raise interesting questions for students of criminal justice, despite the obvious political overtones present in each trial.

Army occupation of the defeated southern states proved to be the flashpoint for an explosive 1868 impeachment trial of President Andrew Johnson. As the successor to President Lincoln, who was assassinated on April 14, 1865, Johnson became commander-in-chief of the Army and thus responsible for the military government of the South. Within the chain of command was his Secretary of War, Edwin Stanton, who had been appointed by Lincoln and who sympathized with the members of Congress who looked forward to black citizens voting in the southern states. The commanding general of the Army was Ulysses S. Grant, the national hero who led the Union to victory and accepted General Robert E. Lee's surrender at Appomattox Court House, Virginia. General Grant was generally viewed as a likely Republican candidate in the 1868 presidential election campaign. He was also allied with the "radical" congressional group that advocated delaying readmission of the Southern states to the federal Union until the voting rights and freedom of black freedmen was assured.

President Johnson favored prompt readmission of the southern states, and was generally opposed to federal power being used to gain substantial social changes in the conquered states. He had been generous in granting pardons to former Confederate leaders, and he used his influence to gain recognition of newly elected state governments in the South. Some historians of the period have termed Johnson a racist, while others picture him as a champion for the constitutional powers of the president who stopped, or at least delayed, congressional domination of the federal government. There is no lack of evidence that President Johnson acted with determination to remove "radical" military officers from command of the military districts through which the former Confederate states were governed. These generals were replaced by others who believed in a more benign approach to the South's newly emergent white supremacists. Ultimately, he discharged Secretary of War Stanton from office, having prevailed upon General Grant to accept an interim appointment as Secretary of War. Unwisely, he delivered speeches and gave press interviews attacking the "radical" faction of the Republican Party in Congress.

Earlier, Congress had passed a Tenure of Office Act, which required that before the president might dismiss a governmental officer who had been appointed with senatorial approval, he was required to obtain the advice and consent of the Senate to the removal. There was an immediate but premature reaction to the president's action. The House of Representatives considered but rejected a motion to file impeachment charges in December 1867. However, one month later the Senate refused to concur in Secretary Stanton's discharge and General Grant, persuaded that Stanton was thus restored to office, vacated the War Office to Stanton. Within two weeks of these events, the House voted to file impeachment charges against

the president, and formal charges were presented to the Senate on March 4, 1868.

The impeachment trial began on March 23, and proved to be the social event of the Washington season. Ladies crowded the Senate gallery, rustling in taffeta and crinolines, as the opposing counsel debated the constitutionality of the Tenure of Office Act and whether President Johnson had conspired with others to violate the laws of the United States. By the time testimony concluded and the lawyers had finished their closing arguments, it was the first week in May and the Senate, as the Court of Impeachment, adjourned for 10 days. When the senators reassembled they voted on the least controversial article of the charges, and it was discovered that there was one vote less than the two-thirds majority required for conviction. A similar fate met the charge that President Johnson had violated the Tenure of Office Act by dismissing Secretary Stanton. Seven Republican senators voted with the Democratic Party senators, resulting in the President's acquittal. Having lost on these matters, the House managers of the prosecution withdrew the remaining charges.

Several reasons have been suggested for Johnson's acquittal. One is that the members of the Senate disliked and mistrusted the president pro tempore of the Senate, Benjamin F. Wade, who would have become president if Johnson had been convicted. Wade advocated women's rights, high tariffs, and permitting black Americans to vote. While these positions were in accord with the wishes of the radical Republicans, it alienated many of their moderate Republican party associates. Another factor was the legislative history of the Tenure of Office Act, which clearly showed that Secretary Stanton was removed from its protective provisions before it was passed by Congress. In addition, a number of senators felt that conviction should occur only if the accused's actions made him subject to a criminal indictment. Finally, the American people appeared to have lost their enthusiasm for radical reconstruction of the southern states prior to the time President Johnson's impeachment was tried.

Like many other impeachments, the trial of President Johnson may be seen as meaning many—and contradictory—things. At least in the short run, it meant that the "radical" Republican wish to establish black majority governments in the South would be delayed. It also vindicated the executive branch's control of the Army, even though the Tenure of Office Act continued on the statute books and was not held unconstitutional.[1] On the other hand, the election of General Grant to the presidency in November of 1868, and the growing power of Congress in the direction of southern state reconstruction, both suggest that President Johnson won but a short-lived victory. Most historians agree that the presidency entered a period of declining power following this aborted impeachment effort, not to be reversed until the dynamic presidential leadership of Theodore Roosevelt (1901-1909).

Questions

1. Do you believe that the impeachment and trial of President Bill Clinton will have the same long-term impact as the Johnson impeachment did? What reasons can you give for your conclusion?

2. Should impeachment proceedings be conditioned upon there being an "indictable offense" that has been charged against the president, or some other official? To what degree should the president's opposition to the will of Congress subject him to the impeachment and conviction process?

3. Recall that President Richard M. Nixon resigned from office in 1974 after being told that his party would no longer support him after it was learned, from tape-recorded evidence, that he may have conspired to obstruct justice in regard to the Watergate burglaries. Does impeachment serve as a lever to ensure ethical behavior, even when it is no more than a threat?

4. Impeachment and conviction simply remove a public official from office, thereby removing from him any immunity from prosecution. What normally would follow a conviction by the Senate is a trial of the indictable offense by the federal or state court exercising criminal jurisdiction. Should evidence submitted in the impeachment proceeding be admissible in such a subsequent criminal trial?

Sources: There is a well-written study of the Johnson impeachment by Gene Smith, *High Crimes and Misdemeanors: The Impeachment and Trial of Andrew Johnson* (New York: William Morrow & Co., 1977); equally well-written, but more scholarly in focus, are Hans L. Trefousse, *Impeachment of a President: Andrew Johnson, the Blacks, and Reconstruction,* 2d ed. (New York: Fordham University Press, 1999); and Michael Les Benedict, *The Impeachment and Trial of Andrew Johnson* (New York: Norton, 1973).

[1] Subsequently, the U.S. Supreme Court has held that the president may legally discharge a postmaster without obtaining senatorial approval; however, when an official is appointed by joint action of Congress and the president to serve on an independent commission, the consent of the appointing authorities must be obtained. *Myer v. United States*, 272 U.S. 52 (1926); *Humphrey's Executor v. United States*, 295 U.S. 602 (1935).

Union army success in the field introduced still another area for expanded government activity. Generals charged with the control of Southern populations recently reclaimed for the Union were faced with the vast problem of maintaining law and order, while at the same time dealing with the human suffering and despair produced by the war and Confederate defeat. Dealing with blacks after the Emancipation Proclamation was a special problem delegated early to the Freedman's Bureau, which had the monumental task of educating, training, and sustaining former slaves as they made the difficult transition from perpetual servitude into a wage-earning labor system. To do all these things required an entirely new way of doing business in government offices. At the beginning of the war, the State Department filing system was the same as it had been under the first Secretary of State, Thomas Jefferson: a cubbyhole for each nation recognized by the United States. By the end of the war, the State Department was a vast array of specialized offices and bureaus, each with its own peculiar system of maintaining records. Prior to the Civil War, the Treasury Department (and particularly the Customs Service) was the only federal executive agency of any size. After the war, there remained a vast array of administrative bureaus, each charged with a particular function in the operation of the national state.

Effective Police and Burgeoning National Enterprise

Given the extent of disaffection in the North and the limited experience with government administration, it came as something of a surprise that the Union of loyal states did not disintegrate, but instead reshaped itself into a cohesive nation waging a successful campaign against a determined enemy. The surrender at Appomattox terminated the southern concept of states' rights and ended once and for all the idea that secession could be done peacefully. The Union was one and indivisible, but it was also a different Union than had existed in 1860. Constitutionally, the foundation for growing federal power existed in the post-Civil War amendments, which altered the position of the states and the federal government. But even more than this took place in the bustle of the war years. Americans discovered that government was capable of undertaking a wide spectrum of tasks hitherto left to private enterprise or not done at all. Jeffersonian preferences for small and limited government were submerged in the need to establish effective and coordinated guidance of a nation at war. The lessons of the Civil War remained after Appomattox as guides for the evolution of a new bureaucracy at both the state and federal levels.

Despite the discovery of administrative efficiency, Americans did not wholeheartedly embrace government intervention into all areas of national life. The philosophy of social Darwinism emerged during the war years to produce fascination with laissez-faire economics. Essentially, social

Darwinism applied to human society the rules of evolution developed by scientist Charles Darwin to explain the diversity among animals and plants. Darwin's suggestion that human beings might well be products of primate evolution drew the full fire of religious fundamentalists who held a literal belief in the biblical account of creation. While that debate raged, English philosopher Herbert Spencer took up Darwin's theme that survival belonged to the life form that proved to be the fittest. He concluded that the human species would be improved under free competition, for then only the fittest would survive to produce offspring. The ultimate in social Darwinism was the suggestion by Thomas Malthus, who studied population statistics and calmly observed that high birth rate was limited by the starvation of children who were unfit to survive. A true follower of social Darwinism strongly objected to poor relief in any form, because it merely perpetuated the genetic strain of those unable to compete, and thus frustrated the natural selection method by which only the fit lived on to reproduce their kind.

Social Darwinism particularly attracted American businessmen who emerged from the war with profits ready for investment in westward expansion and industrial enterprise. These robber barons (who are sometimes more sympathetically called "captains of industry") set forth to establish vast personal fortunes in the construction and operation of railroads (Cornelius Vanderbilt and Colis P. Huntington), steel works (Andrew Carnegie), and oil refineries (John D. Rockefeller). Their leadership and daring established new levels of achievement in American business, but their methods led to the establishment of governmental agencies at the federal and state levels designed to limit the worst aspects of free competition, and to prevent economic competition from victimizing large segments of the population. The first federal regulatory agency was the Interstate Commerce Commission (1887), created by Congress to regulate railroad rates for goods carried in interstate commerce.

Gradually increased economic activity altered the criminal law, both at the federal and state levels. A favorite speculative device of the robber barons was to issue shares of a corporation's stock that represented assets far beyond those in its possession. This "watering" of stock was a trap for the unwary. At first it was considered a shrewd, but otherwise unobjectionable, bit of sharp dealing. Eventually, both state governments and the United States Congress found it necessary to legislate controls over security markets and to impose penal sanctions on those who traded upon public naïveté. Another competitive technique was to establish business combinations or pools that gave one company, or a group of companies, a monopoly in a critical field. Called "forestalling" by an earlier generation, such practices were as old as Athens. In 1890, Congress passed the Sherman Antitrust Act, the first federal law dealing with the problem. Supplemented by newer legislation to deal with later forms of monopolistic organization, the Sherman Act remains one of the primary statutes for the enforcement of fair competition today. It provided for civil remedies to competitors wronged by a monopoly, and it also contained criminal sanctions by means of fines against convicted corporations, their officers, and their directors. Investigation and prosecution of offenses involving securities regulation or monopolistic practices required a very special expertise. In these fields and many others, specialized skills, such as accounting and knowledge of marketing practices, were essential. Law enforcement became more complex and more demanding in terms of professional training for its personnel.

A rapidly expanding national economy made it difficult to enforce law at the state level and, gradually, federal legislation was enacted based upon the constitutional power granted to Congress by the Interstate Commerce Clause. Originally expounded in the 1824 case of *Gibbons v. Ogden* (9 Wheaton 1), the full potential of the Interstate Commerce Clause was not realized until late in American history. It was the events of the second half of the nineteenth century that triggered the enactment of statutes that imposed penalties on those who conducted illegal activities across state boundaries. These statutes included the Mann White Slave Traffic Act of 1910, which made it a federal offense to transport women across state lines for immoral purposes, and the Pure Food and Drug Act of 1906, which imposed federal standards for foodstuffs and medicines carried in interstate commerce.

In earlier times, the federal power to regulate interstate commerce had not involved the prohibition of certain types of goods from the interstate trade. However, during the reforms of the Progressive period (1901-1913), the Supreme Court approved federal actions that denied access of certain products to interstate commerce. When this prohibition involved criminal sanctions, it represented a new type of federal police power. First recognized in *Champion v. Ames* (188 U.S. 321, 1903), a Supreme Court case upholding federal penalties for sending lottery tickets through the mails, federal police power became a focal point for growing criminal justice jurisdiction. In a related development, the Supreme Court in 1904 approved the use of the federal taxing power as a means of eliminating butter-colored margarine from interstate commerce (*McCray v. United States*, 195 U.S. 27).

During and after the Civil War, counterfeiting paper money became a major federal problem. The United States Secret Service was organized in the Treasury Department on July 5, 1865, with William P. Wood as its first chief. A personal friend of Secretary of War Edwin Stanton, Wood had been active in Union spy and detective work during the war. Originally his agency was restricted to the investigation of counterfeiting and was assigned 10 operatives for that purpose. In 1867, the Secret Service was given statutory authority to investigate cases of fraud against the federal government. As the only investigative agency of the United States, the Secret Service was prevailed upon to expand its authority whenever a vague provision in federal statutes permitted. Thus, it was assigned to investigate the Ku Klux Klan in the South during Reconstruction, and during the Spanish-American and First World Wars it served as the primary agency for gathering intelligence as well as preventing espionage and sabotage. In 1876, agents of the Secret

Service uncovered a plot to steal President Lincoln's body from his burial vault and to hold it ransom for the release of counterfeiter Ben Boyd from Joliet Federal Prison. Prompt action prevented success of the plan, and the culprits were turned over to state authorities for prosecution. Also beyond the agency's statutory authority was the job of protecting the president. In 1894, agents of the Secret Service foiled an attempt on President Grover Cleveland's life, but public opinion was alarmed when it was discovered that its agents guarded President William McKinley's private residence in Massachusetts (1898). The assassination of McKinley in 1901 created growing support for statutory approval of Secret Service protection, but not until passage of the Sundry Civil Expense Act of 1907 did Congress finally act in the matter.

When newly-installed President Calvin Coolidge needed a reliable and incorruptible agency to investigate the Teapot Dome bribery scandals,[4] he turned to the Secret Service. As a Treasury Department unit, the Secret Service was not subject to influence from Attorney General Harry Daugherty, one of the participants in the swindle and a holdover cabinet member from the corrupt Harding administration. This rebuff to the Bureau of Investigation of the Justice Department was only temporary. When Coolidge's new Attorney General, Harlan Fiske Stone, appointed J. Edgar Hoover to the directorship of the bureau, that agency began its rise to preeminence that would eclipse the investigative activities of the Secret Service. Ironically, the bureau, originally established in 1907, was itself a product of the Secret Service; eight agents transferred from the older agency formed the initial personnel of the Justice Department's infant Bureau of Investigation.

The evolution of federal law was doubtless the most significant criminal justice event from 1865 to 1910, but substantial segments of crime remained entirely within state jurisdiction. The major violent felonies, such as murder, rape, and robbery, remained punishable only by state law, as did property offenses such as larceny, arson, and burglary. After 1876, Union troops were withdrawn from the former states of the Confederacy, and during a period of extreme violence and terrorism, blacks gave up their right to vote and were held in subjection to white political authority. One lasting legacy of the military occupation of the South is the Posse Comitatus Act of 1883, which continues to provide criminal penalties against any army officer or enlisted person who engages in civilian police activities.

This dispersal of criminal law enforcement among the states remained part of the United States Constitution after the Civil War, and exists to the present day. It raises complex issues when an offense is both contrary to state law and also subject to federal sanctions. Cooperation between several states becomes a necessity in the detection and prosecution of crimes that are subject to state law but are committed in more than one state. It is no wonder that the framers of the British North America Act (1867), in preparing a framework for the Dominion of Canada, established a uniform criminal law for all of Canada and provided for the Royal Canadian Mounted Police as the single law enforcement entity in their federal union.

If the new United States was an arena for building fortunes, it was also a society in which there were serious disparities in living conditions. The heavy influx of European immigrants after the war resulted in a surplus of labor and a resulting reduction in wages. Desperate workers sent their wives into sewing factories and their children into industrial enterprises, attempting to secure enough through joint labor to support their large families. Housing was limited and expensive, causing urban workers to live cramped into apartments without light or ventilation. Disease flourished and men and women grew violent. Those who formed the "respectable" members of society became alarmed at the growing crime rate, the dangerous state of public health, and the human suffering that surrounded them. Never in the history of the United States had there been such a wide gap between the rich and the poor, and never had there been so many at the poverty level. Farmers also felt the economic crunch. Dependent upon railroads to transport their goods to markets, they were forced to pay high rates at a time when crops were bringing modest returns, and money was scarce and expensive to borrow. From these conditions arose labor organizations in the industrial areas and farmers' political and cooperative groups in the countryside. To protect their property, businessmen employed a growing number of private police forces, the most prominent being that established by George Pinkerton. Generally sympathetic to business interests, public officials at the state and federal levels tended to place their emphasis on maintaining law and order and protecting private property. It was during these years that the United States came closest to a full-scale class struggle between the interests of capital and those of the farmer and working class.

An "Open Spot" in Government: Political Corruption

Rapid social and economic growth leaves institutions in a state of disarray. Old bureaucratic methods are abandoned before new techniques can be developed and applied to changing needs. The American Civil War and the Reconstruction period were times when this disorientation was highly visible, and the confusion left a number of "open spots" for ambitious and unscrupulous individuals to exploit. A general decline in public morality characterized the years from 1865 to 1900, and corruption of the political process stalked the land.

As a consequence of the war itself, southern politics became dominated by an unlikely combination of illiterate freed blacks, southern scalawags (those who remained loyal to the Union throughout the War), and northern carpetbaggers (adventurers who moved south to seek their political fortunes). All southern whites who had served in Confederate civil or military positions were barred from office by virtue of the strict rules of Congress, which required clear proof of continued loyalty during the war. "Reconstructed" southern legislatures remained in control of the once-rebellious states until they were readmitted to the Union and until presidential pardons restored the political rights of former Confederates. Despite their inexperience and vulnerability to bribery, the Reconstruction legislatures did yeoman work in caring for the needs of their devastated states. Public schools were established for the first time, new railroad lines were built, and economic recovery began as a free labor system was implemented. However, there were numerous instances of extravagant expenditures; solid gold fixtures were purchased to decorate the legislative halls of southern states whose inhabitants were in imminent danger of starvation.

Although the irresponsibility of Southern reconstruction legislatures was strongly criticized, it was a pale reflection of the moral decay in northern political life. It was generally accepted that state legislatures were closely allied with the economic interests of expanding commerce and industry. Monopolies were granted to the corporations or individuals who offered the highest bribes to the legislators. At the national level, Congress deemed the people's interest best served by vast grants of the most valuable lands in the West to railroad entrepreneurs. The administration of the Union war hero, President Ulysses S. Grant, was shaken by a series of scandals involving theft of whiskey tax revenues and bribery in the disposition of Indian trading post privileges. Crime was becoming nonviolent, was directed toward the acquisition of substantial property interests, and frequently involved some form of theft from the government.

This period in American history is best exemplified by the rise of the city machine, a political organization that operated on the premise that the path to office was to provide jobs or other valuable services to a majority of the voters. The machine was itself the result of growing complexity in the American system of government. As more immigrants flooded into the United States and became naturalized citizens, politics became the only way in which they could gain relief from their difficult financial situations. Many needed jobs and found themselves appointed police officers by the aldermen of their local wards. Others started small businesses and benefited from the influence of their political ward leaders in obtaining contracts from city governments and institutions. In turn, they loyally voted for the politicians who provided these economic rewards. Many foreign-born citizens merely adapted old ways of conducting business to the American scene. They had previously enjoyed the protection of nobles or gentry in exchange for their labor or political support. It was easy to make similar arrangements with native-born political leaders in the United States. From the American politician's standpoint, the new voters were to be preferred for their reliability; they were not likely to be dissuaded from their allegiance by reformist attacks upon the ward bosses.

This arrangement gave birth to such colorful characters as William Marcy Tweed, reputed in history as the "Boss" of New York City from 1866 to 1871. Beginning as the foreman of a volunteer fire company, Tweed became a prominent figure in Democratic Party politics and a member of Tammany Hall. Tweed's initiation into political life began with his election as an alderman for New York County in 1851. After serving one term, he was elected to the House of Representatives but found the office uninteresting. By 1856 he was back in New York City, having been elected to the Board of Supervisors, and shortly thereafter he was to play a major role in the erection of the New York County courthouse, authorized by legislative act in 1858. A physical monument to political corruption, Tweed's courthouse was projected to cost no more than $150,000. When construction was stopped by reforming newspaper editors and irate citizens in 1871, the estimated expenditures for the partially completed building ranged from $3,200,000 to $8,224,000. The inflated costs were, for the most part, attributable to the self-dealing of the Tweed Ring and a fraudulent but profitable system of contracting. When the city needed goods or services, a contract would be issued to a favored firm, which inflated its cost estimates by at least 50 percent. The difference between the fair price and the amount paid by the city was divided between the fraudulent contractor and the politician who awarded the contract.

As an indication of the law's inadequacy, it should be noted that Boss Tweed served only one year in prison, convicted of the misdemeanor of failing to properly audit the city's accounts. The remaining three years he spent in prison before his death were caused by his inability to raise bail and obtain release from arrest in civil actions pending against him to reclaim the city's funds. While imprisonment for debt was a thing of the past, demands for high bail in politically sensitive cases were still very much available.

The Tweed case also provides a glimpse into the informality of prison discipline in the case of favored inmates. While he was held at the Ludlow Street Jail, it was Tweed's practice to take a ride with the warden and keepers to Central Park, where he was permitted to walk with his son. After their promenade, the entire group went to Tweed's residence, where dinner was served to the prison officials and the entire family. After the cigars were finished, Tweed and his jailers returned to the jail. But in December 1875, when the warden, keepers, and family relaxed downstairs, Tweed slipped out the back of the house and headed for parts unknown. He was later discovered in Spain, identified by Spanish police officials who recognized him through one of Thomas Nast's cartoons.

One final matter must be noted; New York City aldermen controlled the appointment of municipal police officers within their wards. While this was not of great financial consideration, it did mean that police officers owed their positions and their continuity in office to Tammany Hall. Professional police activity was subject to direction from the same political groups that engaged in widespread graft and theft; as a consequence, selected criminals might enjoy protection for a price paid into the party's pocket, or into a politician's private treasury.

Summary

Post-Civil War America passed through several decades that were undoubtedly the darkest area of national history, and criminal justice was heavily influenced by the political corruption of the day. While many explanations have been suggested, the most plausible would seem to be that the nation had grown well beyond its earlier political simplicity. Economic growth outstripped governmental control, leaving only a system of favoritism and bribes. The tremendous expansion of government during the war had created opportunities for profiteering that were the foundation for later political corruption and economic exploitation. The changing nature of the electorate, which now contained large numbers of immigrants and recently freed blacks, required new techniques of political leadership and manipulation, and gave rise to a new type of professional politician who dealt in favors and took payment in votes.

A wide divergence between the wealthy and the poor laborer meant that the law was more rigidly enforced against the impoverished. Politicians elected by the votes of the poor were quick to accept financial favors or bribes from the rich. If political office was bought by patronage, it was also a capital investment that yielded good profits in terms of bribes and business advantage. In a very real sense, the politicians of Boss Tweed's era were brokers of economic and political power; in the spirit of the times, they made more than adequate commissions on their services.

Those years also marked a time of divergence in American cultures. Temperance agitation succeeded in imposing prohibition in many of the states, but it could not stamp out alcohol in cities dominated by hard-drinking immigrant majorities who held political control. States like New York would stretch their constitutional powers to the ultimate (and take over the city police), just as the Confederates and Union antagonists did before and during the Civil War. However, state political power was inadequate to deal with the complex interstate problems of economic control and regulation that faced the United States. Problems of interstate flight of criminals and the exchange of information on crime became more acute. Crime itself became infinitely more complex and subtle, leading to the rise of white-collar crime. It was difficult to tell the criminal from the upright citizen, and easier to suspect everyone's motives and attribute all action to greed.

Endnotes

1   See Chapter 10.

2   Constitution of the United States, Amendment XIV, sec. 1.

³   Before his opinion in *Dred Scott*, Chief Justice Taney had undermined a number of Marshall Court precedents upholding private property rights; his uncharacteristic upholding of the master's property rights in *Dred Scott* led contemporaries to comment that he was a strong advocate of private property rights, but only as they existed in slaves.

⁴   These involved the acceptance of bribes by Interior Secretary Albert B. Fall and other high-ranking officials in the Harding administration, which resulted in the lease of federal oil reserves to a number of private oil companies. Uncovered after Harding's death in 1923, the corrupt practices resulted in a series of trials that did not end until 1928.

References

Two good general surveys of the period are James M. McPherson, *Ordeal by Fire: The Civil War and Reconstruction*, 1st ed. (New York: Alfred Knopf, 1982); and James G. Randall and David Donald, *The Civil War and Reconstruction*, 2nd ed. revised (Lexington, MA: D.C. Heath, 1969). On constitutional changes, see James G. Randall, *Constitutional Problems under Lincoln*, revised ed. (Urbana: University of Illinois Press, 1951); Harold M. Hyman, *A More Perfect Union: The Impact of the Civil War and Reconstruction on the Constitution* (Boston: Houghton, Mifflin Co., 1975); Harold M. Hyman and William M. Wiecek, *Equal Justice Under Law: Constitutional Development 1835-1875* (New York: Harper & Row, 1982); and Rembert W. Patrick, *The Reconstruction of the Nation* (New York: Oxford University Press, 1967).

On the rise of big business and its operations, see Matthew Josephson, *The Robber Barons: The Great American Capitalists, 1861-1901* (New York: Harcourt, Brace & World, 1962). Among the best detailed studies are Louis M. Hacker, *The World of Carnegie: 1865-1901*, 1st ed. (Philadelphia: Lippincott, 1968); David Freeman Hawke, *John D.: The Founding Father of the Rockefellers* (New York: Harper & Row, 1980); Harold C. Livesay, *Andrew Carnegie and the Rise of Big Business* (Boston: Little, Brown & Co., 1975); and Allan Nevins, *John D. Rockefeller: The Heroic Age of American Enterprise*, 2 vols. (New York: Charles Scribner's Sons, 1940).

For a general understanding of farmer-railroad issues and the rise of agrarian reform movements, see John D. Hicks, *The Populist Revolt: A History of the Farmer's Alliance and the Populist Party* (Lincoln: University of Nebraska Press, 1959). Violent confrontations between organized labor and businesses are discussed in Samuel Yellen, *American Labor Struggles* (New York: S.A. Russell, 1956). Also of value are Richard Hofstadter, *The Age of Reform: From Bryan to F.D.R.* (New York: Alfred Knopf, 1955); Norman Pollack, *The Populist Response to Industrial America: Midwestern Populist Thought* (New York: W.W. Norton, 1962).

For discussions of the U.S. Secret Service, see Walter S. Bowen and Harry E. Neal, *The United States Secret Service* (Philadelphia: Chilton Co., 1960); and Philip H. Melanson, *The Politics of Protection: The U.S. Secret Service in the Terrorist Age* (New York: Praeger, 1984). For a history of nongovernmental security, see M. Lipson, "Private Security: A Retrospective," *The Annals of the American Academy of Political and Social Sciences* 498, no. 7: 11-22.

On social Darwinism and its American evolution, see Richard Hofstadter, *Social Darwinism in American Thought*, revised ed. (New York: G. Braziller, 1959).

There is an extensive body of literature on Boss Tweed and his ring. See William Alan Bales, *Tiger in the Streets* (New York: Dodd, Mead & Co., 1962); Alexander B. Callow, Jr., *The Tweed Ring* (New York: Oxford University Press, 1966); Leo Hershkowitz, *Tweed's New York: Another Look* (Garden City, NY: Anchor Press, 1977); Denis T. Lynch, *Boss Tweed: The Story of a Grim Generation* (New York: Arno Press, 1974); and Seymour J. Mandelbaum, *Boss Tweed's New York* (New York: John Wiley and Sons, 1965). For a lively discussion of the courthouse and its builders, see Alexander B. Callow, Jr., "The House that Tweed Built," *American Heritage* 16 (December 1965): 65-69.

For evolution of legal principles of substantive and procedural criminal due process, see Kermit L. Hall, *The Magic Mirror: Law in American History* (New York: Oxford University Press, 1989); and Kermit L. Hall, William M. Wiecek, and Paul Finkelman, *American Legal History: Cases and Materials* (New York: Oxford University Press, 1991).

Societal definition of crime in nineteenth-century America and governmental response are traced in Lawrence M. Friedman, *Crime and Punishment in American History* (New York: Basic Books, 1993), Chapters 4-6.

Notes and Problems

1. Why does war have a tendency to expose the vulnerable points in political and legal institutions? How did the Union manage to survive while maintaining its constitutional forms? Is the Constitution "suspended" in time of war? Should it be?

2. What impact did the Civil War have on criminal justice? Did it hamstring local authorities by the limits of the Fourteenth Amendment? Did it facilitate federal-state cooperation? To what extent did crime go unpunished because of a lack of federal or state authority?

3. Should government attempt to regulate business enterprise? If it does so, should it resort to criminal sanctions? How do you imprison a corporation? Do economic offenses fit into the usual definition of criminal activity? If everyone agrees that a given form of competition is acceptable, should government condemn it?

4. As class distinctions widened after the Civil War, did class struggle manifest itself as it did in Britain in the 1830-1866 period? What role did the police organizations play in suppressing disorder? In protecting industrial property? In enforcing unpopular laws like Prohibition?

5. Was Tweed's ring, and like organizations, the only practical system of governing a large and culturally diverse city? Why were the nativist reformers so unsuccessful in breaking the immigrant-ring alliance?

Chapter 12

Penology and Corrections in Modern America

During the American Civil War (1861-1865), American interest in penology did not disappear, but it occupied a minor place in the public conscience. When the Friends of Penal Reform held a national meeting at Philadelphia in the autumn of 1859, only eight states and three prison societies were represented. Yet the basis for postwar developments was being laid. In 1862, young Enoch Wines was appointed secretary of the New York Prison Association, bringing new and enthusiastic leadership to that group. In association with Theodore Dwight, Wines undertook an ambitious survey of penal institutions in the northern United States and several Canadian provinces, leading to their 1867 publication of the *Report on the Prisons and Reformatories of the United States and Canada*, which was made to the Legislature of New York in January 1867. This work restated, in emphatic and expansive terms, the New York Prison Association's firm commitment to rehabilitation within prison walls. Widely read and enthusiastically received, the *Report* launched New York State into a program of reformatory discipline that culminated in the construction and operation of the Elmira Reformatory, completed in 1877. Throughout the nation, a number of states awoke to the need for centralized administration of their penal institutions, a step in the direction of insulation from political appointments and also toward the encouragement of the new cadre of professional prison administrators. These reforms came in the wake of a growing number of prison commitments immediately after the Civil War and went hand-in-hand with problems generated by overcrowding and budgetary restraints.

The National Prison Congress of 1870

The new era in penology was ushered in by the first National Prison Congress, held in Cincinnati in 1870. A gathering of wardens, prison officials, and interested academics working in the area of penology, the Cincinnati Congress promulgated a Declaration of Principles that stressed the need for a pro-

Penology and Corrections in Modern America

1820	Peter Oxenbridge Thacher and John Augustus conduct initial experiments with parole of convicts.
1859	Friends of Penal Reform meet in Philadelphia.
1867	Enoch Wines and Theodore Dwight's *Report on the Prisons and Reformatories of the United States and Canada* published, urging that rehabilitation be the goal of American prisons.
1870	The first National Prison Congress meets in Cincinnati.
1877	New York State establishes a reformatory at Elmira, with Zebulon R. Brockway as its warden.
1886	Elmira Reformatory begins publication of its local newspaper, *The Summary.*
1890	An English translation of Gabriel Tarde's *Penal Philosophy* is published by the American Institute of Criminal Law and Criminology.
1894	New York Constitution amended to abolish contract prison labor.
1896	Volunteer Prison League organized under the leadership of Maud Ballington Booth.
1899	Cesare Lombroso's *Crime: Causes and Remedies* published.
1899	Juvenile courts introduced in Denver, Colorado, and Chicago, Illinois.
1908	The Borstal system adopted in England as a means of combating juvenile crime.
1913-1920	Mutual Welfare League implemented by Auburn (New York) Prison, attempting to give prisoners responsibility for their discipline and communal life.
1914-1918	The First World War is fought in Europe; the United States enters in April 1917.
1929	The Federal Bureau of Prisons is established.
1929-1941	The United States suffers a major economic crisis, known as the Depression.

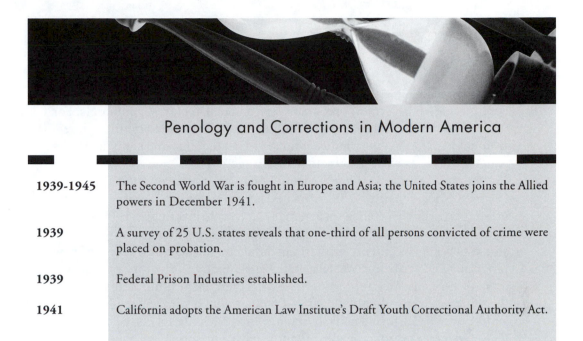

Penology and Corrections in Modern America

1939-1945	The Second World War is fought in Europe and Asia; the United States joins the Allied powers in December 1941.
1939	A survey of 25 U.S. states reveals that one-third of all persons convicted of crime were placed on probation.
1939	Federal Prison Industries established.
1941	California adopts the American Law Institute's Draft Youth Correctional Authority Act.

fessional prison civil service under centralized control of a state board. It asked for the institution of a progressive form of prison discipline, echoing the Dwight-Wines report of 1867, with its reliance on the Crofton, or Irish, system.[1] The declaration was based upon a paper by Zebulon R. Brockway titled "The Ideal of a True Prison System for a State," which caught the attention of the Congress. The young prison warden from Detroit advocated a reformatory program that would prepare inmates for release and reduce the crime rate. Stressing that the central aim of a true prison system should be the protection of society against crime, and not the punishment of criminals, Brockway argued for indeterminate sentencing and for the creation of an impartial board that would decide when it was safe to return inmates to society. While in prison, the inmates were to be provided with a simple but adequate lifestyle. Each would have a separate room for sleeping, with access to a dining hall that operated as a restaurant. A library and public hall would permit reading and other forms of entertainment, as well as a room for religious services. Industrial and agricultural departments would be established, as appropriate to the location of the prison, and these would be run as efficient business organizations, returning profits to the institution and providing training in craft skills to the inmates. The speech catapulted Brockway to the leadership of his profession. When New York State established its new reformatory at Elmira in 1877, the state chose Brockway to preside over the operations of this new and expanded facility for rehabilitation.

Yearly meetings of the National Prison Congress provided an opportunity for the exchange of information and new ideas in penology. Many meetings were graced by observers and speakers from Britain and continental

Europe who were anxious to obtain the latest details of American work in reformatory prison discipline. Largely through the initiative of Wines, who continued to serve as Secretary of the New York Prison Association, an International Congress on Prison Reform met in London in July 1872. It drew the participation of 22 nations, including the United States, and resulted in a number of foreign prison reform programs based upon Brockway's proposals. For the next 20 years, American innovations drew worldwide attention; international meetings on penology continued to devote time and study to American experiments with reformatory discipline.

Meetings of the National Prison Congress, designated the American Prison Association after 1908, attracted participation from more states and offered progressively richer programs. The Seattle meeting of 1909 attracted delegations from 34 states. This widespread participation by professional penologists and prison staff encouraged thorough discussion of new programs and facilities. Western states developed reformatory prison systems at an unusually rapid rate, drawing their inspiration and guidance from the more heavily populated and industrialized states in the Northeast and Midwest. California and Colorado, which had only recently entered the Union, became regional leaders in reformative prison discipline.

After 1908 the international penology movement began to divide sharply into two opposing factions. The Anglo-American group continued to support rehabilitation as the primary goal of penology. Continental Europe, on the other hand, came under the influence of the positivist school, headed by Cesare Lombroso, a medical doctor from Turin, Italy, who broke new ground with a theory of criminology that stressed heredity as one of the major sources of crime. Positivism moved European prison reform in the direction of providing harsh sanctions in the case of habitual offenders but, at the same time, toward more lenient treatment and extensive aftercare provisions for those who were first offenders.

The Rise and Fall of Prison Industries

The foundation of the penitentiary movement was productive labor by the inmates. This served the function of familiarizing inmates with the discipline of work and providing them with useful skills. At the same time, to the extent that prison industries made a profit, they reduced the cost of the institution to the taxpayers. Industrial work was seen as a way of reducing the crime rate, because it was widely believed that poverty was one of the primary causes of crime. Initially some early efforts, such as those of Elizabeth Fry,[2] attempted to use only institutional resources in developing an industrial program. However, it soon became apparent that there were profits to be made in making outside arrangements with private industrial concerns. Contract labor was a system that made convicts available to entrepreneurs for work within prison walls or on prison-run farms or camps. Under this arrangement, the lessee or contractor provided machinery, trained the inmates, and supervised their work. An alternative method was the price-piece system, in which the outside firm provided only the raw materials and was obligated to pay a fixed price for each unit of goods produced by the prison inmates. This arrangement required the prison to make capital investments for machinery, and it also placed the management burdens on prison officials.

Because prison industry competed directly with manufacturers that employed free labor, it was highly vulnerable to political attack as private entrepreneurs grew in number and achieved more political influence. In the case of Britain, the first threat to prison industry was posed by the Reform Act of 1832, which, for the first time, extended the right to vote to the substantial population of the industrial midlands. Within the United States, where industrialization was not as extensive as in Britain, the challenge to prison industrial programs was not mounted before 1850 and did not become a matter of concern until after the Civil War. Then, for the first time, industrial production began to equal agricultural production.

Faced with the need to answer manufacturers' complaints, prison administrators initially turned to the lease system, whereby convicts were supplied to a businessman for labor on his premises rather than in the prison. This shifted the responsibility for safekeeping to the lessor. It also relieved the pressure on overcrowded penitentiary facilities. However, it did not lessen the charge that favored individuals were given the benefit of using convict labor. Ultimately, penitentiary wardens fell back on the state-use system, which employed convict labor within prison walls, setting them to tasks that either served specific state needs or produced goods that did not compete with products of free labor. For example, after the introduction of motor vehicle licensing, many prisons were assigned the task of manufacturing license plates. Other prisons used their convicts to provide janitorial services in public buildings. In a number of states, convicts worked on road and bridge construction projects.

American prisons met their strongest opposition from the young but rapidly growing labor movement, born after the Civil War and attaining national strength with the establishment of the Knights of Labor in 1878 and the American Federation of Labor in 1886. The use of convict labor at a fraction of free labor cost resulted in decreased wages in the industries. The voice of organized labor combined with the voices of manufacturers unable to acquire convict labor. This resulted in growing pressure to limit the use of prison industry. By 1873 American prisons were no longer able to "pay their way," or to cover their operating expenses, through the profits from inmate labor. Contract labor also drew the criticism of the National Anti-Contract Labor Association, which in 1883 met in Chicago and went on record as opposing all forms of contract labor. The New York State legislature, despite its recognition of the reformatory value of labor, imposed sharp restrictions on private contractors' use of inmate labor, but this partial eradication of contract labor did not dispel denunciations of the practice. In 1894, the state constitution was amended to abolish contract prison labor. By 1897, all of New York prison industry was limited to the production of goods required under the state-use formula. In only a few instances did individual states manage to survive this rapid contraction of prison industries. Minnesota, having established a cheap source of binder twine (used in threshing), had a form of prison labor that met the needs of voting citizens in the farming industry. As a consequence, this particular form of prison industry proved virtually unassailable by organized labor.

American prison administrators adapted as well as they could to the changed political times. At the urging of Brockway, the National Prison Association adopted the piece-price system as an alternative to contract labor. By 1887 New York State had adopted piece-price as its preferred system of dealing with inmate labor. When strict provisions were imposed by state law on all forms of contract labor, Brockway was ready with a plan for military training of the most advanced inmates. Within 14 hours of receiving notice of the anti-contract labor laws, he had a system for military drill in place, defusing the danger of resentment and avoiding discipline problems that would arise from enforced idleness. Later, wardens in the Midwest pioneered the idea of organized sports programs, and the idea spread to the Northeast and Far West within a short period (1910-1915). From 1900 to 1930, there were rapidly decreasing opportunities for the use of convict labor. A survey of 27 penal institutions in 1928 revealed that two had more than 50 percent of their inmate population idle; three had unemployment rates ranging from 30 percent to 50 percent, and six had from 20 percent to 30 percent of their inmates without work. The bad situation changed for the worse when Congress passed the Hawes-Cooper legislation (1929), permitting states to exclude convict-made goods carried in interstate commerce. The one bright spot was the creation of the Federal Prison Industries, Inc., in 1939. Established through the efforts of James V. Bennett (director of the Federal Bureau of Prisons) and Eleanor Roosevelt, the new corporation capitalized on the state-use premise by requiring federal agencies to procure supplies (whenever possible) from Federal Prison Industries. In 1939 the corporation reported a profit of $568,000. With the outbreak of World War II and an influx of federal agency orders, the future of Federal Prison Industries, Inc., was secure.

While emergency measures and arrangements helped to provide alternatives to prison industries abolished through political pressure, the rehabilitative functions of prison labor were threatened. In the early 1870s, prison labor helped support the prisons, but it also provided training in craft and trade skills that would be useful upon the inmate's release. Recourse to military drill on one hand or the state-use system on the other provided prisoners with few skills that could be adapted to industrial use outside prison walls. To this extent, the rehabilitative goals adopted at Cincinnati in 1870 were victim to the hostile political climate of the 1880s.

Organized labor exerted a minimal political influence in the South, where states were in the initial stages of recovery from the Civil War. For the most part, they were free to deal with their growing prison populations through a variety of leasing arrangements. Responsibility for prison discipline was shifted to those who leased convict labor, and lessors found profit in operating southern penitentiaries. The inmates, predominantly black, survived harsh conditions in prison camps established near road and canal construction projects, or in isolated areas where logging operations were conducted. Many were shackled with chains during night hours, and a few performed their daily labor shackled together in chain gangs. The absence of secure sleeping quarters led many lessors of convict labor to use heavy wooden wagons as mobile cells, crowding inmates into wagons and supplying them with a minimum of ventilation, food, and water. It was common to use open pits, caves, or mine shafts as sleeping facilities. Statistics provide partial verification of the harsh conditions facing southern convicts. Rough estimates of death rates in northern and southern prisons, prepared in 1888, show that three times as many deaths occurred among southern prisoners than in the case of their northern contemporaries.

Southern prison conditions did not improve until the Populist political parties began to take control of state governments in the 1890s. Throughout the nation, Populism represented the growing complaints of farmers against the financial interests of the North and East, but southern populism can also be seen as the product of regional grievances against wealthy and influential politicians (known as Bourbons), who used their political influence for private gain. One aspect of that favoritism was the provision of prison labor for use on the farms and in logging camps of Bourbon leaders. So strong was the resentment that white southern farmers joined black farmers in electing Populist candidates to office. When they succeeded in gaining office, the end of convict leasing was at hand, and there was increased resort to state-use activities. In 1893 Louisiana made an effort to establish a reformatory penitentiary system. Although the attempt was short-lived, it was quickly followed by the development of plantation prison farms, operated by the state under conditions far superior to those under the convict leasing system. Mississippi ended the convict lease system by an 1895 constitutional amendment.

Prisoners working in rock quarry.

Corbis Images

Southern experiments with plantation prison farms were to prove the new direction of prison labor. A general need for road construction, reforestation, park development, and state-use agriculture led states in the North and the

West to follow the southern example. In 1906, Colorado began an honor-camp program for prisoners approaching parole. The inmates were assigned road building tasks and supervised by a single unarmed guard. Although there were escapes, they did not detract from the excellent record and accomplishments of these prison camps. During World War I, prison labor camps were used extensively in both the United States and in Europe, relieving the shortage of labor due to wartime conditions. The camps were recognized as a legitimate alternative to penitentiary commitment. From 1915 to 1920, the American Prison Congress paid particular interest to road construction camps and farm camps, and as late as 1959 surveys showed that most rehabilitation took place in rural prison camps.

Reformatory Prison Discipline at Elmira

With the 1877 establishment of the Elmira (New York) Reformatory, American penology had an opportunity to put its rehabilitative theories into practice. Central to the initial success of the effort was the first General Superintendent, Zebulon R. Brockway, who spent 20 years at Elmira, working with the prisoners on a highly individualized basis. The newly arrived inmate, usually a male first offender between the ages of 16 and 30, was given a general explanation of the prison discipline system. He also received an interview with Brockway, who tried to determine the new arrival's psychological makeup and potential for reform. Brockway's extensive notes on each inmate indicate that most were from poor, but not impoverished, homes; most lived at home when their offense was committed; almost all read with difficulty or were illiterate; and a large majority were common laborers or partially trained mechanics. It was Brockway's usual practice to place the newcomer in the second (or intermediate) grade in the reformatory's three-tier ranking system. This provided a limited number of privileges, which could be withdrawn by Brockway and eventually result in assignment to the third grade. At the same time, behavior and job performance that met established standards would earn advancement to the first grade, from which prisoners were eligible for parole or early release.

Throughout an inmate's time at the Elmira Reformatory, the general superintendent was readily available. Each evening brought an opportunity to raise grievances or to discuss other matters with Brockway, and it is estimated that with interviewing new arrivals and dealing with inmates in the evening, he spoke to between 40 and 50 men per day. By this extraordinary effort to become familiar with each inmate, Brockway developed a close individual relationship with his charges; observers noted that he was, at the same time, "friend, minister and prisonmaster."[3] His personal acquaintance with the prisoners meant that he was in a particularly strong position to assess punishments. It was the rule that only the general superintendent could withhold an inmate's privileges or order punishment.

Discipline at Elmira was firmly based on a refinement of the mark system of progressive prison discipline popularized by Captain Alexander Maconochie and the Irish prison director, Sir Walter Crofton. However, Brockway found it necessary to establish more clear-cut differentiation between the grades, and to provide a more detailed method for assigning marks. Keepers were required to submit weekly reports on the progress of each inmate, giving Brockway an assessment of the individual's behavior, willingness to work, and quality of performance. Nine marks could be assigned per month: three for demeanor, three for labor, and three for progress in the prison school. A half-year distinguished by nine marks in each month entitled the prisoner to promotion to the next grade.

Promotion to the higher grade was an achievement rewarded by improved eating arrangements, more distinctive clothing, and greater freedom within the reformatory walls. Those prisoners in the third, or lowest, grade were denied the privilege of having visitors, of writing or receiving letters, or of borrowing books from the library. Inmates in this grade were served meals in their rooms by inmate waiters, and they were not permitted tea or coffee. Their uniform was made of a dark red cloth, and they wore no caps. Those in the second grade were permitted visitors and allowed to write and receive letters; they could also borrow books from the library. Although they were required to eat meals in their rooms, they were permitted tea and coffee. Second grade prisoners wore a civilian style suit of dark colored material and wore a scotch cap. First, or highest, grade inmates were permitted all of the privileges of the other two grades. In addition, they were permitted to eat in the dining hall, and they wore a distinctive blue uniform with a navy cap. Distinctions in grade were also shown in assignment to work details, the lower grades being assigned more menial tasks while the first grade inmates were provided with jobs that would improve their skills and opportunities for employment when they were released.

Educational advancement was one of the unique contributions of Brockway's system at Elmira. Undoubtedly, the meager educational achievements of his incoming prisoners caused him to make a connection between criminal activity and lack of education in his young charges. He proceeded to make educational attainment part of the mark system for promotion, and at the same time he retained public school teachers, attorneys, and college teachers on a part-time basis, establishing a vigorous multilevel curriculum. By 1891 Elmira Reformatory's library had 3,970 volumes on its shelves and a collection of 650 periodicals for inmate reading. In 1886 a prison newspaper, *The Summary*, was instituted to provide coverage of local, national, and world news that would otherwise be unavailable in the reformatory. This rich resource of reading material and skillful instruction provided ample opportunity for inmate education, just as the promise of promotion in grade and possible early release gave ample incentive for diligence in study.

A New York statute permitted the managers of Elmira Reformatory to establish the term of imprisonment; for all intents and purposes this provided a system of indeterminate sentences. In the first 25 years of operation more than one-third of the young men committed were released on parole within 15 months, and another one-third were released on parole between 15 and 24 months after their arrival at Elmira. The other third were paroled in less than or slightly more than three years. Parole lasted six months, during which time the prison officials played an active role in finding employment for the parolees and in locating them in permanent residences.

Symbolic of the high point of rehabilitative imprisonment in the United States, Elmira Reformatory fell victim to two external threats to prison reform: (1) the abrupt cessation of prison industry in response to pressures from organized labor; and (2) the rapidly growing incarceration rate, which overwhelmed prisons and reformatories alike and made rehabilitation extremely difficult (if not impossible). Built with 500 cells to house an equal number of inmates, Elmira by 1899 had an average population of 1,500 prisoners. Its workshops, subjected to a slowdown by successive anti-prison labor statutes, were unable to provide eight hours of work per day for inmates skilled in glass blowing, chair making, and the production of tobacco pipes. A German visitor to Elmira in 1927 criticized the lack of adequate housing, the absence of productive labor, the lack of full-time teachers, and the long nightly lockup from six in the evening until six the following morning. What had once been a sterling example of successful application of rehabilitative techniques had become, over the course of time, simply another prison with all of the problems that have plagued administrators and frustrated reformers over the long history of prisons and the movements to reform them.

Criminology and Prison Reform

As the noble effort at Elmira was being overwhelmed by unemployment and high incarceration rates, European penologists became skeptical about the American emphasis on rehabilitation. To a degree, the declining success of Brockway's program was responsible for this change in attitude, but the main reason was the rise and popularization of positivism, a new school of criminology based on the work of an Italian medical doctor, Cesare Lombroso. A surgeon by training, Lombroso worked for some time as a medical officer in the army. During that early phase of his career, he noticed that soldiers who had been tattooed were more likely to engage in criminal activities. Later, Lombroso worked in prison hospitals, giving him access to a large number of criminals and providing him with the opportunity to observe and measure facial, cranial, and physiological features, many of which he identified as being typical of a genetic criminal type. Publishing his major work *Crime: Causes and Remedies* in 1899, he argued that there was a specific "criminal type" that could be distinguished from noncriminal individuals through a number of physical characteristics. The criminal subspecies was a throwback to an earlier stage of evolution; in the male it was characterized by physical violence, and in the female it was typified by promiscuity. Because there was a biological basis for criminal behavior, it followed that rehabilitative efforts would fail whenever they were directed at born criminals. Lombroso and his followers contended that either capital punishment or life imprisonment were the only ways to treat "born criminals." For noncriminals found guilty of criminal acts, the usual graduation of penalties coupled with rehabilitative techniques were appropriate.

Cesare Lombroso (1836-1909)—Italian physician and psychiatrist—argued that there were "criminal types" distinguishable by physical characteristics.

Lombroso's new approach to criminology launched a series of investigations into the causes of crime, all based on the biological characteristics of convicted individuals and the recidivism rates of born criminals. Positivism was to result in European penology abandoning rehabilitation in the case of confirmed criminals, dividing the mainstream of Anglo-American penology from these new developments on the European Continent. Lombroso had a minimal impact upon American and British thought concerning crime and its punishment. More influential was the work of the sociological school of criminology, which viewed crime as a product of individual personality coupled with a number of societal factors. Gabriel Tarde's *Penal Philosophy*, translated into English and printed by the American Institute of Criminal Law and Criminology in 1890, argued that, even though the individual was morally responsible for his or her criminal acts, slums, the existence of a criminal underworld, and depravity within prison walls all conditioned people to a life of crime. Tarde also developed a law of imitation, which asserted that individuals were drawn into crime through their association with others engaged in criminal activity. Those who are inferior in age, social class, or intelligence will imitate the behavioral patterns of their superiors.

American penologists were first exposed to Lombroso's theories by Professor Charles R. Henderson when he addressed the St. Paul meeting of the National Prison Association in 1894. Stubborn opposition to positivist criminology was almost immediate, based upon the strong feeling that all people were responsible for their acts and, if sane, reformable by penological methods. Ironically, the American evidence assembled by Robert Dugdale concerning the Jukes family,[4] then in its fifth American edition, contained more evidence of hereditary criminality than emerged from Lombroso's statistics. What American penology could not ignore was the gradual incursion of scientific analysis into the study of crime, its prevention, and its cure. As early as 1851, Henry Mayhew in England described the social background of crime and explored the impact of various forms of punishment. Social origins of criminal behavior, being popularized by Tarde and others, had earlier been the subject of the French philosopher Adolphe Quetelet in the 1830s, and a classic statistical study of the causes of crime was in the course of preparation by the English scholar Charles Goring.[5]

Rejection of Lombroso's predestination concept of crime did not lead American penologists to oppose scientific methods of dealing with inmates, their discipline, and their correction. As the twentieth century opened, a new era began in which the impact of science on prison reform was much more pronounced than was the influence of religion in the first three quarters of the nineteenth century. Reformers recognized that psychological methods, including group therapy sessions, could be valuable additions to the prison's educational and reformatory programs. By the 1930s, F. Lovell Bixby and other psychologists were actively working in group therapy among young offenders who had been convicted of serious crimes (1932 to 1945), and numerous social workers as well as volunteers from religious organizations participated in counseling sessions for inmates. As Max Grunhut commented, "even in prison the obligations of man to man still exist."[6]

One of the most significant contributions of social science to penology has been the recognition of a specific kind of infrastructure among the inmates of a prison. Donald Clemmer[7] described a process by which a prisoner, through fear of guards and relationships with other prisoners, seeks out a small protective group and thereafter becomes progressively more hostile to the corrections program. Clemmer termed this phenomenon "prisonization," and it has become a recognized aspect of any scientific approach to prison sociology. Recent work in penology and prison sociology has provided valuable insights into the complex web of human relationships present in every prison and reformatory. For the most part, it establishes once more the value of Brockway's approach of individualized attention and patient encouragement in the direction of readjustment and eventual release.

The Mutual Welfare League

Never has inmate infrastructure come under closer public scrutiny than it did during the Mutual Welfare League experiment (1913-1920). This concept was developed by researcher Thomas Mott Osborne after he spent a week among the inmates of Auburn Prison in September 1913. Although Osborne's identity was known to the inmates, he was nevertheless able to observe their relationships and concerns. From this he became convinced that prisoners should be made responsible for group discipline and for decisions concerning their communal life. Previously, similar experiments had been tried. In 1887 Colonel Gardiner Tufts, superintendent of the Concord (Massachusetts) Reformatory, established societies and clubs for prisoners who had advanced to the first grade and hence were approaching parole. In 1896, Maud Ballington Booth developed the Volunteer Prison League, which brought evangelical Christianity to the prisons and organized inmate converts into league units. However, never before had self-government been attempted on such a broad scale as that proposed by Osborne in the Mutual Welfare League.

Subsequently, Osborne instituted the Mutual Welfare League at Auburn Prison during his time as warden there and on later assignments as warden at New York's Sing Sing Prison at Ossining and the U.S. Naval Prison at Portsmouth, New Hampshire. League officers were elected by prisoners and were responsible for supervising prison workshops and assigning punishments for infractions of the league's rules. Any failure to obey the rules or submit to league discipline immediately placed the prisoner back in the charge of prison officials and subject to the old prison routine. While the league was in full operation, it achieved some notable results. Escapes, mental problems, and injuries from fights all decreased markedly. Over a period of five years under Mutual Welfare League operations, shop production at Sing Sing almost doubled. Like many innovations, the league prospered under the leadership of its originator, and Osborne was widely credited with substantial success; few other wardens were able to duplicate the program and its achievements. By 1920, however, public resistance, legislative opposition, and inmate misgivings began to undermine the league. Thereafter it survived as a useful organization for planning athletic activities and inmate social events. Abroad, the idea was adopted in the German province of Thuringia, and from 1923 to 1933 it was used as a mode of discipline with prisoners at the probationary stage immediately preceding their release.

Parole and Probation

Essential to the success of a parole, or early release, program was maintaining a system that would provide aftercare to released prison inmates. In Europe this function was performed by government agencies, but in the United States private charitable groups were almost entirely responsible for the welfare of paroled inmates. Most prominent in this work were the Salvation Army's Prison Gate Movement; the Volunteers of America (a successor to Booth's Volunteer Prison League); and the Central Howard Association, established in Chicago to provide parole services wherever another agency was not involved in assisting parolees. During the calendar year 1944, the Salvation Army handled more than 10,000 former prison inmates, providing a sizeable supplement to the limited amount of government activity with paroled convicts.

By 1898, about 25 states in the United States had a parole law in operation, but the slow development of indeterminate sentencing and the assignment of arbitrary minimum and maximum penalties hampered flexibility in administering the law. The organized bench and bar, intent upon the need for certainty and for protection against judicial inconsistencies, preferred definite terms of sentencing. Law schools reflected the new scientific attitudes and stressed standardization, rather than individualization, in criminal law administration. Legal professionalism and lack of sympathy for the aims of prison rehabilitation did much to limit the effectiveness of parole in the states.

Throughout the first quarter of the twentieth century parole continued to grow, and studies of the systems of early release and parole stressed the need for more vigorous supervision of parolees. Parole boards instituted systems of psychological testing and interviewing, aimed at identifying inmates who were likely to harm society if released on parole. The growing pressures of overcrowding resulted in a general release of most inmates after they had served the minimum time of their sentence. In 1915, Wisconsin launched a work-release program designed to release inmates for work outside the prison during daylight hours, but requiring them to return to spend the night behind bars. This system of work release spread to North and South Carolina in the 1950s and to most of the other states in the 1960s.

Probation also played a significant role in reducing prison overcrowding in the United States. In utilizing probation, a sentencing judge continues his or her control of the case, placing the convicted criminal in the charge of a probation officer. Failure to meet any rules of probation can result in immediate imprisonment. After a period of good behavior, the probationer is released and his or her sentence is commuted. Probation has a long history in America, going back to the time of Judge Peter Oxenbridge Thacher and John Augustus (c. 1820), but it became commonplace only from 1912 to 1933. During that time the number of probation officers in the nation increased from 200 to 4,000. When 25 states were surveyed in 1939, it was found that about one-third of all persons convicted of crime were placed on probation. Only 30 percent of those placed on probation were later sent to prison, either for violation of probation or for some subsequent offense.

Juvenile Delinquency

Increased study of the origins of crime pointed to the influence of environmental and social factors on juvenile delinquency, or criminal activity of juveniles. The response of the criminal justice system was to establish a special court for the trial of youthful offenders and special correctional programs for their rehabilitation. The cities of Chicago and Denver in the United States were among the first (1899) to use juvenile courts designed to provide a separate system of criminal justice for young offenders, as well as to provide social services and aftercare to young men and women committed to reform schools or houses of refuge.

Several studies undertaken from 1930 to 1950 focused on the causes and remedies for juvenile delinquency. They found that young men and women were led into criminal activity through a combination of social factors and emotional instability. Among a group of 111 families living under adverse conditions, 45 percent of the children were delinquent, and within that group 91 percent were found to be under some form of emotional stress. More than adult crime, juvenile delinquency was found to be group conditioned. One of the innovative suggestions that emerged from this period was the American Law Institute's Draft Youth Correctional Authority Act (1940), which proposed that juvenile delinquency matters be removed from the court system and placed under the supervision of a Youth Correctional Authority, which would have available to it all of the facilities of social work and psychological counseling needed for an effective youth corrections program. Adopted by California in 1941, the Draft Youth Correctional Act has served as a basis for a number of similar programs in other states.

American developments in the control of juvenile delinquency have paralleled British establishment and operation of the Borstal system, which provided a group of correctional facilities for youth and stressed rehabilitation through vocational training. Formalized by the Prevention of Crime Act of 1908, the Borstal system originated through the efforts of Sir Evelyn Ruggles-Brise at Borstal in Kent. It made special training available to young offenders ranging in age from 16 to 21. Girls were trained in domestic work and boys were assigned to labor parties. Eventually, both young men and women progressed to workshops where they learned skills that would be useful upon their release. The Borstal system relied upon a group of more than 1,000 paid and volunteer associates who worked with those discharged from the training facilities, finding them jobs and otherwise easing their adjustment to society.

Criminal activity among young people has occupied an increasing amount of law enforcement time since the 1950s. During and after World War II, juvenile delinquency became a subject for state, national, and international study. In practice, it has resulted in the development of a large and expert bureaucracy devoted to the study of youthful crime and the evolution of techniques for its control and correction. To a considerable degree, this work has occurred outside the scope of American prison reform, and thus it has lacked the formative influence that earlier efforts with youthful offenders had on the reform of adult correctional procedures.

Recent Developments in American Penology

It is difficult to fully appreciate the impact of the Federal Bureau of Prisons, which was established in 1929. A succession of outstanding directors, including Sanford Bates and James V. Bennett, spearheaded the United States' effort to provide prisons for a large number of offenders. For the first time, the federal government ended its reliance on state prison facilities to maintain those who violated federal criminal laws. The Depression caused an increase in federal convictions, particularly for violation of the Prohibition Amendment and for related gangland activities. As a consequence, the Federal Bureau of Prisons became one of the leading agencies in operating a classification system for a wide spectrum of inmates requiring imprisonment at the maximum security level, as well as for individuals who could safely be placed in minimum-security camp-like facilities. The federal prison constructed at Lewisburg, Pennsylvania, in 1930 provided a variety of confinement facilities within one institution, ranging from medium security to maximum security. Beyond being an outstanding model for differentiated treatment of inmates, the Federal Bureau of Prisons pioneered new and innovative methods of rehabilitation and parole. Its establishment and operation of Federal Prison Industries, Inc., gave encouragement to state prison officials in their efforts to make effective use of the state-use method of prison industry.

TIME CAPSULE

Private Prisons

As the use of incarceration as a form of punishment increased in the nineteenth-century United States, states and local jurisdictions built up systems of government jails and prisons. Then, during the 1980s, some jurisdictions in the United States reverted to earlier practice and made contracts with private firms (such as Corrections Corporation of America) to build and manage prison facilities. This move was primarily instigated by conditions of severe overcrowding; it was argued that private operators could gain financing for new prisons less expensively and could bring the units into operation more quickly. Furthermore, once the new facilities were ready, costs to the government for management of prisons by private contractors would be less because of lower pay and fewer benefits for correctional officers and less training for personnel. Private contractors could realize scaled profits when their operations covered several jurisdictions, and their concern for profit would promote efficient management. Not being burdened by governmental bureaucracy, they could be creative in facility design and in management techniques. On a more theoretical level, libertarians argue that government functions should be as minimal as possible.

Delegating responsibility for incarceration of convicted offenders to private enterprise, however, raises serious ethical and legal questions. Should private contractors be allowed to profit from punishment? Is it just that private individuals decide the conditions and length of incarceration (through discipline rules, "good time" decisions, "earned time," etc.)? Should nongovernmental employees be allowed to use coercive force, even lethal force, against inmates (e.g., during riots or attempted escapes)? Is there a vested interest of private contractors to keep inmates incarcerated longer in order to increase their profits? Should not custodians be held responsible to governmental supervisors rather than to the bureaucracy of a private enterprise?

There are at least two well-litigated constitutional challenges to the operation of private prisons. The first arises from prisoner misconceptions concerning the legal consequences of being assigned to a prison outside the state of conviction. Because there are a limited number of private corporations operating prisons, these complaints find their origin in the fact that, on occasion, prisoners are transported to distant private prisons to serve their sentences. Hawaiian convicts have been transferred to a California private prison; Montana inmates find themselves in Tennessee. However, the courts have consistently rejected prisoner pleas that these transfers are unconstitutional. In some instances the petitions have asserted that punishment for escape is illegal, because the inmates prior to their escape were entitled to their freedom because of the interstate transfer.

The second constitutional issue involving private prisons may create more serious problems in future years. This involves the question of qualified immunity from liability under 42 U.S.C. § 1983, which awards damages against individuals who deprive a person of his or her rights under the Fourteenth Amendment "under color of State law." Previously, private prisoner guards were judged to occupy the position of government-employed correctional officers. As such, they were entitled to qualified immunity from suit under § 1983. However, in 1997 the U.S. Supreme Court held, in a 5-4 decision, that private prison guards were not entitled to qualified immunity (*Richardson v. McKnight*, 521 U.S. 399, 1997). Because this may substantially increase the cost of doing business as a private prison operator, it may again be economically advantageous for state and local governments to once more operate official prisons rather than utilize private prison facilities. Alternatively, there may be some intermediate solution, whereby public officials will serve as supervisory personnel, and thereby provide the necessary state connection upon which qualified immunity may be based.

These complications have clouded the future for private prison operations in the United States. However, it is clear that without private prisons the public prison systems will become overcrowded. This will generate complaints that the inadequate public facilities impose unconstitutional "cruel and unusual punishment."

A growing concern with recidivism (or repeat offenses) generated interest in methods of identifying prisoners. In the 1890s a method of identification based upon the Bertillon measurements of facial characteristics was used in obtaining positive identification. In use since 1883, the Bertillon system of identification resulted in a centralized file for the nation, maintained at Sing Sing Prison after 1892. In 1901 New York prison authorities adopted the fingerprint methods developed by Scotland Yard, and by 1907 the federal government established a centralized clearinghouse for fingerprints in its newly established Bureau of Investigation. Careful statistical analysis was applied to prison records in the years after 1930, giving rise to a wide variation in findings concerning recidivism. In 1930, Sheldon and Eleanor Glueck published *Five Hundred Criminal Careers*,[8] based upon their study at Concord (Massachusetts) Reformatory, where they discovered a repeat offense rate of 80 percent. Thirty-five years later, Daniel Glaser[9] surveyed the federal prison rates and reported a 31 percent recidivism rate, attributable, in his opinion, to the Federal Bureau of Prisons' recourse to early release programs. Despite the wide disparity in these findings, it is clear that repeat offenses are common despite extensive efforts at inmate counseling and rehabilitation. At the same time, American penology continues to seek a method of individualized treatment that will effectively neutralize the criminal tendencies of prison inmates.

TIME CAPSULE

Foucault—On Prison "Reformation"

Foucault notes that French prisons, turned to the process of "reformation" in the nineteenth century, became instruments to exercise the technology of changing individual personality. Their efforts at classification, their application of an elaborate system of discipline and rewards, and their exercise of subtle coercion laid the ground for a more closely regimented society outside prison walls. It was no accident that prisons looked like similar institutions—the schools, military barracks, and hospitals for the treatment of disease. The modern prison maximizes physical control and conducts a total and persistent education. Once within the prison, the convict becomes subject to new rules, and to punishments established not by law but by prison officials.[1]

Penology has long recognized the concept that exemplary behavior by a prisoner should shorten the time of imprisonment, and yet is not Foucault correct that this eliminates both the certainty of punishment and the legality of prison discipline that thereby operates outside the legal and judicial system?

Foucault is somewhat inconsistent here. He argues that prison discipline produces compliant workers once the convicts are released outside the prison's walls; on the other hand, he asserts that the delinquents who are shaped by the prison experience are frequently found among the recidivists. Are the inmates changed by prison discipline, or do they merely shape themselves to appear "reformed" and gain early release, and thereafter behave as they wish?

[1]   Michael Foucault, *Discipline and Punish*, pp.248, 252-254.

Outbreaks of prison violence, both before and after World War II, demonstrate that concern for the conditions of imprisonment is essential if any rehabilitation is to take place. Staff must be competent, adequately paid, and able to engage inmates in useful and challenging activity. There is a growing tendency to rely upon specially trained corrections officers rather than on prison guards provided with a minimum of training and professional pride. Riots and prisoner rights movements have alerted prison management to the need to give serious consideration to inmate complaints and to rectify the difficulties long before they rise to the point of crisis and confrontation.

Two centuries after the reform effort was launched by John Howard, penal institutions continue to provide a fertile ground for study and new programs. The social sciences have provided insights into prisoner psychology and the causes of crime that enlighten prison officials and guide law enforcement authorities in their work. The key to successful rehabilitation of criminals continues to elude Anglo-American penologists. At the same time, they have steadfastly, on the basis of religion and morality, refused to accept Cesare Lombroso's conclusion that there is a subspecies of humans that commit crime and cannot be reformed. American penology continues to hope for, and work toward, a better program for the rehabilitation of criminals and the betterment of our society.

Summary

The National Prison Congress of 1870 restated in emphatic terms an earlier emphasis on rehabilitation as the primary aim of penitentiary sentences. Inspired by the keynote address of Zebulon R. Brockway, the 1870 meeting instituted an era of expanded prison industry, increased educational opportunities within prison walls, and the systematic use of the progressive system of prison discipline, originated by Sir Walter Crofton and applied by Brockway at the New York State Reformatory at Elmira. Unfortunately, prison industry, one of the vital parts of the rehabilitative system, was vigorously opposed by competing industrialists and organized labor. This caused the virtual elimination of prison industry, except for state-use items, by 1890.

Later developments in penology included the establishment of the federal prison system, providing a much larger group of inmates and greater opportunity for classification and the establishment of prisons with graduated security. Thomas Mott Osborne's Mutual Welfare League sparked studies of inmate infrastructure and illustrated the need to avoid disciplinary problems and riots by communication between inmates and wardens. Southern prison systems, largely unaffected by late nineteenth-century penal reforms, moved from extensive leasing of convict labor to a new and widely copied institution of prison farms. The farms provided a healthy method of using labor to support the penal system and have become one of the more effective systems of inmate rehabilitation throughout the United States. Parole and probation have provided partial solutions to the problem of prison crowding, but private charitable organizations have played the major role in implementing post-release programs. With the rise of juvenile delinquency immediately before and after World War II, there has been a general effort to provide special facilities for young offenders, and substantial study has taken place concerning the sources of juvenile crime and techniques for its punishment.

The 1870 National Prison Congress initiated a period of international influence for American penology that lasted until the turn of the century, when Cesare Lombroso, the Italian criminologist, changed the focus of European penology with his theory that criminal behavior is hereditary, and rehabilitation, in many cases, is impossible. While American criminologists and penologists have examined possible hereditary origins of crime, the major emphasis of American penology has continued to be rehabilitation along with modification of environmental and cultural factors that tend to breed criminal activity.

Endnotes

[1]   See discussion in Chapter 9.

[2]   See Chapter 9.

[3]   Alexander Winter, *The New York State Reformatory at Elmira* (London: Swan Sonnenschein & Co., 1891), p. 37.

[4]   Robert Dugdale, *The Jukes: A Study in Crime, Pauperism, Disease and Heredity*, 5th ed. (New York: G.P. Putnam's, 1891).

[5]   Charles Goring, *The English Convict: A Statistical Study* (London: H.M. Stationery Office, 1913).

[6]   Max Grunhut, *Penal Reform: A Comparative Study* (Oxford: The Clarendon Press, 1948; reprint ed., Montclair, NJ: Patterson Smith, 1972), p. 250.

[7]   Donald Clemmer, *The Prison Community* (Boston: Christopher Publishing House, 1940).

[8]   Sheldon and Eleanor Glueck, *Five Hundred Criminal Careers* (New York: Knopf, 1930; reprinted, Millwood, NY: Kraus Reprints, 1975).

[9]   Daniel Glaser, *The Effectiveness of a Prison and Parole System* (Indianapolis: Bobbs-Merrill, 1964).

References

Two general works are invaluable for an understanding of the modern development of penology. They are Max Grunhut, *Penal Reform: A Comparative Study* (Oxford: Clarendon Press, 1948; reprinted, Montclair, NJ: Patterson Smith, 1972); and Blake McKelvey, *American Prisons: A History of Good Intentions* (Montclair, NJ: Patterson Smith, 1977). Also of value is a survey by Torsten Erikkson, *The Reformers: An Historical Survey of Pioneer Experiments in the Treatment of Criminals*, trans. Catherine Djurklou (New York: Elsevier, 1976).

On Brockway and his work at Elmira Reformatory, see Alexander Winter, *The New York State Reformatory at Elmira* (London: Swan Sonnenschein & Co., 1891) and Zebulon R. Brockway, *Fifty Years of Prison Service: An Autobiography* (New York: Charities Publishing Co., 1912).

Further details on the new schools of criminology are available in Hermann Mannhein, ed., *Pioneers in Criminology*, 2d ed. (Montclair, NJ: Patterson Smith, 1972); Cesare Lombroso, *Crime: Its Causes and its Remedies*, trans. Henry P. Horton (Boston: Little, Brown & Co., 1911; reprint, Montclair, NJ: Patterson Smith, 1968); and Enrico Ferri, *Criminal Sociology* (New York: D. Appleton & Co., 1898).

For a comprehensive historical analysis of penology theory, see Samuel H. Pillsbury, "Understanding Penal Reform: The Dynamic of Change," *Journal of Criminal Law and Criminology* 80 (1989): 726-780. The case for a retributive system of correction is forcefully presented by David Fogel, *We Are the Living Proof: The Justice Model for Corrections* (Cincinnati, OH: Anderson Publishing Co., 1982). The need to continue the attempt to rehabilitate criminals is argued in Francis T. Cullen and Karen E. Gilbert, *Reaffirming Rehabilitation* (Cincinnati, OH: Anderson Publishing Co., 1982). An overview of current controversies regarding corrections is provided by Alexis M. Durham III, *Crisis and Reform: Current Issues in American Punishment* (Boston: Little, Brown & Co., 1994).

The development of juvenile justice is reviewed in "History of the Control and Prevention of Juvenile Delinquency in the United States," in Barry Krisberg and James F. Austin, *Reinventing Juvenile Justice* (Newbury Park, CA: Sage Publications, 1993); and in Clifford Dorne and Kenneth Gewerth, *American Juvenile Justice: Cases, Legislations and Comments* (San Francisco: Austin and Winfield, 1998). Legal issues and possible future trends in juvenile delinquency are discussed by Jay S. Albanese, *Dealing with Delinquency: The Future of Juvenile Justice* (Chicago: Nelson-Hall Publishers, 1993).

Recent books have revived the dispute about the degree to which innate characteristics determine criminal behavior: for example, James Q. Wilson and Richard J. Herrnstein, *Crime and Human Nature* (New York: Simon and Schuster, 1985); Charles Murray and Richard J. Herrnstein, *The Bell Curve: Intelligence and Class Structure in American Life* (New York: The Free Press, 1994); David Shichor, *Punishment for Profit: Private Prisons/Public Concerns* (Thousand Oaks, CA: Sage Publications, 1995); Douglas C. McDonald, ed., *Private Prisons and the Public Interest* (New Brunswick, NJ: Rutgers University Press, 1990); and Charles H. Logan. *Private Prisons: Cons and Pros* (New York: Oxford University Press, 1990).

Notes and Problems

1. Prison industries provide gainful employment, contribute to the cost of prison maintenance, and can serve a rehabilitative purpose. In the light of opposition by organized labor and the restrictions on transporting prison-made products in interstate commerce, how can prison officials sustain this vital aspect of prison management?

2.   Theories concerning the causes of crime can, and should, have a substantial impact on the operation of correctional institutions. Clearly they show the need to segregate hardened criminals from first-time offenders and to provide some segregation in terms of age, type of criminal activity, sex, and receptivity to rehabilitation. However, should one begin to work on the problem of the hardened repeat criminal to determine whether societal interests demand a permanent solution, either through capital punishment or for continuance of the prison term during the natural life of the convict?

3.   Some recent experiments with human chromosomes have suggested that those inclined to criminal behavior possess a certain chromosome pattern that is determined by heredity. Is it possible that Dugdale's work on the Jukes and Lombroso's concept of the born criminal is finally proved, and that there really is a genetic defect that causes criminal behavior? Should we alter our view of crime and punishment in the light of this proposition? How should we adapt to this new scientific finding?

4.   Prison overcrowding has been a constant threat to effective corrections programs during the twentieth century. The chapter has suggested work camps, forest camps, plantation prison farms, parole, and probation as possible solutions to overcrowding. They have been tried and still prisons are filled to capacity. Should new methods be tried? For example, restrictions on freedom less than imprisonment but still identifiable as punishment, or extremely heavy fines to be paid out of a convict's earnings over an extended period. Could a system of victim compensation be substituted for all or part of a prison term?

5.   Certain New England states have experimented in operating a regional prison authority, with interchange of convicts between the participating states. Each state is responsible for accepting a given group of prisoners and sends its prisoners to other states responsible for convicts imprisoned for other offenses. Does this system offer savings in the operation of prisons that would not normally be available to small states or to those with small prison populations? Does it facilitate classification and individualized treatment of inmates in all of the participating states? Are there constitutional and legal problems in establishing such a regional system?

6.   Indeterminate sentencing provides corrections officials with a powerful stimulant for good behavior and rehabilitation. At the same time, it tends to remove the responsibility of judges and juries to impose sentences in proportion to the serious nature of the crimes. We have seen that the bench and bar tended to resist indeterminate sentencing laws. Were they correct in terms of constitutional law, procedural rights, and protecting the interests of the public? Should corrections officers or parole boards be permitted to second-guess judges and jurors in this area of great concern to public safety?

Chapter 13

The Rise of Law Enforcement Professionalism

The quickening pace of twentieth-century historical change resulted in dramatic alteration of criminal justice professions. Early decades of the century witnessed the introduction of new inventions, such as the telephone, radio, automobile, and airplane, which predictably improved systems of police communication and facilitated mobility of police units. More recently, political and social developments have also made their mark. Constitutional limitations on investigative activity have occurred through federal court decisions and Congressional and state legislative action. Rising demands for equal opportunity by women and racial minority groups have altered the composition of police and correctional units. Also, the growing complexity of governmental regulatory activity has placed new demands on the criminal justice system.

Although the United States emerged from the Spanish-American War (1898) with worldwide interests and power, the sobering reality of this new status was not appreciated until the bloodbaths of World War I (1917-1918) and World War II (1941-1945). In between the two world wars there was a time of malaise, during which national energy and reform impulses waned, materialism reigned supreme, and criminal activity became commonplace in American life. The Depression years (1929-1941) shook national confidence in the inevitability of progress and resulted in many Americans challenging the validity of capitalism and free enterprise. To counter the impact of the Depression, President Franklin D. Roosevelt instituted the New Deal, a pragmatic effort to reestablish confidence in the business world, create regulatory safeguards against excessively harsh competition, and develop legal foundations for a stable national economy.

In the Cold War (1948-1991), the growing power of the Soviet Union, and its seeming success in assembling a group of satellite nations with the People's Republic of China, had a significant impact on American life and policing activities. Increased emphasis on internal security measures designed to limit spy activities (espionage) characterized this period, along with continuing efforts to regulate business practices and strengthen nation-

The Rise of Law Enforcement Professionalism

1879-1883	Identification by anthropometry is developed, but shortly replaced as a means of identification by fingerprinting.
1901	National Police Chiefs Union meets in Chicago; becomes International Association of Chiefs of Police in 1915.
1901-1940	Experiments in blood testing permit classification into four types, and the identification of the Rh factor.
1903	Chief Fred Kohler of the Cincinnati Police Department institutes sunrise court and a system for rehabilitating juvenile delinquents.
1905	Lola Baldwin of the Los Angeles Police Department becomes the first female law enforcement officer appointed in an American police department.
1906	Chief August Vollmer recruits college students into the Berkeley (California) Police Department.
1907	Bureau of Investigation established in U.S. Department of Justice.
1915	University of California at Berkeley establishes a three-year course for training police officers.
1918	J. Edgar Hoover becomes head of General Investigations Division, Bureau of Investigation.
1918-1933	Prohibition of the sale of alcoholic beverages begins as a wartime measure and is adopted as the Eighteenth Amendment to the Constitution; it was repealed by the Twenty-First Amendment in 1933.
1919	Boston Police Strike triggers state legislation prohibiting the unionization of police forces.
1922-1929	Ballistic evidence becomes an accepted form of proof in criminal courts.
1923	"Zone" schools established to provide regional training for law enforcement officers.
1924	Hoover becomes head of the Bureau of Investigation.
1929	A stock market crash forces American participation in a worldwide recession.
1930	San Jose State University (California) establishes a two-year police training curriculum.
1931	Wickersham Commission report on crime is published.

The Rise of Law Enforcement Professionalism

1933	Franklin D. Roosevelt inaugurated as president. The New Deal brings the resources of the federal government to bear on measures to stimulate economic recovery. These include the construction of new local courthouses and jails.
1935	Justice Department's Bureau of Investigation becomes the Federal Bureau of Investigation. FBI Academy established.
1935	Medical examiners introduced in large cities, replacing coroners who served without any significant medical training.
1939-1945	The United States enters World War II in December 1941. Postwar reforms of military justice result in the enactment of the Uniform Code of Military Justice in 1951.
1950-1951	Kefauver Committee hearings on interstate crime televised; officials in the Internal Revenue Service, Treasury Department, and Justice Department removed from their positions.
1953-1954	McCarthy Committee hearings on "un-American" activities broadcast nationally.
May 1954	U.S. Supreme Court orders desegregation of elementary schools in *Brown v. Board of Education*.
1964-1975	American involvement in Vietnam incites violent confrontation between police and student protesters.
1968	Assassination of Rev. Dr. Martin Luther King heightens racial tension and causes unrest in urban areas.
1968	Law Enforcement Assistant Administration (LEAA) established by congressional statute.

al defense. These broad national and international concerns did not diminish efforts in the criminal justice field, where federal, state, and local police agencies conducted a continuing battle against rapidly increasing criminal activity. The Kefauver Committee hearings on interstate crime (1950-1951) were carried on national television and resulted in sweeping removals of federal officials in the Internal Revenue Service, Treasury Department, and Justice Department. In 1953-1954, Senator Joseph McCarthy's Senate investigating committee provided televised coverage of individuals testifying concerning espionage during and after World War II.

Civil rights dominated the domestic scene in the late 1950s and 1960s, ushered in by the Supreme Court's 1954 decision in the school desegregation case of *Brown v. Board of Education* (349 U.S. 294). Ultimately, the Supreme Court's opinions undermined the political foundation of racial segregation throughout the United States, and its efforts were supplemented by a series of federal statutes guaranteeing civil rights to all citizens. Coupled with concern for civil rights was a growing awareness of racial distinctions in the administration of criminal justice, as well as a reevaluation of due process and equal protection guarantees for all persons accused of crime.[1] The criminal justice system itself was subjected to careful study and evaluation, encouraged to some degree by the passage of the Federal Law Enforcement Assistance Act (LEAA) of 1968.

The FBI: Paradigm and Paradox

No police agency has been more controversial than the Federal Bureau of Investigation, and none has made a greater impression upon the law enforcement profession in the twentieth century. Established in 1907 as the Bureau of Investigation of the Justice Department, the FBI was active in countering German espionage before and during World War I. On the eve of America's entry into that conflict, a young law school graduate, J. Edgar Hoover, began his professional career as a law clerk in the Department of Justice. Soon marked for his ability and diligence, Hoover was made head of the General Investigation Division in 1918. As head of this division, Hoover was in charge of prosecutions of espionage agents as well as the investigations of Communist and Socialist groups and individuals that combined to hinder the war effort after the Bolshevik Revolution of October 1917. With the close of the war in November 1918, a series of strikes and terrorist attacks generated strong public opinion against the Communist Party and its affiliated organizations. During the Red Scare (1918-1922), a number of aliens residing in the United States were deported after their Communist associations were verified by the Department of Justice. Hoover played an active role in these prosecutions, becoming a recognized authority on the Communist Party and its American operations.

Despite its commendable investigative work during the war, the Bureau of Investigation was riddled with political appointees. Standards of conduct were low and police work tended to be shoddy. In addition, the bureau's intervention in a steel strike led by William Z. Foster (later head of the Communist Party USA) enhanced its reputation for being antilabor and an instrumentality for strikebreaking. It was against this background that President Harding, in September 1921, appointed William J. Burns, owner of the large strikebreaking private detective agency, to be director. Almost simultaneously Hoover was named assistant director, and during Burns' tenure he was kept busy with the extensive investigation and prosecution of the Ku Klux

Klan resurgence in the southern states. Hoover learned by bitter experience how difficult it was to secure convictions from southern juries and how deeply racism and violence marked southern society.

Hoover's eventual elevation to the directorship was a direct result of the Teapot Dome scandal, in which high-ranking officials in the Harding administration were found to have conspired to sell valuable oil leases on government lands in return for extensive bribes from oil drilling companies. Although the Bureau of Investigation was innocent of any implication in the scandal, it was discovered that its agents had cooperated with Director Burns in a plot to discredit Senator Burton K. Wheeler of Montana. Wheeler was chairman of the Senate Committee assigned to investigate Teapot Dome, and exposure of this Justice Department attempt to embarrass the Senate investigation led to public outrage. President Coolidge, who succeeded to office at Harding's death, inherited the Teapot Dome mess and the related illegal practices in the bureau and Department of Justice. Harlan F. Stone, Coolidge's new attorney general, named Hoover to be bureau director. Hoover's acceptance on May 10, 1924, was on the condition that Stone would guarantee him freedom from political influence, that he would have sole authority to deal with discipline within the bureau, that a rigid chain of command would be instituted in which Hoover would be responsible only to the attorney general, and that FBI employees would channel their complaints to Hoover and be answerable only to him. Thus began an association between the Bureau of Investigation and Director J. Edgar Hoover, that for better or worse would dominate federal law enforcement from that time until Hoover's death on May 1, 1972.

J. Edgar Hoover (1895-1972)—Director of the FBI from 1924 until his death in 1972.

Corbis Images

Prohibition ushered in times of criminal activity, violence, and corruption rarely seen in American history. Individuals avoided the ban on alcoholic beverages by making their own beer, "bathtub gin," and moonshine; lawbreaking became a home-based industry. This contempt for an unenforceable statute encouraged public enthusiasm for those who broke the law flagrantly and still escaped punishment. The neighborhood speakeasy (illegal saloon) was as much a mark of American life in the 1920s as the fast-living flapper and the racy sports car were. By 1924, criminal elements organized themselves into rival gangs, vying for control of speakeasy operations, prostitution rings, and other sources of profit and power. Inevitably, police departments were drawn into the circle of criminal activity; encouraged to condone activities that violated prohibition laws, they took the expedient step and accepted bribes to cooperate fully with the underworld in a large number of "joint ventures."

The FBI had no investigative jurisdiction over most of this cesspool of crime, and the federal prohibition law had been assigned to agents of the Treasury Department for enforcement purposes. The limited scope of federal criminal law (and, thus, investigative jurisdiction) is evidenced by the 1928 report on bureau activities. By far the largest number of cases prosecuted were the 2,549 indictments and 2,055 convictions under the National Motor Vehicle Theft Act. Next in magnitude were the 923 cases involving fugitives from justice apprehended by the bureau. Carrying women across state lines for immoral purposes (prohibited by the Mann Act of 1910) was the basis for 602 indictments and 469 convictions. These were followed by investigations involving violation of the bankruptcy laws, embezzlements under the National Bank Act, and larceny of goods being carried in interstate commerce.

Congress gradually extended federal criminal law, relying on constitutional grants of power to the federal government and reacting to the rapidly unfolding national economy and the nationwide scope of criminal activity that was based on exploitation of gaps between state and federal criminal law. Expanded bureau jurisdiction came from statutory authorization, but it also resulted from a willingness on the part of Hoover and his superiors to use existing federal statutes as vehicles for authorizing necessary expansion of bureau activity. For example, using FBI agents for counterintelligence work before World War II was based on an obscure statute permitting the State Department to conduct such investigations in support of its diplomatic activities.

In the first five years of Hoover's directorship, the Bureau of Investigation assumed greater responsibility, while simultaneously being subjected to a steady reduction in personnel. This may have been due to Hoover's intention to eliminate from the ranks of special agents any individuals who did not have either law degrees or degrees in accounting. It also demonstrated his preference for a small, highly productive, and cost-effective agency. As such, the management of the bureau appealed to economy-minded members of Congress. On the other hand, the underworld was given clear notice that killing an agent of the bureau was not an acceptable means of budget reduction. When Special Agent Edward B. Shanahan was shot and killed by professional auto thief Martin J. Durkin, Hoover made it clear that the culprit was to be caught in his interstate flight. Agents in Illinois, California, Arizona, and New Mexico participated in the manhunt before Durkin was apprehended in Texas and turned over to state authorities for trial.

The bureau, renamed the Federal Bureau of Investigation (FBI) in 1935, was the focus of public attention in the 1930s, as its agents tracked down and secured the imprisonment of such legendary underworld characters as

George "Machine Gun" Kelly (who named the FBI "G-Men"), John Dillinger, "Ma" Barker, Alvin Kirpis, and Bonnie Parker and Clyde Barrow. However, the case that touched America's heart was the 1932 kidnapping and subsequent murder of Charles Lindbergh, Jr. The infant son of the "Lone Eagle," who was the first pilot to fly solo and nonstop across the Atlantic Ocean from New York to Paris in 1927, and Anne Morrow Lindbergh, the daughter of millionaire Dwight Morrow, was abducted from his parents' New Jersey mansion. Ransom payments were made amidst the full glare of national press coverage, but the child was found murdered. Based on certain interstate aspects of the case, the bureau provided investigative assistance and its laboratories exhausted the scope of forensic science in efforts to locate the kidnapper/murderer. Not until 1936, when Bruno Hauptmann attempted to pass gold certificates that were withdrawn from circulation in 1934, was the ransom money located in his apartment and his conviction secured. Subsequent federal legislation authorized earlier involvement by the bureau in kidnapping cases, and many states amended their kidnapping laws to impose capital punishment for kidnappings that resulted in death.

American entry into World War II found the FBI already active in the area of combating espionage and sabotage in the United States, having been assigned those tasks by President Roosevelt in 1936. In addition, the bureau was given responsibility for countering Axis activities in Central and South America through its Special Intelligence Service, which worked closely with Army and Naval Intelligence. However, the FBI did not have any jurisdiction or responsibility for the security of information concerning the Manhattan Project (the research groups engaged in theoretical and developmental activities concerning the atomic bomb) until after the war. Efforts to isolate this highly secret project from the bureau and other agencies involved in counterintelligence investigations resulted in the project's vulnerability to a number of security leaks and the transmission of classified information to the Soviet Union. Ultimately, a series of disclosures and espionage trials led to the prosecution and conviction of Julius and Ethel Rosenberg in 1951 and their executions for espionage in 1953. In addition to the Rosenberg trial, the postwar years were marked by the FBI's participation in investigations and convictions of Alger Hiss, a high-level State Department employee charged with espionage for the Soviet Union.

The postwar years and the beginning phases of the Cold War were also marked by a rapidly rising crime rate, attributable in large degree to illegal behavior by individuals below the age of 18. The FBI estimated that 43 percent of the crimes reported were attributable to persons in this age group and that over half of the juvenile delinquents were under the age of 15. In response to this challenge, Hoover established a Juvenile Delinquency Instructor's School to assist state and local police agencies in the prevention and investigation of juvenile crime. Responding to the increase of crime among adults, Hoover criticized growing liberality in granting parole and probation. He referred to leading correctional theorists as "gushing, well-wishing, mawkish sentimentalists,"[2] which drew their sharp counterattacks. In his defense, it should be pointed out that many of the FBI's most-wanted criminals were released from prison on parole after having served the bare minimum time for their sentences. These were hard core criminals who had taxed bureau resources greatly and who had been put behind bars at great risk to Hoover's agents in the field.

A series of circumstances was responsible for turning Hoover from bureaucratic neutrality in his early years into a quasi-political figure after 1945. He had been close to President Franklin Delano Roosevelt and a strong right hand to the president throughout the critical war years. However, he had stood firmly against the massive relocation of the Japanese and Japanese-American population of the western states, asserting that all of the dangerous subversive elements had been interned by his agents at the beginning of the war. With the arrival of peace, Hoover discovered that the new President, Harry Truman, did not share his understanding of the extent to which agents of the Soviet Union had infiltrated both civil and military agencies of the federal government. Hoover's frustration at Truman's attitude, supplemented by his personal friendship for Senator Joseph McCarthy of Wisconsin, drew him into the political quagmire of the McCarthy hearings and identified him with ultraconservative political elements. At the same time, President Truman's institution of a widespread internal security program saddled Hoover's bureau with the responsibility of investigating most federal government employees for security clearances. This task was added to the already substantial workload of the FBI in criminal and counterintelligence investigations.

After a brief respite from political pressure during the Eisenhower administration, Hoover faced some of his sharpest critics during the presidency of John F. Kennedy. Attorney General Robert F. Kennedy opposed Hoover for both ideological and personal reasons, their relationship ultimately coming to public attention over the responsibility of the attorney general for authorizing wiretapping of prominent political leaders. Throughout this debate, Hoover insisted that he instituted wiretaps legally and only after authorization by the attorney general; Kennedy was not pleased when Hoover's position was supported by documentation within FBI files. Public concern about wiretapping and other activities perceived as violations of privacy resulted in stronger statutory safeguards.

President Kennedy's assassination in November 1963 brought Lyndon B. Johnson, a one-time neighbor and close friend of Hoover, into the White House. For a time, Hoover's political stance drew less public attention, but the appointment of Ramsay Clark as Attorney General pitted the director against his boss. Clark was a strong advocate of civil liberties, and a Washington wit described him as "a conscientious objector in the war against crime." During this phase of his career, Hoover became the subject of hostile interest on the part of the press, some reporters going to the length of inspecting his trash for evidence of misbehavior.

J. Edgar Hoover and his Federal Bureau of Investigation attracted harsh criticism from the press during their time, and to a degree they remain controversial today. While some of the criticisms are justified, the critics often overlook the magnitude of the bureau's contributions to twentieth-century American law enforcement.

The contributions made to law enforcement by Hoover's FBI include:

Personnel and management. There was virtual freedom from political influence in the appointment of special agents and other employees in Hoover's FBI. Discipline was tight, and all personnel were expected to conduct themselves with dignity and decorum, even when off duty. The smallest lapse might be brought to the attention of the director, and attempts to appeal outside bureau channels or to secure political support were dealt with harshly. For the most part, FBI disciplinary measures did not draw public or political attention, but a few agents who were disciplined or discharged by Hoover wrote books critical of him and the bureau. Special agents were carefully selected from among graduates of law schools or graduates of accountancy programs; they were trained extensively both in formal schools and on the job by their veteran colleagues. Both agents and clerical employees were loyal to the "company," the euphemism used in daily discourse to deflect public curiosity about the individual's work. Management of field offices was marked by decentralization of authority to Special Agents in Charge, but each office was inspected at irregular intervals to ensure that bureau directives and procedures were being followed. Advancement, like appointment, was kept free of political influence. Personnel procedures were outside the normal federal civil service system, giving the director and his subordinates broad discretion in disciplining and rewarding personnel.

Investigative practices. FBI investigative work was thorough, persistent, and results-oriented. It earned the bureau a reputation for always apprehending its criminal, no matter what resources and time were required to do so. Agents were trained to use the most advanced scientific techniques to solve crimes. The FBI Laboratory was then, as now, the leading forensic and identification facility in the nation. Meticulous intelligence files were maintained, both in regard to criminal activity and in the counterintelligence field; these raw files were carefully cross-indexed and provided a treasure of materials concerning individuals who had come to FBI investigative attention. With all of this attention to investigative procedures, the FBI became a leading police agency in extending procedural rights and guarantees to suspects. Long before the Warren Court began its enumeration of protections guaranteed to accused persons, the bureau had implemented those rules in its operations manuals.

Law enforcement liaison and training. The FBI Academy, established in 1935, was designed to provide training for state and local government police officials, a function it has performed with distinction for many years. The bureau also publishes a *Law Enforcement Bulletin* for circulation among academy graduates and chiefs of police throughout the nation. Its laboratory and the central fingerprint identification bureau (established in 1924) provided invaluable support to police activities nationwide. The bureau served as a model for countless federal law enforcement organizations and activities. For example, when the United States Air Force found itself in need of an investigative agency in 1948, it organized its Office of Special Investigations (1951) along bureau lines, drawing its first director from the ranks of the FBI.

To a lesser degree, the bureau has influenced police and investigative activities at state and local levels. FBI investigative jurisdiction is limited to federal crimes, and most of the violent felonies and capital crimes have remained within the jurisdictions of state and local police. Obviously, the bureau has no responsibility for street patrol and traffic control, and it does not deal with riots and public disturbances. In these and many other areas, state and local officials must look elsewhere for their models of good police practices.

State and Local Law Enforcement

Absent any useful federal model, and given the similarity of law enforcement activities throughout the United States, police executives have recognized the value of exchanging police intelligence; they also need to compare their programs and operating procedures. As early as 1871, the National Police Convention met at St. Louis to discuss the impact of new scientific discoveries on law enforcement. After noting the use of photography, telegraphy, and scientific investigative techniques, the group disbanded, resolving to establish a National Police Association. However, the new association did not materialize and no similar meetings were held until 1893, when the National Police Chiefs Union met in Chicago in conjunction with the Columbian Exposition. This group devoted most of its meeting time to organizing, and it was not until 1901 that it became a strong force for the professionalization of American law enforcement. Under the presidency of Major Richard Sylvester, chief of the Washington, D.C., Police Department, the union instituted a strong program of educational meetings and publications. It was renamed the International Association of Chiefs of Police (IACP) in 1915 and has been a strong influence in law enforcement activities since the second decade of the twentieth century.

Twentieth-century police reform has developed two major functions. The predominant function has been efficiency in law enforcement, which has drawn police leaders to direct their attention to modern management theory, to the study of personnel selection and methods of training, and to improved methods of command and control. During the Progressive period (1901-1920), this effort was carried forward in conjunction with the view that law enforcement officers should also be enlisted to provide certain social services not otherwise available. This second function, that of social servant, was not new in practice; historically, police station houses had been places to shelter and feed vagrants collected from the city streets. The new emphasis, provided by police officials trained in social work, was on providing a wide variety of rehabilitative and reformatory techniques, as well as preventing crime, through police activity. With the rise of new social welfare agencies in the 1930s, this social service function became secondary to the major effort to provide efficient and effective police services.

Police efficiency depended on strong leadership, the elimination of political influence, and the improvement of personnel through careful recruiting and enhanced standards of training. After 1900, local police organizations began to be centralized under a single administrative head, who reported either to a city manager or city commissioner charged with responsibility for public safety. This centralized responsibility was a large step toward limiting political influence in the appointment of officers or the supervision of their work. Many new police executives were inexperienced in law enforcement and were selected for their knowledge of management techniques; others were veteran law enforcement officers, elevated to command by their demonstrated effectiveness and abilities. Many police executives found themselves recruited by police departments that needed the management methods they had pioneered on an earlier assignment. A cadre of nationally known police executives formed the nucleus for a growing police bureaucracy that would dominate modern police history. Typical of this group was August Vollmer, chief of the Berkeley Police Department from 1905-1932, who answered a call to reform the Cleveland Police Department and ended his career as a professor of police science at the University of California. Vollmer's disciple, O.W. Wilson, after a time as chief of the Berkeley Police Department, joined the University of California faculty as professor of criminology and then became the reform superintendent of the Chicago Police Department.

The police executive who took office in the first three decades of the twentieth century found himself confronted with a serious management problem. These were times of change, but the traditional difficulty of instituting an effective street patrol was still a problem. Because the patrol officers were few, the beats were long. Initially, a two-shift system was implemented, requiring 12 hours on the beat for each shift. It was difficult to exercise supervision, even after the introduction of police call boxes, and a 1915 Chicago study suggested that the patrolmen spent most of their time in saloons. Street sergeants charged with ensuring performance of duty found it difficult to locate their men. Most lieutenants did not move from the station house to provide guidance to the sergeants and patrolmen of their platoon. With the introduction of the three-platoon system (that is, three shifts of eight hours each), beats became more manageable and patrolmen less fatigued. This change was pioneered in Cincinnati by Chief Phillip M. Dietsch (1886) but did not become commonplace until after it was instituted by the Philadelphia Police Department in 1912. The Philadelphia authorities estimated that under the old two-platoon system of patrol (two shifts of 12 hours each), every patrolman spent 65 hours per week on the streets and an additional 42 hours per week on station duty or in reserve.

The development of motor vehicles, the two-way radio, and the public telephone resulted in major changes in patrol methods. A patrol officer in an automobile could cover greater distances in a shorter period. The radio was an efficient mode of command and control, permitting the station house to concentrate police forces whenever and wherever needed. The telephone permitted the public to report criminal activity immediately to the station house, which could dispatch aid to the scene or alert its patrol cars to the emergency. Under a system of foot patrol, arrests had been limited to those deemed absolutely essential because the patrol officer had to carry or drag the prisoner back to the station house. A call on the call box produced a horse-drawn patrol wagon or one of the newer motorized "paddy wagons."

The expense of constructing radio facilities resulted in the development of shared communications nets by neighboring police departments. Progress in adopting radio communication systems was rapid. The Detroit Police Department set up the first publicly owned police radio system in 1928, and by 1939 there were 700 municipal police radio stations. By 1959, virtually every police agency had some form of radio communication system. However, the adoption of radio communication did not solve problems of command and control. The number of authorized channels was limited at the outset, and as police communications systems multiplied, it became impossible to assign a channel to each independent department. This factor, coupled with the cost of transmitting equipment, created a need for the sharing of facilities by neighboring police departments. Shared radio facilities, in turn, resulted in a more efficient patrol and crime suppression system because rapid means of transportation had made it possible for criminals to pass quickly from one police jurisdiction to another.

Selection and training of police personnel underwent a dramatic change from 1870 to 1940. In 1870 political appointments meant frequent rotation in office, and few patrolmen expected to make police work their lifetime career. By 1940, more than 81 percent of those leaving police departments did so due to death or retirement. This new occupational longevity created a force that began to develop its own distinct subculture in American life. It created cohesion among the rank and file, but it also imposed new demands for physical training, periodic retraining, and a need for employee benefits (including pensions). Most police administrators, following the lead of the FBI, tried to exclude their departments from civil service regulations. They reasoned that patrolmen protected by tenured appointments would be resistant to discipline. Despite these management views, in 1915 more than half of the 204 largest police departments were included in civil service systems; by 1959, almost three-quarters of municipal police departments made their appointments through civil service.

The connection between law enforcement and higher education was made early in the twentieth century when Chief August Vollmer recruited college students into the Berkeley Police Department (c. 1906). California institutions of higher education pioneered college-level courses in police subjects. A three-year police training program was instituted at the Berkeley campus of the University of California in 1915; a major in criminology was offered in 1933, and in 1951 a School of Criminology offering graduate degrees was established. San Jose State College began a two-year law enforcement curriculum in 1930, and Michigan State College offered a five-year course in police administration in 1935. Traffic management programs, supported by grants from the Kemper Insurance Company and the Automobile Manufacturer's Association, were begun at Northwestern University (1932) and Harvard University (1936). Taking advantage of the free tuition at City University, the New York City Police Department initiated programs at the Baruch School of Business and Public Administration (1955), leading to Bachelor of Business Administration and Master of Public Administration degrees. By 1959, more than 1,150 students were enrolled in the undergraduate program and 100 officers were taking courses toward the graduate degree. Subsequently, this program would be moved to the John Jay College of Criminal Justice, established in 1965. Emphasis on formal education as a qualification for police recruits resulted in more than half of the city police departments in the nation requiring a high school diploma from an applicant by 1959.

Vocational training and research in practical police problems came somewhat later. Zone schools, designed to provide regional police training within each state, began in 1923. The George-Dean Act (1936) provided federal grants-in-aid for vocational training, and in the 1939-1940 fiscal year, more than 9,000 police officers were enrolled in programs funded under that legislation. The Works Progress Administration (WPA) funded 101 police-related projects in the period 1934-1938, allocating $1,275,000 for this purpose and establishing a precedent for federally-funded police research. In addition to the FBI National Academy, designed for training police executives, FBI field schools were established in state, local, and "zone" locations beginning in 1959. Education in these vocational programs focused on and was enhanced by two manuals describing skills and training required in police activities (*Job Analysis of Police Services*, published in 1933 by the California State Education Department, and *Training for Police Service*, published in 1938 by the United States Department of the Interior).

Rising standards of law enforcement were also enhanced by the establishment of state police agencies. The Texas Rangers (1835), Massachusetts

District Police (1879), Arizona Rangers (1901), and New Mexico Mounted Police (1905) were early manifestations of this new move to create police agencies with wide jurisdiction and statewide authority. The Pennsylvania State Constabulary (1903) and New York State Police (1917) were responsible for introducing rigid physical and mental recruiting standards and imposing demanding training and strict disciplinary rules on all officers. Because of their centralized direction, these state police agencies were relatively free from political pressure at the local level. Promotions were based on merit and there were many opportunities for promotions to command area headquarters and substations.

Social Service and Public Relations

At its 1870 Cincinnati meeting, the National Prison Association approved a report to its Standing Committee on Police that endorsed a crime prevention role for the police, based upon social work principles and designed to reinforce the rehabilitative goals established in accordance with Zebulon Brockway's plan (see Chapter 12). One year later, the National Police Convention at St. Louis took up this theme. There, police administrators analyzed social evils and how they influenced criminal behavior. They considered problems of juvenile delinquency, as well as the perennial difficulty of how prostitution could be controlled or eliminated. Theoretical discussion did not materialize into action before the turn of the century, but thereafter police departments became deeply involved in social work activities.

When Fred Kohler became chief of police in Cleveland in 1903, he was disturbed by the high arrest rate for such minor offenses as vagrancy, public intoxication, and disorderly conduct. For the otherwise well-intentioned citizen, arrest and imprisonment could mean the loss of a job and begin the vicious spiral decline of an honest person into a life of crime. Caught between enforcing the law and protecting the innocent, Kohler arranged to convene a sunrise court that would process the cases of all honest working people before they were due to report for work the next day. In 1908, Kohler initiated a golden rule policy, which operated on the premise that no juvenile should be confined in a jail or prison; it also directed officers to reconcile differences between individuals and to issue reprimands in lieu of arrest whenever the circumstances dictated such a course. In effect, Kohler's sunrise courts and policy-restricting arrests diverted minor offenders out of the formal criminal justice system, relieving court dockets and allowing time to prevent and investigate more serious crimes.

The beginning of the policewomen's movement occurred in 1905 with the appointment of Lola Baldwin to the Portland, Oregon, Police Department for service with juvenile offenders apprehended at the Lewis and Clark Exposition. For the next 20 years, women were added to police departments for special assignment with juveniles, for the protection of women and girls, and to assist in interrogating female offenders. These pioneering policewomen were required to meet much higher educational standards than their male counterparts. They also suffered discrimination in receiving lower pay than male officers. Of course, none were assigned to street patrol or to any of the routine police functions of the force. An International Association of Policewomen was organized in 1915 with Alice Stebbins Wells as its president, but with the declining interest in women police officers after 1925, the association soon lost membership and became inactive.

Chief August Vollmer of the Berkeley Police Department was a strong advocate of police participation in social work. Building on his belief that every patrol officer should be a practicing criminologist, Vollmer felt that police should strive for better schools, recreational facilities for the poor, and better housing for those likely to fall into criminal activity. Various departments accepted the challenge and became active in raising money for the relief of the poor and destitute. They organized boy police clubs, worked with school safety patrols, and ran clinics to help young people stop smoking.

All of these activities enhanced police public relations that had been badly neglected, causing public misunderstanding of police functions and capabilities. For years the police had been the object of wry humor. However, by 1915 the jokes wore thin, and the International Association of Chiefs of Police became worried about the way police were depicted in the new motion pictures; the "Keystone Kops," with their awkward antics, were not the ideal model. Also harmful to the image of police was the Wickersham Commission's 1931 multivolume report; its most dramatic disclosure was the extent and brutality of the "third degree," as practiced throughout most American police departments.

Scientific Criminal Investigation

The twentieth century has produced phenomenal growth in the scientific aspects of detective work. August Vollmer recognized this as early as 1916 when he, as chief of the Berkeley Police Department, joined with Dr. Albert Schneider to establish the first crime laboratory in an American police department. Earlier times witnessed some work in forensic science, which deals with the application of the physical and biological sciences, as well as social science, to the investigation of crime. As early as 1248, a Chinese handbook appeared on the subject of forensic medicine; between 1510 and 1590, Ambroise Pare of France and two Italian anatomists, Fortunato Fidelis of Palermo and Paolo Zacchia of Rome, were active in the field. However, the scientific revolution of the seventeenth and eighteenth centuries formed a necessary foundation on which to base a truly definitive science of forensic medicine. Specifically, the modern disciplines of physiology, anatomy, physics, and chemistry came into their own, and they collectively provided highly effective instruments for the detection of crime and the identification of criminals. While much of the testing fell to the scientists retained by police departments, it was the responsibility of police investigators to become aware of the methods of preserving physical evidence and to exercise good judgment in determining which scientific investigations were appropriate.

Criminal justice professionals had long needed a method for the identification of individuals engaged in a life of crime. Investigation frequently involves matching similar modes of operation in otherwise unrelated crimes; prison officials need means of determining recidivism, and judges need to identify repeat offenders. The first step in providing certainty in identification was taken by a clerk in the Sûreté Archives in Paris. Alphonse Bertillon came from a family dominated by medical doctors, naturalists, and mathematicians, but his unassuming air and lack of personal grace resulted in his being assigned an obscure job as assistant clerk in the record room. It was his task to file identifying data on all criminals apprehended and convicted throughout the nation, and this tedious task was rendered distasteful by his realization that virtually all of the descriptions were so vague that they were useless. In 1879, he decided, on the basis of his observations and knowledge of science, that no two people could have exactly the same physical measurements. If enough measurements were taken, a high degree of individuality could be developed for each person contained within a police agency's files. Within a few years, he was given permission to begin his measurements and was provided with a small staff of technicians to process persons to be calibrated. By February 1883, his technique proved successful and was reported in the newspapers as anthropometry or "bertillonage." Bertillon's methods gained immediate attention. In the United States, they were widely adopted and a central file of measurements was developed at Sing Sing Prison for the purpose of identifying multiple offenders.

Ironically, Bertillon's fame was destined to be short-lived, for anthropometry was rapidly replaced by the use of fingerprinting. Fingerprinting seems to have originated in Asia. Henry Faulds, a Scottish physician working in Japan, noticed the practice of identifying pottery and sealing documents through the use of handprints and fingerprints. William Herschel, a British official in India, discovered that he could prevent his employees from drawing a second salary by requiring them to place the inked impressions of two forefingers of the right hand opposite their names in the payroll records. The two men noticed the similarity of their discoveries when Faulds published an article on fingerprinting in *Nature* magazine on October 28, 1880. In 1892, Sir Francis Galton published *Finger Prints*,[3] a book-length monograph that contained a basic system of classification. Galton's system was expanded into a practical method of categorization that was widely adopted throughout the world by 1903. An 1894 report to the British Home Secretary proclaimed the value of fingerprints for identification. It claimed that there was only one chance in 64,000 that the print from the same finger of two persons would be identical, and it was inconceivable that two people would have the same prints on two or three fingers.

American fingerprinting efficiency was increased in 1924 when federal prisoner identification files, maintained at the Federal Prison at Leavenworth, were combined with the files formerly maintained by the International Association of Chiefs of Police at Sing Sing. The consolidated fingerprint bureau, later to be relocated to the Federal Bureau of Investigation in Washington, proved invaluable not only for criminal investigation but also for the identification of the victims of accidents and natural disasters. Emphasis on law and order in the years 1935 and 1936 led to a short-lived campaign for a universal fingerprinting system that would bring all Americans into the FBI fingerprint files. Although that particular effort was far from successful, the passage of time and growing practices of fingerprinting persons wishing to get married, enter professional practice, or join the armed forces have provided virtually complete coverage for identification purposes. Because a variant form of classification (i.e., depending on the characteristics of each finger, rather than all 10) is used for criminal investigative work, the identification files are, for the most part, inaccessible for forensic purposes. A new development in fingerprint analysis involves the microscopic comparison of pores within the ridges of fingerprints, permitting identifications when only a portion of a fingerprint is available for comparison.

The origins of modern forensic medicine predate fingerprinting by about a century, having their inception with the work of Johann Ludwig Casper, Mathieu J.B. Orfila, and Marie G.A. Devergie, all of whom made major contributions during the first half of the nineteenth century. In the 1870s, a Frenchman, Albert Florence, developed a definitive chemical test for the presence of human semen, and in the same decade Ambroise Tardieu discovered dot-like blood spots under the pleura that were characteristic of death by rapid suffocation. In 1882, an Austrian, Eduard von Hoffmann, discovered that persons burned alive had soot in their windpipes and lungs and carbon monoxide in their blood. A 1931 study by John Glaister of Glasgow provided a wealth of information about human hair and its value for investigative work.

Supporting anatomical work was a vastly expanded technology concerning human blood. A German physician, Paul Uhlenhuth, developed a test with blood serums in 1901 that permitted the scientist to distinguish one species of animal blood from another and, hence, made it possible to identify human blood stains and distinguish them from the blood of most other animals. A year earlier, his countryman, Karl Landsteiner, had discovered that human blood cells could be grouped into what came to be known as A, B, and O types. In 1927 Landsteiner, in conjunction with other scientists, developed 12 additional typing characteristics of human blood and then isolated the Rh factor in 1940. In connection with this theoretical research, other scientists devised methods for dissolving blood stains into solutions that could be analyzed in the laboratory. More recent advances in blood chemistry make it possible to positively establish paternity, using a number of tests to determine genetically related human leukocyte antigens. Closely related to blood typing is the use of DNA (deoxyribonucleic acid) matching in criminal investigation. DNA is located in all human cells, and its precise configuration is determined by heredity. First used to establish paternity, the reliability of the test is such that it is now accepted as extremely persuasive evidence in criminal prosecutions. While blood is the most common material subjected to DNA comparison, virtually any cellular material can be used. Recently DNA testing established that a woman who claimed to be Anastasia, the lost Grand Duchess of Russia, could not possibly have been the child of Nicholas II and his wife, Alexandra. All of the parties were dead at the time the test occurred, the bones of the royal parents having recently been exhumed in Russia. This shows the degree to which DNA testing has advanced the science of identification and forensic investigation.

TIME CAPSULE

Revision through Technology

New forensic methods can, in a sense, rewrite history. With increasing frequency, articles appear in newspapers and journals that document tragic instances in which a person convicted of a felony is later exonerated through use of DNA "fingerprinting" of old pieces of evidence. For example, in 1985 Ronald Cotton was sentenced to life in prison for the rape of a woman in North Carolina, primarily on the basis of eyewitness testimony. From prison Cotton continually protested that he was innocent and eventually won a second trial; by then DNA analysis was possible and it proved that he was not the rapist (*The State,* Columbia, SC, September 24, 2000: A4). In a similar case in South Carolina, Perry Mitchell was released from prison after serving more than 14 years (*The State*, Columbia, SC, August 15, 1998: A1). According to an article in *U.S. News & World Report* (October 25, 1999: 33), around 70 convicted persons have been exonerated by DNA testing. The evident fallibility of investigation and trial procedures sends shudders through the criminal justice system. Although there are no documented cases in which an innocent person has been executed, there are now proposals that all death row inmates be given a right to have the evidence against them subjected to DNA testing and that police be required to preserve evidence for possible analysis.

Just as the innocent can profit from retroactive examination, the guilty can lose. Use of DNA can also help police to clear up old unsolved cases. By analysis of preserved evidence and by matching the DNA profiles to data banks, they can sometimes identify the perpetrator years after the crime. The obvious step of performing DNA tests on all arrestees runs into opposition both because of the high cost and because of fears of an unwarranted invasion of privacy. There is concern, too, that the probative value of DNA evidence can be questionable because of faulty police procedures in gathering material evidence, an incomplete chain of custody, or inaccurate analyses in laboratories. This form of rewriting history may increase markedly if other courts agree with the September, 2000 decision of federal district Judge Albert V. Bryan in Alexandria, Virginia, who held that inmates who claimed they were wrongfully convicted had a constitutional right to request DNA testing.

Dentistry, long recognized as a system of identification, has become an invaluable part of forensic science. There may be some doubt about the legend that William the Conqueror's bite was so distinctive that it was accepted as the seal for official documents, but there can be no question that Paul Revere identified the corpse of General Joseph Warren through examining a silver dental bridge he had made for the officer 10 months before his death in the American Revolution. A famous American murder case, involving the killing and dismemberment of Dr. George Parkman (1850), was solved through the discovery and identification of the victim's dentures in the ashes of the accused's furnace. By 1870, dental evidence was widely accepted in criminal trials throughout Europe and the United States.

Teeth are one of the most important means of identification. During the early years of life, the growth of primary teeth and their replacement by permanent teeth aid in establishing the age of a corpse; this can be confirmed by measuring the specific gravity of the teeth, which changes with increased age. The size, alignment, and color of the teeth vary with the race of an individual, as do the arch of the mouth and the shape of the jaw. Abnormal functions of the jaw may provide telltale scratches or indentations on the teeth, as may the deceased's occupation; tailors tend to chew pins, and carpenters mar their teeth by chewing nails. When teeth are subjected to professional care, their fillings, crowns, and dentures provide clues to the region or nation in which the dentist received his or her training, and some dentures may even have the Social Security number of their owner impressed in the supporting material.

Because teeth are virtually unique, bite marks are useful for investigative purposes. Whether on the body of a victim or inflicted on the accused by the victim, bite marks can link a suspect to the crime. Bite marks may fade quickly and lose many of their identifying characteristics shortly after the bite occurs, or they may vary according to the angle and pressure of the bite. To deal with certain variables, an impression can be taken of the biter's teeth and a set of teeth cast and mounted on an apparatus that revolves and can be subjected to varying pressure. An infinite number of bites can be simulated in an attempt to reproduce the bite inflicted at the crime scene.

Toxicology, or the study of poisons, is another area in which science has provided continuing assistance in police work. Arsenic, one of the foremost causes of death by poisoning in the early nineteenth century, formed the subject of extensive research by Mathieu J.B. Orfila, the French forensic scientist. Orfila developed several tests for the identification of arsenic in the bodies of victims, but in 1932 James Marsh, an English researcher, provided a definitive method for isolating arsenic from organic compounds. Through the Marsh method, arsenic in body organs could be detected even if it was only 1/1000th of a milligram. The identification and isolation of organic poisons such as nicotine, aconine, and morphine proved to be more difficult, but Jean Servais Stas, one of the leading French forensic scientists, succeeded in doing this and in developing a number of confirming tests. By 1955, there were more than 30 different methods of testing for morphine poisoning. When it was impossible to isolate the poison, its presence in body organs could be demonstrated by injection into laboratory animals; this method was developed by Ambroise Tardieu in 1863. Tranquilizer poisons became a threat after the Second World War, and extensive research has been necessary to allow their isolation or identification by laboratory means.

Ballistics is another field in which scientific investigation has long provided assistance to the detective. Bow Street Runner Henry Goddard is credited with the first use of ballistics to solve a murder (1835). Noting a peculiar bluish hue to the bullet removed from the victim, Goddard compared the bullet to the residue found in the bullet mold used in the accused's house. An imperfection in the mold also was characteristic of the bullet, and Goddard had his man. The English case of *Regina v. Richardson* (1860) involved evidence of newspaper wadding in a two-barreled muzzle-loading pistol. One wad, found in the victim's wound, contained material printed in the *London Times* for March 27, 1854; the second wad, found unfired in the accused's pistol, carried printed matter from the same issue.

For nearly a century, the value of ballistics evidence was known to police investigators. Marks on bullets and cartridges, along with analysis of powder and its deposits on the victim's skin, were all accepted as useful forms of evidence. However, it was the misuse of ballistics evidence that brought Charles E. Waite into the systematic study of firearms, ammunition, and powders. A dimwitted farmhand in upstate New York was prosecuted and convicted of killing his employer with a .22 caliber pistol; only the concerned interest of a prison warden and a volunteer social worker saved the man from execution. Waite was asked to review the evidence, and he discovered that the man's pistol could not have fired the fatal shots. Waite, horrified at the possible miscarriage of justice in future cases, began to assemble technical details and samples from prominent American gun manufacturers (1920-1922) and then, learning that two-thirds of American firearms were imported, supplemented his collection from foreign sources. By the time of his death in 1926, Philip O. Gravelle and Dr. Calvin Goodard had joined him in the enterprise, and between them they were responsible for establishing the Bureau of Forensic Ballistics in New York City. Careful attention to maintaining a centralized file of ballistics information proved worthwhile in 1929, when police investigators were able to use ballistics evidence to identify a machine gun used in the famous St. Valentine's Day Massacre of seven gangland leaders by members of a rival Chicago gang.

Countless other scientific advances have contributed to the efficiency and accuracy of criminal investigation. Belgian law enforcement officials used photography just four years after its invention by Louis Daguerre in 1839, and Alphonse Bertillon was responsible for establishing standards of crime scene photography by the Sûreté. Advanced techniques of physical and chemical analysis have permitted the examination of textile fibers, dust and dirt, automobile tires, and ash residues in investigative work. Handwriting patterns have long been a method of identifying blackmailers, kidnappers, and other literate wrongdoers, and with the development of typewriters, centralized files were established that permitted the recognition of manufacturer and model. With some degree of luck, imperfections in the typeface actually permitted the investigators to determine whether a given machine prepared a certain document. The development of computers as word processors has virtually eliminated such accuracy in identifying documents produced by a given individual. However, access to a computer, coupled with word content analysis[4] may provide circumstantial evidence of authorship. Computerized access to information, along with the popularity of communication by e-mail, provide more promising methods for tracing individual involvement in criminal conspiracies or acts of terrorism. The forensic opportunities and investigative challenges presented by cyberspace have yet to be fully explored, but they reemphasize the fact that science is a critical component of law enforcement activity.

Rapid expansion of scientific methods of investigation has placed special demands on the training and financial resources of police agencies. Use of these sophisticated techniques requires a high level of formal education, a comprehensive knowledge of modern science, and the ability to work with highly trained professionals in anatomy, physiology, chemistry, and physics. Under this pressure, the old American system of elected coroners began to give way to trained medical examiners after 1935, and the work of the police detective soon became a matter of coordinating the investigations of many professional scientists and applying their discoveries for the solution of the case at hand.

Subculture, Police Riots, and Unionism

From the middle years of the 1960s to about 1975, the United States passed through a series of domestic upheavals, generated by racial tension, the growing unpopularity of the war in Vietnam, and the uncomfortable prospect of declining economic opportunities for American youth. Beginning with the Free Speech Movement (1964) on the Berkeley campus of the University of California, college and university students exhibited a growing tendency to demonstrate their opposition to university, state, and national policies. The civil rights movements, long restrained by Martin Luther King Jr.'s emphasis on nonviolent protests, began to meet with violent opposition that generated a series of riots in major American cities. One of the most spectacular ghetto uprisings occurred in Washington, D.C., in the wake of King's 1968 assassination. Despite sincere efforts on the part of leaders from both racial groups, tension and violence persisted, leaving cities highly vulnerable to widespread disorder and looting. Caught in the crossfire (in regard to both university-based violence and urban ghetto disorder) were the police departments. As one black leader pointed out, police officers on the beat were

Civil rights issues with black communities and anti-Vietnam war sentiments from
college students led to controversial confrontations between citizens and the
police in the 1960s, further expanding the gulf between police and the people they
were supposed to be serving.

the personification of white society maintaining order, and this made them
the most convenient scapegoats for American racial injustice.

Racial tension was not the only cause of conflict between police organizations and society. The escalation of the war in Vietnam after 1964 caused
a growing peace movement, concentrated for the most part among young,
middle-class college students. As demonstrations became increasingly violent, university authorities abandoned their traditional system of self-discipline and called upon municipal and state police forces to restore order on
their campuses. Historically there has always been some animosity between
"town and gown," but the arrival of tactical patrol forces in riot gear was
unprecedented. The inevitable confrontations, resulting in injury and some
deaths, focused public attention on law enforcement methods and resulted
in some telling criticism of police management.

The new and unwelcome notoriety drove police professionals of all ranks further into the protection of their unique subculture. For nearly a century, the "new police forces" slowly evolved into a distinctive organization, a unique social pattern, and a characteristic mindset that sociologists have identified as a subculture in American life. Initially, this was the product of wearing a distinctive uniform, reinforced by authorization to carry and use firearms. Police officers were required to enforce a broad spectrum of laws, ranging from the apprehension and arrest of felons to breaking up tavern brawls, mediating household fights, and suppressing prostitution, excessive drinking, and disorderly behavior. All in all, the police were expected to impose on the civilian population a standard of conduct dictated by principles of Victorian morality that they, in many cases, did not practice themselves. To avoid inconsistency between official and private behavior, police officers and their families became isolated in their social lives, congregating with other officers and their families.

With the advent of the automobile, officers were charged with administering rules of the road. This also brought about the introduction of automotive patrol, which increased the isolation of police officers from the public. Under street patrol conditions, the local patrol officer met the citizens who lived on his beat. It was the essence of walking patrol that he prevented crime by knowing all the inhabitants of his territory and by noticing changes in individuals and circumstances that might be suspicious. The patrol car precluded familiarity with the honest residents and accentuated the feeling that, outside the car itself, the world and its inhabitants were all suspicious.

The social origins of police recruits also had a bearing on the development of the police subculture. While there were a small number of college graduates in police work before World War II, the postwar period saw a return to high school graduates as the norm. Studies have shown that recruits tend to be drawn from working-class (blue-collar) families and that they are motivated toward upward mobility. For the most part, they are conservative in their political and social views, and by background and training, they place a high premium on orderly behavior. They are quick to resent seeming challenges to their authority, and they are impatient and harsh in their views of middle-class college and university students who, by their standards, behave improperly. The "town-gown" polarizations of the Vietnam era have decreased markedly since the fall of Saigon to the North Vietnamese in 1975. As college graduates increasingly enter the law enforcement field, it seems less likely that such attitudes will persist in professional law enforcement. However, economic and social unrest in ghetto communities has triggered a new form of mob violence that has ominous racial overtones. Efforts to recruit minority law enforcement officers seem to have had a limited impact on the frequency of these urban uprisings. However, techniques of crowd control have been substantially improved, and law enforcement managers are increasingly aware of the need to maintain good community relations.

Police officers develop strong bonds to each other and their departments. In part, this can be attributed to the fact that all levels of authority, from patrol officer to precinct chief (and, in some cases, even police chief or commissioner), started at the entry level. Unlike the military services, there is no division between officers and enlisted men in terms of career progression. Leadership is exercised by officers who have long years of experience and, thus, perhaps great empathy with the circumstances of the patrol officer on the beat or the detective in the squad room. Except at the very highest levels of command, there is virtually no opportunity for transfer from one department to another. An intricate relationship of competition and camaraderie develops among the officers in a given precinct or division. Police officers are highly protective of each other, and entire organizations can be aroused by the injury or death of one of their members.

This brief summary of academic study concerning police subculture provides a basis upon which to look at the student riots and racial violence of the 1960s and 1970s. At the outset, it is helpful to recall that the Metropolitan Police of London and the Municipal Police of New York and other American cities have faced difficulties in controlling riotous behavior. Those who have studied the violence of the 1960s and 1970s conclude that regular army units were most effective in dealing with rioting. National Guard troops were less effective, but still superior to police, even when police were specially trained and organized into riot control units.

The key seems to be in the nature of police work and the additional skills needed for the suppression of a riotous assembly. Police officers are trained to act either alone or in small groups. In fact, police work is one of the few activities in which individual discretion increases as one moves down the chain of authority. Police deal with individuals, seeking suspicious behavior and reacting aggressively to challenges to their authority. They aim to make arrests and determine blame. Control of a riot, on the other hand, requires the concerted, disciplined use of gradually increasing force, which is designed to disperse the disorderly crowd and restore order. Military troops acting under strong command direction that stresses dispersal and disengagement are conditioned to work as a team and to use only the weapons and anti-crowd methods authorized by their officers. However, American federal law prevents the use of federal troops in most riot situations. In recent years, National Guard units have received expanded training in crowd control techniques; yet the first line of defense remains the local or state police departments. Realistically, a decision must be made about whether riot control will remain with the police; if it does, some extensive retraining will be required.

Lack of police training, serious mistakes in tactical application of force, and perhaps even overpreparedness by political leaders and police officials generated serious citizen-police clashes in the student riots and ghetto uprisings of the 1960s and 1970s. Charges of police brutality were given increased credibility by established incidents of police officers breaking into riot themselves, beating innocent bystanders and using tear gas indiscriminately. A substantial portion of police misbehavior can be explained by the clash of student and ghetto cultures with the police subculture. Poor police leadership may also have been involved. In the face of overwhelming hostility and physical injury to themselves or their colleagues, police officers broke ranks, venting their fears and frustrations on any person in the vicinity of the riot.

In the aftermath of the 1960s, professional police officers have taken two significant steps. First, they have begun to realize the need to organize themselves politically to protect their interests against hostile forces. An example of their success was the 1967 defeat of New York City Mayor John V. Lindsay's proposed civilian review board. This board was intended to remove from police disciplinary procedures complaints concerning officers accused of brutality and using excessive force. The Patrolmen's Benevolent Association (PBA), representing an overwhelming majority of city police officers, successfully launched a public attack on the civilian review board, securing its rejection by the voters. In a number of other cities across the United States, similar political action by police groups reasserted police independence and professionalism and rejected the contention that outside surveillance was necessary.

Second, the historical reluctance to join police labor unions has begun to disappear. Since 1919, American police officers and city governments have lived in the shadow of the Boston Police Strike. Historians differ concerning the degree to which crime increased during the time that Boston was without police protection. Indeed, there are some suggestions that law enforcement has never been the major part of police work, that most police activity involves the rendition of such social services as getting a cat down from a tree, bringing habitual drunkards into a station house cell for a night's sleep, and similar non-crime-related services.

Whatever the truth may be concerning the Boston Police Strike, it is clear that, thereafter, unionism was considered contrary to public safety and a threat to command and control of police departments. The Boston situation and subsequent efforts at unionization after World War II were generated by stagnation of police salaries in a rapidly inflating economy. However, the new wave of union enthusiasm among police officers is based not only upon economic concerns but also upon the perception of police officers that they have lost the support of the public and that their political superiors and the courts are determined to hinder them in their work. A confrontation between penologists and criminologists on one hand, and J. Edgar Hoover and police professionals on the other, was a recurrent theme of the 1960s and 1970s. Understandably, the police officer who has risked his or her life in apprehending a dangerous felon does not take kindly to the culprit's receiving a light sentence or probation.

Police organizations have, in the past, centered around benevolent or fraternal organizations. The New York City Patrolmen's Benevolent Association, founded in 1892, successfully lobbied in 1900 and 1901 for an eight-hour workday. Other local police clubs were organized in Buffalo, Rochester, and Milwaukee before 1915, when the Fraternal Order of Police (FOP) established its first lodge in Pittsburgh. By 1941, the FOP had 169 local lodges, and that number increased to 194 by 1959. In 1969, the FOP boasted 733 affiliated lodges and 80,000 members. The International Conference of Police Associations in 1972 reported more than 100 local and state affiliated organizations, comprised of more than 158,000 members. To date, these growing police organizations have been active in working for the welfare of their members in the political arena and in serving as bargaining agents concerning conditions of employment. They have the potential to lobby for police benefits and increased wages and perhaps even to resort to strikes to attain these objectives. Police organizations present police concerns to voters and can provide powerful arguments for increased emphasis on law and order. They also continue to have increasing control over the command and personnel policies and decisions of their respective departments.

Police agencies throughout the United States have also been profoundly affected by the establishment of the Law Enforcement Assistance Administration (LEAA), chartered by the Omnibus Crime Control and Safe Streets Act of 1968. The LEAA provided a method for channeling federal assistance to state and local law enforcement agencies. A series of block grants provided police administrators with opportunities to experiment with new methods of management and operations, and many departments secured new and otherwise unattainable equipment. However, perhaps the most significant impact was in the elevation of educational standards for police officers. The Law Enforcement Education Program (LEEP) provided federal grants for the establishment of criminal justice education programs in institutions of higher education. It grew rapidly, serving 20,602 students in 1969 with an expenditure of $6.5 million; by 1974, more than 100,000 students were enrolled in a program funded in excess of $44 million.

Reviewing the variety of offerings in its 1975 report on the LEAA, the Twentieth Century Fund suggested that many programs merely moved vocational training into university classrooms. Classes on interrogation techniques, they suggested, belonged in departmental or zone schools, but future police officers should be exposed to the challenges of a broad liberal arts education. Fortunately, many programs provided a general education in addition to attention to police-related subjects that were suitable for university discussion. A growing number of police professionals took advantage of LEAA-sponsored criminal justice programs and earned undergraduate and graduate degrees in off-duty hours. Two benefits of such education are obvious. The insularity of police subcultural influences may well be softened by educational contact with other segments of contemporary society. Also, police professionals will be better equipped to deal with the highly sophisticated investigative techniques of the twentieth century. At the same time, they will be sensitive to the delicate balance that must be achieved if police activity is to be both effective and publicly acceptable in our multiracial and rapidly diversifying society of the future.

The Impact of the September 11 Terrorist Attacks

One year after the al Qaeda terrorist attacks on the Pentagon and World Trade Center, it is difficult to assess the full impact these events will have on law enforcement and its role in American life. In the wake of those disasters, the response of police and fire departments was heroic. It cannot fail to vastly enhance the general public's respect for law enforcement professionals. At the same time, the widespread demand for enhanced security measures may well provide greater leeway for increasingly vigorous police measures and procedures. Already we have seen airport security moved into the sphere of federal law enforcement, and heightened administrative control over immigration and the activities of aliens resident within the United States. There is also evidence of counterproductive investigative competition between the FBI and the CIA, and a censurable failure to coordinate and exchange information. The magnitude of governmental inadequacy in the face of potential terrorist threats cannot fail to have a sobering, yet perhaps energizing, impact on global law enforcement activity as we enter the twenty-first century.

Summary

With its emphasis on strong management, organizational discipline, and scientific investigative techniques, the Federal Bureau of Investigation has had a formative influence on twentieth-century police activities. Long identified with J. Edgar Hoover, its late director, the bureau has encouraged cooperation between police agencies and the role of the federal government in providing training for police leadership. State police agencies established during the first two decades of this century have served similar coordinating and training functions within their states.

Modern inventions, particularly the automobile and radio, have revolutionized the system of street patrol and permitted rapid improvement in the command and control of police units. Scientific methods of criminal investigation, proliferating rapidly since 1880, have placed a premium on training police officers to coordinate and evaluate scientific procedures and findings.

Social service responsibilities have become a growing part of police activities. There is a growing emphasis on eliminating the sources of crime and increasing efforts to build public confidence and pride in the police. Through the use of the sunrise court and the golden rule policy, minor offenders are diverted from the formal criminal justice system, leaving more time for the prosecution of major criminal activity.

A number of factors in modern life have contributed to the rise of a unique police subculture, which imposes limits on the efficiency of local and state police in dealing with riots. At the same time, strong anti-police attitudes on the part of some segments of the public and efforts to impose popular control over police disciplinary procedures have generated solidarity among professional law enforcement officers. The traditional fraternal organizations have gained new power, and a long-standing antipathy to police unionization may give way to pressures for unionization. Most recently, the Law Enforcement Assistance Administration's grants have resulted in a higher level of education among police officers and, thus, a greater level of interaction and understanding of the needs and attitudes of the general public.

Endnotes

[1]   To be discussed at length in Chapter 14.

[2]   Quoted in Ralph de Toledano, *J. Edgar Hoover: The Man in His Time* (New Rochelle: Arlington House, 1973), p. 261.

[3]   Sir Francis Galton, *Fingerprints* (London: Macmillan Co., 1892; reprint ed., New York: Da Capo Press, 1965).

[4]   Word content analysis uses mathematical probability theory to match a questioned document with a control document authored by an individual. Identification of an author is based upon the likelihood that any individual is likely to use the same words and phrases when discussing a given subject.

References

On the Federal Bureau of Investigation, see Don Whitehead, *The FBI Story* (New York: Random House, 1956); Ralph de Toledano, *J. Edgar Hoover: The Man in His Time* (New Rochelle, NY: Arlington House, 1973); Athan G. Theoharis, "The Presidency and the Federal Bureau of Investigation: The Conflict of Intelligence and Legality, *Criminal Justice History* 2 (1981): 131-160; and Frederick L. Collins, *The FBI in Peace and War* (New York: Books, Inc., 1943). Two critical studies are Max Lowenthal, *The Federal Bureau of Investigation* (New York: William Sloane, 1950); and William W. Turner, *Hoover's FBI: The Men and the Myth* (Los Angeles: Sherbourne Press, 1970).

Police professionalism and social work efforts are best set forth in Eric H. Monkkonen, *Police in Urban America, 1860-1920* (Cambridge: Cambridge University Press, 1981); and Samuel Walker, *A Critical History of Police Reform: The Emergence of Professionalism* (Lexington, MA: Lexington Books, 1977). Also useful are William J. Bopp, *The Police Rebellion: A Quest for Blue Power* (Springfield, IL: Charles C Thomas, 1971); Hervey A. Juris and Peter Feuille, *Police Unionism: Power and Impact in Public Sector Bargaining* (Lexington, MA: Lexington Books, 1973); Barbara Raffer Price, *Police Professionalism: Rhetoric and Action* (Lexington, MA: Lexington Books, 1977); and August Vollmer, *The Police and Modern Society* (Berkeley: University of California Press, 1936; reprint, Montclair, NJ: Patterson Smith, 1971).

No student of scientific criminal investigation should miss Jurgen Thorwald, *The Century of the Detective*, trans. Richard and Clara Winston (New York: Harcourt, Brace & World, Inc., 1964), an outstanding narrative of cases and experiments that advanced forensic science. A thorough introduction to criminal investigation is James W. Osterberg and Richard H. Ward, *Criminal Investigation: A Method for Reconstructing the Past*, 3d ed. (Cincinnati, OH: Anderson Publishing Co., 2000); and in Richard Saferstein, *Criminalistics: An Introduction to Forensic Science* (Englewood Cliffs, NJ: Prentice-Hall, 1998). For coverage of evidence issues, see Andre A. Moenssens, James E. Starrs, Carol E. Henderson, and Fred E. Inbau, *Scientific Evidence in Civil and Criminal Cases*, 4th ed. (Westburg, NY: The Foundation Press, 1995).

Useful insights into police subculture and behavior can be found in Jerome H. Skolnick and Thomas C. Grey, eds., *Police in America* (Boston: Little, Brown & Co., 1975); Rodney Stark, *Police Riots: Collective Violence and Law Enforcement* (Belmont, CA: Wadsworth Publishing Co,. 1972); James Q. Wilson, *Varieties of Police Behavior: The Management of Law and Order in Eight Communities* (Cambridge, MA: Harvard University Press, 1968); and William A. Westley, *Violence and the Police: A Sociological Study of Law, Custom and Morality* (Cambridge, MA: The MIT Press, 1970). On the relationship of police work to crime, see James Q. Wilson, *Thinking About Crime* (New York: Basic Books, 1975). Police unionism and the growing "blue power" movement is traced in Hervey A. Juris and Peter Feuille, *Police Unionism: Power and Impact in Public-Sector Bargaining* (Lexington, MA: Lexington Books, 1973); and William J. Bopp, *The Police Rebellion: A Quest for Blue Power* (Springfield, IL: Charles C Thomas, 1971). On the Law Enforcement Assistance Administration, see *Law Enforcement: The Federal Role* (Report of the Twentieth Century Fund Task Force on the Law Enforcement Assistance Administration) (New York: McGraw-Hill Book Co., 1976).

For historical development of the Mafia, see Dwight C. Smith, Jr., "Some Things That May Be More Important to Understand about Organized Crime and the Cosa Nostra," *University of Florida Law Review* 24, no. 1 (1971): 181-185; and Eric J. Hobsbawm, "Mafia," in *Primitive Rebels: Studies in Archaic Forms of Social Movement in the 19th and 20th Centuries* (New York: Norton and Company, 1965), 90-98.

Issues concerning police unions are discussed in William A. Geller. ed., *Police Leadership in America: Crisis and Opportunity* (New York: Praeger, 1985). Police misconduct is traced in Victor E. Kappeler, Richard D. Sluder, and Geoffrey P. Alpert, "A History of Police Deviance: The Forging of an Occupation," in *Forces of Deviance: Understanding the Dark Side of Policing* (Prospect Heights, IL: Waveland Press, Inc., 1994); and Lawrence W. Sherman, *Scandal and Reform: Controlling Police Corruption* (Berkeley: University of California Press, 1978). Recent efforts to limit and respond to corruption in police organizations are explored in Knapp Commission (New York City), *Knapp Commission Report on Police Corruption* (New York: George Braziller, 1972); and Harry W. More and Peter Charles Unsinger, eds., *Managerial Control of the Police: Internal Affairs and Audits* (Springfield, IL: Charles C Thomas, 1992). Increasingly police are facing civil lawsuits and criminal prosecution; points of vulnerability are discussed in Rolando V. del Carmen, *Civil Liabilities in American Policing: A Text for Law Enforcement Personnel* (Englewood Cliffs, NJ: Prentice Hall, 1991). For an overview of current controversies concerning police function, see Roger G. Dunham and Geoffrey P. Alpert, *Critical Issues in Policing: Contemporary Readings* (Prospect Heights, IL: Waveland Press, Inc., 1993).

Notes and Problems

1. This chapter has raised several issues in connection with police professionalization, but there is some difficulty in pinpointing what that professionalism is. Certainly it is distinguishable from the learned professions of medicine, law, theology, and teaching, but it shares with them the characteristics of having a unique body of knowledge, a shared career experience, a sense of vocational unity, and a monopoly of certain activities denied to the general public. So defined, has police professionalism increased since 1850, and what factors have been most significant in this development?

2.   Assume that you are a university official charged by the Law Enforcement Assistance Administration with designing a proposed criminal justice degree program that would award a bachelor's degree to candidates for police or corrections appointments. What subjects would you include and why? How would you balance vocational skill enhancement with traditional liberal arts subjects? If your college or university has a criminal justice program, how well does it match your requirements? Should it be changed?

3.   A number of scholarly writers on police rioting and violence have suggested (with a battery of statistics to support them) that violence is a way of life for the patrol officer assigned to law enforcement activities. This has alienated substantial portions of the public, particularly young people and blacks. If we accept that viewpoint as correct, what steps could be taken to control excessive use of force? Is this not an important factor in retaining public support, which in turn is an essential ingredient in law enforcement? Should police administrators, for example, consider returning to foot patrol? should they emphasize public assistance and public education programs? Would it help to make a sharp differentiation between patrol duties and traffic enforcement activities?

4.   American constitutional and statutory law prohibits the use of federal troops in the suppression of riots. Only on the request of a state governor, asking for federal assistance, may the president authorize federal units to participate. Yet we have seen that military discipline is critical to the controlled dispersement of rioters and protesters, and that the controlled use of large units is a difficult task for police commanders and a strain on the training and instincts of police officers. How should we plan to assure public safety against rioting and looting? If police units are to be utilized, how must their training be conducted or supplemented?

5.   A perennial problem since the establishment of the "new police" has been the supervision and effectiveness of patrol duties. In its initial state, patrol was considered to provide a police presence throughout urban areas, discouraging crime by making it more difficult. As a practical matter, recent attempts to increase patrol officers in a given area either drive criminals to other locations or provide a mere temporary drop in reported crime. Does patrol perform any useful purpose other than giving the public some assurance that the police are available if trouble should develop? Is the expense of patrol worth the minimal public relations benefits that it gives?

6.   James Q. Wilson's point that very small proportions of police work are involved in law enforcement seems to be well taken. Should police be expected to shelter lost children, help the habitual drunk, get cats out of trees, and help the person who locks their keys in their car? If they stop doing that, who will take their place? The evidence seems to indicate that most patrol officers appreciate opportunities to be of assistance. Conversely, they dislike confrontations with offenders of minor traffic regulations and try to minimize the harsh feelings generated by those encounters. If their duties are sharply limited to law enforcement and crime prevention, will a different type of officer be attracted to police work, and would that be desirable?

7. Increasingly, principles of business management and organization have been brought into police administration. How useful are principles of span of control, chain of command, grouping of similar activities under one executive, and employee participation in generating policy? How different is police administration from business administration and other aspects of public sector management?

Chapter 14

Globalization, Human Rights, and Personal Laws in Criminal Justice

Since World War II ended in 1945, there has been a vast expansion both in the means of communication and transportation and in their speed and availability. This has caused significant changes in all phases of the American criminal justice system. Academic and professional studies within the same five decades greatly expanded our understanding of crime, and led to the creation of more effective international institutions to exchange police intelligence and to achieve greater cooperation in law enforcement. This has required greater interaction between national police agencies, as well as a broader understanding of the diversity of cultures of foreign nations, and increased familiarity with different systems of law and its enforcement.

Success in the Second World War was achieved through the Allied Powers' joint efforts to defeat the imperialist ambitions of Nazi Germany, Fascist Italy, and warlord-dominated Japan. At a relatively early stage, the Big Three (the United States, Britain, and the Soviet Union) began to discuss the eventual establishment of a permanent international organization that would preserve world peace and foster closer relations and cooperation between all nations. Coordination of war planning had drawn the three major powers into a functioning relationship, despite their sharp political and ideological differences. It was hoped that these shared goals would foster continued cooperation in a peaceful postwar world. Ultimately the Allies succeeded in founding the United Nations in December 1945, and its principal headquarters was located in New York City. The United Nations General Assembly, composed of delegations from all the member nations, and the UN Security Council, consisting of representatives of the major world nations (the U.S., Britain, France, Russia, and China), have been located in New York City since 1946. Certain international agencies, established under the League of Nations before World War II, continued to function as part of the United Nations. Included within this group is the International Court of Justice, also known as the World Court, which is located at the Hague in the

TIME LINE

Globalization, Human Rights, and Personal Laws in Criminal Justice

1923	The International Criminal Police Organization is organized with headquarters in Vienna, Austria.
1938	Germany seizes control of the Republic of Austria; a new National Socialist government is installed in Vienna.
September 1, 1939	Germany invades Poland; Britain and France declare war two days later.
June 22, 1940	France surrenders to Germany; a puppet government is installed in southern France at Vichy, and Germany occupies northern France, including Paris.
June 22, 1941	Germany invades the Soviet Union.
August 14, 1941	The Atlantic Charter, issued by the United States and Britain, proclaims that after the defeat of Nazi Germany's tyranny, the signatories look forward to a lasting peace in which all national boundaries will be respected and that "all men in all lands may live out their lives in freedom from fear and want."
December 7, 1941	Japan launches an aerial attack on the United States Naval Base at Pearl Harbor, and the United States Congress declares war the following day.
October 1943	The United States, Britain, and the Soviet Union meet in Moscow, denounce the atrocities of Nazi Germany, and promise trial of the perpetrators by the peoples wronged by these acts.
March 24, 1945	The Allied powers meeting at Yalta, in the Crimea, call for the establishment of a United Nations conference to be held at San Francisco in April and to plan for a worldwide organization to maintain peace.
June 4, 1944	After defeating German and Italian forces in North Africa and Italy, American and British units enter Rome.
June 6, 1944	American and British forces land in Normandy (D-Day).
May 7, 1945	Germany surrenders.
September 2, 1945	After the detonation of an atomic bomb at Hiroshima and a second bomb at Nagasaki, Japan surrenders and World War II ends.
April 25, 1945	Conference in San Francisco lays the groundwork for the establishment of the United Nations.
November 20, 1945-October 16, 1946	Trial of major German war criminals takes place at Nuremberg.
1947	India granted independence from Great Britain.
December 10, 1948	UN General Assembly proclaims the Universal Declaration of Human Rights.

Globalization, Human Rights, and Personal Laws in Criminal Justice

1949	The North Atlantic Treaty Organization (NATO) is formed as a mutual defense pact between the U.S. and the nations of western Europe.
November 4, 1950	The Council of Europe agrees to the European Convention for the Protection of Human Rights and Fundamental Freedoms. The Convention establishes a European Commission on Human Rights and a European Court of Human Rights.
1950	Indonesia gains independence from the Netherlands.
1953	European Coal and Steel Community established; forms the basis for the later European Economic Community (EEC) and European Union (EU).
1953-1968	Earl Warren serves as Chief Justice of the United States Supreme Court.
June 19, 1961	U.S. Supreme Court decision in *Mapp v. Ohio*.
June 11, 1966	U.S. Supreme Court decision in *Miranda v. Arizona*.
June 12, 1967	U.S. Supreme Court decision in *United States v. Wade*.
1968-1986	Warren Burger serves as Chief Justice of the United States Supreme Court.
June 24, 1972	U.S. Supreme Court decision in *Furman v. Georgia*.
July 2, 1976	U.S. Supreme Court decision in *Gregg v. Georgia*.
August 1, 1975	The Helsinki Accords establish a nonbinding international statement concerning human rights.
1975	European Economic Community establishes the first unit of Trevi, dedicated to the establishment of a secure system of communication concerning terrorist activities.
1984	Luxembourg General Assembly of Interpol agrees to take some terrorist cases.
1986	William H. Rehnquist becomes Chief Justice of the U.S. Supreme Court.
June 3, 1992	Australia High Court issues judgment in *Mabo v. Queensland*.
May 1997	Dusko Tadic found guilty of war crimes and sentenced to a 20-year prison term by the Yugoslav War Crimes Tribunal.
January 17, 2001	Verdict and sentence announced in Lockerbie bombing case.
June 11, 2001	Timothy McVeigh, who bombed the Murrah Federal Building in Oklahoma City in 1995, killing 168 people, executed at the Terra Haute Federal Prison.

Netherlands. This Court continues to play a major role in establishing principles of international law, which regulate the way in which nations conduct themselves diplomatically and assist in the peaceful settlement of international disputes. The World Court operates as an arbitral tribunal. As such, it derives its jurisdiction through the consent of the nations, which submit their dispute to the tribunal and agree to abide by its decision. In addition to the World Court, there are a number of subordinate UN organizations and agencies located throughout the world that foster the exchange of information among nations. Two UN Committees are of particular interest to the American criminal justice community: the Committee on Crime Prevention and Criminal Justice and the Committee on Narcotic Drugs. The United Nations Interregional Crime and Justice Research Institute (UNICR) is another part of the United Nations that is of special concern to the law enforcement and academic communities.

The Second World War also triggered heightened international concern for human rights, and for the punishment of war crimes and crimes against humanity. As Allied troops drove Nazi armies from occupied Poland, the first grim remains of Nazi concentration and death camps greeted them. Horrendous piles of cremated remains testified to the fanatic intensity and widespread scope of Hitler's campaign to eliminate the Jewish population of Europe. Skeleton-like survivors with registration numbers burned into their skin recounted the degradation and terror that haunted their daily existence. Yet this was but part of the massive murder campaign against hordes of civilians and soldiers deemed to be inferior beings by the leaders of the Third Reich. Captured Nazi documents confirmed that elite units of the German Army followed the advancing front-line troops into Poland and Russia. They were assigned to routinely execute captured Polish and Russian soldiers, and to deal in a similar way with all Jewish civilians discovered in conquered territories. Postwar investigations placed the total number of executed Jews at about six million; less accurate computations suggest that more than four million prisoners of war and enemy civilians were executed or permitted to die through starvation, exposure to the elements, or medical neglect. In addition, a virtual army of prisoners of war and political dissidents were assigned to slave labor units in Germany and elsewhere. Few of these laborers survived to the end of the war.

These crimes, other crimes against humanity, and infractions of the laws of war were the subject of a trial of 22 Nazi leaders by an international court convened by Britain, France, the United States, and the Soviet Union. The proceedings before the International Tribunal at Nuremberg, or Nuremberg trials, focused world attention upon the need to define human rights more precisely and to establish standards of humane national behavior. Despite the historic trial at Nuremberg and lesser-known trials of Japanese wartime leaders, crimes against humanity have persisted. Most recently these have included tribal genocide in Rwanda, and fratricidal and religious "ethnic cleansing" in states of the former Yugoslavia. Countless other violations of human rights have occurred at national levels that have escaped international investigation and punishment because they have been classified as "internal" national concerns. However, a number of worldwide organizations have played a significant role in calling attention to these offenses against humanity, thereby directing international attention and protests against the perpetrators. Most prominent in this endeavor has been the American organization known as Amnesty International.

Even as the victorious nations of World War II united to advance the cause of human rights and to punish war crimes, they themselves experienced political and ethnic fragmentation and polarization. This is particularly true in the case of the former world empires when colonies sought independence from a European "mother country." Yet even within the domestic territory of former imperial nations, there have been strong forces for self-determination that threaten to divide these world powers into smaller quasi-political units.

The former British Empire provides a good example of the way in which these forces have played a critical role in the postwar world. In the course of granting independence to the subcontinent of India, the British were required to partition their former colony into two new nations, Pakistan and India. After Britain's withdrawal from the territory of the two new sovereign states, the ethnic and religious tensions between Muslim Pakistan and Hindu India persisted. Rivalries from the old colonial period had simply been converted into international tensions and boundary disputes that still threaten the peace of South Asia.

Racial apartheid in the colony of South Africa persisted well beyond the Second World War despite public opinion in Britain. Given the self-determination granted to the dominions by the British imperial constitution, it was possible for South Africa to remain within the Commonwealth despite strong feeling in the British Isles against racial segregation and white minority rule. Even after the establishment of a predominantly black government under Nelson Mandela in (1994), South Africa remains within the empire, yet her trading patterns and economic well-being depend far more upon contact with sub-Saharan Africa than they do on the political tie to Britain.

Even the British overseas possessions most closely allied with the culture of the British Isles sought and gained greater autonomy within the Empire. Postwar British imperial legislation has almost eliminated the constitutional links that bind Canada and Australia to the mother country. The British decision to join the European Economic Community in 1971 was a belated recognition that Britain's future economic prosperity would lie more with sister nations of Europe than with the scattered and increasingly more independent Commonwealth peoples. Finally, as the British Empire has drifted apart, the smoldering fires of regional self-determination in Scotland and Wales have, within the past five years, resulted in grants of limited autonomy to the people of Scotland and more limited recognition of Welsh political independence.

This British experience is paralleled by that of other former colonial powers. Virtually all of sub-Saharan Africa gained independence from the former empires of Britain, France, Belgium, and Portugal. Within many of these newly independent African nations are ethnic, tribal, and religious divisions that threaten even more extensive fragmentation. The resulting political turmoil only exacerbates the financial instability and grinding poverty that is characteristic of so many of these new nation-states. Many Middle Eastern nations, themselves a product of the disintegration of the Ottoman Empire after 1919, have experienced a resurgence of fundamentalism in their traditional Islamic religion. These countries have legal systems based on the Koran and other holy books of the Muslim faith. The western fringe of the Pacific Basin has also not been immune to the chaotic legacy of a post-colonial era. The Philippine Republic, which achieved independence from the United States in 1946, continues to be divided by religious and ethnic quarrels that fuel a persistent guerilla war against its government. Indonesia, after winning independence from the Netherlands after World War II, has also suffered from similar religious and ethnic divisions that threaten its political stability and economic development.

Within the United States, Canada, and Australia, indigenous peoples have begun to work politically toward achieving a limited political and legal autonomy. Although each nation's response has been quite different, claims for recognition of tribal rights and for some level of self-government have resulted in new accommodations by both state and national governments. In the United States, Native Americans (Indians and Eskimo groups) have been given limited autonomy in certain fields of governmental action. These include the administration of criminal justice in regard to minor offenses, and the establishment of tribal courts to deal with civil controversies among tribe members and trials of minor misdemeanors committed by tribe members on the tribal reservations.

American criminal justice professionals have much to learn concerning other criminal justice systems—both international and intranational. As the world has grown smaller and national systems have become more complex, there is an imperative need to broaden and share criminal justice knowledge and appreciate cultural and ethnic differences.

The Nuremberg Trials

The nineteenth and early twentieth centuries were noteworthy for a number of attempts to set forth more humane rules concerning the conduct of armed warfare. In May 1863 Professor Francis Lieber of Columbia University published a proposed code of military conduct. Shortly thereafter the code was adopted by the Union and regulated discipline in United States units throughout the Civil War. Lieber's code also detailed the rights of prisoners of war, the duties owed to noncombatant civilian enemies, and the principles governing partisans and spies captured by military forces. Within a year after Lieber's code was adopted by the United States, 12 European nations signed a convention designed to provide more humane treatment for the wounded by armies in the field. Two Hague Conventions, ratified by most European nations and by the United States, were put into effect in 1899 and 1904; among many other provisions, the 1904 convention restricted the aerial bombardment of cities that were devoid of military significance. After the bloodbath of World War I, the 1927 Kellogg-Briand Pact united 44 nations in a formal renunciation of war as an instrument of national policy. However, virtually all of these international agreements focused on the distinction between military personnel and the civilian population. They also assumed that all troops were well-fed and disciplined in stable military units.

Yet despite deep concern about humanitarian rules of warfare, and even renouncing the use of war entirely, did not result in concrete accomplishments. In many ways, the peace conferences and resulting conventions simply overemphasized diplomatic form without coming to grips with the brutal realities of combat. Much remained to be done, and ambiguities had to be resolved. None of these efforts defined the meaning of a "just war," nor did any condemn nations that launched a war of aggression. Humane treatment of prisoners, stipulated in Lieber's code, was subjected to the exception that prisoners might be executed when a commander's combat necessities made it impossible for him to encumber himself with prisoners. At least some of these matters had been brought to international attention during World War I (1914-1918). Atrocities against the Belgian civilian population went unpunished, and the German emperor was not brought to trial for launching an aggressive war. The newly created German Republic brought several military officers and enlisted personnel to trial in 1919 and 1920. Most escaped conviction on pleas of following superior orders, and those convicted received light prison sentences. The exalted sentiments of international diplomacy appear to have no consequence in the behavior of troops or their commanders, and violation of the rules of international war drew no significant punishment.

Against this background it is not surprising that Nazi Germany felt free to conduct itself in an extraordinarily cruel manner toward prisoners of war and civilian populations. After occupying Poland in the fall of 1939, the German authorities killed virtually all of the Polish leadership classes and deported vast numbers of Poles as slave labor. Many German Army officers were appalled at the devastation wrought on Warsaw and the mistreatment of the Polish population. Early in 1940, the American embassy in Berlin reported the wholesale deportation of German Jews to Poland. After Hitler declared war on the Soviet Union, the embassy told of Russian prisoners of war freezing or starving to death. In October 1941 President Franklin Roosevelt and British Prime Minister Winston Churchill condemned Germany's execution of innocent hostages captured in the occupied nations. On January 13, 1942, the exiled governments of occupied Europe, meeting at St. James's Palace in London, organized an Inter-Allied Commission for the Punishment of War Crimes.

Smoke spotted in Poland and eastern Germany earlier in the war puzzled Allied intelligence agencies. As the Soviet Red Army advanced into Poland, it came upon a grisly scene—the German death camp at Mydanek, located near Lublin. Subsequent Allied advances in Poland and Germany confirmed the fact that about six million Jews had met their deaths at the hands of Hitler's military and police organizations. Evidence submitted before the Nuremberg tribunal by Russian prosecutors showed that the treatment of Russian military and civilian personnel was the result of high-level directives issued by Hitler's personal military staff. Captured Russian soldiers were held in open-air detention camps during the winter months; they either froze or starved to death. Civilian and military prisoners were torn to pieces by dogs, others were used for target practice, and infants were drowned in buckets of water. As German forces advanced into Russia, they captured Jews among the civilian population. Newborn children were killed immediately, and many people were not gassed before they were placed alive into the crematory ovens. These atrocities were sanctioned by Hitler's "Barbarossa Order" of May 13, 1941, which permitted extensive retaliatory action against the Soviet civilian population, removing them from the protections of international law, and officially exempting German forces from complying with the laws of war. Meticulously maintained German records indicate that more than 3,900,000 Soviet soldiers fell into German hands, but that only 1,100,000 remained alive in the closing months of the conflict, and many of those were dying of typhus.

Well before Germany's formal surrender on May 8, 1945, the United States, Britain, France, and the Soviet Union began to prepare for the trial of German war criminals. Prosecuting teams assembled in April 1945, and with the assistance of military investigators began to collect evidence of Nazi atrocities. Beginning in June, the lead prosecutors, including Associate Justice Robert H. Jackson of the U.S. Supreme Court, assembled lists of major German leaders whose actions indicated that they deserved prosecution as war criminals. Ultimately 24 individuals were included in this group. They included Hermann Goering, Hitler's Deputy Führer; Admiral Karl Doenitz, Hitler's successor as head of the German state; and Field Marshals Alfred Jodl and Wilhelm Keitel of Hitler's personal military staff. Unfortunately neither the prosecutorial staff nor military intelligence sources were consulted before the final list was fixed in August. As a consequence, industrialist Gustav Krupp was included among those indicted before the International Military Tribunal. At war's end and throughout most of the war, the vast Krupp steel manufactory was under the management of Krupp's son, Alfried. Gustav Krupp was senile, inarticulate, and incontinent when the trial was about to begin. His attorney successfully moved that his case be severed from the group of major war criminals, and ultimately the charges were dropped. However, the International Tribunal subsequently refused to substitute Alfried Krupp to stand trial in his father's place. The tribunal reasoned that the defense counsel for Alfried Krupp lacked adequate time to prepare a defense.

Consequently, Alfried was dropped from the list of defendants but added to a group of lesser figures to be tried after the major trials were concluded.

The trial began on November 20 with the reading of the indictment filed against the defendants. Count one charged them with conspiracy to wage aggressive war. Waging aggressive war formed the basis for count two. The third count charged them with crimes against the law of war, focusing on the treatment of prisoners of war and the maltreatment of civilians contrary to the accepted rules of law. The fourth count charged crimes against humanity. On the next day, Justice Jackson delivered his opening statement to the Tribunal. He called attention to the groundbreaking nature of the trials about to begin, asserting:

> That four great nations, flushed with victory and stung with injury, stay the hand of vengeance and voluntarily submit their captive enemies to the judgment of the law, is one of the most significant tributes that power has ever paid to reason.

Aware of the historical nature of the proceedings, he continued:

> The wrongs we seek to condemn and punish have been so calculated, so malignant, and so devastating, that civilization cannot tolerate their being ignored, because it cannot survive their being repeated.

Jackson continued by citing captured German documents, which proved Hitler's long-standing intention to invade Poland and detailed the circumstances of its announcement to his military staff. Pointing to the extermination activities of German SS units in the invasion of Russia, Jackson quoted reports that at Kiev 33,771 Jews had been killed at the massacre of Baba Yev, and that at the 1943 destruction of the Warsaw Ghetto 56,065 Jews had been shot or burned to death, and countless others destroyed by blasting the sewers and tunnels in which they were hiding.

If captured documents provided Jackson with proof against the defendants, they also forced both prosecutors and judges to read lengthy quotations from written reports, letters, and memoranda. Indeed, it was the German penchant for record-keeping that was to provide some of the most credible evidence against the defendants, but it was oral testimony and photographic materials that would create the greatest impression on the defendants and the watching world. Shortly after the trials began, a motion picture was shown that depicted the concentration camps at Dachau, Buchenwald, and Bergen-Belsen. One scene documented a mass burial—a virtual cascade of corpses being dumped into mass graves by bulldozers. The accused sitting together in the dock were stunned, and Hermann Goering later commented that "they showed that awful film, and it just spoiled everything." Shortly after the tribunal viewed the film, German General Erwin Lahousen began his testimony for the prosecution. Lahousen had served as a section chief and personal assistant to Admiral Wilhelm Canaris, the senior officer in Hitler's headquarters staff. Although Admiral Canaris' diary had been destroyed, Lahousen had a copy in his possession, and from it he testified concerning German plans to eradicate the intellectual and religious leadership of Poland. When his military staff objected that the German Army would balk at participation in such a violation of the rules of war, Hitler replied that if that were the case, the SS or Security Police that accompanied the Army units would carry out the executions for them. Lahousen also confirmed that the brutal treatment of Russian soldiers and political commissars had been discussed and approved in advance by Hitler's personal military staff.

Erich von dem Bach-Zelewski, a former lieutenant general in command of SS units on the Russian front, also testified for the prosecution. He was also in charge of anti-partisan units operating in the Eastern Front, and took part in suppressing the Warsaw Ghetto uprising. Otto Ohlendorf, former commander of Einsatzgruppe D of the SS, testified that in the year beginning in June 1941 his unit liquidated 90,000 men, women, and children on the Eastern Front. A German construction manager described the execution of about 5,000 Jews near Dubno in the Ukraine. American prosecutors also provided documentary details concerning medical experiments performed on inmates in the concentration camps, and a prisoner held at Buchenwald testified that prisoners with tattooed skin were killed to supply colorful skin lampshades for Ilse Koch, the camp commander's wife. One of Adolph Eichmann's assistants submitted an affidavit that four million Jews were killed in concentration and death camps, and another two million were liquidated by the Einsatzgruppen and other SS agencies.

After American and British prosecutors completed submission of their documentary evidence and finished presentation of their witnesses' testimony, the defendants were given an opportunity to testify. The first to take the stand was Hermann Goering, a Luftwaffe ace from World War I who served as commander-in-chief of Hitler's air force and also as Deputy Führer. In 12 days of testimony and cross examination, Goering admitted that he was involved in setting up concentration camps for the incarceration of prewar enemies of the Nazi regime. He justified Germany's invasion of Poland and other countries, claiming that military necessity demanded these initiatives. When 75 Royal Air Force officers escaped from a German prisoner of war camp, two-thirds were executed by orders relayed from Hitler by Goering.

During cross-examination Goering was quick-witted and frustrated the best efforts of Justice Jackson and other prosecutors. Yet Goering's own testimony readily convicted him of conspiracy to wage an aggressive war, of waging an aggressive war, and of crimes against the law of war, as charged in the indictment. His final triumph, after he was sentenced to death by hanging and denied a soldier's death before a firing squad, was to poison himself in his prison cell.

At the conclusion of the Nuremberg trials of the major war criminals, Hermann Goering was convicted on all four counts of the indictment. The other defendants were more fortunate and three were acquitted of all charges. Including Goering, 11 of the defendants were sentenced to death. Goering committed suicide on the morning of October 16, 1946, the day scheduled for the executions. The other nine were hung in the prison gymnasium, but Martin Bormann, who had been tried in absentia, did not meet the gallows that day. Rudolf Hess, considered by many trial observers to be mentally ill, was sentenced to life in prison; he shared that sentence with Walther Funk and Admiral Erich Raeder. Admiral Karl Doenitz was sentenced to 10 years in prison, and Baldur von Schirach received a 20-year sentence. Those imprisoned for life and for terms of years were removed to Spandau Prison in the British sector. The acquitted defendants enjoyed a brief time of freedom before they were arrested and prosecuted by German authorities for offenses against German law.

In the hindsight of history, the Nuremberg trials have been criticized for being a "victors' tribunal" in which only the defeated were subjected to punishment. The complaint rings particularly true in regard to the Soviet Union, which during the early stages of the war had massacred captured officers of the Polish Army in the Katyn Forest, but doubtless none of the victorious armies were completely free of offending against the Nuremberg indictment charges. A second criticism is that the defendants were punished for crimes that were only made specific at the termination of the war. Of course it is true that some offenses were inadequately defined by international treaty when World War II began, and others were based on Allied announcements during the course of the war. As such, the Nuremberg trials might be seen as violative of American constitutional principles—prohibitions against bills of attainder and ex post facto laws.[1] However, the massive neglect of humane treatment for prisoners of war, coupled with the wholesale execution of Jews in Germany and in the occupied nations, could never be rendered innocent by the failure to condemn these practices by specific treaty provisions. They were clearly offenses against the general law of nations, and would have been so considered well before 1939. Finally, the third criticism is that the procedures at Nuremberg inadequately protected the rights of the accused. This is perhaps the most valid criticism. The documentary evidence was not fully translated at the start of the trial, and defense counsel not only had difficulty accessing the materials but also had the additional obstacle of translating it from English. Because German defense counsel were not skilled in Anglo-American criminal trial techniques, their cross-examination of prosecution witnesses was awkward and ineffective. In addition, much of the evidence introduced before the Nuremberg tribunal was in the form of affidavits submitted by eyewitnesses. Few of these witnesses were made available for cross-examination by defense counsel, denying the accused the right to confront these witnesses who provided evidence against them.

Conceding that these departures from American constitutional standards for criminal procedure violated Anglo-American norms of due process, the remarkable thing is that trials were held at all and that some of the leadership class of Nazi Germany were either acquitted outright or subjected to imprisonment rather than executed. At the early stages of the war, both Winston Churchill and Joseph Stalin advocated summary execution for the Nazi leaders. It was American pressure for a trial, long favored by Secretary of War Henry L. Stimson, that resulted in the Nuremberg proceedings. Because the trial was based upon a procedure that melded Anglo-American (common law) principles with the inquisitorial prosecution methods of Continental Europe, it is readily apparent that neither American nor European standards could be satisfied. However, the trials at Nuremberg left little doubt concerning the culpability of those convicted. They also provided a new level of due process for the civilian and military leadership of nations defeated in war. As the American chief prosecutor, Justice Robert Jackson, observed after the conclusion of the trials, "[T]here can be no responsible denial of those crimes in the future, and no tradition of martyrdom of the Nazi leaders can arise among an informed people."

Never Say Never—War Crimes and Crimes against Humanity after Nuremberg

It would be gratifying to think that the Nuremberg trials deterred future war crimes and offenses against humanity, yet that has certainly not been true in the second half of the twentieth century. Joseph Stalin's purges in the Soviet Union began in 1937, continued until his death in 1953, and accounted for about four million deaths. Five million Chinese died in the cultural revolution that shook the People's Republic from 1966 through 1976. Two million were butchered in Cambodia (1975-1979), and 30,000 people "disappeared" in Argentina in the 1970s. Dictator Idi Amin exterminated three-quarters of a million Ugandans from 1971 until his fall from power in 1987; and Iraq gassed 100,000 Kurdish dissidents in 1987-1988.

Most recently the dissolution of the former state of Yugoslavia has resulted in a series of bloody wars among the resulting national states in the Balkans. These have been marked by mass executions of civilian noncombatants, widespread rape of women, and extensive maltreatment and execution of prisoners of war. Because these confrontations have occurred across national boundaries or involved adjoining nations, the international community has been directly concerned with policing conflicts and preventing these atrocities—initially in Bosnia-Herzogovina and subsequently in Kosovo.

This area of the Balkans has a long history of ethnic tension exacerbated by religious differences. In 1389 western portions of what later became Yugoslavia—now Croatia and Slovenia—were Roman Catholic in religion, while the eastern areas (Bosnia, Serbia, Montenegro, and Macedonia) were Eastern Orthodox. When the territory was conquered by the Ottoman Empire in 1389, many of the residents became Muslim to avoid persecution. Thus, the Muslims' descendants are considered traitors, even today after the passage of 600 years. Nazi occupation in World War II took advantage of these ethnic and religious divisions, and the Croatians, seeing an opportunity for independence, collaborated with the Germans and established concentration camps for Serbs. At the end of World War II, the Serbs retaliated by murdering more than 100,000 Croatian prisoners.

Violent warfare in former Yugoslavia has been partially suppressed by peacekeeping forces sent to the area by NATO, the military alliance of Western European nations. Prior to international involvement, the Serbs had virtually expelled all non-Serbs from Bosnia through a program of ethnic cleansing—the murder or forcible exile of all non-Serbian residents. One town badly affected by this policy was the Muslim enclave of Kozarac, where Dusko Tadic, a Serb, owned and operated a bar built with funds borrowed from Muslim neighbors. After Kozarac fell to Serb forces, Tadic helped identify Muslim intellectuals and other leaders who were immediately executed. It was rumored that Tadic had provided targeting information to Serb artillerists prior to the fall of Kozarac, and there were reports that Tadic appeared frequently at concentration camps to partake in the interrogation and torture of the Muslim prisoners. However, Tadic quarreled with a Serbian warlord and thought it wise to send his wife and daughter to Germany. Shortly thereafter, he joined them in their self-imposed exile. In February 1994 Tadic was arrested by German police on the suspicion of having committed war crimes. Shortly thereafter he was turned over the Yugoslavia War Crimes Tribunal, which had been established in May 1993 by the United Nations Security Council.

The trial of Dusko Tadic took place at The Hague in the Netherlands and was six months long. It was based almost entirely upon eyewitness testimony, much of which was uncorroborated. One witness testified that she saw him murder a Muslim prisoner, and another stated that she saw him cut the throats of two Muslims who were formerly police officers. Tadic's sister-in-law testified that he had a violent temper, and that he was known as a dangerous and cruel streetfighter. She also verified his whereabouts in the vicinity of the concentration camp for Kozarac Muslims, undermining his alibi that he was away from Bosnia during the times in question. Unlike the evidentiary situation at Nuremberg, the proof against Tadic lacked documentary support, and witnesses favorable to Tadic were not available. His Serbian superiors were protected by the Serbian government, and most of the Muslims who had witnessed his activities were dead. Although the trial ended on October 25, 1996, the tribunal's decision was not announced until the following May. Tadic was found guilty of 11 of the 34 counts alleged in his indictment, but acquitted of all the specific murder charges. He was acquitted of a charge of castrating a Muslim neighbor, and of killing another by discharging the contents of a fire extinguisher into his throat. Tadic was sentenced to a 20-year prison term, thus becoming the first person to be tried and convicted by the tribunal.

The activities of the Yugoslavia War Crimes Tribunal have been hampered by the fact that Serbian leaders responsible for ethnic cleansing in Bosnia, and subsequently in Kosovo, have not been surrendered by the Belgrade government. Unlike the Allied situation at the end of World War II, the NATO peacekeeping forces do not control conquered enemy territory, and thus do not have ready access to accused war criminals, witnesses, or extensive documentation. Rather they are involved in maintaining the military status quo while diplomatic negotiations continue. Aggressive action to secure custody of indicted war criminals may well hinder the peacekeeping mission, endanger the lives of NATO soldiers, and very likely complicate discussions with Serb leaders, many of whom are indicted war criminals. Given these difficulties, the main achievement of the War Crimes Tribunal may well be informing the world of human rights violations and breaches of international law in former Yugoslavia.

International Cooperation
in the Suppression of Terrorism

Terrorism by private individuals is certainly not of recent origin, but the complicity of national states in the sponsorship of terrorism has changed the complexion of the violence. It has also led to new and growing challenges to the criminal justice system, both in the United States and abroad. Sophisticated investigative techniques have emerged for the analysis of bomb casings and explosives. The rising number of attacks on aircraft have vastly altered security precautions on both domestic and foreign flights, and in 2001 a significant trial of Libyan terrorists took place in the Netherlands before three Scottish judges. The trial of the so-called Lockerbie defendants marked a new phase in the pursuit and prosecution of terrorist defendants—the Libyan government surrendered to international pressure and delivered them to the Dutch authorities for trial and possible punishment.

On December 21, 1988, Pan Am Flight 103 exploded in the sky above Lockerbie, Scotland. All the passengers and crew, totaling 276 persons, were killed, and the village of Lockerbie lost residents as airplane fragments crashed to the ground. At the time it was known that Pan Am Flight 103 originated in Malta, and had made intermediate stops at Frankfurt and London before it took off for New York City. Forensic evidence indicated that the bomb particles were of Libyan origin, and further investigation led to the identification of Ali Mohmed al-Megrahi and Al Amin Khalifa Fhimah and implicated them in the placement of the bomb. After the imposition of economic sanctions against Libya, the government of Colonel Quaddafi agreed to deliver the two men to international authorities, provided that they would be tried in the Netherlands before Scottish judges. The trial lasted nine months and was held at Camp Zeist, a former NATO base in the Netherlands.

Understandably, after 12 years the evidence against the defendants was limited, and their identification as persons involved in the preparation of a bomb and its placement in Flight 103 was uncertain. Nevertheless, the court found al-Megrahi guilty and sentenced him to life imprisonment, which was mandatory under Scottish law. After imposing the sentence, the judges told Megrahi that they would recommend he be eligible for parole in 20 years. This was the strongest penalty that was available to the court. The second defendant was acquitted, the only evidence against him being diary entries indicating a meeting with Megrahi and his acquisition of suitcase luggage tags. Unlike the record on Megrahi, there was no connection established between Fhimah and the Libyan intelligence service. Two prosecution witnesses, a Libyan secret service informant and a Swiss electronics firm owner, were considered to have given unreliable and untruthful testimony that the judges discounted. On the other hand, Megrahi had dealt with the Swiss electronics firm Mebo, and it was a Mebo timer that triggered the Lockerbie bomb. Within the suitcase that held the bomb, investigators found clothing very likely purchased by Megrahi at a clothing store in Malta. If Megrahi loses his appeals to a higher Scottish court, he will serve his sentence at a prison in Glasgow.

The conclusion of the Camp Zeist trial provides insight into the utility of criminal justice systems as instruments to combat terrorism. Newspaper comments of the day suggested that formal rules of evidence and procedure make it difficult to secure justice against accused terrorists. Others argued that the measured use of military force is a more appropriate and more effective response to discourage nations that adopt terrorism as a national policy. Undoubtedly the sparsity of the evidence and documentation, coupled with Libya's initial refusal to surrender those accused of this crime, were partially responsible for the acquittal. On the other hand, one of the accused was tried, found guilty, and sentenced to life imprisonment with a possibility of parole after 20 years.

Beginning in 1986, the United States government has made violence against American nationals a federal criminal offense, and the United States District Courts have been given jurisdiction to try individuals who, either within the nation or abroad, commit violent acts that (1) intimidate or coerce a civilian population, (2) attempt to influence the policy of a government by intimidation or coercion, or (3) attempt to affect the conduct of a government by assassination or kidnapping. In addition, providing material support to terrorists has also been designated a crime.[2] Despite these provisions to discourage terrorist activities, it is quite clear that no criminal justice remedies in this area can be effective unless there is international cooperation leading to the prompt extradition of suspected terrorists from their host countries.

Aftermath of the September 11 Terrorist Attacks

On September 11, 2001, two commercial airliners were diverted by fundamentalist Muslim terrorists belonging to Osama bin Laden's al Qaeda network. The aircraft, including the crew and passengers, were subsequently crashed into the twin towers of the World Trade Center, located in the financial district of New York City. The heat and fire from exploding aviation fuel caused the deaths of virtually all individuals on the upper floors of the buildings, and many others, including police officers and firefighters, died when the two buildings collapsed. Shortly after these disasters, another commercial airliner, under the control of other al Qaeda operatives, crashed into the Pentagon, the U.S. Defense Department's command and communication center near Washington, D.C. A fourth airliner, also under al Qaeda control, later crashed in western Pennsylvania. Apparently its passengers, alerted to the earlier attacks via cell phone conversations, were able to overpower the terrorists, but were not able to fly the aircraft or land it safely. It is believed that the fourth plane was going to be crashed into the White House. The immediate death toll from these three terrorist attacks was 2,937 individuals, including numerous foreign nationals working for firms located in the World Trade Center. The environmental damage may also ultimately exact a heavy toll through shortened lives of the survivors.

In the aftermath of these attacks, the United States launched a military incursion into Afghanistan, where the de facto government under the Taliban militia had permitted al Qaeda training activities and after the attacks had refused to surrender bin Laden and other terrorist leaders. The military action continues, and President George W. Bush announced an expanded "war on terrorism," to reach other nations believed to harbor terrorist organizations.

While other nations have indicated reluctance to support American expansion of military action, it is noteworthy that there has been substantial cooperation in the investigation of al Qaeda activities leading to the September 11 attacks. Antiterrorist investigations in the United States, Europe, and Asia have identified al Qaeda cells and operatives, leading to their arrest and detention. As this effort continues, it is becoming clear that multinational police and intelligence cooperation has been vastly accelerated in response to these disasters. Of course, in the year following the attacks there has been little opportunity to implement new systems for the cross-national exchange of police intelligence, nor has there been time for the negotiation of multilateral international conventions and treaties dealing with this worldwide threat to national and personal security.

The Continuing Role of Interpol

Among the international organizations involved in global law enforcement, few are as active as the International Criminal Police Organizations, known since 1956 as Interpol. Established in 1923 as a private organization of senior police officers in Europe, the International Criminal Police Commission served as an informal place for the exchange of information concerning criminals who conducted their activites across national borders. With the fall of the Austrian Republic into Nazi control in 1938, the commission ceased to function at the international level and many of its records were apparently destroyed. At the end of the war, the commission's headquarters was established at Paris, and with the aid of a French government loan, Interpol moved into a new building at Saint-Cloud in 1967.

Shortly after Interpol was situated in its new headquarters, the outbreak of the Cold War resulted in the withdrawal of Eastern Bloc nations from membership. The United States, represented by the Federal Bureau of Investigation, withdrew from membership after 1950. This was in protest of Interpol's identification of individuals who hijacked a Czechoslovakian airliner for a flight to freedom in 1949. The United States resumed membership in 1958, with the Treasury Department and its Secret Service being the main participants in Interpol activities.

Throughout its history, Interpol has been reluctant to serve as a channel for distributing information concerning "political" crimes. Most controversial has been its refusal to assist in the location of Nazi war criminals, many of whom had been convicted in absentia at Nuremberg. On the other hand, Interpol's refusal to assist communist Cuba in searching for President Fulgencio Batista's regime leaders has been widely acclaimed by western nations and the United States. In 1988 Interpol reviewed its policy concerning Nazi war criminals and has since been active in assisting nations seeking to apprehend them. Interpol had also refrained from participating in the investigation of terrorism, deeming terrorist activities "political crimes." However, the 1984 Luxembourg General Assembly of Interpol members agreed to assist in investigating terrorist acts, but provided that the decision to participate would be made on a case-by-case basis.

Unfortunately, the degree of national cooperation with Interpol, as well as compliance with Interpol requests for information, is shaped by the member nations' divergent concepts of criminal law enforcement and by their assessment of the appropriate scope of police activity. In the past two decades, growing international law enforcement needs have increased the value of police cooperation across departmental and national boundaries. That is particularly the case in regard to drug trafficking, as many nations (including the United States) have stationed police officials in other nations, hoping to halt the illegal trade in drugs. Interpol has exercised a growing role in the exchange of police intelligence, in the capture of most-wanted criminals, and in the location of missing persons. Cross-national efforts to control drug trafficking, solve terrorism cases, and enforce laws against smuggling have also increased the frequency of using the extensive files maintained by Interpol. The organization has thus expanded from a European institution to a police intelligence activity that has global recognition and impact.

TIME CAPSULE

Drug Trafficking and Criminal Justice

Global law enforcement has been confronted with its most serious challenge in the frustrating effort to stamp out the international trade in narcotics. As the nation providing the largest market for illegal drugs, the United States has been deeply involved in diplomatic and law enforcement efforts to restrict the supply of addictive illegal drugs. American efforts have included providing financial subsidies to governments and individuals designed to reduce the acreage devoted to the growth of plants used in the manufacture of drugs. In addition, the Drug Enforcement Administration (DEA) maintains overseas branches devoted to assisting local and national police forces in suppressing the production and distribution of illegal narcotics. At the United Nations and at all levels of international diplomacy, there has been a steady increase in sharing information and initiatives designed to decrease the use and abuse of drugs.

The literature on drugs, their abuse, and the nature and wisdom of governmental controls is vast. These subjects are of vital concern to criminal justice professionals, to lawmakers at all levels of government, and to the academic community. United States government reports for 1997 indicated that drug-induced deaths increased 47 percent between 1990 and 1994. As of 1997, there were approximately 14,000 deaths per year attributable to the use of illegal drugs, and the national cost in social, health, and criminal activities was estimated at $67 billion. In the U.S. Virgin Islands, 75 percent of the burglaries in 1993 were attributed to the drug trade, and in Puerto Rico the following year, 60 percent of the murders were drug-related. When the United States Customs Service discovered drugs in shipments of garments imported from Jamaica, the subsequent embargo closed a factory that employed 550 workers. Statistically, the trade in illegal drugs is a major part of the world economy, and its costs heavily impact the economic life of both recipient and supplier nations. Unquestionably this is an area of human conduct that threatens to undermine public order and social stability. It is very clearly a stimulant for both violent and property-related crimes, and it also serves as an investment vehicle for the profits gained from organized criminal activity.

A United Nations Convention against Illicit Traffic in Narcotics, issued in 1988, has increased international police cooperation. For example, by 1990 there was a sharp drop in the amount of drugs seized on the high seas, due in large measure to active participation by many nations in the search for drugs being carried by ship. However, the financial strength of the drug traffickers is such that movement from one nation of operations to another is not difficult. When Mexico succumbed to United States pressure and began to suppress opium poppy cultivation, the cartels moved their farming efforts to Guatemala. In 1985 only 212 hectares of Guatemalan land were used for poppy farming; by 1991 the poppy growing area in Guatemala had increased to 1,145 hectares, and farm income increased 120 percent. Working with the U.S. Drug Enforcement Administration, Guatemala decreased its poppy farms to a total of 39 hectares by 1995.

The habitual use of habit-forming drugs is not a new development. Alcoholic beverages were used in prehistoric times, and opium was used in Asia many centuries before European traders carried it to the West. Rising standards of living in industrialized nations have provided the financial means for individuals to access illegal drugs, and the supply has increased to meet that demand. At the same time, the complexity of modern life, coupled with challenges to established values, has introduced tensions in mass psychology that make drug use even more attractive. With increased communication and transportation links between drug-producing nations and drug-consuming populations, it is not surprising that the post-World War II era has seen the rise of the international narcotics trade as a major concern of the world's criminal justice systems.

Questions and Problems

1. In most areas of law enforcement, all nations share a similar viewpoint toward a particular crime. However, because some nations produce illegal drugs and others are involuntary consumers, can we anticipate good cooperation in limiting this traffic? Because organized crime frequently infiltrates government institutions, including police activities, isn't this a threat to international cooperation also? Even at the national policy level, will the legitimate governmental concerns of a drug-exporting nation be served by suppression of the drug trade?

2. Supply and demand economics in the drug trade work against effective law enforcement. The more effective police work is—the more it succeeds in seizing illegal drugs and jailing distributors—the more profitable the sale of the remaining narcotics becomes. It has been suggested that legalizing all narcotics would kill drug trafficking by destroying the profits to be made. Is that true? Would easy access to habit-forming drugs inhibit the use of those substances? Even if the profits per transaction were less, would the increased volume encourage more individuals to enter the trade? Remember that the most successful mercantile operations are those that depend, not upon highly profitable sale of individual items, but rather on making very modest profits from the sale of a vast quantity of items.

3. Given what you know about international police organization and cooperation, what steps would make global control of drug-trafficking more effective?

Suggestions for Additional Reading

A good history of the drug trade is contained in William B. Allister's *Drug Diplomacy in the Twentieth Century: An International History* (London: Routledge, 2000). Also of value are H. Richard Friman, *NarcoDiplomacy: Exporting the U.S. War on Drugs* (Ithaca: Cornell University Press, 1996); Ivelaw L. Griffith, *The Political Economy of Drugs in the Caribbean* (Houndmills, England: Macmillan Press, 2000); and Ivelaw L. Griffith, *Drugs and Security in the Caribbean* (University Park: Penn State University Press, 1997); Robert W. Ferguson, *Drug Abuse Control* (Boston: Holbrook Press, Inc., 1975); and Peter Dale Scott and Jonathan Marshall, *Cocaine Politics: Drugs, Armies and the CIA in Central America* (Berkeley: University of California, 1991). Rebecca Stetoff, *The Drug Enforcement Administration* (New York: Chelsea House, 1989), provides a closer, but dated, discussion of the DEA.

Policing international criminal activities has a long way to go before it will proceed without disagreements and tension. Professor Malcolm Anderson points out that without a harmonization of criminal law procedures—such as the U.S.-British common rules concerning drug trafficking and policing this threat to national life—there is a limited amount of success that can be achieved through international organizations such as Interpol. There is also strong Anglo-American and British skepticism concerning the centralized police systems of Europe, which place inordinate stress on the assembly of large dossiers of information on *all* citizens, not only those who have criminal records.

The reluctance of Interpol to deal with terrorism prior to 1984 has resulted in the rise of other institutions for the exchange of international police information. Under the category of European Political Cooperation activity, sponsored by the European Union, three so-called Trevi groups have emerged as focal points for inter-European cooperation in law enforcement. Trevi 1 was organized in 1975 to establish a secure communications system that would relay information concerning terrorists and their activities. Trevi 2, established later, is dedicated to the exchange of information on police methods and systems, and Trevi 3 deals with approaches to serious crime other than terrorism.

Making Law More Humane: Declarations of Human Rights and the Rule of Law

The shadow of the Holocaust and Germany's racial cleansing on the Russian front darkened Allied victory celebrations and provided a priority mission for the newly formed United Nations. At its first session, the UN General Assembly gave to the Economic and Social Council (UNESCO) the task of preparing a bill of rights that would reflect international endorsement of the rights of mankind. Two years later, on December 10, 1948, the resulting document was proclaimed by the General Assembly, and the world had its Universal Declaration of Human Rights. While the concept of individual human dignity originated in the Renaissance, the idea grew and matured during the Enlightenment of the seventeenth and eighteenth centuries. More specifically, the concept owed much to the writings of John Locke, Jean-Jacques Rousseau, Thomas Paine, and Thomas Jefferson. It was manifested in both legal and political documents, such as the English Bill of Rights of 1689, the American Declaration of Independence, and the French Revolution's Declaration of the Rights of Man and the Citizen (1789). As Professor Louis Henkin has pointed out, the ideal of human rights was given universal acclaim by the United Nations action and met with widespread international approval. However, he notes that the behavior of national governments has left much to be desired in their maltreatment of subjects and citizens. There have been severe violations of human rights on virtually every continent, and they will undoubtedly continue to occur well into the future.

In addition, the United States Senate has blocked ratification of the declaration, reflecting more widespread apprehension that such an action would result in a loss of national sovereignty on one hand, or would, on the other hand, risk the danger of treaty-based modification of the American constitutional system. This reluctance to embrace the Universal Declaration has proved to be an embarrassment in the conduct of American foreign relations, which frequently stresses the need for respect for human rights. Furthermore, the absence of support by the most powerful nation in the world today is a hindrance to the advocates of stronger protections for individual freedom and dignity.

The preamble to the Universal Declaration of Human Rights announces that "recognition of the inherent dignity and of the equal and inalienable rights of all members of the human family is the foundation of freedom, justice and peace in the world," and that "disregard and contempt for human rights have resulted in barbarous acts which have outraged the conscience of mankind." It affirms that the member states have pledged themselves to work together for the promotion of "universal respect for and observance of human rights and fundamental freedoms."

Two provisions have direct relevance to law enforcement activities. Article 9 prohibits arbitrary arrest, detention, or exile; and Article 12 protects the right of privacy in one's home, family, or correspondence. Still others deal with the conduct of criminal trials. Article 5 prohibits the used of torture or cruel, inhuman, or degrading treatment or punishment; Articles 6 and 7 guarantee that an individual will be recognized as a person before the law and be afforded equal protection of the law. Those accused of a criminal offense are to be presumed innocent until proven guilty by an independent and impartial tribunal, and there are to be no ex post facto criminal laws and no bills of attainder (Articles 10 and 11).[3]

Finally, the Universal Declaration proclaims a number of freedoms that are comparable to those of the United States Constitution's Bill of Rights and the Declaration of Independence. These include the right to life, liberty, and the security of the person (Article 3); freedom of thought, conscience, and religion; and the right to form associations, or to refrain from joining such groups (Articles 18, 19, and 20). In addition to these rights familiar to Americans, the Declaration of Rights provides for access to social security and such economic, social, and cultural rights as are indispensable to human dignity (Article 22). There are guarantees of a right to work, to receive equal pay for equal work, and to receive remuneration that is adequate to support an individual and his or her family at a level consonant with human dignity (Article 23). Other guarantees provide for unemployment and old age relief, for a free education to the secondary school level, for freedom of travel, and for the right to marry (Articles 13, 16, 25(1), and 26). Some of these rights are not contained in the U.S. Constitution, but have been recognized in U.S. Supreme Court decisions or through the enactment of statutes by Congress. However, several of the economic rights are beyond the scope of either the Constitution itself or American practice. Quite possibly, it is these areas that, from an American standpoint, may undermine the free enterprise system that may be the stumbling block to American ratification of the Universal Declaration.

TIME CAPSULE

Universal Declaration of Human Rights (1948)

...Whereas Member States have pledged themselves to achieve, in cooperation with the United Nations, the promotion of universal respect for and observance of human rights and fundamental freedoms . . .

Now, therefore, the General Assembly Proclaims this Universal Declaration of Human Rights as a common standard of achievement for all people and all nations . . .

Article 1. All human beings are born free and equal in dignity and rights. They are endowed with reason and conscience and should act toward one another in a spirit of brotherhood.

Article 2. Everyone is entitled to all the rights and freedoms set forth in this Declaration, without distinction of any kind, such as race, color, sex, language, religion, political or other opinion, national or social origin, property, birth or other status. Furthermore, no distinction shall be made on the basis of political, jurisdictional or international status of the country or territory to which a person belongs, whether it be independent, non-self-governing or under any other limitation of sovereignty.

Article 3. Everyone has the right to life, liberty, and the security of person. . . .

Article 5. No one shall be subjected to torture or to cruel, inhuman or degrading treatment or punishment. . . .

Article 7. All are equal before the law and are entitled without any discrimination to equal protection of the law. All are entitled to equal protection against any discrimination in violation of this Declaration and against any incitement to such discrimination.

Article 8. Everyone has the right to an effective remedy by the competent national tribunals for acts violating the fundamental rights granted him by the constitution or by law.

Article 9. No one shall be subjected to arbitrary arrest, detention or exile.

Article 10. Everyone is entitled in full equality to a fair and public hearing by an independent and impartial tribunal, in the determination of his rights and obligations and of any criminal charge against him.

Article 11. (1) Everyone charged with a penal offense has the right to be presumed innocent until proved guilty according to law in a public trial at which he has had all the guarantees necessary for his defense.

(2) No one shall be held guilty of any penal offense on account of any act or omission which did not constitute a penal offense, under national or international law, at the time when it was committed. Nor shall a heavier penalty be imposed than the one that was applicable at the time the penal offense was committed.

Article 12. No one shall be subjected to arbitrary interference with his privacy, family, home or correspondence, nor to attacks upon his honor and reputation. Everyone has the right to the protection of the law against such interference or attacks. . . .

Article 17. (1) Everyone has the right to own property alone as well as in association with others.

(2) No one shall be arbitrarily deprived of his property.

Article 18. Everyone has the right to freedom of thought, conscience and religion; this right includes freedom to change his religion or belief, either alone or in community with others and in public or private, to manifest his religion or belief in teaching, practice, worship and observance.

Article 19. Everyone has the right to freedom of opinion and expression; this right includes freedom to hold opinions without interference and to seek, receive and impart information and ideas through any media and regardless of frontiers.

Article 20. (1) Everyone has the right to freedom of peaceful assembly and association.

(2) No one may be compelled to belong to an association. . . .

Article 25. (1) Everyone has the right to a standard of living adequate for the health and well-being of himself and of his family, including food, clothing, housing and medical care and necessary social services, and the right to security in the event of unemployment, sickness, disability, widowhood, old age or other lack of livelihood in circumstances beyond his control.

(2) Motherhood and childhood are entitled to special care and assistance. All children, whether born in or out of wedlock, shall enjoy the same social protection.

Source: The Human Rights Reader: Major Political Writings, Essays, Speeches and Documents from the Bible to the Present, ed. Micheline Ishay (New York: Routledge, 1997), pp. 408-412.

Questions

1. To what extent do these declarations parallel provisions in the U.S. Declaration of Independence or Constitution? Which are different, and have more recent U.S. Supreme Court decisions recognized these rights, in their entirety or in part?

2. Are some of these rights incompatible with a capitalist system, or more pertinent to socialist systems of government and society?

3. To what degree is the United States bound by these provisions or affected by them? If all applied to our criminal justice system, would the enforcement of law and the punishment of crimes be altered?

Human Rights and American Criminal Justice

Despite the American reluctance to ratify the Universal Declaration of Human Rights, there has been a trend within the criminal justice system to provide greater protections for individuals accused of crime. Most significant has been the groundbreaking postwar work of the Supreme Court under the leadership of Chief Justice Earl Warren. Prior to American entry into World War II (1941), the Court had began to apply some of the procedural requirements of the federal Bill of Rights to state law enforcement activity and the conduct of state criminal trials. The war itself provided motivation to a long-overdue revision of disciplinary procedures in the armed forces, and to apply more of the Constitution's due process guarantees to courts-martial. A new manual for courts-martial and a new substantive criminal law code for the armed services was issued in 1951, just two years before Earl Warren was confirmed as chief justice.

TIME CAPSULE

Military Trials under the Uniform Code of Military Justice

Traditionally, members of the United States armed forces have been subject to the jurisdiction of courts-martial rather than trial in civilian state or federal courts. Court-martial procedures differ from those guaranteed by the Fifth Amendment, and outside observers have frequently asserted that commanding officers, who press charges and convene courts-martial, have exerted too much influence over the courts' decisions and sentences. Criticism of court-martial procedures peaked during and after the First and Second World Wars, because many civilians were drafted or enlisted into military service and thus found themselves subject to military discipline and courts-martial. Understandably, both the general public and members of Congress were concerned about the state of military law in the United States.

During and after American participation in World War I, a sharp disagreement over military law developed between the Army's Judge Advocate General, Enoch Crowder, and his young assistant, Brigadier General Samuel Ansell. Major General Crowder viewed the military justice system as a part of the Army's disciplinary and command system. General Ansell argued that courts-martial should conform to the rules and procedures established for criminal trials in civil courts. Legal professionals tended to adopt Ansell's position, believing that the accused enjoyed more protection when tried in civilian courts. Ansell also sought a greater participation of law professionals in the Army's appellate process. He sought a three-man court of military appeals to be established in the Army Judge Advocate General's office;

this court would decide appeals from court-martial decisions, and recommend modifications of the sentence or clemency to the president. Ansell proclaimed that a democratic Army required a military justice system that followed set procedures and was controlled by law. Lawyers, judges, and bar associations supported Ansell's views, but General Crowder enjoyed steady encouragement from the line officers of the Army, including General John J. Pershing, commander of the victorious American Expeditionary Force in France. As interest began to wane after the Armistice, General Ansell decided to resign from the Army, and with his departure the struggle to reform court-martial procedure dissipated.

However, World War II rekindled American interest in reforming military law. In addition, continuing international commitments of the United States throughout the world meant that American soldiers, sailors and airmen would continue to be subject to court-martial jurisdiction. President Harry S. Truman appointed a committee to study the state of military justice and to recommend changes to Congress. Chaired by Yale Law School Professor Edmund H. Morgan, the committee was sworn in on August 18, 1948, and began its work. By the end of 1948 it had agreed upon a draft proposal, which called for review of court-martial findings and sentences by service boards of review established for each military service. A higher level of review would be conducted by a court of three law-trained civilians.[1]

When the new code was made public in the spring of 1949, the press and the bar associations criticized the report for not going far enough in achieving reform. Most judge advocate officers and career military and naval officers felt that the proposed changes went too far and undermined military discipline. Historian Jonathan Lurie points out that the proposal, as submitted by the Morgan Committee and subsequently approved

by Congress, had been modified to satisfy many of the objections put forth by the military and naval services. However, it was quite clear that the success of these reform measures depended upon continued civilian interest and pressure on Congress.[2] The commencement of the Korean War in June 1950 deflected immediate attention on the proposed new code, but even as it did so it established the need for a revision of the old Articles of War. On May 22, 1951, President Truman appointed Robert Quinn, George Latimer, and Paul Brosnan to be the first three judges of the new Court of Military Appeals, and the new system of military justice was in full operation.[3]

The new code, known as the Uniform Code of Military Justice 1951, applied to all of the armed forces, which since 1948 had been united under a single Secretary of Defense while retaining their separate departmental secretaries. It required that each general court-martial have a law-trained officer assigned as a law officer. When the UCMJ 1951 was revised in 1984, the law officer was renamed a military judge. His or her function—to serve as the officer providing rulings on the law—has continued, but in 1984 it was expanded to permit trial by the military judge sitting without a jury in non-capital cases, if requested by the accused. The law officer proposal was one of the reforms sought by General Ansell in 1919. Another 1951 change in court-martial procedure was the provision allowing enlisted members to serve on a court-martial, provided that the enlisted person made a timely request. Congress also enacted into law the Morgan Committee's proposal that there be a three-judge civilian Court of Military Appeals. This tribunal would review the decisions of the service Courts of Military Review.[4]

The Supreme Court of the United States and other federal courts historically exercised collateral review of court-martial decisions by issuing writs of habeas corpus in appropriate cases. This procedure was used during the Civil War in several cases, including *Ex parte Milligan*. The *Milligan* case established that military tribunals might not constitutionally try civilians within territories where civil courts were open and functioning; this is the so-called open court doctrine. Habeas corpus oversight was supplemented in the 1984 amendment of the Uniform Code of Military Justice, which authorized the Supreme Court to review the decisions of the Court of Military Appeals through the issuance of a writ of certiorari. The writ of certiorari is issued at the Court's discretion on the petition of a party wishing to appeal. The availability of the certiorari procedure permits direct appellate review of the decisions made by the Court of Military Appeals, and thus ensures greater conformity with civilian criminal procedures.[5]

Even after a half-century of revision, the Uniform Code of Military Justice 1984 is a distinctive body of law. In addition to defining and sanctioning felonies and misdemeanors recognized in American state and federal courts, the UCMJ 1984 prohibits and punishes a number of strictly military offenses. For example, there are specific provisions for punishing sentries who neglect their duties; there are penalties for being absent without leave; and there are severe punishments for desertion in the face of the enemy. Among the more controversial offenses are the two "general articles," one reads as follows:

> Article 134. Though not specifically mentioned in this chapter, all disorders and neglects to the prejudice of good order and discipline in the armed forces, all conduct of a nature to bring discredit upon the armed forces, and crimes and offenses not capital, of which persons subject to this chapter may be guilty, shall be taken cognizance of by a general, special or sum-

mary court-martial, according to the nature and degree of the offense, and shall be punished in the discretion of the court.

The other, Article 133, deals with conduct unbecoming an officer and a gentleman, expanded in editorial notes to include female officers of the armed forces. It prohibits "action or behavior in an official or private capacity which, in dishonoring or disgracing the officer personally, seriously compromises the person's standing as an officer." The notes indicate that these activities include acts of dishonesty, unfair dealing, indecency, indecorum, lawlessness, injustice, or cruelty.

Questions

1. Do the provisions of Article 134 conflict with Article I, Section 9 and Article I, Section 10 of the U.S. Constitution prohibiting bills of attainder? Are they "void for vagueness" under the due process provisions of the Fifth Amendment, in that they fail to warn about acts that will be considered crimes?

2. If a member of the armed forces is guilty of any other offense against provisions of the code, may he or she not be subject to prosecution underArticles 133 or 134? Is neglect of duty normally considered a criminal offense? Should it be? Are there wartime situations when neglect can properly be considered a criminal act?

3. Should Article 133 be recast to more accurately define those types of behavior that are considered "unbecoming"? Would that be rendered difficult if, as the notes suggest, both men and women are covered by the article? What is "indecorum"? Should it be included within the other examples, which seem to indicate immorality rather than mere impoliteness? Are there wartime situations that might create a need for this type of disciplinary provision? If not, should it be eliminated?

Notes

1. Jonathan Lurie, *Arming Military Justice, Vol. 1, The Origins of the United States Court of Military Appeals, 1775-1950* (Princeton: Princeton University Press, 1992), pp. 75-77, 81, 85, 91-92, 97-99, 114, 125-126.

2. Lurie, *Arming Military Justice,* pp. 129-137, 145-146, 149-150, 161, 171, 199, 201-203, 206-207, 257.

3. Jonathan Lurie, *Pursuing Military Justice: Volume 2, The History of the United States Court of Appeals for the Armed Services, 1951-1980* (Princeton: Princeton University Press, 1998), 22.

4. Lurie, *Arming Military Justice,* 112-113, 169; *Manual for Courts Martial, 1984,* sec. 2, 106-107.

5. Lurie, *Arming Military Justice,* 165-166, 184; *Manual for Courts-Martial, 1984,* sec. 2, 195; David A. Schlueter, *Military Criminal Justice: Practice and Procedure,* 3rd edition (Charlottesville: The Michie Company, 1992), secs. 17-16 and 17-17; see also William B. Aycock and Seymour W. Wurfel, *Military Law under the Uniform Code of Military Justice* (Chapel Hill: University of North Carolina Press, 1955), Chapter 15.

It was one of the Warren Court's achievements that it was able to use its opinions to implement new concepts of federalism in the field of criminal procedure. The Court applied federal standards on a case-by-case basis to state police methods and court procedures. The result was that virtually all of the provisions of the Federal Bill of Rights (Amendments I through VIII) were held applicable to the states. Among the more significant cases are *Mapp v. Ohio* (367 U.S. 643, 1961), *Miranda v. Arizona* (384 U.S. 436, 1966), and *United States v. Wade* (388 U.S. 218, 1967). These cases applied federal standards in the areas of search and seizure, the assistance of counsel to persons suspected of crime, and the manner in which police used lineups to identify suspects. When Chief Justice Warren E. Burger succeeded Earl Warren in 1968, some of the steps toward nationalizing criminal trial and investigatory procedures were modified, but the interest in ensuring fair and humane criminal justice persisted. State death penalty trials were halted by the Burger Court's decision in *Furman v. Georgia* (408

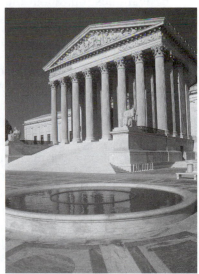

Corbis Images

The U.S. Supreme Court Building in Washington, D.C. houses the highest court in the nation. Despite the swing of judicial philosophy from a "liberal" Supreme Court to a bench ostensibly committed to "law and order," the past three decades have witnessed growing judicial concern with the operation of the criminal justice system.

U.S. 238, 1972), in part due to the Court's recognition that an inordinate number of black defendants were sentenced to death by state courts throughout the United States. After the states introduced a double trial procedure for capital cases,[4] the U.S. Supreme Court upheld the imposition of the death penalty (*Gregg v. Georgia*, 428 U.S. 153, 1976). However, even after the introduction of this separate "sentencing hearing," Associate Justices William J. Brennan Jr. and Thurgood Marshall remained opposed to the imposition of capital punishment. They considered this sanction to be "cruel and unusual punishment," and hence contrary to the Eighth Amendment to the Constitution.

Capital Punishment, DNA Evidence, and the Impact of World Opinion

Increasingly, the United States has assumed the role of being the only industrialized western nation to continue the practice of capital punishment. Not frequently, this has halted the extradition of fugitives from American justice who reside in Europe. More importantly, the availability of DNA (deoxyribonucleic acid) evidence[5] has provided a powerful basis on which to challenge death sentences. This type of evidence, coupled with confessions by other persons exonerating a prisoner on death row, has raised some critical questions about the ability of the American criminal trial to determine guilt. At least 85 death row convictions were reversed between 1973 and 2000, and public awareness of this fact has begun to have an impact. Surveys in 1960 reflected that 38 percent of Americans were in favor of the death penalty. That approval rating increased to a peak of 80 percent in 1994. In the year 2000, about 66 percent of the Americans polled answered that they were in favor of the death penalty. If the death penalty review process continues to generate conviction reversals, the American public will continue to lose confidence in the reliability of the criminal trial, and we can anticipate an upsurge of public opinion favoring abolition of the death penalty.

DNA is a genetic indicator that occurs in all bodily structures and fluids—from bones to blood, and all other organic matter. Except for identical twins, who are conceived when a single fertilized human egg divides into two embryos, it is almost statistically impossible for two persons to have the same DNA in their body cells. The slow decomposition of bone matter after death makes it possible to reopen the cases of long-dead victims and their convicted murderers. Archaeologists have used DNA sampling to determine family relationships between the pharaohs of Egypt, and even more remarkably, they have been able to trace the genetic affinity between modern Jews, the patriarchs of biblical times, and a tribe in Africa that has traditionally (and correctly) asserted its descent from a Jewish ancestor. In American civil law, DNA comparisons are used widely to resolve issues of paternity contested in our family courts. Few homicide trials are devoid of some evidence that involves DNA comparisons. Even a single hair found at a crime scene may determine a verdict. With such widespread use and the reliability of proof fixed between 94 and 99.5 percent, it is inevitable that DNA research will continue to play a significant role in criminal justice—both in providing more accurate proof at trial, and in reversing those convictions in which DNA was not used or was used improperly.

Should capital punishment be ended in the United States because of rising public objections, criminal justice practice will once more be altered because of social disillusionment with antiquated methods of proof. That has happened at least twice before—when Peter the Chanter in the thirteenth century pointed out the many erroneous convictions based on ordeal evidence, and in the eighteenth century when Enlightenment philosophers attacked the use of torture to obtain "proof" in the inquisitorial method. In both cases, it was the cumulative impact of wrongful convictions that triggered reform. There is a Hungarian proverb that deserves American criminal justice's consideration: "If one person calls you a horse, laugh at him. If a second person calls you a horse, think about it. If a third person calls you a horse, maybe you should buy a saddle."[6] In regard to capital punishment, DNA may well be the third person.

Personalization and the "Jurisdictional Maze" of Native American Tribal Justice

As criminal justice concerns have become more globalized in the past five decades, they have also been affected by a variety of demands for racial and ethnic self-determination, both within and among nation states. This particularization of criminal justice is in part due to heightened public sensitivity to the plight of indigenous peoples throughout the world. Perhaps the most sweeping recognition of aboriginal rights occurred in Australia in 1992, when the High Court of Australia took a substantial step toward eliminating the paramount land title of the British Crown based upon discovery and settlement. The Meriam Islands in the Torres Strait, off the northern coast of Queensland, had long been settled by an agricultural people who established an advanced system of land use and ownership. When their titles were threatened by new settlers asserting ownership of the land, they began a court proceeding to assert their prior entitlement to the land based upon their local customs and usages. Ultimately the High Court upheld not only Mer land titles, but also noted that native title on the Australian mainland would be subject to judicial confirmation (*Mabo v. Queensland*, 175 Commonwealth Law Reports 1 (1992). The High Court's included the extensive hunting territories of aboriginal tribes, many of which contained both valuable mineral resources and scarce farm and pasture lands.

Within the United States the quasi-independent status of American Indian tribes has been reaffirmed, and tribal councils have been given greater autonomy in administering local reservation affairs. In 1924, Indians both on and off the reservations were granted U.S. citizenship, and the Bureau of Indian Affairs began to authorize the establishment of criminal justice systems on each tribal reservation. Native American concerns for the welfare and cultural heritage of Indian children have been partially answered by Congress's enactment of the Indian Child Welfare Act of 1978, which confers on tribal courts exclusive jurisdiction over the adoption of Indian children.[7]

Within the past decade, the United States Supreme Court has taken a close look at the jurisdiction of American Indian tribal courts and the related law enforcement authority of Indian police departments. Traditionally, the status of Indians has been a matter of federal government concern, with states exercising virtually no criminal justice functions within Indian country. This tribal autonomy was first recognized by the Supreme Court under Chief Justice John Marshall. In opinions dating from 1823 through 1832 (*Johnston v. McIntosh*, 1823; *Cherokee Nation v. Georgia*, 1831; and *Worcester v. Georgia*, 1832), the Court recognized Indian tribes as "dependent sovereign nations." As such, they retained appropriate portions of their prior sovereignty and were under the protection of the United States government. In keeping with this doctrine, the Department of the Interior promulgated a uniform code of laws governing life on Indian reservations. However, in the 1930s increased demands for self-determination resulted in federal approval of tribal criminal codes, and the establishment of tribal courts and law enforcement agencies. At first restricted to limited misdemeanor jurisdiction, the tribal courts were permitted to sentence offenders to no more than six months in prison and to impose fines of not more than $500. A 1986 federal statute increased the sentencing limits of tribal courts to imprisonment of one year and imposition of fines not more than $5,000. In 1990 and 1991, additional congressional legislation authorized tribal courts to hear criminal cases against Indians who were not members of their tribe; however, non-Indians are still not subject to the jurisdiction of tribal courts or tribal law enforcement agencies.

Although federal law enforcement officers and the federal courts are empowered to enforce sanctions against more serious crimes committed by Indians and others on tribal reservations, the division of law enforcement and prosecutorial authority can result in awkward overlaps between tribal criminal justice and that administered by United States Attorneys and Federal District Courts. For example, the United States Supreme Court has recognized that constitutional guarantees against double jeopardy do not preclude federal prosecution of an Indian already convicted by an Indian tribal court of a lesser included offense within the same crime. Because the tribal court is viewed as representing a separate sovereignty, there cannot be double jeopardy in such a case (*United States v. Antelope*, 430 U.S. 641, 1977). The rationale for the ruling in *Antelope* is based on the premise that as a one-time independent people, each Indian tribe retained those aspects of sovereignty not surrendered to the United States by treaty, statute, or assumption of dependent status (see *United States v. Wheeler*, 435 U.S. 313, 1978). However, in the same term, the U.S. Supreme Court rejected the argument that Indian tribes possess inherent sovereignty to impose criminal sanctions upon non-Indians resident within their reservations (*Oliphant v. Suquamish Indian Tribe*, 435 U.S. 191, 1978).

The limited extension of tribal court jurisdiction to all Indians, regardless of tribal affiliation, has simplified law enforcement problems. However, there remains the difficult law enforcement task of distinguishing between Indians and non-Indians for purposes of apprehension and arrest. To a large degree this reintroduces the dichotomy between personal law and territorial law, which has largely disappeared in Western Europe since the Middle Ages.[8] With the extension of tribal court jurisdiction to include Indians who are not tribe members, there has been a modest return to the recognition of a territorial basis for law enforcement. That is, the tribal court exercises criminal law jurisdiction over all Indians within its reservation. However, it lacks jurisdiction over all non-Indians. The uncertainties inherent in a system of personal law weaken the ability of Indian tribal law enforcement agencies to operate effectively to ensure law and order in the reservations. Because these complications are based on the long-standing "dependent sovereign nation" characterization of the Indian tribes, they are likely to persist and demand periodic reconsideration by federal agencies and Congress.[9]

One possible solution to this problem might be to provide for the issuance of federal marshals' commissions to tribal law enforcement officers. This would permit detention and arrest of non-Indian offenders on a reservation, and would also authorize the prosecution of cases before a local United States Magistrate or federal marshal commissions. No significant change in jurisdiction would be involved, because the federal courts currently have authority over the more serious crimes committed on the reservations. On the other hand, tribal law enforcement officers would be protected from accusations of false arrest should they mistakenly arrest a non-Indian.

Summary

The beginning of the twenty-first century finds American criminal justice at an interesting stage of development. Globalization provides new opportunities and new challenges; unquestionably, it also points to the need for more effective communication and cooperation between policing agencies—across local, state, and international boundaries. We can anticipate that systems of international cooperation, such as Interpol, the UN agencies studying crime, and related regional organizations, will increase greatly in significance and in volume of requests processed. The current stress on the recognition and protection of human rights will continue to affect police practice and trial procedures, demanding that law enforcement professionals and prosecutors work more closely to ensure that investigative methods conform to local and national standards. Perhaps most significantly, in the years ahead international terrorism, drug trafficking, and the clarification of law enforcement roles and functions will remain critical issues in the field of criminal justice.

Endnotes

1   As discussed earlier, an ex post facto law operates retroactively to make criminal an action that was legal at the time the accused took part in the activity. A bill of attainder is a statutory provision that both defines a crime and convicts an individual that it declares guilty of the crime defined in the statute.

2   See 18 U.S. Code §§ 2331-2339B.

3   See the definition of these terms in note 2, above.

4   In the approved procedure, a court trying a capital punishment case must first obtain a jury verdict that the accused is guilty of a crime that might be punishable by death. Once guilt has been determined, the jury then decides whether death is the appropriate sanction, guided by new and separate evidence introduced for that purpose.

5   See Chapter 13, pp. 229-230.

6   Quoted by Milton M. Klein, in *South Carolina Legal History*, Herbert A. Johnson, ed. (Columbia: University of South Carolina Southern Studies Program, 1980), p. 20.

7   25 U. S. Code §§ 1901-1963.

8   See the discussion in Chapter 3, above.

9   See *Johnson v. McIntosh*, 8 Wheaton 543 (1823), *Cherokee Nation v. Georgia*, 5 Peters 1 (1831), and *Worcester v. Georgia*, 6 Peters 515 (1832), in Herbert A. Johnson, *The Chief Justiceship of John Marshall, 1801-1835* (Columbia: University of South Carolina Press, 1997), pp. 248-255.

References

On the Nuremberg trials, see Telford Taylor, *The Anatomy of the Nuremberg Trials: A Personal Memoir* (New York: Alfred A. Knopf, 1992); and Theodor Meron, *War Crimes Law Comes of Age: Essays* (Oxford: Clarendon Press, 1998). The Tadic trial and the Yugoslavia War Crimes Tribunal are discussed in Michael P. Scharf, *Balkan Justice: The Story Behind the First International War Crimes Tribunal Since Nuremberg* (Durham, NC: Carolina Academic Press, 1997); and Gary Jonathan Bass, *Stay the Hand of Vengeance: The Politics of War Crimes Tribunals* (Princeton, NJ: Princeton University Press, 2000). Aryeh Neier, *War Crimes: Brutality, Genocide, Terror, and the Struggle for Justice* (New York: Times Books, 1998), provides a good discussion of both Rwanda and Bosnia.

On terrorism, Paul Wilkinson and Brian M. Jenkins, eds., *Aviation Terrorism and Security* (London: Frank Cass, 1999) provides a valuable discussion of the Lockerbie incident, and points to the increasing threat of aircraft bombings and skyjacking.

For a careful and scholarly discussion of Interpol, see Malcolm Anderson, *Policing the World: Interpol and the Politics of International Police Cooperation* (Oxford: Clarendon Press, 1989). Also of value is Malcolm Anderson, *Policing Across National Boundaries* (London: Pinter Publishers, 1994). More sensational but considerably less reliable are Trevor Meldal-Johnssen and Vaughn Young, *The Interpol Connection: An Inquiry into the International Criminal Police Organization* (New York: The Dial Press, 1979); and Omar V. Garrison, *The Secret World of Interpol* (Glasgow: William Maclellan, 1977).

Basic to the study of international human rights is the useful anthology dealing with the subject from biblical times to 1996, *The Human Rights Reader: Major Political Writings, Essays, Speeches and Documents from the Bible to the Present*, ed. Micheline Ishay (New York: Routledge, 1997). Of equal significance is the excellent commentary, article by article on the UN Declaration, Asbjorn Eide, et al., eds., *The Universal Declaration of Human Rights: A Commentary* , (London: Scandinavian University Press, 1992). Louis Henkin, *The Age of Rights* (New York: Columbia University Press, 1990), provides a series of the author's essays on both the American approach to human rights and international understandings and practices. Natalie K. Havener, *Human Rights Treaties and the Senate: A History of Opposition* (Chapel Hill, NC: University of North Carolina Press, 1990), explores in-depth the origins and consequences of U.S. failure to ratify the Universal Declaration and related international human rights proposals. For historical background of the French Declaration of the Rights of Man and Citizens, see Dale Van Kley, ed., *The French Idea of Freedom: The Old Regime and the Declaration of Rights of 1789.* (Stanford, CA: Stanford University Press, 1994); in this volume, see David A. Bell, "Safeguarding the Rights of the Accused: Lawyers and Political Trials in France, 1716-1789," pp. 234-264, an essay of particular interest regarding Old Regime criminal procedure and its impact on the French Declaration of Rights,.

Clovis C. Morrison, Jr., *The Dynamics of Development in the European Human Rights Convention System* (The Hague: Martinus Nijhoff Publishers, 1981), is a dated but good discussion of the work of the European Court of Human Rights.

The current state of the death penalty in the United States and abroad is surveyed in Roger G. Hood, *The Death Penalty: A World-Wide Perspective,* 2nd ed. (Oxford: Clarendon Press, 1996); Hugo A. Bedau, *The Death Penalty in America,* 3rd ed. (New York: Oxford University Press, 1982); Hugo A. Bedau, *The Death Penalty in America: Current Controversies* (New York: Oxford University Press, 1997); and Jim Dwyer et al., *Actual Innocence: Five Days to Execution and other Dispatches from the Wrongly Accused,* 1st ed. (New York: Doubleday, 2000). Also of value is Michelle McKee, "Tinkering with the Machinery of Death: Understanding Why the United State's Use of the Death Penalty Violates Customary International Law," *Buffalo Human Rights Law Review* 6 (2000): 153-182.

There is a vast and growing body of materials on DNA and its forensic uses. Among the more useful articles are Paul E. Tracy and Vincent Morgan, "Big Brother and His Science Kit: DNA Databases for 21st Century Crime Control," *Journal of Criminal Law and Criminology* 90 (2000): 635-690; and Michael N. Schmitt and Laura H. Crocker, "DNA Typing: Novel Scientific Evidence in the Military Courts," *Air Force Law Review* 32 (1990): 227-330. On post-trial relief and DNA, see Josephine Linker Hart and Guilford M. Dudley, "Available Post-Trial Relief after a State Criminal Conviction when Newly Discovered Evidence Establishes 'Actual Innocence'," *University of Arkansas at Little Rock Law Review* 22 (2000): 629-646.

Notes and Problems

1. Why is the United States Senate reluctant to ratify the Universal Declaration of Human Rights? There is an important question concerning the federal union that arises when treaties touch upon matters of internal concern. In *Missouri v. Holland* (252 U.S. 416, 1920), the United States Supreme Court upheld the con-

stitutionality of the Migratory Bird Treaty, a multilateral agreement between the United States, Canada, and Mexico to protect waterfowl and other birds during migration. Normally restrictions on hunting are matters of state concern, but the Supreme Court pointed out that the federal government may do things by treaty that Congress cannot accomplish through a statute. What would be the constitutional significance of the federal government's ratification of the Universal Declaration of Human Rights? Note that the terms of the Universal Declaration simply establish rights, and that virtually no federal legislation would be required to put the Declaration into force. Would ratification result in new federal rules concerning human rights, and would those laws be enacted by the president as the chief diplomat, subject only to obtaining the consent of the Senate through ratification?

2. The availability of DNA testing has raised the possibility of using DNA databanks much in the way we use fingerprinting, both for identification purposes and in aid of criminal investigation. While the idea may have some appeal in terms of law enforcement, it also raises questions concerning the privacy of individual citizens. Those are important considerations, and how would you deal with those factors? Then add to this difficulty the cost of DNA testing and analysis, which at current prices may run well more than $200 per person. In their article cited in the Reference section above, Paul Tracy and Vincent Morgan point out that most criminal activity in the United States does not involve violent crime. Rather it is property crime, in which the perpetrators rarely leave telltale fragments of hair, fingernails, semen, or blood. In other words, there is a real question of whether the few "matches" to be made by DNA would turn out to be cost-effective, given the high cost of "DNA-printing" the entire U.S. population. Some restrictions on the scope and size of the databanks seem likely. What sort of limits do you think would be justified?

3. Where do you stand on capital punishment? Is the current system of investigation, prosecution, jury trial, and extensive appellate review sufficient to guarantee the guilt of the accused person? What if the convicted person had given a free and voluntary confession in the case—would that always be an indication of guilt? Assuming that 10 percent of capital punishment convictions were shown to be in error, would you advocate a change in the death penalty? What if the percentage were 25 percent or 50 percent?

4. Anglo-American investigative practice is based on maintaining records on individuals who have been convicted of criminal activity. European practice in general deals with creating dossiers covering the activities of all citizens, whether or not they have committed a crime. Which of the two practices complies with the principle that one is innocent until proven guilty? Which of the two is more likely to deter criminal activity? Which of the two constitutes a greater intrusion into the privacy of the individual? Does this mean that the use of international police intelligence requires that each law enforcement agency interpret the meaning of an individual having a police "file"? Add to this the fact that police in European nations work under the supervision of magistrates who direct the manner in which a dossier is documented prior to the actu-

al trial of the case. Does this mean that the preliminary findings of such a magistrate, who is legally trained, should be more accurate than the unsupervised investigative conclusions of an Anglo-American police department?

5. When dealing with the definition of crimes, the user of foreign materials must be careful to understand the approach of the originating nation to the elements of the crime as well as to the serious nature of the crime. For example, an Asian nation may well provide for more serious sanctions against a person who kills a parent. There might be some variation in what is considered premeditation. These and other issues have to be considered in evaluating incoming police intelligence. Given these problems, will American investigative agencies need specialists in foreign legal and criminal justice systems? How does a small town police department of a chief and five officers deal with this staffing problem?

6. One troubling question that arises in connection with violations of the law of war is whether an accused is innocent when he or she was simply "following superior orders." Is that a defense if the accused is charged with killing unarmed and defenseless civilians? Assuming that the American position is that superior orders are no defense, then is the superior officer likewise guilty? Is a commanding general, several levels of command removed from the individual, also guilty? Is the president of the United States, as commander-in-chief of the armed forces, also culpable?

Chapter 15

Epilogue

No single volume can aspire to give full treatment to the vast and fascinating history of criminal justice in the Western world, but the previous chapters provide sufficient basis for drawing tentative conclusions concerning crime, modes of law enforcement, and methods of punishment. In retrospect it becomes apparent that there is a "layering" process of criminal justice knowledge and practice. Beginning with ancient society's initial dislike of violence and vengeance, the social chaos of self-help and indiscriminate vengeance, particular cultures have evolved characteristic ways of solving their crime problems. Imperfect though their techniques might have been, they formed new stages in the history of crime and punishment and provided succeeding generations with a stronger basis on which to construct still another "layer." Through examining a number of cultural histories, it is possible to trace the transfer of ideas and crime control methods across societal lines. Criminal justice systems are social institutions that respond to the cultural requirements of each distinct human society. However, at the same time, humankind does not exist within hermetically sealed social and cultural enclaves. There are constant cross-cultural exchanges of ideas, moral preferences, and techniques of social and political control. Even in the midst of great diversity, humankind is one, and individual societies do not hesitate to borrow from others the institutions that offer solutions to pressing human problems.

Chronologically there is also an increase and expansion. While crime changes its character slowly, society's attitude toward antisocial behavior has been remarkably altered over the past three millennia. Initially, violent behavior and homicide were matters of greatest concern, and connected with the suppression of those crimes there was the public need to suppress an individual's psychological impulse toward revenge. Ancient societies, perhaps because of their recent emergence from systems of group property, did not worry about most property-related crime, except to the extent that it might result in physical violence. Growing commercial activity changed that, raising the protection of property to a high priority in criminal law. It also spawned a new group of economic crimes, such as counterfeiting, use of false weights, and monopolizing necessary goods in the marketplace. Opportunities for fraud and theft presented themselves to medieval clerics and nineteenth-century American politicians, but their societies reacted slowly to penalize behavior that preyed upon the gullibility of the devout or the weaknesses of American municipal government. Today, criminal law is hard-pressed to deal with the burgeoning possibilities for larceny through computer systems or by use of stolen credit cards and checkbooks. Social and technological change inevitably lead to new forms of antisocial behavior, and gradually a culture's definition of what is criminal must expand to forbid these activities.

Definitions of crime change constantly, usually to include offenses previously tolerated as being beneath notice by the criminal law. Traditional prohibitions against violent crime (murder, rape, robbery, assault, and battery) and those against property-related crime (larceny, arson, and burglary) tend to persist through time periods and across cultural lines. However, sanctions against what have become known as victimless crimes vary over time and between cultures. Prosecutions for prostitution, adultery, fornication, bigamy, sodomy, and excessive use of alcohol or habit-forming drugs all fall within this category. And it is possible to include municipal ordinances against overtime automobile parking, driving at excessive speeds, littering the streets, and failure to restrain a dog with a leash in that same category. Over the course of history, the concept of crime has been greatly expanded to include this wide and bewildering variety of lesser offenses. In part this reflects a heavy reliance on legal processes to regulate individual conduct. With the rise of class distinctions and class consciousness, penal sanctions have been used to enforce the standards of law and order generally accepted by the politically dominant class. The result has been that the concept of crime has been stretched out of shape, and it no longer is restricted to the bare minimum of prohibitions necessary for a peaceful society. This proliferation of offenses vastly diffuses the law enforcement process, reducing its effectiveness in dealing with major felonies and obscuring the moral distinction that society must maintain between minor misdoings and the major offenses that violate the universal law of civilized humankind.

Law enforcement systems also demonstrate cross-cultural and chronological layering. Emphasis on self-help was natural to a culture that was not differentiated into vocational groups and in which there was an absence of formal police and judicial institutions. At its best, self-help was limited by the relative physical prowess of the victim and the accused, and at its worst it led to vengeance and the blood feud. The transfer of police responsibility to the community eliminated some of the defects and temptations of the self-help system, but inefficient justices of the peace and lethargic constables provided little security. Their shortcomings as detectives led to the rise of the professional thief-catcher, available for hire by the victim. By the early nineteenth century, law enforcement was sorely in need of change. The newly established modern municipal police forces emphasized protective patrol and public investigations of criminal activity. However, that modern urban police system has found an increasing number of tasks assigned to it.

The invention and widespread adoption of the automobile as a means of transportation has required police supervision of traffic and enforcement of rules of the road. Reformers, anxious to eradicate the supposed social origins of crime, have called upon police departments to institute social action programs. Politicians, businesspeople, and even university presidents call upon police officials to supply officers trained in crowd control. Sociologists have estimated that a very small portion of modern police activity deals with the prevention or investigation of crime. Much more time is involved with helping to coax cats down from the tops of trees and providing a warm cell for drunks to sleep off their evening on the town. Indeed, if police officers were not available for these tasks, where in modern society could one find a substitute service?

It may very well be that the community service activities of police organizations are what is needed to bring police officers out of a subcultural pattern that may separate them from the society they serve. Police officers bear a heavy responsibility when they are given a virtual monopoly of violence in their jurisdiction. Better armed and equipped to deal with crime, better prepared now than in the 1960s to deal with student riots and ghetto uprisings, they nevertheless need the confidence and full cooperation of the people if they are to be effective agents for law and order. Advanced education will provide a broader perspective on the needs of society and the role that the criminal justice system should play in the community. It will facilitate the adoption of new systems of communication, transportation, and criminal investigation. Hopefully it will bridge the gap between law enforcement officers on one side and the criminologists and penal reformers on the other. Allied agencies in the war against crime should not waste resources fighting each other.

The prison system is of fairly recent origin in the history of criminal justice, but it reflects the full spectrum of historical attitudes toward crime. In its retributive aspects, the prison inflicts pain on the convict through deprivation of freedom, through hard labor, and through other coercive means. Crime must be adequately punished by the state; if the prison is not sufficiently punitive, a system of private revenge will arise to supplement it. Since the eighteenth century reformers have paid increasing attention to rehabilitation. This recognizes the social need to reclaim criminals and return them to the ranks of the law-abiding. A tremendous task of restructuring human behavior has been undertaken by the rehabilitative prison and, not surprisingly, recidivism rates show there is little hope for success. The idealism of nineteenth-century prison reformers has degenerated into valiant attempts at retaining educational and vocational training in the face of budget cuts and public hostility.

The public, fearful of a rising crime rate, demands longer and harsher sentences but refuses to supply the expanded prison facilities required to meet those demands. One manifestation of this need to "warehouse" offenders, and thereby to protect society, has been the establishment of mandatory minimum sentences for certain violent crimes. Parole for good behavior has been sharply restricted, limiting the use of parole and early release as rewards for exemplary behavior behind bars. Recidivism has become a matter of public concern, and some states have enacted three-strikes laws, under which any three felony convictions can result in a life sentence without the possibility of parole. Unfortunately, lawmakers have enacted many of these increased sanctions into law without giving adequate attention to the degree to which they will influence plea bargaining, prison discipline, or jury behavior.

There is a serious need for professional penologists to realistically reassess their goals and to provide the general public with accurate cost estimates for a program of long prison sentences. The activism of the federal courts in examining the physical conditions of state prisons and the growing judicial interest in humane systems of prison discipline promise to have a major impact on prison administration in the years ahead. In addition, the federal judiciary has made a concerted effort to equalize the application of sanctions imposed in United States courts. This effort has provided sentencing guidelines for federal district courts exercising criminal jurisdiction. Although this initiative has eliminated much of the individual judge's discretion in imposing punishment, it also provides a less flexible system of penalties. As such, sentencing guidelines may also assist in prison overcrowding.

Ultimately, increasing the severity of imprisonment may find its limits not in public compassion, but rather in the economic realities of costs. In the past, penology has found ways to conserve costs through the use of minimum-security prisons for offenders who have not been convicted of violent crimes or whose rehabilitation is more likely to occur in less restrictive confinement. Public reaction to these practices and increased demands for harsh and vengeful prison terms may well accelerate costs beyond what society is willing to pay.

There is an even more pressing moral issue, raised by growing evidence that prosecutorial and evidentiary systems are unable to prevent wrongful convictions of crime in death penalty cases. To a large degree, the recent development of DNA evidence has heightened public awareness of these miscarriages of justice, but reversals of death sentences based on other evidence has also become increasingly common. Fortunately, a number of executions have been stayed, but doubtless many others were carried out before the evidence came to light. The tragedy of these cases will inevitably erode public confidence in the criminal justice system. International pressures for abolishing the death penalty in the United States reinforce this moral demand for its suspension and ultimate abolition.

A less alarming issue is raised by the much larger number of sentences that do not involve the death penalty. If wrongful, these convictions unjustly deprive the individual of months and years of freedom. They may decisively foreclose career choices; they may make parenthood unwise or impossible; they may, through length or vigor of confinement, undermine physical, mental, or spiritual health. Even without the shadow of capital punishment, these are catastrophic losses that no system of compensation, no matter how generous, can reimburse or justify. Time is not money—it is far more precious.

Criminology must ultimately confront the problem of what causes crime within society. Neither the imposition of harsh sanctions nor the improvement of law enforcement seems to have had a permanent deterrent effect. It is interesting that when men and women find themselves isolated from a formal criminal justice system—as happened during the nineteenth-century American experience of the Overland Trail—there is virtually no crime. And the absence of law enforcement officials and courts may generate a grass roots vigilante movement to provide a rough and ready form of justice based on local community standards. The historical record suggests that crime may be inevitable, but there is also a powerful societal need for order, security, and justice. This is the force that sustains not only the formal criminal justice system, but also the basic cultural values that support modern life.

Medieval alchemists spent their lives seeking the reaction that would convert base metals, such as iron and copper, into gold. They never succeeded, but they laid the basis for the modern science of chemistry, which enriches the lives of all. Students of criminal justice search for methods to combat crime, and they doubtless will find new and more effective ways of preventing, investigating, and punishing criminal activity. But when they attempt to eliminate the causes of crime, they must look beyond the criminal justice system and examine society itself. People turn to crime for a variety of reasons, and painstaking study has begun to provide insight into those basic causes of criminal behavior. Certainly we cannot dismiss Lombroso's suggestion that genetics may condition one to crime, but it seems clear that heredity plays a minor role. The link of criminal activity to young men belonging to what society deems an "underdog" social group (Irish in the nineteenth century, blacks in the twentieth century) should suggest that the vibrant, rebellious energy of youth, combined with resentment against realized or imagined slights, is an explosive mixture that frequently results in crime. And we must wonder too about the clerics of fourteenth-century England, isolated from criminal prosecution by their status, and the nobility of Renaissance Italy, licensed to rape inferior class women by a criminal justice system that overlooked such sexist activities. Can it not be said that exemption from prosecution and punishment is a strong incentive to commit major offenses against society?

Like the alchemists of old, we have been attempting the impossible in our efforts to eradicate crime, and we have been working in the wrong places. Crime is an integral part of our society. It will continue to exist as long as two human beings walk the face of the earth. Criminals are not an isolated or special group, but even in their most deviant behavior they are shaped by the society and culture they share with the general population. Seeking to understand the "criminal mind," we must first look within ourselves to find the emotions and states of mind that could lead to antisocial behavior, and also to discover the social and psychological inhibitions that deter us from unacceptable or even criminal actions. Because no individual lives in isolation, it will also be necessary to examine society and discover that there the inequities, injustices, and dehumanizing experiences that turn men and women to rebellion and crime. Closer attention to the humanities and social sciences will offer new insights into human yearnings and aspirations, and help both the student and the practitioner of criminal justice to better understand the lawbreaker. Consider once more Elizabeth Fry and Captain Alexander Maconochie. The gentle Quaker woman found a way to alter the attitude of desperate female convicts; she appealed to their love and concern for the hungry, naked, and sickly children they had brought into prison life. The Royal Navy captain turned prison warden held out hope to the hardened criminals in a penal colony, and the mere promise of earlier release reformed their behavior and brought order to their society. Sharing a convict's humanity, we hold within ourselves not only an explanation for the existence of crime, but also ample capacity to exercise compassion toward its perpetrator.

Index

Winthrop, John, 127
Wiretaps, 284
Wirz, Henry, 239-240
Witchcraft cases, 55, 129
Women
   likelihood of committing crimes, 10
   Newgate Prison reform, 185-187
   policewomen's movement, 290-291
Wood, William P., 246
Worcester v. Georgia (1832), 338
Word content analysis, 297, 304n. 4
Work-release program (Wisconsin, 1915), 268
Works Progress Administration (WPA), 289
World Court, 312
Writ de odio et atia, 73

Writ of habeas corpus, 103
Writs of Assistance Case (1761), 163

Yale, D.E.C., 100
Youthful offenders, 184, 194-195
   see also Juvenile delinquency; Juvenile reformatories
   criminal activity increasing among, 269
Yugoslavia (former), 312-313, 320-322
Yugoslavia War Crimes Tribunal, 322

Zacchia, Paolo, 291
Zenger, John Peter, 165-167, 168
Zone schools, 289